Emmett N. McFarland

Professor of Business Education and Office Administration
Central Missouri State University

SECRETARIAL PROCEDURES:

Office Administration and Automated Systems

Reston Publishing Company, Inc.
A Prentice-Hall Company
Reston, Virginia

Library of Congress Cataloging in Publication Data

McFarland, Emmett N.
    Secretarial procedures.

    1. Office practice.   2. Secretaries.   3. Office
practice—Automation.   I. Title.
HF5547.5.M39 1985   651.3'74   84-11650
ISBN 0-8359-6957-6

Copyright 1985 by
Reston Publishing Company, Inc.
A Prentice-Hall Company
Reston, Virginia 22090

10 9 8 7 6 5 4 3 2 1

Printed in the United States of America

CONTENTS

Preface

Acknowledgments

PART I, 1

Chapter 1   The Organizational Structure and the Secretarial Role, 2

Introduction, 3
Types of Organizations, 3
Legal Forms of Business
   Organizations, 4
Managers, 5
Organizational Charts, 7
Departmental Functions, 9
Secretarial Positions, 14
Role of the Secretary, 17
Summary, 21
Questions, 23
Projects, 24
Cases, 24

PART II, 25

Chapter 2   Automated Office Systems, 26

Introduction, 27
Word and Data Processing, 27
Work Stations, 32
Word Processors, 33

Computers, 38
Input-Output, 40
Communication Links, 40
Teleconferencing, 40
Reprographics, 41
Micrographics, 43
Summary, 46
Questions, 46
Projects, 47
Cases, 47

Chapter 3   Office Environment, 48

Introduction, 49
Office Layout, 49
Modular Furniture, 51
Chairs, 56
Other Environmental Factors, 58
Summary, 62
Questions, 63
Projects, 64
Cases, 64

Chapter 4   Time Management, 66

Introduction, 67
Time Wasters, 67
Keeping a Time Log, 76
Analyzing the Time Log, 76
Planning, 79
Summary, 82
Questions, 82
Projects, 83
Cases, 84

PART III, 85

Chapter 5   Arranging Meetings, 86

Introduction, 87
Scheduling Meetings, 87

Notifying Participants, 88
Checking the Agenda, 95
Selecting a Place, 96
Equipment, 97
Supplies, 98
Refreshments, 100
Preparing the Program, 100
Final Checks, 101
Interruptions, 103
Follow Up, 104
Summary, 106
Questions, 106
Projects, 107
Cases, 108

Chapter 6   Travel Arrangements, 110

Introduction, 111
Travel Agencies, 111
Making Reservations, 112
Air Travel, 112
Rail, Bus, and Automobile Travel,
    120
Room Reservations, 120
Car Rental, 121
Foreign Travel, 122
Canceling Reservations, 124
Itinerary, 124
Financial Arrangements, 125
Summary, 128
Questions, 128
Projects, 131
Cases, 132

Chapter 7   Telephone Use, 134

Introduction, 135
Telephone Personality, 135
Listening, 137
Planning the Call, 137
Preferences of Your Boss, 138
Placing Calls, 138
Answering Calls, 140

Screening Calls, 143
Placing a Caller on Hold, 145
Taking Messages, 146
Transferring Calls, 147
Ending Conversations, 148
Long-Distance Calls, 149
International Calls, 152
Time Zones, 154
Summary, 154
Questions, 154
Projects, 156
Cases, 157

PART IV, 159

Chapter 8   Communication Services, 160

Introduction, 161
Telephone Directories, 162
Directory Assistance, 164
Telephones, 165
Custom Calling Services, 168
Private Branch Exchange
   (PBX), 168
Central Exchange (Centrex), 169
Computer Controlled PBX
   Features, 169
Wide Area Telecommunications
   Service (WATS), 171
Alternative Long-Distance
   Services, 171
Federal Telecommunications
   System (FTS), 172
Tie-Lines, 173
Facsimile, 173
Telegraph Services, 174
Telex and Telex II (TWX), 175
Summary, 177
Questions, 178
Projects, 179
Cases, 181

Chapter 9   Postal Services, 182

Introduction, 183
Classes of Domestic Mail, 183
Special Services, 189
Ancillary Services, 196
Equipment, 198
ZIP Code System, 200
Internal Pickup and Delivery, 200
Alternative Delivery Methods, 201
Summary, 202
Questions, 203
Projects, 204
Cases, 205

Chapter 10   Processing Mail, 206

Introduction, 207
Incoming Mail, 207
Outgoing Mail, 218
Summary, 224
Questions, 224
Projects, 225
Cases, 226

PART V, 227

Chapter 11   Writing Principles, 228

Introduction, 229
Tone, 229
Conciseness, 238
Concrete Words, 241
Grammar, 242
Proofreading, 252
Summary, 252
Questions, 253
Projects, 254
Cases, 259

Chapter 12   Writing Procedures, 260

Introduction, 261
Order Letters, 261
Request Letters, 265
Responses to Requests and
    Inquiries, 268
Claim Letters, 273
Goodwill Letters, 277
Invitations, 280
News Releases, 282
Summary, 284
Questions, 284
Projects, 285
Cases, 286

Chapter 13   Preparing Reports, 288

Introduction, 289
Graphic Aids, 290
Typing the Report, 309
Preliminary Pages, 312
Supplementary Sections, 315
Informal Reports, 316
Summary, 319
Questions, 319
Projects, 320
Cases, 322

PART VI, 323

Chapter 14   Reference Material, 324

Introduction, 325
Types of Libraries, 326
Library Resources, 327
Data Bases, 341
Microform, 343
Selecting Specific Sources, 344
Library Assistance, 344

Chapter 15 Taking and Preparing Minutes, 348

Introduction, 349
Prior Planning, 349
Recording the Proceedings, 350
Content of the Minutes, 352
Assisting Others with Minutes, 360
Typing the Minutes, 360
Follow-Up Duties, 364
Summary, 366
Questions, 368
Projects, 370
Cases, 370

Chapter 16 Supplies, 372

Introduction, 373
Supplies, 373
Description of the Supplies
   Needed, 374
Quality, 374
Quantity, 374
Determining the Price, 375
When to Order, 375
Procedures for Obtaining
   Supplies, 376
Receiving Supplies, 378
Storage, 377
Types of Supplies Used in Most
   Offices, 378
Summary, 389
Questions, 389
Projects, 390
Cases, 390

PART VII, 393

Chapter 17 Human Relations, 394

Introduction, 395
Tact, 395

Listening, 396
Nonverbal Communication, 399
Ethics, 402
Empathy, 405
Remembering Names, 406
Vocal Presentation, 406
Office Etiquette, 410
Summary, 413
Questions, 414
Projects, 415
Cases, 416

Chapter 18   Appointments, 418

Introduction, 419
Appointments, 419
Visitors, 427
Meetings, 436
Summary, 438
Questions, 438
Projects, 440
Cases, 440

Chapter 19   Interoffice Relationships, 442

Introduction, 443
Starting a New Position, 443
Formality, 446
Forming Opinions, 446
Working for More Than One
    Executive, 447
Loyalty, 448
Performing Questionable
    Tasks, 449
Becoming Compatible with the
    Boss, 450
Confidential Information, 451
Accepting Criticism, 452
Expressing Opinions About
    Others, 453
Mutual Consideration and
    Respect, 453
Plan Your Suggestions, 454

Making Decisions, 455
Confrontations, 456
Summary, 456
Questions, 457
Projects, 458
Cases, 459

Chapter 20   Financial and Legal Assistance, 460

Introduction, 461
Notary Public, 461
Signing the Supervisor's Name, 466
Financial Responsibilities, 468
Records Retention, 476
Destroying Confidential Information, 477
Privacy, 477
Subpoenas, 478
Cautions, 478
Summary, 479
Questions, 480
Projects, 481
Cases, 481

PART VIII, 483

Chapter 21   Selecting and Securing a Position, 484

Introduction, 485
Self-Analysis, 486
Identifying Duties, 486
Identifying Strengths, 489
Selecting Businesses, 492
Sources of Job Openings, 492
Learning About the Company, 495
The Resume, 496
The Letter of Application, 501
Typing the Letter and Resume, 503
Interviewing, 504
Application Blank, 511
Follow-Up Procedures, 514

Accepting a Position, 515
Rejecting a Position, 515
Summary, 515
Questions, 516
Projects, 517
Cases, 518

Chapter 22   Career Goals, 520

Introduction, 521
Professional Development, 521
Promotions, 524
Determining Your Career
    Direction, 526
Leaving a Position, 530
Summary, 530
Questions, 531
Projects, 531
Cases, 532

PREFACE

Secretarial Procedures: Office Administration and Automated Systems emphasizes the practical aspects of the tasks performed by the secretarial and administrative staff. The book thoroughly covers topics relating to most secretarial duties including areas normally not covered in other secretarial or administrative procedures courses. It is appropriate as a textbook for a capstone course in secretarial, office, and administrative procedures offered at two- and four-year colleges and business schools and as a reference book for those already working in the secretarial and administrative areas.

Organizational structures, the classifications of secretarial positions, and the general role of the secretary as a member of a team are discussed in chapter 1. Succeeding chapters provide preliminary training and general knowledge concerning technologies, office environment, mail services, telephone and telegraph services, reference material, supplies, and writing principles.

Human relations in general are covered in chapter 17; the human relations skills essential to effectively interact with the public and with co-workers are covered in chapters 18 and 19.

The knowledge and skills frequently needed by secretaries are comprehensively covered in the chapters on managing time, understanding the law, using the telephone, processing mail, composing, arranging meetings, preparing minutes, preparing reports, and making travel arrangements.

The employment process is covered in detail in chapter 21. Chapter 22 helps the secretary become cognizant of the qualities necessary for success and offers concrete suggestions that will aid the secretary in advancing professionally.

Questions, projects, and cases are presented at the end of each chapter and are designed to reinforce and enhance the material covered.

ACKNOWLEDGMENTS

My thanks to all who assisted and cooperated in preparing this book. Special acknowledgment is made to Jane Bucks, Hilda Higgins, Kenneth Higgs, Dolores Kitterman, Michael Lewark, Janet O'Brien, Bettie Simmons, Jill Smith, and the following businesses and organizations:

Administrative Management Society

American Pad and Paper Company

Cramer Inc.

Dow Jones & Company, Inc.

Esselte Pendaflex Corporation

Eye Com Systems, Inc.

Gestetner Corporation

Hallmark Cards Incorporated

Hilton Hotels Corporation

Honeywell Inc.

International Business Machines Corporation

Libraries Unlimited, Inc.

Marquis Who's Who, Inc.

Mead-Hatcher Inc.

Moody's Investors Service

Official Airline Guides, Inc.

Red Carpet Travel Agency

Ricoh of America, Inc.

Shredex™, Inc.

Southwestern Bell Telephone Company

Steelcase Inc.

United Missouri Bank of Warrensburg

The H. W. Wilson Company

The Mutual Benefit Life Insurance Company

The New York Times Company

Tops Business Forms

United States Postal Service

Waddell & Reed, Inc./United Investors Life

Wang Laboratories, Inc.

Western Union

Xerox Corporation

Emmett N. McFarland

PART I

CHAPTER 1

The Organizational Structure and the Secretarial Role

All organizations are similar in that they all have objectives, they all have some type of organizational structure, and they all have managers who are responsible for carrying out organizational functions.

The objectives of an organization are concerned with providing services and goods to organization members or to others outside the organization. They are accomplished through the interaction of managers and workers at all levels in the organization. Everyone in the organization needs to understand the responsibility, authority, and accountability relationships within the organization.

This chapter will help you understand the types and legal forms of organizations, the different levels of authority, the general functions of the managers and various departments, and the organizational structure. Different classifications of secretarial positions will be discussed, as well as the general role of the secretary in assisting managers in carrying out their duties.

TYPES OF ORGANIZATIONS

The organizations with which one may be associated can be classified into three basic categories:

1. Profit-oriented businesses that are privately owned and operated as proprietorships, partnerships, and corporations.
2. Service-oriented agencies and associations that are either publicly or privately controlled, such as churches, fraternal organizations, and the

YMCA, and that are usually operated as nonprofit corporations.

3. Service-oriented agencies, such as public colleges, city and police departments, and departments of education, that are created and controlled by some level of government.

LEGAL FORMS OF BUSINESS ORGANIZATIONS

The legal form of an organization refers to the type of ownership. Sole proprietorships, partnerships, and corporations are the most predominant legal forms of business organizations.

Sole Proprietorship

A sole proprietorship is a firm owned by one person who usually actively participates in managing and operating the business. From a legal standpoint, the sole proprietor owns all the firm's assets, owes all the firm's debts, and has the right to all the firm's profits.

Partnership

As defined by the Uniform Partnership Act, a partnership is an association of two or more persons who will carry on as co-owners of a business by voluntary legal agreement (called the Articles of Copartnership). Instead of one person owning the business, at least two people own all the assets, owe all the liabilities, and have an equity (claim against the assets) in the business.

Although any kind of business may be a partnership, partnerships are often formed by professionals such as doctors, lawyers, and architects.

Corporation

A corporation is a legal entity separate and apart from its owners and is created by state charter. As a separate entity, the corporation can be dealt with separately just like an individual. It can hold, buy, sell, and exchange property in the corporation's name. In a sole proprietorship or partnership, property must be held in the name of the individual owners.

The ownership of the corporation is divided into equal parts known as shares of stock. The stock is owned by stockholders who elect officers to manage the corporation. When certain stockholders own the majority of the voting stock, they can and often do elect themselves as managers.

Organizations of all types have managers who have the authority and responsibility to accomplish the organization's objectives. Planning, organizing, controlling, staffing, and directing are the classic functions of management at all levels.

The *planning function* involves setting goals or objectives. The long-range goals for the organization are usually developed at the high management levels, are communicated throughout the organization, and serve as a guide for the activities of all parts of the organization. The lower-level managers are primarily responsible for outlining and implementing the steps to be taken to accomplish the objectives developed at higher levels.

The *organizing function* of the manager involves visualizing the entire process and determining the resources needed to accomplish the established plans. The resources include the individuals needed to perform specific tasks, as well as the equipment, materials, and procedures required to effectively accomplish the plans.

The *controlling process* involves determining whether people and the various parts of an organization are progressing toward the established objectives. The controlling process consists of the following three basic steps, which apply to the people and processes being controlled:

1. Establish standards to be used in measuring the progress toward accomplishing the goals.
2. Measure performance against the standards.
3. Identify deviations and take corrective action.

The manager's controlling function, then, is to ensure that activities are providing the desired results.

For maximum efficiency, the manager must have subordinates who are qualified to complete their assigned tasks. The manager's *staffing function* usually involves determining the personnel needed to carry out the work and participating in interviewing and selecting those who appear qualified.

The manager has the important function of *directing* the activities in his or her area. The manager must provide leadership, solve problems, answer questions, supervise subordinates, and make numerous decisions to ensure the day-to-day activities are successfully completed.

The managers of a business organization are appointed by the owners; those of nonprofit and government organizations are appointed by elected officials or some type of governing body.

Although most large organizations have managers who occupy several levels of authority and are responsible for a variety of different people and functions, management typically has three levels. Fewer managers

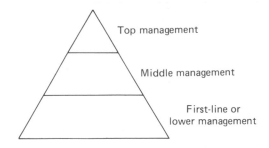

FIGURE 1-1. Pyramidal nature of management.

are at the top of the organization than at the bottom; thus, the typical organizational structure is pyramidal as shown in figure 1-1.

Top Management

The top management group in most large organizations is made up of the president or chief executive officer (CEO) along with the vice presidents. In some cases, the board of directors is also thought of as a part of the top management of corporations. In many organizations, an executive or senior vice president is second in command and thus has authority over the other vice presidents. Companies frequently have vice presidents for several areas, such as production, marketing, personnel, finance, and research and development.

In federal and state governments, other titles are used. For example, at the federal level, the Secretary of Commerce is a member of the President's cabinet. At the state level, the director of the department of agriculture may be considered a member of the top management group.

Top management is responsible for the overall management of the organization and shapes the organization's direction, mission, and strategy.

Middle Management

The middle management group is made up of all managers below the rank of vice president but above the first-line or supervisory level. The titles of middle managers vary considerably and have different meanings in different organizations. For example, a regional manager in one company could be the equivalent of a district manager in another firm.

In universities, the deans of the various colleges are considered middle managers. Assistant secretaries or directors of agencies at the federal and state government levels are frequently considered middle managers.

Regardless of the title, middle managers must supervise other managers and are responsible for translating top management's overall policies into operational procedures and methods.

First-Line Management

First-line managers or supervisors are those at the lowest management level. Supervisors are the links between the rest of management and the workers. First-line managers are responsible for supervising the nonmanagement workers who carry out the tasks necessary to accomplish the mission of the organization.

ORGANIZATIONAL CHARTS

An organizational chart is the implement generally used to show the formal structure of an organization. It gives the position titles and the chain of command or line of authority from the top of the organization to the bottom. Organizational charts help employees see where their jobs are in the hierarchical structure and how their jobs relate to others in the organization.

The typical organizational chart has a rectangular box at the top showing the individual who holds the most authority and who has the final responsibility for managing the organization. While in most organizations this position is held by the president, it is sometimes held by the board of directors or the chairman of the board.

All of the positions at the next level of authority are placed horizontally on the chart below the position shown at the top of the pyramidal arrangement. The same procedure is followed to show the positions at the other echelons. In large organizations, the chart may show numerous hierarchical levels.

All managers in an organization have the authority that comes with the position; thus, the person who occupies a manager's position has its formal authority only as long as he or she remains in the position. Authority gives the manager the right to make decisions that commit an organization's resources, the right to give orders, and the right to issue directives to others.

Lines are used on the organizational chart to show the types of authority relationships among the various decision-making levels in the organization. These levels represent the chain of command.

Line Authority

The thickness and position of the lines indicate the authority of the person holding a particular position. Authority flows downward and line authority is indicated on an organizational chart by a heavy line connecting the superior and the subordinate. The heavy line represents a direct supervisory relationship. As figure 1-2 illustrates, the president has direct authori-

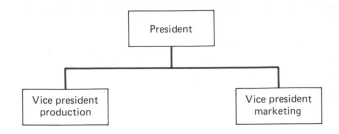

FIGURE 1-2. Line authority.

ty over the vice president of production and the vice president of market-ing. The vice presidents have no authority over each other.

Staff Authority

Staff authority is advisory in nature. Staff departments give advice or provide technical assistance to other departments but do not have direct control over the personnel or activities of those in other departments. The only people over whom the head of a staff department has line authority are those within his or her department. The staff departments are usually high on the organizational chart and frequently report to the president or executive vice president. In many organizations, the legal department is a staff department and might appear on the organizational chart as shown in figure 1-3.

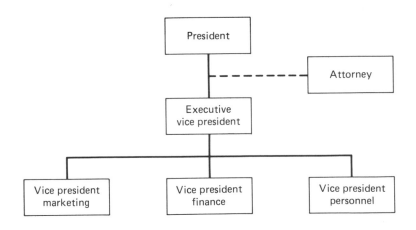

FIGURE 1-3. Staff authority.

Functional Authority

Functional authority is delegated to an individual or department over specific activities in other departments. For example, the personnel department usually has functional authority for the recruitment, selection, and performance appraisal activities of the operating departments. The functional authority of a personnel department is illustrated in figure 1-4.

Span of Control

An important aspect of organizational structure is the span of control or the number of subordinates reporting to a manager. A flat or wide organization is characterized by fewer levels of authority with more subordinates reporting to a manager. A tall or narrow organization is characterized by a number of hierarchical levels with fewer subordinates reporting to a manager. A formal organization is usually described in terms of the degree of "tallness" or "flatness"; it is not simply one or the other. These two organizational structures are illustrated in figure 1-5.

Communication Channels

In addition to showing who reports to whom, how many subordinates work for each manager, and the types of authority relationships, the organizational chart shows the formal communication channels. The hierarchical positioning of people in the organization can significantly influence how, with whom, and why they communicate. In some organizations, the lines of communication rigidly follow the formal lines of authority; in others, much business is transacted informally.

Regardless of the type of organization, the messages between the manager and others flow in upward, downward, and horizontal directions; however, most of the manager's objectives will be accomplished by working with those in his or her line of command.

DEPARTMENTAL FUNCTIONS

The secretary, as well as all others, needs to view the organization as a whole and to see how the parts of the organization relate to and depend on one another. Organizational objectives are accomplished through a cooperative effort; therefore, a basic understanding of the functions performed by the various departments is essential. The number and types of departments found in an organization depend on several factors, including the size of the organization and the nature of the business. A brief explanation

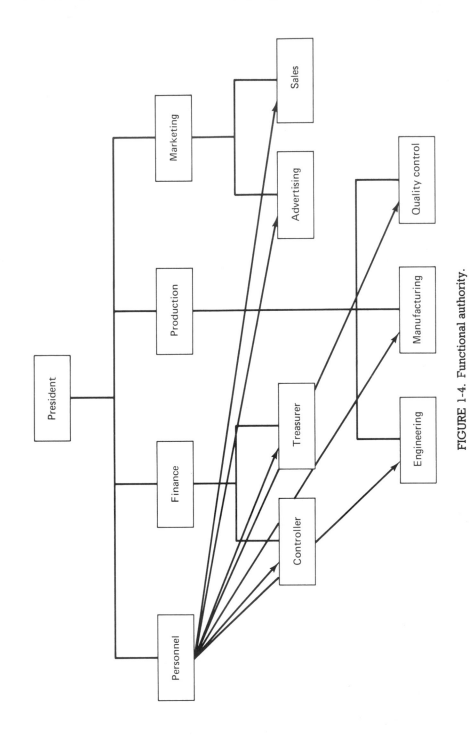

FIGURE 1-4. Functional authority.

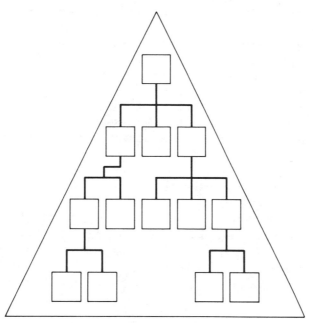

Narrow span of control

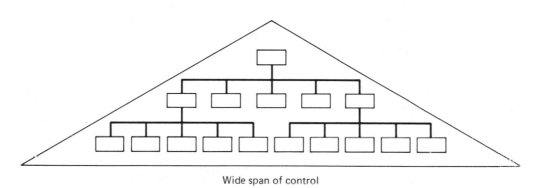

Wide span of control

FIGURE 1-5. Span of control.

of the departments frequently found in businesses is given in the following section.

Purchasing

In industrial organizations, the purchasing manager usually reports to the president, executive vice president, or some other executive with a broad view of the objectives of the company. In schools, government units, and other organizations that operate under a fixed budget, the purchasing manager usually reports to the top financial officer.

The purchasing department is responsible for having materials, supplies, and equipment available in the proper quantity and quality, at the proper time and place, and at the proper price. Therefore, purchasing is a managerial area that includes planning and policy activities such as researching the proper selection of materials and sources; developing procedures, methods, and forms necessary to carry out the policies; following up to ensure proper delivery; and inspecting incoming shipments to make sure they are correct.

In addition, the purchasing department coordinates the activities of that department with traffic, storekeeping, accounting, and other divisions to facilitate operations.

The purchasing department of a small organization may consist of the manager and a clerical staff. Large organizations may have one or more assistant managers, directors, or managers of different areas, buyers, and clerical workers.

Finance

The finance department examines, analyzes, and interprets financial data to advise top management and department managers. It must consider the financial implications of decisions made by all departments.

In addition to serving in an advisory capacity, the finance department performs all accounting functions and prepares the required statements and reports.

Personnel

The personnel director has line authority within the personnel department and directs the activities of the department's staff.

As mentioned earlier, the personnel department performs staff functions for line managers at all levels by assisting with recruiting, hiring, training, evaluating, compensating, counseling, promoting, and firing employees. The personnel department also assists line managers in complying with occupational safety and equal employment laws and may administer benefit programs such as health and accident insurance, retirement, and vacation.

Marketing

Marketing involves the performance of the activities that direct the flow of goods and services from producer to consumer. The top marketing executive is usually a vice president; however, the title is sometimes marketing manager. The top executive in the marketing department carries out the classic functions of management by coordinating the activities of the different departmental areas.

Advertising and sales are almost always two functional areas in the marketing department, and they are headed by managers. The structure of the marketing department in an industrial firm is often similar to that shown in figure 1-6.

The *advertising/promotion department* makes plans and decisions regarding developing, implementing, and managing an advertising/promotion program. The department manager is responsible for setting advertising/promotion goals, preparing budgets, determining the message content, selecting the media, and measuring the effectiveness of the overall program.

The *sales manager* coordinates the personal selling functions with the overall marketing plan. In addition to recruiting, selecting, and training sales personnel, the sales manager establishes sales goals and motivates the sales staff.

The manager of the *product planning department* works with other departments in the organization, such as finance and production, to answer questions such as the following:

- Does a demand exist for the product?
- Does the company have the expertise required to develop the product?
- Can the product be produced with existing facilities?
- Could the resources required to produce the item be used more profitably in some other way?
- Is the product compatible with the other products of the company and the company image?
- What is the extent of the competition?

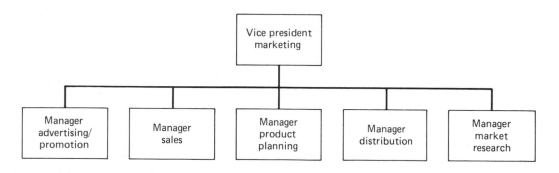

FIGURE 1-6. Marketing department structure.

The *marketing research department* provides management with information needed to make marketing decisions that will result in the company remaining competitive. The data, such as the company's position in the industry and the extent of the demand for certain products, are generally provided on a continuing basis and periodic reports are prepared regarding sales campaigns and similar types of activities.

The *distribution department* selects the channels to follow to get the product or service to the customer and coordinates the transportation and storage functions.

Production

The primary objective of the production area is to produce a good or service of the highest quality possible at the lowest cost possible.

The top production executive is almost always a vice president. Frequently, managers head departments such as engineering, tool and design, scheduling, production control, manufacturing, quality control, inventory, and maintenance.

Administrative Services

A number of large organizations concentrate many of the routine office operations in an area called administrative services. The area may be headed by a top-level executive with the title of vice president or by a middle-level executive with the title of manager.

The services performed by the division vary considerably, but they frequently include mailing, information (word and data) processing, reprographics, forms, records management, and other types of services that can be performed more efficiently by a staff of specialists than by individual departments.

SECRETARIAL POSITIONS

Secretarial positions are identified in several ways. In some companies, the different positions are classified by number or letter, such as *secretary I* or *secretary–level A.* In other companies, the position may be identified by including the title of the person for whom the secretary works, such as *secretary to the vice president of production.*

The Administrative Management Society classifies the three general secretarial positions as *secretary–level B, secretary–level A,* and *execu-*

tive secretary/administrative assistant and describes them in the following way.*

Secretary–Level B performs a limited range of secretarial duties in a small company or for a supervisor in a larger firm. May take dictation and transcribe from notes or dictating equipment with speed and accuracy. Screens calls, makes appointments, handles travel arrangements, answers routine correspondence, and maintains filing systems.

Secretary–Level A performs an unlimited range of secretarial duties for middle management personnel or for more than one individual. Composes and/or takes and transcribes complex and confidential correspondence. Position requires a knowledge of company policy and procedure and above-average secretarial and administrative skills.

Executive Secretary/Administrative Assistant. Performs a full range of secretarial and administrative duties for high-level member of executive staff. Handles project-oriented duties and may be held accountable for the timely completion of these tasks. Relieves the executive of routine administrative detail. Position requires an in-depth knowledge of company practice, structure and a high degree of technical skill.

Companies that have word processing centers or secretaries who spend most of their time using sophisticated word processing equipment usually have positions identified as *correspondence secretary* or *word processing operator.* The Administrative Management Society describes two word processing positions in the following way.

Word Processing Operator. Uses word processing equipment to input, edit, customize, and deliver medium-to-complex typed documents with established quality and time standards. Proofreads and edits own work. Incumbent is familiar with department terminology and company practices. Equipment includes the uses of microprocessor-based, standalone, or shared-logic word processing systems utilizing a CRT screen. May also perform general secretarial duties.

Lead Word Processing Operator. Utilizes full scope of equipment capabilities to produce and revise complicated documents, such as lengthy technical and statistical reports, from complex source information, including the retrieval of text and data. Leads the activities of lower-level operators.

*Source: Administrative Management Society, *AMS 37th Annual Office Salaries Directory,* copyright 1983 by Administrative Office Management Society, Willow Grove, PA. Reprinted by permission.

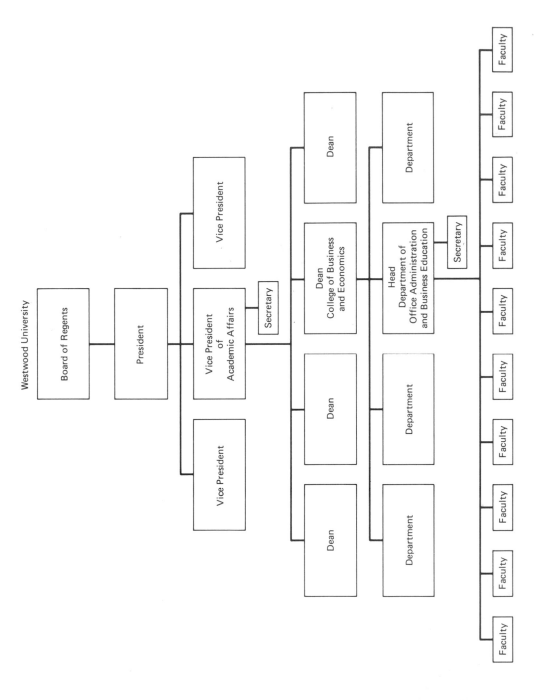

FIGURE 1-7. Abbreviated organizational chart of a hypothetical university.

Several secretarial positions have titles that specifically identify the area of work. For example, those who work as secretaries in legal offices are often referred to as legal secretaries, those who work in medical offices as medical secretaries, and so forth.

ROLE OF THE SECRETARY

With a basic understanding of the types of organizations and the levels of authority shown in the organizational chart, we are now ready to consider how the secretary fits into the organizational structure.

As a student, you probably are more familiar with an academic organization than you are with a business organization; therefore, let us review the organizational structure and examine the role of the secretary at two levels by considering a hypothetical university, Westwood.

By looking at the abbreviated organizational chart shown in figure 1-7, we observe that the board of regents is the governing body for Westwood. The president is the chief administrative officer and is the only one who reports directly to the board of regents.

At Westwood, the president has line authority over three vice presidents, one of whom is the vice president of academic affairs, and perhaps staff administrators whose positions are not shown on this chart. The president and three vice presidents constitute the top level of management at Westwood.

Each of the vice presidents has line authority over personnel in his or her area. The vice president of academic affairs has line authority over the four academic areas, known as colleges, as well as other areas not shown on the chart. The college of business and economics, as well as each of the other colleges, is headed by a dean. The deans of the colleges are considered middle managers.

The dean of the college of business and economics has line authority over the head of the department of office administration and business education, the heads of the other departments in the college, and the office staff not shown on the chart.

The department heads represent the lowest management level in the academic area at Westwood. They have line authority over the faculty members in their departments and over the departmental secretary.

The level at which a secretarial position appears on the organizational chart depends on the position of the person to whom she reports.* Secretaries work for administrators at all levels at Westwood, but let us examine the two positions shown on the chart.

---

*Because the English language lacks a generic singular pronoun signifying *he* or *she,* the feminine pronouns *her* and *she* are used in this text for succinctness.

```
┌─────────────────────────────────────────────────────────────────┐
│                          JOB DESCRIPTION                          │
│                                                                   │
│   Classification:  Secretary                                      │
│                                                                   │
│   Reports to:  Head of the Office Administration and Business     │
│                Education Department                               │
│                                                                   │
│   Duties and Responsibilities:                                    │
│                                                                   │
│       Serves as receptionist for the department.                  │
│                                                                   │
│       Schedules appointments for the department head.             │
│                                                                   │
│       Answers the telephone and takes messages for the            │
│       department head and faculty members.                        │
│                                                                   │
│       Routes mail and other documents to the faculty members      │
│       in the department.                                          │
│                                                                   │
│       Assists the department head in the preparation of           │
│       departmental reports.                                       │
│                                                                   │
│       Maintains records of equipment in the offices and           │
│       classrooms.                                                 │
│                                                                   │
│       Types and duplicates tests for faculty, as time permits.    │
│                                                                   │
│       Attends departmental meetings and records the minutes.      │
│                                                                   │
│       Takes dictation and types correspondence.                   │
│                                                                   │
│       Processes the student evaluations of the faculty in the     │
│       department.                                                 │
│                                                                   │
│       Files.                                                      │
│                                                                   │
│   Qualifications:                                                 │
│                                                                   │
│       Ability to relate effectively to faculty and students.      │
│                                                                   │
│       Must be able to type 50 words per minute and take           │
│       shorthand at 80 words per minute.                           │
│                                                                   │
│       Clerical or stenographic experience desirable.              │
│                                                                   │
└─────────────────────────────────────────────────────────────────┘
```

FIGURE 1-8. Job description for a secretary to a first-level administrator.

At Westwood, the secretaries do not supervise other secretaries or clerical workers; therefore, they do not have line authority.

The job description of the secretary who reports to the head of the department of office administration and business education is shown in figure 1-8.

The description shows the qualifications expected or required and the duties to be performed in addition to the title of the person to whom she reports. Only minimum qualifications are required of secretaries holding positions at this level at Westwood. The duties listed on the description indicate that the tasks are routine and that the person holding the position has limited opportunities to perform creative and administrative types of work.

```
┌─────────────────────────────────────────────────────────────────────┐
│                          JOB DESCRIPTION                              │
│                                                                       │
│  Classification:  Head, Department of Office Administration and Business Education │
│                                                                       │
│  Reports to:  Dean, College of Business and Economics                 │
│                                                                       │
│  Duties and Responsibilities:                                         │
│                                                                       │
│      Coordinates the activities of the ten department faculty members.│
│                                                                       │
│      Coordinates the selection of staff members.                      │
│                                                                       │
│      Evaluates staff members.                                         │
│                                                                       │
│      Schedules the teaching assignments.                              │
│                                                                       │
│      Coordinates the preparation of the departmental budget.          │
│                                                                       │
│      Initiates orders for equipment.                                  │
│                                                                       │
│      Coordinates the use of the equipment and arranges for its maintenance. │
│                                                                       │
│      Represents the department at the weekly meetings of the department heads. │
│                                                                       │
│      Represents the department at the monthly meetings of the Administrative │
│      Council conducted by the Vice President for Academic Affairs.     │
│                                                                       │
│      Supervises the student evaluations of the faculty.               │
│                                                                       │
│      Corresponds with prospective students.                           │
│                                                                       │
│      Confers with students concerning academic grievances.            │
│                                                                       │
│      Assists in making curriculum recommendations.                    │
│                                                                       │
│      Conducts departmental meetings.                                  │
│                                                                       │
│      Advises students and prospective students.                       │
│                                                                       │
└─────────────────────────────────────────────────────────────────────┘
```

FIGURE 1-9. Job description for a first-level administrator.

Although the job description for a secretary outlines the duties and responsibilities of the position, a secretary can often determine much more about the people with whom she will be working and the types of duties she will be performing by looking at the job description of the person to whom she reports.

As indicated earlier, most of the manager's objectives are accomplished by working with those in his or her line of command. Therefore, when we look at the organizational chart and the job description shown in figure 1-9 for the head of the department of office administration and business education, we can conclude that most of the work carried on in that office will involve frequent contact with faculty members and students in the department and perhaps occasional contact with the person-

```
JOB DESCRIPTION

Classification:  Secretary

Reports to:  Vice President of Academic Affairs

Duties and Responsibilities:

    Coordinates the vice president's appointments and work schedule.

    Schedules and makes the logistical arrangements for committee meetings
    and conferences chaired by the vice president, as well as for those that are
    chaired by people who report directly to the vice president.

    Attends and records minutes of committee meetings.

    Assists in preparing special projects and programs.

    Collates reports submitted by the various colleges.

    Assists in preparing materials for meetings and presentations.

    Manages logistics for travel and assists in preparing and monitoring the
    travel budgets.

    Assists with the meetings of committees that are chaired by the vice president
    and by those who report directly to the vice president.

    Acts as receptionist for five-person office.

    Keeps detailed records.

    Receives, screens, and answers inquiries.

    Maintains office supply inventory.

    Operates on-line computer terminal and word processor.

    Prepares and distributes routine correspondence, forms, and other material.

    Takes and transcribes dictation.

Qualifications:

    Ability to relate effectively to faculty and administrators.

    Must be able to type 60 words per minute and take shorthand 120 words per
    minute.

    Working knowledge of the use of the computer and word processor.

    Excellent verbal and communication skills required.

    Four-year degree with a major in office administration desirable.
```

FIGURE 1-10. Job description for a secretary to a high-level administrator.

nel in the office of the dean of the college of business and economics. The secretary in the department seldom has contact with top-level administrators at Westwood.

The secretary for whom the vice president of academic affairs has line authority is much higher on the organizational chart, even though both positions have the classification of *secretary* shown on the job description. When we look at the job description shown in figure 1-10, we find that the qualifications of the secretary holding this position are much higher than those for the secretary at the lower level.

The secretary performing the duties listed on the description for this position needs to be highly skilled in many areas. Most of the duties listed are not routine and most of them require a high level of administrative ability. The secretary needs to be able to work with minimum supervision.

As shown in figure 1-11, the duties of the vice president are extensive and involve working with numerous individuals and groups at Westwood. The secretary to the vice president is actively involved in coordinating many of the activities and needs a great deal of expertise in the communication and human relations skills.

The vice president of academic affairs has line authority to the deans of the colleges; therefore, the secretary has frequent contact with middle-level administrators and some contact with other vice presidents and the president at the top administrative level. The job description indicates that several support personnel and committees report to the vice president. The secretary must also work closely with these groups.

The organizational chart shows the lines of authority and the formal communication channels; however, the working relationships in an organization depend to a considerable extent on the people involved. Effective managers, and those who work closely with them, realize that they accomplish their objectives primarily through the efforts of others and that the willingness of others to accept and respond favorably to the authority is essential. Generally, the work in the organization flows more smoothly when a spirit of cooperation and respect prevails than when people are expected to respond simply because someone in a position of authority has demanded it.

Although the secretary does not have line authority, she assists the executive in working with staff members at all levels. The way she performs her functions has a distinct impact on the organization's operations. Because the secretary holds a strategic position, her performance directly relates to how the manager's performance will be viewed by superiors, peers, and subordinates. The ultimate objective of an effective managerial–secretarial team is to develop a smooth working relationship that will allow the functions to be conducted as efficiently as possible.

Summary

All organizations, regardless of the type and legal form, have objectives that are carried out by managers who have the authority and responsibility

```
JOB DESCRIPTION

Classification:  Vice President of Academic Affairs

Reports to:  President of the University

Basic Function:  To manage all aspects of the academic program, selected universitywide
                 functions and processes, and all instructional and academic support
                 budgets.

Duties and Responsibilities:

    Supervises and coordinates work of four colleges, educational media services, six
    primary support services and programs, and other miscellaneous academic programs
    and services.

    Provides leadership for development of academic programs and faculty development.

    Manages and supervises faculty and graduate assistant personnel procedures, including
    recruitment, hiring, evaluation, and termination.

    Supervises management of personnel records of all persons included in the faculty
    EEO file, and reports annually on all personnel actions to comply with affirmative
    action requirements.

    Manages office of academic affairs with functions including budget, curriculum
    processing, catalogs, schedules, space assignment, external and internal reports, annual
    report, various faculty and staff meetings, faculty development, intra-university
    communication, and university calendar.

    Supervises academic support and development offices and programs including admissions,
    registrar, academic advising, college skills, testing, textbook services, and international
    student advising.

    Manages and/or supervises preparation and implementation of budgets for all academic
    departments and academic support services.

    Develops, implements, or supervises major developmental projects, such as academic
    reorganization and accreditation self-studies.

    Coordinates work of various academic and universitywide committees and the council
    of deans.

    Supervises development of policy related to academic standards, academic standing,
    admissions, and records.

    Supervises academic institutional research.

    Coordinates and/or supervises academic long-range planning.

    Supervises academic publications, including class schedules, catalogs, faculty handbook,
    and various program brochures.

    Represents the University externally in matters related to academic affairs.
```

FIGURE 1-11. Job description for a vice president.

for the functions of planning, organizing, controlling, staffing, and directing. The organizational chart is a graphic presentation that shows the line and staff relationships of the people involved in carrying out the objectives, as well as the formal channels of communication.

The role of the secretary in the organizational structure depends on the level of the manager to whom she reports. However, at all levels, the secretary assists the manager in carrying out his or her functions so that the objectives of the organization can be accomplished.

————————————— Questions —————————————

1. What are the three basic classifications of organizations?

2. May a partnership have more than two co-owners?

3. How does a corporation differ from a sole proprietorship and a partnership?

4. Must the managers always be part owners of the organization?

5. List the five functions of management.

6. Which function of management involves determining whether people and the various parts of the organization are progressing toward the established objectives?

7. Do lower-level managers have the primary responsibility for setting long-range goals for the organization? Discuss.

8. Is the CEO always the owner or major stockholder of an organization?

9. Discuss the differences between the role of middle managers and first-line managers.

10. Does a manager at the second level in an organization have line authority to all managers below that level? Explain.

11. Explain what is meant by "Authority comes with the position."

12. Does the head of a staff department have line authority over anyone? Explain.

13. Discuss the difference between "flat" and "tall" organizational structures.

14. What determines the number and types of departments in an organization?

15. Do all organizations have departments? Discuss.

16. Name a department that would not be found in a service-oriented business.

17. Why do some organizations have an administrative services department?

18. Does the title of the secretarial position always accurately indicate the level of the position? Discuss.

19. According to the definition of the Administrative Management Society, is *secretary–level B* or *secretary–level A* the higher-level position?

20. Does a manager work more closely with those at a higher level or those at a lower level to accomplish organizational objectives?

21. Discuss the parts of a job description.

22. Does a secretary ever have line authority? Explain.

—————————————————— Projects ——————————————————

1. Conduct library research and write a report on the advantages and disadvantages of the sole proprietorship, partnership, and corporate forms of business organizations.

2. Use the following information as you prepare an organizational chart for the controller's division of the Stonner Corporation. The supervisors of budgeting, cost analysis, cost accounting, general accounting, accounts payable, and payroll report to the manager of accounting and budgets. The supervisors of budget estimating, cost reduction, standard hour rating, and capital equipment report to the manager of industrial engineering. The managers, the supervisor of auditors (a staff position), and an executive secretary report directly to the controller.

3. Look at the Sunday edition of a metropolitan newspaper and list the skills requested in the advertisements for a secretary. Also list the titles used for the positions to be filled.

—————————————————— Cases ——————————————————

1. Vicki has worked for five years as private secretary to a vice president of the company. Much of her time is spent typing correspondence and reports. Julie, a private secretary to another vice president, plans to resign. Rather than hire a replacement for Julie, the president of the company has decided to purchase word processing equipment and have Vicki work for the two vice presidents. Vicki does not believe she will be happy working for two executives. What should she do?

2. Monica Pernell works as secretary to Edward Owsley, the sole proprietor of the business. Mr. Owsley expects Monica to perform many tasks, such as typing term papers for his children, that are not related to the business. Since Mr. Owsley considers Monica's salary a business expense for tax purposes, should she refuse to perform the non-business-related tasks?

3. Joan and Bettie both work as private secretaries to vice presidents of the Wilson Company. Joan is well-qualified and her work is always of high quality. Bettie has minimal skills and much of the work she completes cannot be used; however, she is always willing to retype the letters, reports, and so forth that contain errors. Can the company justify paying them the same salary?

PART II

CHAPTER 2

Automated Office Systems

Secretaries continue to perform the same general types of activities they have performed for many years. They continue to create correspondence and documents. They continue to store and retrieve information. They continue to do research for executives and perform numerous other functions. Today, however, they are often expected to perform many of the duties by using modern technologies and often work in one of these environments:

1. Using a standalone word processor or microcomputer that is located in the office (local) and that might or might not be connected to a computer located somewhere else.

2. Using a terminal connected to a host computer not located in the office (remote).

3. Using a local, individual work station that is some combination of the first two and that may contain additional word processing, data processing, and communication capabilities.

Many of the technologies you may expect to use in the modern office will be discussed in this chapter.

WORD AND DATA PROCESSING

Both word processing and data processing systems are used to process information, and much of the terminology, media, and equipment is similar. Word processing is generally used to refer to text material, such as letters and reports, and data processing often is used to refer to information processing that involves computation problems. Much of the equipment can be interfaced so that information may be exchanged between word processing systems and computers.

The keyboard, video display, central processing unit, and printer are the hardware of the word processing and computer systems.

Keyboard

The keyboard is an input device for word and data processors. It has character keys that are essentially the same as those on a standard typewriter. The keyboard also includes other keys needed to use the various features of the system.

The keyboard for a word processor is shown in figures 2-1 (a) and (b) and includes the following:

- *Cursory position keys.* The cursor is a beam of light that indicates where the next character or symbol keyboarded will appear on the screen. The cursor is a moving typeguide and serves the same purpose as the type position indicator found on a standard typewriter. The cursor can be moved vertically as well as horizontally across the screen where characters or symbols have been entered.

- *Operation keys.* Operation keys are used to instruct the word processor to perform electronically the formatting, locating, editing, or other procedures.

- *Transaction keys.* Transaction keys are used to inform the system when an operation is to be completed or canceled. On some processors the *execute* key is used to inform the system that a sequence is acceptable and the *cancel* key is used to end a function.

Display Screen

The televisionlike screen found on display systems is usually a cathode ray tube (CRT), which is also referred to as the video display terminal (VDT). A display screen and keyboard are shown in figure 2-2.

Display screens come in several colors, configurations, and sizes. The viewing screen load may range from only a few lines to more than one page, depending on the system used.

The screen displays the following:

- Information as it is keyed in.
- Information that has been previously keyed in and retrieved for review.
- System communications to the operator.

Character Keys

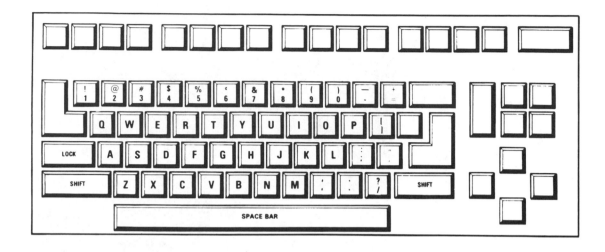

Special Function Keys for Operations

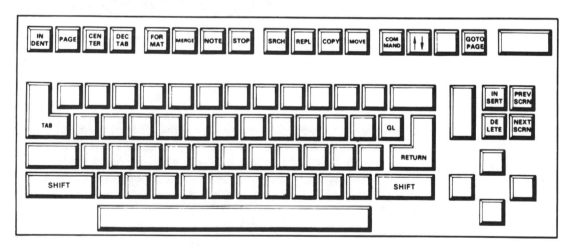

FIGURE 2-1. Word processor keyboard. (Courtesy of Wang Laboratories, Inc.)

Central Processing Unit (CPU)

The CPU contains the "logic" that controls the entire system. Information is stored in the memory circuits and through operator commands can be transferred in and out of memory to a storage device or an output unit such as a printer or transmitted to another system.

FIGURE 2-2. Display screen and keyboard.

Printer

A printer looks very much like a typewriter without a keyboard and is the unit that produces the hard (printed) copy. A printer on a word processor may print out hundreds of pages a day at speeds of anywhere from 40 characters per second up to hundreds of characters per second; therefore, the print device needs to be more efficient than that found on standard typewriters.

Some printers are bidirectional; that is, they print one line from left to right and the next line from right to left. A line printer prints an entire line of text at a time. Although some printing techniques are faster than others, not all printers produce the same quality type.

The characters may be produced on paper in several ways, including using the dot-matrix printer or the daisy wheel printer. With the *dot-matrix printer,* electrically driven pins are used to punch characterlike figures of dots through the ribbon of the unit onto the paper. With the *daisy wheel printer,* a separate letter is contained on each petal of a disk that resembles a daisy, as shown in figure 2-3.

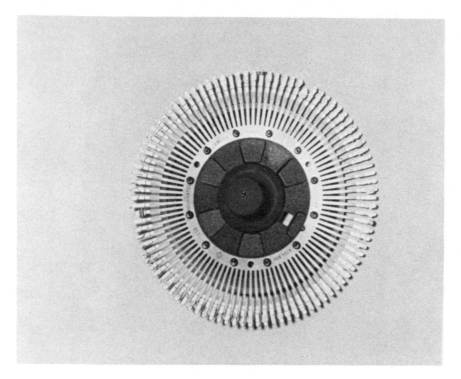

FIGURE 2-3. Daisy wheel printer.

Software

The software used with the systems are the media used to store the instructions or programs that cause the word or data processing systems to execute the user's commands.

Disk

The storage medium for a system is known as a disk. A floppy disk (also called diskette) is flexible, is coated with a magnetic material, and can store more than 100 pages of material. Floppy disks, such as the one shown in figure 2-4, are used extensively with word processing and data processing systems.

A hard disk is composed of a metal plate sealed in a circular hard plastic case. Thousands of pages of material can be stored on a single hard disk.

FIGURE 2-4. Diskette.

WORK STATIONS

A standalone work station operates independently. It can range from an ordinary typewriter to a highly sophisticated system that uses computer technology and has storage, communications, and other capabilities. The electronic standalone systems found in many offices are comprised of an input unit, control and memory electronics, a storage device, and a typewriter or letter-quality printer.

Shared-logic word processing systems share central control and memory circuitry. Several work station terminals at various locations throughout the company may share a single central computer that contains a CPU, memory, an arithmetic logic unit that performs mathematical functions, and input–output circuits. In many companies where the shared-logic system is used, the terminals are used for both word processing and data processing.

Although many companies use a word processing center that is staffed with specialists, the trend appears to be toward traditional secretarial work stations, with the secretary using word processing equipment and working for more than one executive.

Companies that have word processing centers generally have the centers structured in one of the following three ways:

1. Centralized word processing center serving all users in the organization.

2. Centralized word processing center supplemented by satellite operations that concentrate on work to be completed by a particular segment of the business.

3. Decentralized satellite centers with each serving a particular area of the business.

These three structures are illustrated in figure 2-5.

WORD PROCESSORS

The electronic typewriter is the most basic word processing machine currently found in offices. The electronic typewriter looks very much like a standard electric typewriter with additional keys needed for word processing functions.

All electronic typewriters have an internal memory that is capable of storing keystrokes. The memory size and other capabilities depend on the make and model of the machine.

The memory capacity of an electronic typewriter is stated in characters or number of lines and ranges from only a few characters to several thousand. With some units, the memory is erased if power is interrupted or turned off; others, however, are equipped with a battery backup to preserve information in case of power failures.

Many electronic typewriters feature a visual display, such as the one shown in figure 2-6, so that the typist can see the material and make corrections before the data are printed onto paper. This feature is especially useful during editing. The typist can see what text the machine is looking at in its memory and can make changes before printing the line.

The electronic typewriters have either a single element or a daisy wheel and are usually available with a variety of typefaces and print styles.

Decimal centering, right margin justification, search, replace, word wraparound, and other features found on dedicated text editing machines are also available on some electronic typewriters. However, the entire document cannot be viewed on a screen at one time before it is printed out.

When using some display text editing word processing systems, you begin each major activity by making a selection from a menu, such as the following:

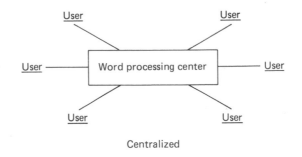

Centralized

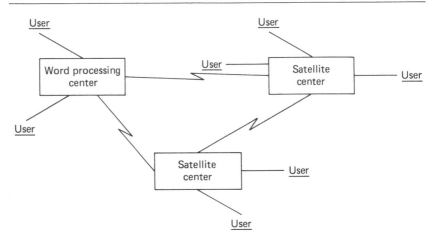

Centralized with satellites

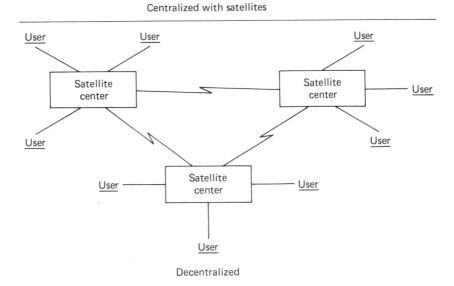

Decentralized

FIGURE 2-5. Word processing center structures.

- Edit old document
- Create new document
- Print document
- Special print functions
- Document filing
- Document index
- Telecommunications
- Other functions

Some word processing features are standard and some are offered as options on certain systems. As a secretary, you need to be aware of the capabilities of the system to which you may have access. You may be able to use many of the features to increase the productivity of your office.

As letters and other documents are being typed, they appear on the terminal screen and any changes, such as deleting, moving, or adding lines or paragraphs or correcting typographical errors, can be made before the copy is transferred to the printer or to some other terminal.

FIGURE 2-6. Xerox® 630 Memorywriter. (Courtesy of the Xerox Corporation)

Features not found on standard typewriters but found on many word processing systems include the following:

- *Wraparound.* Carries a word to the next line when it exceeds the right-hand margin limit; thus, this feature eliminates the necessity for the operator to use the return key.

- *Decimal or align tab.* Aligns the decimal points in columns of numbers or justifies the right-hand margin of columns where no decimal is used.

- *Strikeover.* Replaces incorrect characters, symbols, or spaces on a one-for-one basis.

- *Reformat.* Changes format settings such as margins, lines per page, tab locations, and so forth and automatically readjusts the copy.

- *Right-hand justification.* Aligns right-hand margin of text.

- *Autoscore.* Underlines text as it is being entered.

- *Copy.* Duplicates one part of a document in another location in the same document or in a second document.

- *Move.* Relocates consecutive text from one part of a document to another location in the same document or to a second document.

- *Delete.* Removes a space, character, series of characters or spaces, line, paragraph, or page. The system automatically readjusts the remaining text.

- *Insert.* Adds a space, character, series of characters or spaces, line, paragraph, or page. The system automatically readjusts to accommodate the added text.

- *Hyphenation.* Hyphenates words according to preprogrammed rules.

- *Pagination.* Numbers pages consecutively, even after text has been inserted or deleted and when the format has been changed.

- *Spelling verification.* Searches the copy and highlights the misspelled words by matching the keyboarded word with the words stored in the memory.

- *Global search.* Locates and highlights a specified word or phrase throughout an entire document.

- *Replacement.* Locates one or all instances of defined consecutive text and replaces them with some other text.

- *Headers and footers.* Prints standard text used at the top and bottom of each page in a document at proper locations during the printout.

In addition to the text editing functions performed on the word processor, many secretaries especially appreciate having the opportunity to use the word processor for filing, merging documents, and addressing envelopes.

Filing

Having a word processor in your office does not eliminate the need for filing, but a word processor does change the method of filing documents and saves time and space.

Space is saved because a hard (paper) copy of the document may not be required and the equivalent of more than 100 typed standard pages can be stored electronically on one archived (file) disk.

Some systems allow the operator to assign a document number for identification and retrieval purposes; others automatically assign system-generated numbers. Some systems indicate the date the document was last filed and the number of pages in the file index.

The disks on some small systems may be filled in one day and disks on large-capacity systems are eventually filled and the documents must be deleted from them or moved to an archive disk. When documents that have been filed on an archive disk are needed, they can be electronically copied back to the system disk by performing a retrieval operation at the work station. All of the text, format lines, and other electronic codes are kept with the document; and transferring documents from one disk to another takes only a few seconds. Once the document is back on the system disk, the secretary can perform the operations desired on the document or print a hard copy.

Merge

Secretaries often consider merge one of the most time-saving applications of the word processing system. Rather than type the same basic letter or document numerous times, the secretary can enter everything except the information that is to change into one document and the information that changes into a second document. The information from the two documents can then be merged into one printed document.

Assume, for example, that the same basic letter is to be sent to 50 customers. The secretary would type the basic letter once, minus the variable information, in one document. The variable information, such as the customer's name, address, name used in the salutation, and other relevant information for each customer, would be typed in the second document. During printing, the information from the basic letter and the variable information for each customer would merge into one printed letter. Each customer would receive a personalized letter even though the secretary typed the letter only once.

Addressing Envelopes and Labels

A variable list with names and addresses and other information can be used to address envelopes or labels. The system can be instructed to print only the name and address and omit the other information, such as the date, salutation, and other variable information used in the previous example.

Mathematical Functions

Software packages can be used with many systems to instruct the system to perform mathematical functions, such as add, subtract, multiply, divide, calculate percentages, and accumulate subtotals.

COMPUTERS

The computer is being used by many executives and secretaries for a variety of tasks. Through the use of software packages, it is being used as an appointment calendar, a reminder file, an address and telephone directory, and in numerous other ways.

Appointment Calendar

This capability permits the secretary or executive to set up and electronically maintain a calendar for a department or staff. For example, if your boss wanted to arrange a meeting for a particular time, you could access not only his or her calendar stored in the computer but also the calendars of all those expected to attend the meeting to determine whether or not they would be available. This task may be accomplished at home terminals and from other remote sites, as well as in the office.

Reminder File

Information about assignments, items requiring action, and scheduled events can be stored in the computer and automatically displayed to indicate important meetings, deadlines, or activities for that day or week.

Address and Telephone Directory

Multiple up-to-date lists of names, addresses, phone numbers, and other information about those people the executive frequently contacts can be stored in the computer and can be easily accessed by name, organization, city, and so forth.

Calls received may be read, reviewed, and filed; or the messages can be forwarded to someone else.

Electronic Mail

You or the executive can send and receive messages electronically over interconnected terminals. Once a memorandum or other document is ready to be transmitted, a function key is depressed and the message is sent. A notice indicating that mail has been received appears on the work station screen of the mail recipient and messages may be read, printed out, or acted upon in some other way. If the recipient is not logged on the system, the message will appear at the time of log in.

Reports

When reports contain statistical data, the secretary or executive can use the computer to process the data and present the information in text and graphic forms in only a fraction of the time required if the computer were not used. Suppose, for example, that an executive must submit a report projecting income for the next five years. The executive must assume values for sales revenue, overhead costs, interest rates, cost of materials, repeat business, and so forth. The executive makes a columnar sheet, bar charts, and pie charts containing all of the information and submits the report to the controller who asks that the repeat business be assumed to be 80 percent instead of the 75 percent the executive projected.

The executive must, therefore, recalculate all of the columnar values affected by the change and reconstruct all of the supporting graphic aids. A spread-sheet program on a diskette can be used to transform a micro-computer screen into a huge columnar sheet, permitting the user to work with a large number of interrelated values. Thus, the executive or secretary can change the 75 percent to 80 percent, press a function key, and produce documents reflecting the changes.

Software packages can be used to produce budgets, action and profit plans, sales forecasts, income statements, cash-flow projections, expense reports, job cost analysis, and so forth in text or graphic form on the screen or as hard copy, in black and white or in color, and in letter-quality or in draft-quality print. The user simply inserts the software diskette in the computer and follows the directions appearing on the screen.

Data can be transferred back and forth between word processors and data processors.

With the growing array of inexpensive high-technology software and hardware available to the business executive, the secretary's exposure to such products will parallel her employer's interest in and use of them.

INPUT–OUTPUT

The secretary controls work station components through various combinations of keyboards, the telephone, interchangeable software on magnetic media or boards, switching devices, and networks.

Data input and retrieval methods are getting easier. Optical character recognition (OCRs) readers and voice-input technologies have improved and are less expensive. They are moving into the office-equipment line and out of the computer-center line of equipment.

The OCR scanner reads typed characters optically and records the information on the system's magnetic medium. The document can be called up on a word processing terminal even though the keyboarding may have been done on a typewriter with a different size of type.

COMMUNICATION LINKS

When data are to be sent from one word or data processor to another, obviously some type of communication link is required.

Acoustic- and direct-connect modems are used to link word and data processing systems to the telephone system to allow communications to be sent and received over the telephone. The acoustic modem is a cradle consisting of two rubber cups, one for the mouthpiece and the other for the earphone of a telephone handset. When the handset is placed in the cradle, the signal from the communications circuit of the word or data processing system is coupled to the telephone system. A direct-connect modem connects the communications circuit of the word or data processing system to the telephone system through a hard-wire interface.

A direct cable is often used to connect word and data processors and other equipment within the organization.

TELECONFERENCING

Many organizations use audio teleconferencing as an economical method of communicating with others at various locations without the participants having to leave the office. In-service training, seminars, and other types of meetings can be conducted through speakerphones in offices or a conference room or through telephone systems that allow several individuals to carry on a conversation simultaneously.

The electronic blackboard permits diagrams, illustrations, handwriting, and other visual aids to be transmitted on one telephone line while participants use another telephone line for the conversation.

Videoconferencing is used by executives to talk with a group without traveling to the location where they may be assembled. The use of videoconferencing gives the participants a feeling of being in the same room. Videoteleconferencing is not used extensively but is used by some to introduce a product or discuss important issues with a group without actually traveling.

REPROGRAPHICS

For many years, fluid and stencil (mimeograph) duplicators were used in offices when multiple copies were needed. They are inexpensive reproduction methods; however, they are not used in most offices today. In many offices, they have been replaced by offset duplicators and fiber optic copiers.

Offset

The offset process is a fast and economical way to duplicate when numerous high-quality documents are needed. Many companies use the offset process when duplicating price lists, forms, bulletins, and similar types of documents.

The offset master is a sheet of heavy, coated paper and can be prepared on the typewriter by using a noncorrectable film ribbon or a ribbon made especially for use with the offset. A pencil or soft eraser may be used to correct errors, but the master is usually ruined if more than one correction is made in a particular spot.

Masters can also be prepared on an electronic scanner, such as the one shown in figure 2-7. The scanner is especially useful when the documents to be duplicated include pictures or diagrams and print that is not the standard size found on typewriters.

Various colors of ink can be used, and the copy can be reproduced on paper of various sizes and weights, as well as on both sides.

Copiers

Almost all copiers found in offices today use plain, ordinary paper and the trend in copiers is toward the dry-toned system.

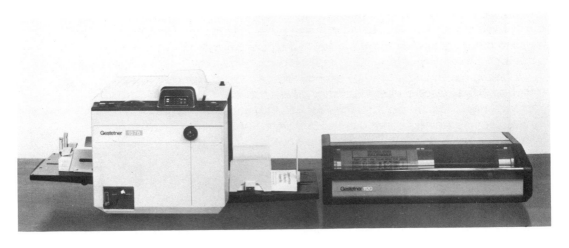

FIGURE 2-7. Offset printer and electronic scanner. (Courtesy of Gestetner Corporation)

Most of the machines are easy to operate; however, you should carefully study the manuals provided for the machines. Not only do you need to know how to operate the machines, you also need to know their capabilities. Many of the copiers have either standard or add-on accessories that enable you to do much more than make the same size copy from an original.

Several of the machines will accept and reproduce documents as large as 11 inches by 17 inches. Some machines reduce the copy by as much as 75 percent and enlarge the copy to more than 125 percent of the original size. Documents can be printed in black, brown, and blue on some machines. If documents of several pages need to be reproduced and collated, the collating and automatic document feed features can save time. Some copiers have feed decks that can hold several hundred sheets of paper. The duplexing feature, which enables copying on both sides of a page, is available on several copiers. A copier with the collating feature is shown in figure 2-8.

In many companies, the use of the copier is controlled in some way, such as one of the following:

- Users record their name, department, and the number of copies made.
- One operator may be solely responsible for the use of the machine.
- Only authorized individuals may have a key to the copier or the room where it is housed.

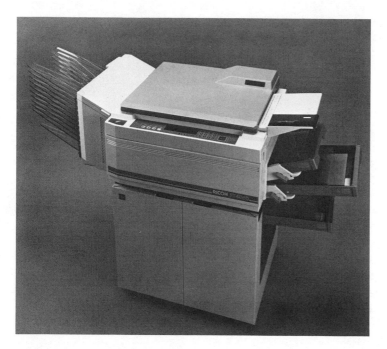

FIGURE 2-8. Copier with collating feature. (Courtesy of Ricoh of America, Inc.)

Intelligent Copier

An intelligent copier is a reproduction device capable of receiving graphic or alphabetic information from a word processor, computer, or other copier and converting the information into printed copy. The intelligent copier and the other equipment can be hard-wired or telecommunication-connected and documents can be sent and received locally or remotely.

MICROGRAPHICS

Microrecording reduces the amount of space needed to store records, may eliminate the need for hard copies, and provides a means of making duplicate copies. The most common types of microforms are films, reels, and cartridges; microfiche; aperture cards; ultrafiche; and jackets.

Microfilm

Microfilm was the first type of microrecord and was used first by the banking industry to photograph customers' checks. The microfilm is made by photographing the original records on 16mm or 35mm (millimeter) film. Microfilm reels are desirable when information is filmed continuously in sequence and does not need to be updated frequently. Changes can be made by cutting and splicing the film, but the process is slow and costly.

Microfiche

The word *microfiche* (pronounced "microfeesh") is a combination of the prefix *micro* (meaning small) and the French word *fiche* (meaning a file index card). The microfiche contains multiple microimages arranged in a grid pattern and is frequently 6 inches by 4 inches, which provides for 98 frames at a 24X reduction. A reduction ratio of 24X means that the image on the film is 1/24th the size of the original record. When a greater reduction ratio is used, more pages can be placed on the microfiche sheet.

A microfiche usually contains a heading at the top to identify the contents. This heading can be read without magnification. The information on a fiche is usually closely related, such as reports, directories, and manuals.

Ultrafiche

Ultrafiche contains images reduced more than 90X; therefore, thousands of images can be placed on a single fiche.

Cartridge

A cartridge is more convenient than a reel since it is self-threading. Furthermore, the film is protected from fingerprints that can mar or damage the film when manual threading is involved. A cartridge is a convenient way to store information by subject. The cartridge can easily be indexed, stored, and retrieved.

Aperture Card

An aperture card is a standard data processing card on which a micro-image can be mounted. The card may contain a single 35mm image or up to eight 16mm images. The aperture card is frequently used for separate units, such as drawings and diagrams, rather than for sequential types of information.

The content of the information contained in the card is printed in the upper margin as well as punched in the card; thus, the card can be stored and retrieved manually or mechanically.

Jacket

Microfilm jackets are plastic carriers with one or more sleeves designed to accept single frames or strips of 16mm or 35mm film. The images can be easily added or removed when the information stored in the jacket needs to be updated, but the images do not need to be removed from the jacket when they are to be read or copied.

Computer-Output-Microfilm (COM)

Large companies use the COM process, which eliminates the need for preparing a hard copy. The output to be stored is sent in electronic coded form to a recorder where it is automatically decoded, photographed, and reduced to microimage size on film. Each of the microimages is automatically coded so that the information may be retrieved. Not only may a document be easily retrieved, a hard copy can be made.

Readers and Printers

Reader equipment, such as that shown in figure 2-9, can be used to illuminate, magnify, and display a microform document on a screen. Micrographic copier devices can be used when a paper copy of a microform document is required; however, the paper copy recreated from the film image is rarely as clear as the original.

FIGURE 2-9. Microfiche reader. (Courtesy of Eye Communication Systems, Inc.)

──────────────── Summary ────────────────

The traditional one-to-one manager–secretary arrangement is no longer found in many offices. Technological advances have simplified many of the tasks the secretary must perform; thus, one secretary often is able to assist several executives in carrying out their functions.

Today, a secretary in many offices is able to create a message or document at her work station, view the entire document, and easily make the necessary changes before printing the copy. Without leaving her desk, she may electronically send the message to a remote location, file the copy on a disk, or through the use of an intelligent copier make multiple copies.

Messages received in the terminal can be captured on a storage device, displayed on a screen for review and revision, or printed on paper. The revised document may be telecommunicated back to the person who sent it so that he or she will be aware of the changes.

As you study the remaining chapters in this text, consider the ways modern technologies may be used to help you and others in the organization work more efficiently.

──────────────── Questions ────────────────

1. Discuss the differences between word processing and data processing.

2. What constitutes the hardware of a data processing system?

3. Why does a word processor or data processor keyboard have more keys than a regular typewriter keyboard?

4. What type of information is displayed on the CRT?

5. Discuss the different types of printers that may be used in data processing.

6. Explain the difference between software and hardware.

7. What is meant by the statement, "A standalone work station operates independently"?

8. Explain the ways in which the word processing function can be structured.

9. Does the visual display on an electronic typewriter serve the same purpose as the screen on a word processor? Explain.

10. What is the purpose of a menu on a word processor?

11. Does all word processing equipment perform the same functions?

12. Discuss the difference between the "copy" and "move" editing functions.

13. What are the advantages of storing data on a floppy disk?

14. How can the computer be used to simplify the scheduling of meetings?

15. What is meant by electronic mail?

16. Can mail always be sent electronically? Explain.

17. How can an OCR reader be used to save time in word and data processing?

18. Discuss the different types of modems.

19. What is the main advantage of teleconferencing?

20. How can masters for documents that are not typewritten be prepared for use on the offset?

21. Are all copiers intelligent copiers? Explain.

22. Discuss the differences between microfiche and ultrafiche.

23. Why would a long report not be stored on an aperture card?

────────────────────── Projects ──────────────────────

1. Look at recent issues of magazines in the business section of your college library and prepare a list of the features of copiers, computers, word processors, and other office equipment promoted by the different manufacturers.

2. Talk with friends who work in offices and make a list of the equipment they use and the features of the equipment they find most useful.

3. Visit your library and learn how to use the readers to view different types of microforms.

────────────────────── Cases ──────────────────────

1. Mary Hanson's boss has decided to buy word processing equipment and believes Mary should learn to use the equipment by enrolling in a word processing course offered by a local junior college. Her boss has offered to have the company pay the fees for the course, but he believes Mary should not expect to be paid to attend the eight-hour sessions that are to be held on three consecutive Saturdays. Is Mary justified in believing she should be paid?

2. Wilma and Elaine are students in a secretarial program at a community college. Wilma works hard to improve her typing speed and accuracy. Elaine tells her that because she plans to work for a company that has word processing equipment she sees no need to work hard to improve her typing skill since corrections can easily be made. Is Elaine's reasoning sound?

CHAPTER 3

Office Environment

The term *ergonomics* is frequently used in discussing office environment. Ergonomics is a science that seeks to adapt work and working conditions to the worker by considering both the physiological and psychological needs of the worker. It is an attempt to establish the best possible relationship between workers and their physical environment.

Many factors, such as layout, furniture, color, temperature, noise, and lighting, that have an impact on the productivity and morale of office workers will be discussed in this chapter.

OFFICE LAYOUT

Everyone is familiar with the traditional office that is a private area with walls which extend from the floor to the ceiling and doors which can be closed and locked. The typical furniture found in these offices is a large wood or metal desk, a typewriter desk or a return on the secretarial desk, a secretarial chair, one or more chairs for visitors, and files or a credenza.

Some company secretaries who work for high-level executives may continue to have traditional private offices. However, the office landscaping or open office concept has been the trend in many companies that have constructed buildings during the past two decades. When the office landscaping layout is used, the office space is arranged in configurations that provide the most economical use of floor space possible.

In many companies using the open office design, the offices of the high-level executives are along the exterior walls and the other offices are located in the interior part of the room, which is often large enough to accommodate 20 or more people. Frequently, glass partitions are used so that the executive and secretary can see each other.

When office space is limited, the functions to be performed by the different employees should be considered when assigning space; therefore, the work areas will not necessarily be the same size. Often, an irregular layout, such as the one shown in figure 3-1, is used to eliminate the monotony of identical rows of offices.

The office arrangement should be aesthetically appealing, but aesthetic considerations should never have priority over practical aspects. The ease with which the functions can be carried on should always have top priority.

FIGURE 3-1. Irregular office layout. (Courtesy of Steelcase Inc.)

Although little empirical evidence is available to indicate whether the open office improves productivity, most current data relating to workers' attitudes toward the plan indicate workers favor the plan. Proponents of the open office design cite the following advantages:

1. *Flexibility.* When office walls are not involved, work areas can be installed or changed rapidly at a fraction of the cost of removing walls. Since the office area can often be reconfigured in only a few hours, the work of those in the area is minimally interrupted.

2. *Space utilization.* With open office landscaping, the worker is not fitted into the space; rather, the space is fitted around the worker to provide the most effective environment possible. As a result, a larger percentage of the office space is used.

3. *Production.* The work areas can be designed to complement work flow and communication between those whose activities are closely related. Work stations can be open and shared by using modules that have pass-throughs between two work stations. As shown in figure 3-2, the CRT is mounted on a carousel and can be shared.

4. *Maintenance.* Costly changes are not necessary in the heating and lighting, ventilation, and air conditioning systems each time the area is rearranged. Fewer light fixtures are needed since the elimination of walls between offices allows a more efficient placement of fixtures. Maintenance costs are also reduced because cleaning is easier.

5. *Capital flow.* Walls are considered part of the building and are depreciated over a fifteen-year period. Panels used with the open plan are depreciated as office equipment over a five-year period; thus, a return on the investment in the open plan furnishings is much faster.

MODULAR FURNITURE

Although traditional furniture may be used in the open office, modular furniture is normally used because it is portable and flexible. Modular furniture consists of components such as partitions, desks, and work surfaces, that can be arranged in a variety of ways to facilitate the performance of tasks as efficiently as possible. As explained in the following sections, components that have been designed for particular functions can be added to the work area as needed.

Desks

The desk is usually 45 in. to 65 in. wide, 24 in. to 30 in. deep, and 29 in. to 30 in. high. It is normally either a single-pedestal or a double-pedestal type;

FIGURE 3-2. Individual work stations can be open and shared. (Courtesy of Steelcase Inc.)

that is, it has drawers on the right or left side or on both sides. Each pedestal usually has two to five drawers ranging in size from a box drawer to a file drawer large enough to accommodate hanging folders. A double-pedestal desk with a center drawer, three file drawers, and two box drawers is shown in figure 3-3.

The type of secretarial desk found in most offices is L-shaped with a left or right machine-height return. The return usually is 36 in. to 42 in. wide, 18 in. to 24 in. deep, and 26 in. high. An L-shaped desk with a left machine-height return with a pedestal is shown in figure 3-4.

Word Processing and Computer Desks

When a display terminal and keyboard are part of the work station, the screen should be at the eye level of the operator and positioned at a

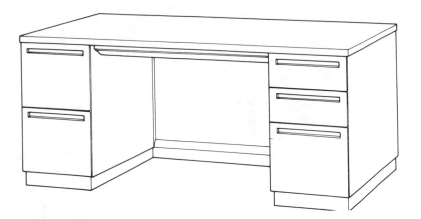

FIGURE 3-3. Double-pedestal desk with a center drawer, three file drawers, and two box drawers.

proper viewing distance. Input keyboards should be at a proper keying height and document copy should be at a comfortable reading angle in line with the keyboard and the screen. Machine-height desks may be used, or desk-height furniture can be converted into an efficient ergonomic work station, as shown in figure 3-5.

Tables and Work Surfaces

Work surfaces that can be used alone or with other components are available in desk and keyboard heights and in numerous widths. When several secretaries work in the same general area or on the same floor of

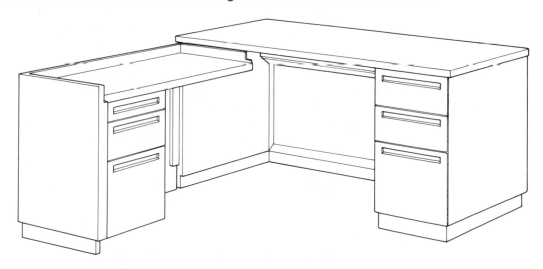

FIGURE 3-4. L-shaped desk with a left machine height return with a pedestal.

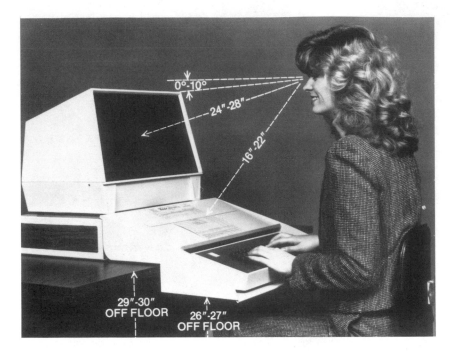

FIGURE 3-5. Efficient ergonomic CRT work station. (Courtesy of Mead-Hatcher Inc.)

the building, tables are often placed in a central location rather than in the separate offices.

Storage

The amount of storage space needed in the office depends on the nature of the work. A credenza or one or more pedestal components are often part of the work station. The credenza may be only a few feet long or may extend six or more feet. Most modular credenzas have hinged doors or drawers or a combination of drawers and doors, as illustrated in figure 3-6.

In many offices, the trend is toward using a storage station that is created by combining upper storage units along with the pedestal components, as shown in figure 3-7.

When a large quantity of material must be filed in the office area, lateral files are often used. The lateral file, also known as a side file, opens from the long side of the cabinet. The lateral file appears to be a bookshelf with doors or a chest of drawers, as shown in figure 3-8.

Because the long side opens out, lateral files require less depth and are particularly suited to narrow spaces. They are available in numerous shapes and sizes and normally have two to five drawers.

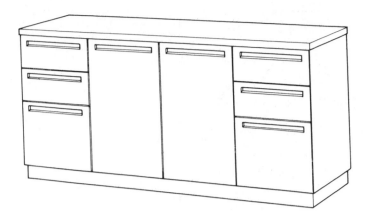

FIGURE 3-6. Credenza with hinged doors and drawers.

FIGURE 3-7. Storage station with upper and lower units.

FIGURE 3-8. Lateral file.

When space is not limited, traditional drawer files may be used. They, too, vary in height, width, depth, and number and size of drawers. The card, letter, and legal sizes are the most common sizes of file cabinet drawers; however, cabinets with drawers appropriate for filing virtually all types of things are available.

Vertical storage units or bookcases are used in many offices for reference books, magazines, journals, and other items that cannot easily be stored in drawers or files.

Partitions

Although files, bookcases, and other items are sometimes used to separate the work areas in the open office, acoustical partitions are often used. The partitions are available in a variety of shapes, heights, colors, and patterns. They help create audio and visual privacy as well as enhance the area's appearance.

CHAIRS

Correct seating is essential to comfort. Most office chairs are designed to fit closely to the body's contours, and an ergonomically designed secretarial chair can be adjusted so that the various parts of the chair are

FIGURE 3-9. Secretarial chairs should be adjustable. (Courtesy of Cramer, Inc.)

appropriately positioned for the one using the chair. An inappropriately designed chair can reduce productivity, cause you to tire quickly, and result in physical discomfort, such as muscle fatigue, backaches, and headaches.

The seat height and the back height and angle of the chair need to be adjustable, as shown in figure 3-9. Most secretarial chairs have a height of at least 16 inches and allow for a four- or five-inch adjustment in the height. The pneumatic system found on some chairs makes the adjustment to the correct height easy and smooth. This automatic adjustment feature is especially useful when more than one person must use the same work station.

The backrest should provide continuous support. Some chairs are designed to permit the backrest to be locked at the desired angle when a lever is placed in one position and to move freely with the natural movements of the body when the lever is placed in another position.

The chair should be padded and have soft edges that eliminate pressure points behind the knees. It should allow free blood circulation regardless of your position in the chair.

The chair should be a swivel type and should have casters that roll freely when someone is sitting in the chair but roll slowly when the chair is unoccupied. A chair mat made of material such as vinyl, acrylic, or polycarbonate will ease chair movement at the desk or work station and protect office carpeting.

When most of your tasks involve typing or performing other work that requires you to bring your eyes and arms to the work, the chair need not have arms. However, a chair with arms can help reduce fatigue when a considerable amount of your time is spent looking at a display terminal or at work that must be brought to your eyes. Therefore, in many offices, the secretary needs two chairs—one with arms and one without arms—in her work area.

OTHER ENVIRONMENTAL FACTORS

In addition to the layout and furnishings of the office, other factors, such as noise, color, and temperature, can have an impact on the secretary's productivity and morale and should be considered.

Color

Color has a psychological effect on office workers and thus influences production, attitudes, and morale. Color also has an effect on office visitors.

Blue and green are regarded as cool colors and tend to have a calming effect on people. The cool colors are appropriate for offices with southern exposures. Warm colors, such as yellow, brown, tan, and pink, often are used in offices with northern exposures. Natural tints (e.g., beige, off-white, and buff) are light colors and are needed in offices where extensive detailed work on white paper is involved. Gray is not recommended for offices since it tends to have a sleep-producing effect.

Constant exposure to extremely bright and contrasting colors can cause the eyes to become tired quickly and frequently results in tension and headaches.

In addition to producing a psychological effect, colors can be used to change the perceptions people have concerning the dimensions of a room. Light colors make a room appear larger. Long, narrow offices appear wider when dark colors are used on the end walls and light colors are used on the side walls. Dark colors make the ceiling appear lower. One wall may be painted a different color from the others to make a square room more attractive.

The most desirable color or colors for an office depends on the functions to be performed in the office, its size, its location in the building, and the climate of the geographic area.

Lighting

Good lighting can improve productivity, reduce errors, and minimize eye fatigue and headaches. Lighting can also be used to differentiate one space from another in open office layouts.

Direct glare should be eliminated and the lighting should be uniformly distributed in your working area. In the open office environment, illumination often includes ambient lighting supplemented by task lighting. You have the right to expect the proper amount and quality of lighting for your area, even though you probably will not have any input concerning the type of lighting used for the building.

Temperature and Air Quality

The ideal working temperature in an office is about 68° Fahrenheit when the humidity is in the range of 40% to 60%. To conserve energy, many companies set the thermostat a few degrees lower in the winter and several degrees higher in the summer. The temperature level will usually not please everyone and is often a source of irritation to some employees. When you find the temperature is uncomfortable, you should try to adjust to the situation by wearing appropriate clothing. In extreme situations where your productivity is adversely affected, you may need to ask for permission to use a space heater or a fan.

The air conditioning system and other devices are used in many offices to clean the air of dust, dirt, and odors. To further reduce office pollution, many companies restrict smoking to certain areas. Should you have to work in the proximity of someone who smokes and you find the smoke offensive, you should courteously ask the person to abstain. When you have a good working relationship with the person, he or she will usually comply. If you smoke, you should demonstrate the same courtesy toward the other person. If the other person asks you whether you object to his or her smoking, you should answer truthfully.

Keep in mind, too, that other odors, such as perfume and deodorants, are also offensive to some people and thus should be used in moderation, especially when you must work closely with others in areas that are not well-ventilated.

Noise

The noise level is an environmental factor that has an effect on office productivity. Although absolute silence is not desirable in the office, some types of noise can be distracting and cause fatigue and nervous conditions. When the noise interferes with your being able to concentrate or work comfortably, you should attempt to have something done to correct the situation.

Excessive noise is caused primarily by the layout of the work area, machines, surface coverings, and people. Sometimes people with related tasks can be assigned to the same work area to isolate certain types of noises and to reduce the amount of traffic. Sound-absorbing (acoustical) materials used on the ceiling, floor, and partitions, as shown in figure 3-10, greatly reduce the noise level. Low ceilings shorten sound paths and help reduce the noise level. Hard surfaces, such as metal, wood, and glass, reflect sounds; soft surfaces, such as porous ceiling tiles and partitions, draperies, and carpeting, absorb sounds.

Sound-absorbent pads can be placed under typewriters and other machines to help reduce the noise. Sound-absorbing covers can be placed over some types of equipment.

FIGURE 3-10. Decorative acoustical panels help keep sound at a comfortable level. (Courtesy of Steelcase Inc.)

People working in the same area should be considerate of others. Do not carry on loud conversations. When talking on the telephone, speak distinctly and loudly enough to be heard easily by the one with whom you are talking, but keep your voice low enough to avoid disturbing others. If possible, operate noisy machines at times when you believe the noise will be least disturbing to others.

Avoid vigorously chewing or popping gum, slamming drawers or doors, tapping pencils on the desk, or any other noisy habits that could be annoying to others.

When certain types of work are being performed, music can reduce the monotony and contribute to a pleasant work atmosphere. The music may be transmitted throughout the offices by a speaker system over which you have no control. However, when you have control over the music for your area, you should keep it low enough that it does not distract others. The music should be conducive to the type of work being performed. Instrumental music is usually preferred in office situations. The music should not be continuous; rather, it should be provided at the times when fatigue most frequently occurs.

Periodically check with others concerning the appropriateness of the volume and type of music.

Safety

Since the enactment of the Occupational Safety and Health Act of 1970, most businesses involved in interstate commerce have established safety programs and endeavor to make all employees aware of safety precautions through meetings, safety brochures, posters, bulletin boards, and so forth. The cooperation of employees in helping to identify and eliminate potential accident situations is essential if the programs are to be effective.

As a secretary, you should be aware of the office hazards that can cause accidents, that create discomfort or inconvenience, and that can be costly in terms of hospital and medical benefits as well as in a loss of office productivity.

Most office accidents are caused by tripping on carpets, extension cords, or other objects on the floor or by slipping on wet or waxed floors. Floor space should be clean, well-lighted, and free from debris that can cause a fall. Coffee, water, or other liquids spilled on the floor should be removed immediately.

Office equipment can be a hazard when not operated according to the instructions. Do not attempt to repair electrical equipment without turning it off and unless you have the proper knowledge. All electrical equipment (e.g., typewriters, word processors, copiers, coffeemakers) should be properly grounded. Frayed cords should be replaced. Avoid catching jewelry, hair, garments, and fingers in the moving parts of the machines you are operating.

Be careful when using the paper cutter. Always secure the lever when the cutter is not in use. Use the proper instruments when opening packages and envelopes to avoid paper cuts. Store sharp objects, such as razor blades, in a container.

Flammable liquids should be properly stored. Space heaters and other electrical appliances should be carefully used and should be turned off when no one is in the area. Do not leave a burning cigarette unattended.

Desk and file drawers should not be left open, and the work area should be arranged so that you can move around conveniently. Do not store supplies, books, or other items on high shelves or in hard-to-reach areas. Always seek assistance when moving heavy equipment or furniture.

Know the action to take in case of fires, tornadoes, and other catastrophic situations. Know where fire extinguishers are located and know how to use them.

Emergency telephone numbers should be kept near the telephone and should include the following: hospital, ambulance, and fire and police departments. Also maintain a file of the names and telephone numbers of relatives or friends to be contacted should an emergency arise involving someone in your work area.

Keep in mind, too, that accidents which occur away from the office have a serious impact on the company. Try to avoid unsafe conditions and situations at all times.

Privacy

Whether your work area is of the traditional type or is part of the open office plan, it should provide for the basic needs of privacy, individuality, status, and belonging.

Privacy does not necessarily mean being alone. Rather, it means that you should be able to regulate your interaction with others. You should be able to carry on a confidential conversation, concentrate on your work without being interrupted by coworkers, and work without being distracted by excessive noise. When confidential work must be performed on a typewriter, computer, or word processor, you may place the machine so that you will be facing the passageway, as shown in figure 3-11. With this arrangement, the screen images are visible only to the one using the machine and access to the area is restricted.

In many companies, employees are encouraged to use desk and wall accessories, pictures, plants, and other items to personalize their work areas. The things you do to personalize your area should not interfere with the aesthetic atmosphere of the other offices in the area and should always be appropriate for a business setting.

Secretaries to executives of equal rank should have offices that reflect a comparable degree of prestige. A secretary to a vice president should not necessarily have the same office equipment as a secretary to a supervisor, but she should have an office that reflects her superior rank in the organizational hierarchy.

The open office design often enables the secretary to identify with other employees and have a feeling of belonging to a group that is not possible in a traditional private office.

Summary

Ergonomics is the study of the relationship between employees and their physical environment. To be as productive as possible, the secretary must have a work area that permits her to perform her duties comfortably and efficiently.

The types of work the secretary is expected to perform should be considered when designing the work area. Some secretaries may need

FIGURE 3-11. The word processor can be placed so that it will not be facing the passageway. (Courtesy of Waddell & Reed, Inc./United Investors Life)

only a desk, a typewriter, a chair, and a small amount of storage space. Other secretaries may need a more complex work area that includes space for word or data processing equipment, large work areas, and extensive storage facilities.

Office landscaping and modular furniture are becoming more popular because offices, people, and machines can easily be moved within an organization with a minimum of disturbance and at less cost than when permanent walls are involved.

—————————— Questions ——————————

1. Define "ergonomics."
2. What is meant by "office layout"?
3. Why is an irregular arrangement frequently used in an open office layout?
4. List the possible advantages of an open office layout.
5. How does modular furniture differ from traditional furniture?

6. Name the furniture components found in many offices.

7. Discuss the features of word processing and computer work stations that need to be considered.

8. What are lateral files and when are they often used?

9. What are acoustical partitions?

10. Describe an ergonomically designed secretarial chair.

11. Should a secretarial chair have arms? Discuss.

12. Discuss the possible consequences of poor lighting.

13. When is noise in an office considered excessive? Discuss.

14. List several sources of noise in the office and discuss possible ways to reduce or eliminate the noise caused by each one.

15. Discuss the importance of color in an office.

16. Does "privacy" mean being alone? Explain.

Projects

1. Visit an office furniture store or borrow a catalog from the college purchasing office and list the features of the different types of office chairs, desks, and files.

2. As a group project, plan and draw a scale model of an ideal office layout for a secretary who must work for three executives. List the assumptions you make concerning the type of work to be performed and write a report justifying the furniture and equipment selected.

3. Talk with friends and prepare a list of what they consider to be the advantages and disadvantages of both traditional and open office designs.

Cases

1. Ruth and her boss work in an area that is not separated by a partition. Frequently when Ruth is talking on the telephone her boss interrupts and makes comments such as "be sure to ask ..." or "tell her ...." As a result, Ruth has trouble concentrating on the conversation and often has to ask the person with whom she is talking to repeat what has been said. Should Ruth ask her boss not to interrupt, or should she handle the problem in some other way?

2. Angie and Jane must share a small office. Angie does not smoke and when she suggested that Jane not smoke in the office, Jane responded by saying, "If I don't smoke, I'll be extremely unpleasant and hard to get along with. What do you prefer?" How should Angie respond?

3. The Windsor Company is moving to a new office building where the open office arrangement will be used. The preliminary plans indicate that Lisa and Kathy will have adjacent work stations. Lisa does not particularly care for Kathy and believes that they will have difficulty working near each other. Should Lisa express her concern to her boss?

CHAPTER 4

Time Management

INTRODUCTION

Time is money; therefore, all employees have the responsibility of making sure that the time they spend on the job is productive. The ability to use time effectively is one of the greatest skills a secretary can possess. As a secretary, you need to be aware of the things that have an impact on the quantity and quality of work you perform, and you need to be able to establish priorities and plan your activities intelligently.

This chapter is designed to help you learn to use your time effectively and efficiently.

TIME WASTERS

Many things can interfere with your performance on the job. By carefully studying the time wasters discussed in this section, you should be able to take action that will increase your productivity.

Telephone Use

Even though the telephone is one of the greatest time-saving devices ever invented, frequently it does not serve that purpose. All of us have made and received telephone calls and realized at the conclusion of the conversation that nothing was accomplished and that if prior thought had been given, the call need not have been made. Most of us fail to ask, "Is this call necessary?" We simply make the call. We must, of course, answer the phone or offend the caller or give the impression of being unavailable; but we can do several things to minimize the time wasted in using the telephone.

Before placing a call, you should plan your message just as you would if you were writing a memorandum or letter. To appear organized, to avoid discussing extraneous matters, and to obviate the need for a follow-up call, you should note the subjects you need to discuss and the questions you need to ask or answer. Have on your desk the files, correspondence, or background information that you are likely to need.

You will spend less time making telephone calls by looking up the numbers and making several of your calls at one time. When you know that the people you need to call are usually in their offices at only a certain time of the day, you should plan to make the calls at that time.

For some people, the length of the phone calls is as much of a time waster as the number of calls. If the call involves a routine matter, you should immediately get to the point and then end the conversation. The nature of your job and your relationship with other people you talk to on the phone may require a certain amount of "small talk." But if you spend much time discussing things not related to the specific purpose of the call, you are wasting time.

When you first realize that a telephone call is not going to result in the desired information, you should immediately suggest that either you or or the other person call back or send the information.

If the person with whom you are talking is the type who likes to visit, here are some statements that may help to shorten the conversation and keep it related to the purpose of the call:

"I have a report I must finish before Ms. Davis goes to a meeting."

"Mr. Wilson is waiting for me to give him this information."

"Here's what I called about."

"I'm in a hurry, but I need to know ...."

By acting businesslike and using subtle techniques, you can let those with whom you must talk know that you do not have the time nor the desire to carry on lengthy conversations over the telephone.

You should seldom need to make or receive a personal call while at the office. If the need arises, you should always keep the conversation short.

Office Visitors

All office workers have the experience of being interrupted by people. Whether the visitors need to discuss important business-related matters or want to engage in socializing, you must interrupt the task on which you are working. As a result, your chain of thought is broken and you often consume much valuable time as you resume your work after the visitor leaves.

The people with whom the secretary must have frequent interaction include the supervisor and coworkers, as well as customers, suppliers, or others outside the organization. Although you do not want to convey the idea you are aloof or unfriendly, you can minimize the number and the length of the interruptions by making changes in the physical environment or in your behavior.

You do not want to be interrupted each time a coworker passes your desk or the door to your office. You can avoid the interruption by not making eye contact with the other person. If you have a private office, you may need to keep the door closed. By closing your door, you are not necessarily making yourself unavailable; but you are limiting your accessibility.

When you work in an area with several people and have no door to close, you may have frequent interruptions by coworkers who want to socialize. You may be able to turn your desk so that you will not be facing other workers or place some type of divider between your desk and the desks of other. By placing your desk so that you will not be facing a passageway, you can avoid making eye contact without offending coworkers.

Some people may persist in interrupting you while you work. You may need to be firm, but tactful, in order to change the situation. Expressions similar to the following used often enough usually prove effective:

"I'd like to talk about that, but I'm in the middle of a report now."

"Can we discuss it at lunch?"

"I'll be interested in hearing about your weekend when we go on our coffee break."

If your boss interrupts your work frequently, you may be able to suggest that time could be saved by establishing specific times for dictating, placing telephone calls, giving instructions, running errands, and so forth.

When someone outside your organization comes to your office, you should immediately interrupt your work and offer to help. You must be friendly and courteous, but no visitor should expect you to stop your work and engage in unproductive socializing while he or she is waiting to meet with someone else.

When you must have a quiet time to concentrate or complete a project, your only recourse may be to locate an unused office or area where you may work without being interrupted.

Paperwork

A tremendous amount of paper flows through most offices, and the secretary normally has to touch each piece. Much time can be saved if effective procedures are established for handling paperwork.

The cluttered or stacked desk is a common sight in many offices. People have many reasons for letting their desks get piled high with papers. Some believe the cluttered desk gives people the impression that "This person must really be busy." Some are convinced that they do not have time to clear their desk. Others believe that having papers readily accessible is the most efficient way of operating.

Although some people seem to function effectively with cluttered desks and take great pride in being able to locate a particular document instantly, most people realize that shuffling papers and hunting for things is a waste of time. Furthermore, most people find that entering the office in the morning and immediately facing a myriad of papers is not a particularly pleasant experience.

On the other hand, some people spend an inordinate amount of time maintaining a clear desk by filing or placing everything out of sight, even though some of the papers will be needed in a few minutes. They believe that the clear desk provides evidence that they are well-organized and efficient.

Most people find that some things need to be left on the desk throughout the day and that neither a totally clear desk nor one with numerous stacks of papers may be practical.

After the mail has been opened and sorted, you should attempt to handle each piece of paper as few times as possible. Keep the paper moving or at least organized so that you will not have to sort through a stack of paper each time you need a particular document. When at all possible, you should take action on a document rather than build up a backlog of pending items.

You should develop and adhere to a procedure for organizing your desk and processing paperwork that is appropriate for you and your office situation. No one plan is necessarily appropriate for each person, for each office, or for each day.

Crises

Murphy's Law states that "If anything can go wrong, it will." If you find yourself in this situation very often, you need to take measures to control this major time waster. Not only must other work cease while the crisis is solved, frequently much time is wasted in becoming reoriented to the task that was interrupted.

Crises cannot be eliminated entirely, but they can be controlled by proper planning. When you know that most of your crises revolve around a particular person, task, or deadline, you can anticipate the crises and take preventive action.

If you know that you are usually not given some information you need for a report until the last minute, you can often plan your schedule so that when the information is available you can devote all of your time to the report. You need to anticipate that some pages of a lengthy report will need to be revised because your boss wants to make changes or because some errors are detected. Ample time should be scheduled to do the work. You should anticipate that equipment will sometimes fail. When your boss is planning a lengthy trip, you should anticipate that some pressure may be involved in getting material ready for him or her to take along. Changes in flight schedules may have to be accommodated.

With experience, you should be able to plan your work schedule to minimize or eliminate most crisis situations.

Waiting for Others

Plan your work so that you will not waste time waiting for others. Rather than waste time waiting to get in to see your boss or to place or receive a telephone call, you may be able to complete several tasks that take only a few seconds or minutes.

If you have to go to another office to pick up some material, you can telephone and ask that the material be ready when you arrive. You can often plan to use the copying machine during other than peak periods and avoid wasting time by waiting in line.

When you know that you will have to wait, you should take along some work so that you may productively use the time while you wait. Perhaps you can proofread a report or read through the shorthand notes of the minutes of a meeting you attended. You might be able to sketch the outline for a graphic aid or plan your schedule for the next day.

Procrastination

Most people have the tendency at one time or another to put off doing something. Tasks that seem involved, hard, or unpleasant are often postponed. Although to procrastinate is human, it can become an occupational hazard.

When postponing a difficult or unpleasant task, think about what will happen if action is delayed. Avoiding an unpleasant task usually does not make it go away. The task must be completed sometime, and often it tends to appear more unpleasant as time passes. The preoccupation with thinking about the task you are avoiding can interfere with your ability to complete other work. Furthermore, a crisis may be created by delaying action.

If a task seems hard because it is unfamiliar, you should seek the help you need. Perhaps you need to ask for additional instructions or need to talk with someone who has performed a similar task. When you need help, seek it immediately; do not agonize over it.

When a project or task appears formidable, break it down into segments. You may want to start with the easiest segment or the thing you know how to do best, or you may want to complete the least enjoyable segment first to get it out of the way. You need to anticipate the feeling of satisfaction that you will experience once the task is completed. Most people have difficulty enjoying themselves when they have major unpleasant tasks pending.

Making a commitment to someone and promising to have a project completed by a certain date often gives one the impetus needed to start and complete a project.

Delegating Work

Your position determines the extent to which you are able to delegate work. If you supervise other secretaries or clerical workers, you should spend your time on tasks that require your degree of expertise and delegate to others the tasks they may be equally well-qualified to perform. Also, instead of voluntarily or inadvertently accepting problems of subordinates and coworkers, you should encourage them to demonstrate initiative in arriving at a solution. Solving the problems of others may give you a feeling of importance, but it takes away from the time you need to spend on your work and deprives others of the opportunity to grow.

When reports and other documents you prepare are based on data provided by coworkers, you should not have to spend your time checking the accuracy of their work. When you do not have authority over those who consistently provide you with incomplete or incorrect data, you may need to discuss the situation with your supervisor.

Perhaps letters and documents that must be typed as originals can be typed in the word-processing center. Simply because you are familiar with a particular task and feel comfortable or enjoy doing it is not sufficient reason to continue doing it a certain way if it can be done more efficiently in another way.

Biocycles

Most people have times throughout the day and normal work week when they are highly productive and other times when they seem to be able to accomplish very little. Some people work best in the morning while others are most productive in the afternoon. Some poeple have trouble getting started on certain days, such as on Monday morning or the day after a vacation. Some people have difficulty working on detailed assignments for extended periods.

You should be aware of your cycle of productivity and, when possible, plan your work accordingly. If you are an afternoon person, perhaps you can begin your day by completing the routine and pleasant tasks and waiting until the afternoon to do the more difficult work. You may need to plan your work schedule so that you can alternate between difficult and simple tasks.

You may have little flexibility in arranging your schedule so that certain tasks can be performed at your most productive time of the day, but getting plenty of rest, eating regular and balanced meals, and exercising properly will help you be emotionally and physically prepared to perform at your highest level at all times.

Repetitive Tasks

One of the most overlooked opportunities for saving time is the potential for developing a routine for completing repetitive tasks in the office. In many organizations, the repetitive tasks can be accomplished by using word-processing equipment or computers. The alert secretary stays abreast of the equipment to which she has access.

In some offices, forms may be prepared for recurring reports and all the secretary must do is to type in the data that change. Some tasks may be easy to perform but may result in a waste of time. For example, if documents are normally circulated to the same individuals, the routing slips can be duplicated.

If information must be obtained from or supplied to others daily, time can often be saved by establishing a convenient time when a call can be made each day.

When the repetitive work involves the use of a machine, you should develop a thorough understanding of the operation of the machine so that you will not have to continually refer to the manual or ask for assistance.

Numerous time-saving suggestions are given in other chapters of this textbook.

Stress

Pressures of both personal and professional life may become an emotionally disruptive influence. Many illnesses, such as headache, lower back pain, high blood pressure, and heart problems, are enhanced or even caused by reaction to stress. If pressures become too great and exceed acceptable limits, your physical and emotional health can be affected.

You need to be aware of the events that go on around you and how to deal with them. If you find that situations occur and you are continually bothered by the outcome or the way you handled them, you may need to consider more constructive ways of dealing with stress.

Most libraries have books on stress management. You may be able to identify stress outlets that will work for you.

Relaxation

Most people can accomplish more when they are relaxed than when they are tired or tense. Several things may be done to help you relax. When working on a difficult assignment that requires total and extended periods of concentration, you should occasionally leave the work and go for a drink of water or walk around for a few minutes.

Following through with an assignment until it is completed can cause you to experience a feeling of accomplishment and result in your feeling relaxed.

Your mental outlook and the way you feel about yourself and others has much to do with your being able to relax. You need to feel comfortable in your position and with the people with whom you must frequently interact. You need to have confidence in your ability. You need to have a positive outlook and to think in terms of success. Believe in your ability to complete a project. Try to avoid associating with those who cause you to be tense or uncomfortable.

Your personal life should be planned with your professional life in mind so that the things you do away from the office will not adversely affect your job performance.

Secretarial Skills

Much time is wasted when people are not well-qualified and when the work that they complete is not usable. All of us have weaknesses, but we can correct most weaknesses if we have the desire and put forth a conscientious effort. We should not use the excuse, "I have never been good at that"; rather, if our weaknesses have an adverse effect on our work, we should do what is necessary to become proficient. Do not simply avoid tasks at which you are less proficient.

If your work frequently is not usable because of errors on your part, you should take corrective measures. The time spent in typing a letter that is not mailable is wasted even though your willingness to retype it may be commendable. All people must occasionally use the dictionary to look up the meaning and spelling of words; however, if you have to use the dictionary extensively, you should make an effort to learn the spelling and meaning of the words that cause you problems. A list of the words that cause you the most trouble may be prepared and kept readily accessible.

You should never need to use the dictionary to look up the meaning or spelling of a particular word more than one time.

Those who frequently have to use a reference manual to learn how to punctuate correctly may need to purchase a programmed instruction book or enroll in an English course to improve their skills in this area. You should either memorize or prepare a list of the telephone numbers and addresses you use repeatedly. If you spend time looking up the same thing repeatedly, you should use your initiative and creative ability to think of a solution.

When your work involves considerable typing and shorthand, you should be sure you are acceptably competent in these areas. Obviously, a mailable letter typed by someone who has a typing production speed of 45 words a minute is less costly than one typed by someone who is paid the same salary but has a production speed of 15 words a minute. Much time can be wasted when a secretary has trouble taking and transcribing dictation. If your typing and shorthand skills are not acceptable, you should develop a formal program of practice or enroll in a course.

Although your boss would prefer you to ask questions rather than do something incorrectly, you should never waste time by having to ask the same question twice. Develop the habit of writing down information and instructions and develop a filing system so that you will be able to locate the information at a later time.

When the work assignments involve extensive reading, many people waste much time because they do not read rapidly. If you find that you are spending an inordinate amount of time reading and proofreading, you may need to seek assistance in increasing your reading rate.

Thinking

Some people mistakenly believe that "thinking time" is wasted time. The few minutes you spend thinking of the most efficient way to perform a task often considerably reduces the amount of time needed to complete the task. Many companies encourage employees to think by financially rewarding those who recommend better and more efficient ways of doing things.

The most productive employees in a company often are those who spend a considerable amount of time thinking constructively. As a secretary, you should develop the habit of thinking before acting. Before starting to type a letter, think of the number of copies you need. Before starting to type a table, think about what arrangement is best. Before going to an office in another section of the building, think of things you may need to do along the way to avoid making another trip.

In addition to thinking before acting, you should develop the practice of always asking yourself "Could the task have been done more efficiently?"

KEEPING A TIME LOG

Before you can use your time more efficiently, you must determine how you are using it now. Keeping a time log will help you determine whether your time is being spent on tasks that you originate or on those that your boss, coworkers, or other business-related people require.

You should keep a time log for at least one week and should record on it what you are doing every minute of each day. "I don't have time to keep a detailed time log" is a frequent objection; however, without recording all of your activities (e.g., making and answering telephone calls, taking dictation, answering questions) you cannot accurately know how your office time is spent. Unless you record the time throughout the day as you perform the different tasks, you may forget to record some of the activities, overestimate the time spent on some, and underestimate the time spent on others.

When you use a form similar to the one shown in figure 4-1, you will need to spend only a few seconds recording each activity and the time involved. At the end of the day, you will have an accurate record of what you did every minute.

The log can be designed in many different ways. A log with one-minute intervals may be desirable if you must perform numerous tasks that involve short periods of time. A log with 10- or 15-minute intervals may be preferred when only a few lengthy tasks are performed during the day. A log may consist of a sheet with several lines on which you list in sequence the tasks performed and indicate the minutes spent on each one.

ANALYZING THE TIME LOG

At the end of each day, you need to analyze how your time was spent. By using the log that you kept throughout the day, you can easily categorize activities that involved people by completing forms similar to the one illustrated in figure 4-2.

To analyze your telephone calls, prepare one sheet for "Analysis of Telephone Calls Received" and one for "Analysis of Telephone Calls Placed." After you have completed the sheets, ask the following questions concerning each call:

- What was accomplished?
- Was the call assigned the proper priority?
- Could the call have been shortened?
- Could the call have occurred at a more opportune time?

- Could the message have been conveyed more appropriately by using a letter or memorandum?
- Could the call have been avoided with proper planning?

Use three sheets to analyze your time spent with others: "Analysis of Time Spent With Supervisor," "Analysis of Time Spent With Coworkers," "Analysis of Time Spent With Those From Outside the Organization." Ask the previously listed questions concerning each meeting.

- What was accomplished?
- Was the meeting assigned the proper priority?
- Could the meeting have been shortened?
- Could the meeting have occurred at a more opportune time?
- Could the business have been transacted more efficiently by telephone?
- Could the meeting have been avoided with proper planning?

To analyze the other tasks you performed throughout the day, prepare analysis sheets similar to the one illustrated in figure 4-2 for the various types of tasks.

After you have completed an analysis sheet for each type of task, you should ask the following questions:

- What was accomplished?
- Was the task assigned the proper priority?
- Should the task have been completed in less time?
- Did the task need to be completed?
- Should the task have been performed by someone else?

As you analyze your activities at the end of each day, you should list the specific ways in which time was not used efficiently. Also list specific ways in which the time wasted could have been reduced or eliminated. At the end of the week, you should be able to identify specific areas of your work that could be completed in less time, and you should be able to develop a concrete plan for making improvements.

If you find that time has been wasted in several areas of your work, establish priorities and concentrate on using your time more wisely in one area at a time. You may need to solicit the help of your supervisor or coworkers to implement some of the ideas you have for using your time more productively.

TIME LOG

Date ______________________

Time	Person or Activity	Purpose
8:00		
8:05		
8:10		
8:15		
8:20		
8:25		
8:30		
8:35		
8:40		
8:45		
8:50		
8:55		
9:00		
9:05		
9:10		
9:15		
9:20		
9:25		
9:30		
9:35		
9:40		
9:45		
9:50		
9:55		
10:00		
10:05		
10:10		
10:15		
10:20		
10:25		
10:30		
10:35		
10:40		
10:45		
10:50		
10:55		
11:00		
11:05		
11:10		
11:15		
11:20		
11:25		
11:30		
11:35		
11:40		
11:45		
11:50		
11:55		

FIGURE 4-1. Time log.

ANALYSIS OF _____

Priority	Who	Purpose	Time Elapsed

FIGURE 4-2. Analysis form.

PLANNING

Daily, weekly, and long-range planning is essential if you are to accomplish the maximum amount of work in the most efficient way possible.

The first step in developing your plans is to identify and list the tasks that must be completed. Most time-management experts suggest that an "ABC" system be used to assign priorities to the various tasks.

The "A" priority tasks are those of primary concern and those that must be undertaken at a particular time. Examples of "A" priority work include typing letters that must be included in a particular mail pickup, completing material for the supervisor's 10 o'clock meeting, or making a plane reservation for the supervisor's urgent trip to a branch office later in the day. Taking minutes at a staff meeting is an example of an "A" priority task that does not involve an urgency but is one that must be performed at a particular time of the day.

The "B" priority tasks are of secondary importance, but they should be completed as soon as the "A" tasks have been accomplished. Most of the daily tasks the secretary must perform are of the "B" priority type and include routine tasks, such as opening and processing the mail and transcribing dictation.

The "C" priority tasks are of low importance. They should be completed during "slack" periods. Updating the files is an example of a "C" priority task.

When planning your schedule, you must list your "A" priority items first. If you have several "A" priority tasks pending, you must determine the sequence in which they should be performed. The tasks should be listed for specific times on a schedule. Always realistically estimate the amount of time needed to complete a task.

Rather than list the "B" priority items for a specific time on a daily schedule, many secretaries prefer to have a sheet similar to the one illustrated in figure 4-3 on which the tasks are listed at the bottom in the order in which they should be completed. Always estimate the amount of time needed to complete each of these tasks, too. The "C" priority items are normally listed on another sheet.

Many types of printed schedule forms and calendars are available. If none is available that is appropriate for your situation, you should design a form that will aid you in planning your schedule the most effective way possible.

Even when you plan carefully and are well-qualified to perform the tasks, you may find that not enough time is available to complete all of the work and meet all deadlines. When this occurs, to avoid giving your supervisor the impression you are complaining, you should show him or her a copy of your schedule and ask for assistance in deciding the order in which the work should be completed. The supervisor may decide that temporary help is needed, that some of the work can be delegated, or that some of the work can be postponed. Supervisors sometimes become occupied with their work and fail to realize the numerous routine functions the secretary must perform in addition to the specific tasks they assign.

A well-planned schedule may need to be changed several times in a single day. Periodically, things that you had no way of anticipating will force you to reorganize your priorities.

At the end of each day, look over your schedule. If you accurately prepared your list of tasks and you have completed all of them, you know that you have managed your time well. If you have not completed all of the tasks you had scheduled or did not complete them in the time allocated, you need to analyze the reasons and decide what should have been done differently. Consider the uncompleted tasks as you prepare your schedule for the next day.

Most secretaries prefer to plan the next day's schedule before leaving work so that when they arrive at the office the next morning they can begin work immediately. Also, by having the schedule prepared in written form, you do not have to remember overnight the things that must be done the next day.

In addition to the detailed daily schedule, you should keep a weekly and a long-range calendar. A typical desk calendar can normally be used for this purpose. You must keep the calendar conveniently located so that

SCHEDULE

Monday, April 3

Morning	Afternoon
8:00	1:00
8:10	1:10
8:20	1:20
8:30	1:30
8:40	1:40
8:50	1:50
9:00	2:00
9:10	2:10
9:20	2:20
9:30	2:30
9:40	2:40
9:50	2:50
10:00	3:00
10:10	3:10
10:20	3:20
10:30	3:30
10:40	3:40
10:50	3:50
11:00	4:00
11:10	4:10
11:20	4:20
11:30	4:30
11:40	4:40
11:50	4:50

"B" Priority Tasks

FIGURE 4-3. Schedule form.

you can record appointments and tasks as soon as you learn of them. The calendar must be kept current, and you must refer to the calendar each time you prepare your daily schedule.

———————————————— Summary ————————————————

Time is a precious commodity. The secretary, as well as all others, needs to be cognizant of the many things that may interfere with the productive use of her time. Unnecessary time may be used in telephone calls and meetings with the supervisor, coworkers, and those from outside the organization. Time can be wasted when the secretary is not well qualified, relaxed, or organized. Time can also be wasted by not delegating work, by not routinizing procedures for completing repetitive tasks, and by procrastinating.

The secretary should follow a structured plan in an attempt to reduce or eliminate time wasters and thus increase her productivity. A detailed log of the activities performed should be kept for a week. An in-depth analysis of the activities and the time spent on them can help identify time wasters and result in a plan of action that may be taken to use time more wisely.

By prioritizing the tasks that must be performed and by developing a daily, weekly, and long-range schedule, the secretary can maximize the efficient use of her time in the office.

———————————————— Questions ————————————————

1. Why is the effective use of time by all employees important?

2. Discuss the steps that a secretary may take to reduce interruptions caused by people stopping by her desk.

3. What determines whether the time spent talking with others is "wasted"?

4. What can be done to minimize the time you spend on telephone conversations?

5. Why is some socializing expected of those working in an office?

6. What is Murphy's Law?

7. Why is no one procedure for organizing the desk and processing paperwork necessarily appropriate for everyone?

8. Discuss ways to avoid or control crises.

9. Explain how proper planning often minimizes the amount of time wasted in waiting for others.

10. Define "procrastination."

11. List several reasons why people procrastinate.

12. Discuss steps that can sometimes be taken to overcome the habit of procrastinating.

13. What should you do when you must obtain data from coworkers for reports you prepare and these data often are incorrect?

14. Do you agree that all people should plan their most difficult work for the morning hours? Discuss.

15. List several things that may often be done to save time in performing repetitive tasks.

16. When should work not be delegated?

17. Why is being able to relax important?

18. What should be done to avoid having to ask the same question more than one time?

19. Explain what is meant by "thinking time."

20. What is a time log?

21. When keeping a time log, why should one not wait until the end of the day to record the activities and the amount of time spent on each one?

22. Should a time log have 1-, 5-, 10-, or 15-minute intervals? Explain.

23. Outline the steps involved in analyzing the time log.

24. When an analysis of the time log shows that much time is wasted during the work day, what should be done?

25. Describe the procedures involved in assigning priorities to the tasks that must be completed.

26. What should you do when you plan your daily schedule and find that not all of the work can be completed?

———————————————— Projects ————————————————

1. Decide on a realistic hourly rate a full-time office employee with your qualifications might earn. Add to that figure approximately 30 percent to cover the additional costs, such as FICA and unemployment taxes and fringe benefits, incurred by the employer. When you type a letter or perform tasks similar to those in an office, determine the cost of the work.

2. Plan a daily schedule for at least a one-week period. List the tasks to be completed and assign an "A," "B," or "C" priority to each task. At the end of each day evaluate what you accomplished. If you did not complete all of the tasks you planned, analyze the reasons and determine what you should have done differently.

3. Keep a record for several days and note the ways you observe time being wasted by those working in offices and stores.

4. Write a report telling how one or more of the suggestions discussed in this chapter enabled you to use your time more efficiently.

———————————————— Cases ————————————————

1. Mary Beth works as secretary to two executives and frequently does not have work completed when it is needed. Mary Beth always explains the delay by saying that she is overworked. One of the executives told her that she would have sufficient time to complete all of the work if she had better skills and used her time more wisely. What should be Mary Beth's response?

2. Assume that a secretary whose desk is adjacent to yours makes numerous personal phone calls, writes personal letters, and spends time doing things that are not related to the business. As a result of this, she frequently has trouble getting the business-related work completed when it is needed and asks you to help. How should you respond to her request?

3. Lorna Kelly has just started working as a private secretary to Fran Jaggars, a high-level executive, who will be out of the office much of the time. Ms. Jaggars told Lorna that she should decide whether to offer to assist coworkers with some of their work while she is away from the office and Lorna's work load will be light. If Lorna decides to offer to assist others, how can she preclude their taking advantage of her generosity?

PART III

CHAPTER 5

Arranging Meetings

INTRODUCTION

A large part of many executives' work day is spent in meetings. For many of the meetings, the executives assemble in an office or conference room; however, advanced technology in the communications area makes meetings possible for those who may be in different geographical locations.

The secretary's responsibilities concerning meetings of company personnel may include notifying the executives of the time and purpose of the meeting, arranging for conference calls, scheduling equipment needed, and taking notes of the meeting.

Executives are often involved in community and professional organizations and may be responsible for arranging meetings for a group. Secretaries to these executives are often asked to assist with maintaining the mailing lists, sending notices of meetings, reserving rooms and equipment, typing and duplicating programs, and preparing minutes.

The work the secretary may be expected to perform prior to, during, and following the meeting is discussed in this chapter.

SCHEDULING MEETINGS

Generally, meetings should be scheduled as far in advance as possible. The meetings associated with the day-to-day operation of a business often must be called on short notice, but the conventions and large conferences are almost always scheduled a year or more in advance.

Some meetings must be scheduled for a particular time; however, the time of most meetings depends on the availability of those expected to attend. Selecting a time when the maximum attendance possible can be expected is simplified if you have ready access to the schedules of the participants. Some organizations have the schedules of executives stored in a computer to which secretaries have access. In many colleges and universities, the schedules of the professors are on file in the office of the department head or dean. When you do not have ready access to the schedules of those involved, you normally have to call the offices of the participants. This can be a time-consuming process.

Ask your boss to indicate two or three acceptable times for the meeting, especially if several people are involved. If some people are to present data or for some other reason must attend for the meeting to be successful, call the offices of these individuals first. If they are not available at the suggested times, notify your boss.

As you contact those expected to attend, keep a record of the times each would be available. If, after all the people have been contacted, you find that not all can attend at any one time, you should present a typewritten summary of your findings to the executive so that he or she can decide the best time to hold the meeting.

The summary should be in easy-to-read form, such as the following:

```
The following people can attend a budget planning meeting on
March 15 at the times indicated:

                                  10   1   2

Bailey                            x    x   x
Baker                                      x
Fullerton                         x    x   x
Ramsey                            x        x
Walton                                 x
Zimmerman                         x    x   x
```

Once a final date and time have been selected, the individuals should be notified as soon as possible so they can plan their schedules around the meeting.

NOTIFYING PARTICIPANTS

Content of Notices

The accuracy of the notice is extremely important because the time of several individuals may be involved. If you compose the notice, you should have your supervisor approve it before it is duplicated and mailed.

Use the journalist's W's—who, what, when, where, and why—as guides when composing notices. An agenda is often included as part of the notice. Material the executives are expected to read and study prior to a meeting may accompany the notice of a business meeting. If the executives are expected to bring the material to the meeting, be sure to mention that in the notice. You may need to mention in the notice whether the meeting will include lunch or dinner and, if so, the cost.

Methods of Notification

Executives are normally notified of meetings to be held within the company by a telephone call or memorandum. For many other types of meetings, the participants are notified by postcard, letter, or newsletter. Conventions and conferences are often announced in magazines and newspapers.

The form of notification to use usually is determined by the type of meeting to be held, the number of participants, and the time between when the meeting is called and the date of the meeting. Sometimes laws or bylaws stipulate the procedures to be followed in announcing the meeting.

A committee normally plans conventions and large conferences, but as secretary to a member of the committee you may be asked to help prepare and mail the notices. Make sure that the dates on which all stages of the work must be performed are noted on your calendar. Much time may be involved in composing, reproducing, and mailing the notices; therefore, the work should be started long before the deadline.

When social, civic, professional, and other groups hold regularly scheduled meetings, the attendance can often be increased by sending reminders. The members should receive the notices at least two or three days before the meeting and earlier if they are expected to make dinner or hotel reservations.

Telephone

When you notify the participants by telephone, prepare an outline of all the information and be sure to cover all the details in the conversation. Note on the sheet the names of the people with whom you talked, the date, and the time. A record, such as that shown in figure 5-1, can be important should someone not attend the meeting and later indicate he or she did not receive the notice.

Mail

When you are responsible for mailing notices of meetings, you must keep the mailing list up to date. Even though the membership may be

July 15, 1984

Telephone calls made to cancel the Community Recreation Board
Meeting that had been scheduled for July 18. The meeting will
be held at 7:30 p.m. on July 29.

Board Member	Telephone Number	Time Called	Talked With
Barbara Cheney	432-8311	9:00	Bettie Cormier
Arlo Cottrell	455-2295	9:05	Cottrell
Allen Dyer	257-2097	9:08	Barbara Cordero
Joe Hartmann	588-1205	9:12	Kathy Cord
Tony Masser	262-8927	9:15	Pauline McCool
George Naruns	432-6718	11:30	Connie Shatswell
Anna Rose	381-6682	11:33	Rose
Guy Norman	931-2326	2:30	Kathryn Walls

FIGURE 5-1. Keep a record of telephone calls made in regard to meeting changes.

large, the task may be relatively simple and require very little time if you
have access to word-processing equipment. If you put the membership
list on an input medium, the names, addresses, telephone numbers, and
other data can be added, deleted, and changed easily. The information for
the notices can be put on another input medium, and the notice and mailing
list can be merged during the play out.

If you do not have access to word-processing equipment and the
membership changes frequently, you should prepare a three-inch by
five-inch card for each member. The information concerning each
member may consist of only the name and address or may include much
more, such as the telephone number, name of the company for which he or
she works, position title, home and business addresses, membership
number, and numerous other things.

The cards may be filed in any number of ways. A strictly alphabetical
listing may be appropriate for most organizations, but an alphabetical
listing for those in each geographical area or some other arrangement may
be appropriate for some.

The equipment you have available will determine how you prepare
the labels or address the envelopes or cards. The word processor may be
used, or you may have access to an addressing machine. The addresses
may be typed on stencils to be used for duplicating labels, or the labels or
envelopes may be typed individually.

The cards, envelopes, or labels should be addressed well in advance
to avoid a last-minute rush, but remember to make changes that may have

```
┌─────────────────────────────────────────────────────────┐
│                      Regular Meeting                      │
│                         of the                            │
│         Jackson County Office Managers' Association       │
│                                                           │
│   WHEN:                                                   │
│                                                           │
│   WHERE:                                                  │
│                                                           │
│   PROGRAM:                                                │
│                                                           │
│                                                           │
│                                                           │
│                                                           │
│                                                           │
│   COST:                                                   │
│                                                           │
└─────────────────────────────────────────────────────────┘
```

FIGURE 5-2. Cards may be mailed to remind participants of a meeting.

occurred during the interim between the time they were addressed and the time they are mailed.

Postcards are frequently used to remind members of meetings, particularly meetings that are regularly scheduled. A large supply of cards may be printed with the standard information, as illustrated in figure 5-2. The cards can be readily completed by filling in the variable data when monthly or periodic notices are to be mailed.

If the participants are to make a reservation, a double postcard similar to the one shown in figure 5-3 may be used.

Memorandums are used extensively within the company to announce meetings and to remind executives of the meetings that have been arranged by telephone.

Even though the executives may be notified by telephone, a memorandum should usually be sent as a reminder unless the meeting is to take place before the memorandum can be delivered. The memorandum should be sent several days prior to the meeting when the executives have not been notified by telephone.

Those being asked to attend a meeting are frequently interested in knowing who else may be present; therefore, the names of all those to receive the notice are normally typed on the memorandum. Also, when all of the names are typed on the memorandum, it can be duplicated and the copies can be distributed simply by placing a check mark by the name of the individual to receive a particular copy, as shown in figure 5-4.

Leaflets and brochures are often used to notify prospective participants of special meetings, conferences, or seminars. These types of notices can be especially effective when the participants need to be given a

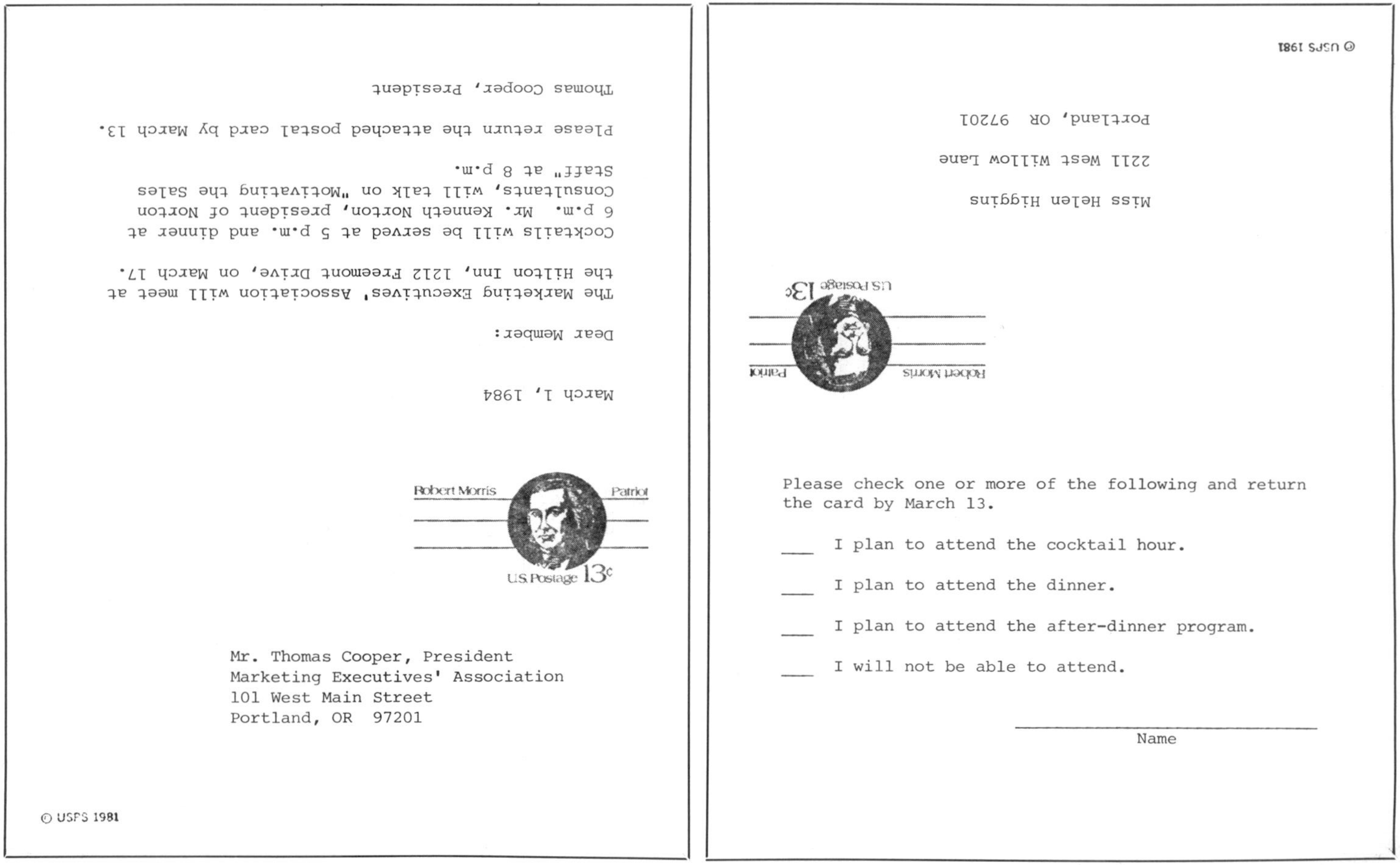

© USPS 1981

Please check one or more of the following and return the card by March 13.

_____ I plan to attend the cocktail hour.

_____ I plan to attend the dinner.

_____ I plan to attend the after-dinner program.

_____ I will not be able to attend.

_____
Name

Robert Morris

U.S. Postage 13¢

Patrix

Miss Helen Higgins

2211 West Willow Lane

Portland, OR 97201

© USPS 1981

Robert Morris

U.S. Postage 13¢

Patrix

Mr. Thomas Cooper, President
Marketing Executives' Association
101 West Main Street
Portland, OR 97201

March 1, 1984

Dear Member:

The Marketing Executives' Association will meet at the Hilton Inn, 1212 Freemont Drive, on March 17.

Cocktails will be served at 5 p.m. and dinner at 6 p.m. Mr. Kenneth Norton, president of Norton Consultants, will talk on "Motivating the Sales Staff" at 8 p.m.

Please return the attached postal card by March 13.

Thomas Cooper, President

FIGURE 5-3. A double postcard encourages members to make reservations.

```
                        M E M O R A N D U M

                                    February 17, 1984


TO:         A. Burthchett
            L. Cade
            C. Freeman
            M. Ryan
            R. Schnake

FROM:       S. Shannon

SUBJECT:    Scholarship Committee Meeting



The Distinguished Scholarship Award Committee will meet at 3 p.m.
on Monday, February 27, in Room 10 of the Education Building.

Please be prepared to discuss the procedures to be used in selecting
the recipients of the scholarships.
```

FIGURE 5-4. Duplicated reminder memorandum.

considerable amount of information in easy-to-read form. Frequently, a reservation form is part of the brochure or leaflet, as illustrated in figure 5-5.

When the group is large or does not meet often, the meetings are sometimes announced by letter. The letters are usually duplicated and no inside address is used. If only a few individuals are to receive the announcement, the names may be arranged in alphabetical order and listed in the inside address section of the letter. "Dear Member," "Dear Board Member," or some other general salutation is normally used when the letters are not addressed to individuals.

The bylaws of corporations and organizations may specify the dates by which notices must be sent and what must be included in the notices. An attorney normally prepares the notices for stockholders' meetings. The public meetings and hearings of some governmental units, such as the city council, must sometimes be published in the newspaper or announced through some other media. If you work for an organization that must announce meetings in a particular way and at a certain time, become thoroughly familiar with the laws or bylaws that apply.

An announcement of a stockholders' meeting usually contains information similar to that shown in figure 5-6.

MANAGEMENT WORKSHOPS

Sponsored by

OFFICE MANAGERS' ASSOCIATION OF DES MOINES

University Inn
1215 Summit Drive
Des Moines, IA

August 1, 1984

    8:30   Registration

    9:30   Personality Development — — Dr. Sally Ritter
                                     Psychologist
                                     Career Development Center

  10:45   Positive Thinking — — Mr. Jim Scott
                             Professor
                             Rawleigh Junior College

  12:00   Lunch

    1:30   Effective Communication — — Dr. Mary McElwain
                                 Associate Professor
                               Rolling Hills University

    2:45   Teamwork — — Mr. Robert Long
                        Management Consultant
                      A. B. Price & Associates

— —

ADVANCE REGISTRATION FORM

Mr.
Mrs.
Ms. _____

Position _____

Organization _____

Address _____

City _____ State _____ ZIP _____

The cost of registration and buffet luncheon is $50.
Make check payable to Office Managers' Association of Des Moines.

Mail registration form and check by July 15 to:

        Ms. Lynda Warnecke, Office Manager
        Homestead Development Company
        233 Grove Drive
        Des Moines, IA   50301

          FIGURE 5-5. Meeting announcement with reservation form attached.

BEST WAY STORES, INC.
Stilwell, Oklahoma

NOTICE OF ANNUAL MEETING OF STOCKHOLDERS
To Be Held June 3, 1984

To the Stockholders of Best Way Stores, Inc.:

Notice is hereby given that the 1984 Annual Meeting of Stockholders of Best Way Stores, Inc., an Oklahoma corporation, will be held Friday, June 8, 1984, at 10 a.m., in the Auditorium, Stilwell High School, Stilwell, Oklahoma, for the following purposes:

1. To elect directors;

2. To consider and act upon a proposal to amend the Certificate of Incorporation of the Company to increase the number of shares of the Company's Common Stock, par value $0.10 per share, which the Company is authorized to issue from 86,000,000 shares to 325,000,000 shares;

3. To consider and act upon a proposal to amend the Certificate of Incorporation of the Company to increase the number of shares of the Company's Preferred Stock, par value $0.10 per share, which the Company is authorized to issue from 4,000,000 shares to 25,000,000 shares; and

4. To transact such other business as may properly come before the meeting or any adjournment thereof.

By Order of the Board of Directors

———————————————

Andrew Willis
Secretary

Stilwell, Oklahoma
May 1, 1984

FIGURE 5-6. Notice of annual stockholders meeting.

CHECKING THE AGENDA

An agenda is the order of business to be discussed. Although the person conducting the meeting normally prepares the agenda, as his or her secretary, you can do several things to assist. If the announcement of the meeting asks members to suggest agenda items, you should keep a record of the suggestions. You should read the minutes of the previous meeting to see if unfinished business needs to be included on the agenda. Make sure the agenda includes items that may be required by the bylaws.

A typical agenda for meetings conducted under parliamentary law is as follows:

    I. Call to Order
   II. Minutes of the Previous Meeting
  III. Reports of Officers
  IV. Reports of Committees
   V. Old Business
  VI. New Business
 VII. Announcements
VIII. Adjournment

The agenda may be mailed to the members or may be given to them as they arrive at the meeting.

SELECTING A PLACE

When you are asked to plan a meeting, your first task is to select an appropriate place. The room must be large enough for all participants to be seated comfortably; therefore, you need to consider the purpose of the meeting, the number of people involved, and the places available.

Since meetings often extend beyond the time originally planned, make sure the room will be available for the entire time it may be needed.

If the participants will be working with documents during the meeting, secure a room with tables and adequate space for each person. Frequently, three or more feet of table space should be allowed for each participant.

You need to consider the arrangement of the room. Will participants be able to see and hear other participants and speakers?

When movies or slides are to be shown, you need to consider the following:

- Can the room be darkened?

- Are adequate electrical outlets available and properly placed?

- Can lights be turned off without shutting off the power to the outlets?

- Will all participants have an unobstructed view of the screen?

When meetings are to be held at a motel or hotel, you should work with the staff in planning the facilities needed. Figure 5-7 shows a meeting being held in a room at a hotel.

FIGURE 5-7. Hotels and motels will make all of the physical arrangements for meetings. (Courtesy of Hilton Hotels Corporation)

If confidential topics are to be discussed, the room should be sound-proof and secure so that those not involved in the meeting will not be able to hear or observe the proceedings.

If the meeting needs to be held at a location different from the one mentioned in the announcement, you should do all that is possible to notify the participants. When the notice is mailed, be sure that the participants will receive it by the date of the meeting. The changes are sometimes announced in the newspaper and on the radio.

When the meeting must be changed to a different room in the same building, notices should be posted in the lobby and in the elevator, as well as on the door of the room where the meeting was to have been held.

EQUIPMENT

You may need to check with several people concerning the equipment that may be needed and to determine what arrangements must be made to secure the equipment. Arrange for the use of projectors and a screen if movies, slides, or transparencies are to be shown. A speaker may need a chalkboard, an easel for charts, and a lectern. A recorder will be needed if the meeting is to be taped. Make sure microphones are placed in locations convenient for the speakers.

Many hotels and motels have equipment (projectors, screens, and so forth) available and provide the equipment free when the room is rented. That may be an important consideration when selecting a location for the meeting.

Anticipate the equipment that will be needed and develop a form similar to the one illustrated in figure 5-8 to use to reserve the room and equipment. Give each person involved a copy and keep a copy for your file.

SUPPLIES

The supplies and materials you are expected to provide for those attending the meeting will vary. For informal meetings held in an executive's office, participants normally bring their own note pads and pens. For large meetings, you should check with the person in charge concerning the supplies that will be needed.

Documents to be used during a meeting in an executive's office may be handed to the people as they enter. If the meeting is held in a conference room, documents and supplies are often placed on the table before the meeting.

When several people are involved and documents are distributed and discussed at various times during the meeting, confusion often prevails. If possible, give all of the documents to be used during the meeting to the participants at one time. The documents may be numbered, lettered, or prepared on paper of different colors so that they can be readily identified.

If you attend the meeting and take minutes, anticipate everything you will need to take to the meeting. You may need to take all or some of the following:

1. Shorthand notebook.
2. Pens and pencils.
3. Bylaws of the organization.
4. Membership list.
5. List of committees.
6. Minutes of previous meeting.
7. Copies of the agenda.
8. Extra copies of material distributed to members prior to the date of the meeting.
9. Material to be distributed.

RESERVATION FORM

Room _____   Date of Request _____

Date of Event _____   Reservation Made With

Time _____   _____
      Begin   End   Name

Event Title _____   _____

Estimated Attendance _____   Telephone Number

_____ Chalkboard

_____ Easel

_____ Lectern

      _____ Floor

      _____ Table

_____ Screen (size _____)

_____ Movie Projector

      _____ 8 mm

      _____ 16 mm

_____ Slide Projector

      _____ 35 mm _____ Remote Control

      _____ 70 mm _____ Remote Control

_____ Projector Stand

_____ Microphone

      _____ Table (number _____)

      _____ Floor (number _____)

_____ Recorder

      _____ Reel

      _____ Cassette

_____ Extension Cord (length _____)

_____ Other _____

      _____

      _____

Diagram of Room Arrangement Preferred

FIGURE 5-8. Equipment reservation form.

100
Secretarial
Procedures:
Office
Administration and
Automated Systems

10. Ballots. If voting is by ballot and several issues are to be voted on, use paper of different colors and have a sufficient number of ballots (already counted) of each color.

11. Tapes or cassettes.

12. *Robert's Rules of Order.*

13. Reference materials or documents.

REFRESHMENTS

When the meeting is held at a hotel, the food service department will provide the refreshments. Prior arrangements should be made and include letting the hotel staff know what refreshments are needed and when they should be delivered. The food service department in some companies will provide the same service. You should ask for a written confirmation.

Frequently, when the meeting is held in the conference room or an executive's office, the participants bring beverages with them to the meeting. If you are expected to make and serve coffee, be sure you have an adequate supply of cups, cream, sugar, and spoons. Napkins should be provided, and a supply of paper towels should be kept handy in case something is spilled. If you expect the meeting to last more than one hour, you probably should place pitchers of water on the table prior to the start of the meeting.

Be familiar with the financial arrangements you are expected to follow. Petty cash funds are sometimes used to pay for the refreshments, especially those provided for visitors. If company personnel are expected to pay, have a container near the refreshments and clearly indicate the amount each one is expected to contribute. The secretary should not be expected to spend her money to pay for refreshments for others.

PREPARING THE PROGRAM

Frequently, the secretary to the person in charge of the program is expected to type and duplicate the program. If you are given this assignment and have not had considerable experience in completing work of this type, you may need to experiment with several formats and seek the opinions of others.

For relatively short programs, a single unfolded page, a page folded in half, and the French fold are commonly used arrangements. The programs for lengthy conferences and conventions are usually planned by committees and are printed commercially. Regardless of how the program is duplicated, a secretary normally types the copy and is responsible for its accuracy.

Observe the following concerning the program that uses the French-fold format and is presented in figure 5-9:

- Each section has one-half inch left-hand and right-hand margins.
- Material is balanced on pages, 1, 2, and 3.
- Hours are aligned vertically.
- Titles of presentations are expressed consistently. The titles could have been typed as follows:
  PERSONALITY DEVELOPMENT
  "Personality Development"
  Personality Development
- Courtesy titles are used with the names of all speakers. Use titles with either all or none of the names on the program. (Consult a reference manual regarding the typing of titles for elected and appointed government officials and titles of religious leaders.)
- Comparable information is given about each speaker.
- Information is given concerning *who, what, when,* and *where.*

A border and type of different sizes, as shown in figure 5-10, can enhance the appearance of the cover of a program.

If the program is being prepared for a fraternal or educational organization, the crest or seal printed on the front gives the program a formal appearance. Numerous other techniques, such as the quality and color of paper and color of ink, can be used to add to the distinctiveness of a program; however, the techniques usually add to the cost of the program.

The program should be attractive, easy to read, and accurate. Misspelled names and incorrect courtesy and position titles can be extremely embarrassing. Two or three people should check the program for accuracy before it is duplicated.

You should always have a few extra programs printed. Always place one or two in the meeting file.

FINAL CHECKS

When a particularly important meeting has been planned several days in advance, your boss may want you to telephone the offices of the executives the day before the meeting to confirm that they are planning to attend. When you telephone do not hint that you believe the executive may have forgotten about the meeting; instead, indicate that you are

102
Secretarial
Procedures:
Office
Administration and
Automated Systems

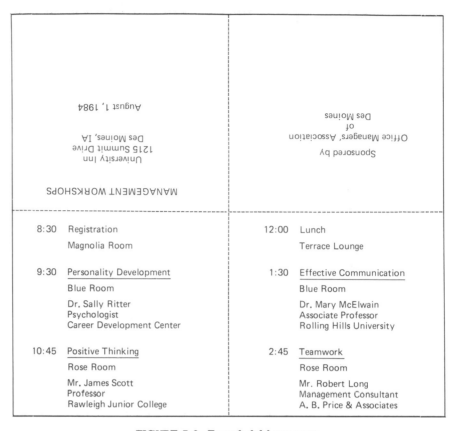

FIGURE 5-9. French-fold program.

checking to see who will be attending. If some executives who indicated they would attend do not arrive for the meeting, you may need to call their offices to remind them.

At least an hour before the meeting, make sure the room is properly arranged and that a sufficient number of chairs are in place. The lighting and temperature should be checked. A room may appear cool when only one or two people are present, but remember that the temperature rises rapidly when the room is filled. When smoking is permitted, ash trays should be provided.

If movies, slides, or transparencies are to be shown, you need to check the following:

- Are the projectors working properly (audio and visual)?
- Are the machines an optimum distance from the screen and are they properly focused?
- Will all participants have an unobstructed view of the screen?
- Will all participants be able to hear?
- Are spare bulbs available and can you or someone else insert them?

College of Business and Economics

AWARDS BANQUET

FIGURE 5-10. A border can enhance the appearance of a program.

All other equipment should also be checked to determine that it is functioning properly.

When you are expected to operate the equipment, study the operator's manual carefully several days in advance and practice operating the machines prior to the meeting. Try to anticipate all adjustments that may need to be made so that you will not become frustrated if the machine does not operate properly during the meeting.

If refreshments are to be provided, you should see that everything that is needed is available.

Make sure that all materials needed during the meeting are readily accessible.

You should have available the name and telephone number of the person to contact if you need assistance before or during the meeting.

INTERRUPTIONS

Interruptions can be annoying and result in a waste of valuable time to those involved in a meeting; however, they are occasionally necessary.

104
Secretarial
Procedures:
Office
Administration and
Automated Systems

If a message must be given to someone while the meeting is in progress, type the message, fold the paper, type the person's name on the outside, and hand the paper to the person conducting the meeting. Be sure the message is clearly and accurately stated. If the person is expected to respond, you may wait; otherwise, you should leave the room as soon as the message is delivered.

You should not have to interrupt the meeting you are attending to answer the telephone. If possible, arrange to have someone answer your telephone when you must attend the meeting. If you must answer the telephone during the meeting, keep the conversation as brief as possible or ask if you may return the call when the meeting ends.

FOLLOW UP

At the close of the meeting, all materials that have been left on chairs or tables should be collected. Copies of the material should be sent to those who may have been absent. Be sure that you have a copy of all documents you need to prepare the minutes or to file.

Unplug or turn off all electrical equipment. You may need to arrange to have movies, slides, or other visual aids or equipment returned.

To help those who will need to plan subsequent meetings for the group, keep a file of all things that may be helpful, such as copies of the notices, the agenda, and programs. Any problems concerning the room, equipment, food service, or any other area should be noted. A list of suggestions for improving meetings can be helpful.

When you return to the office, you should make calendar notations of future meetings or duties to be performed as a result of the meeting.

You may need to write or remind the executive to write thank-you letters to speakers and those who helped with the meeting. You should immediately read through the notes you took during the meeting and write the minutes as soon as possible.

When you made meeting arrangements through hotel personnel and things went particularly well, you may want to write a letter of appreciation.

A summary of the actions taken and the announcements made during informal meetings of executives within the company frequently is sent to those who attended the meeting, as well as to those who were absent. The summary, such as the one shown in figure 5-11, is usually prepared as a memorandum and may be dictated by the executive or written by the secretary if she attended the meeting.

                    M E M O R A N D U M

                                              April 3, 1984

TO: B. Alexander
         S. Bass
         T. Bodenhammer
         H. Handley
         A. Percy
         R. Sullins
         B. Timmons

FROM: Beverly Higgs

SUBJECT: Meeting of the Supervisors

A meeting of the supervisors was held in Mr. Duly's office at 9 a.m. on
Monday, April 2. All supervisors except Alexander were present.

Mr. Duly announced that desk computers are being purchased for all
supervisors and that training sessions will be held from 8 until 12 on
April 27, 28, 29, and 30 at the Modern Computer Company, 1010 Main Street.
Each supervisor is to attend one of the sessions.

The copying machines are being used excessively. Supervisors should make
sure the machines are used only for company business.

Employee tardiness and absenteeism were discussed. Each supervisor is
to submit a memorandum report to Mr. Duly by April 25. The report is to
cover the three-month period from January 1 through March 31 and is to
cover four areas:

1. List each employee and indicate the number of times tardy, the number
    of minutes late each time, and the number of days absent.

2. Show the total number of times employees were tardy and the average
    number of times the employees in the department were tardy.

3. Show the total number of times employees were absent and the average
    number of times the employees in the department were absent.

4. Suggest ways of reducing tardiness and absenteeism in the department.

FIGURE 5-11. Summary in memorandum form.

106
Secretarial
Procedures:
Office
Administration and
Automated Systems

———————————— Summary ————————————

Assisting the executive with meetings gives the secretary an excellent opportunity to demonstrate her efficiency prior to, during, and following the meeting.

The secretary usually assists in scheduling the meetings and is responsible for notifying the participants, scheduling the meeting room and equipment, and ensuring the room is properly prepared.

Often the secretary is expected to attend the meeting and is responsible for follow-up activities, such as writing thank-you letters and preparing and distributing a summary of the meeting.

———————————— Questions ————————————

1. If your boss asks you to schedule a meeting of five particular executives, what determines which one you should contact first?

2. What factors may affect the time for which a meeting is called?

3. When those expected to attend a meeting have conflicting schedules, what should be done?

4. Why must some meetings be announced at a certain time and in a certain way?

5. What determines the form of notification to use?

6. Why is a written notice of a meeting often more desirable than one given over the telephone?

7. When you notify people of a meeting by telephone, what should you do to make sure the complete message is given?

8. Why are people sometimes notified of a meeting by telephone and in writing too?

9. Why are duplicated memorandums normally used to notify executives of meetings to be held within the company?

10. When notifying people by telephone, why should you keep a record of the people with whom you talked, the date, and the time you called?

11. Should a secretary be expected to assist her boss in planning a meeting for an organization in the community? Discuss.

12. Discuss the possible role of the secretary in helping an executive plan a meeting for a professional group.

13. How can sexist salutations be avoided when sending a form letter to the members of an organization?

14. Discuss the procedures to be followed in maintaining an up-to-date mailing list.

15. What may be done to encourage people to make reservations for a meeting or banquet?

16. List the things that need to be considered when selecting a meeting room.

17. What are the advantages of using a form when reserving a room and equipment?

18. What action should be taken when the meeting room must be changed after the meeting notices have been delivered?

19. Discuss the things the secretary should check shortly before the time of the meeting.

20. Explain how the secretary's duties during a formal meeting conducted under parliamentary law differ from her duties during an informal meeting of executives in an office.

21. If several documents are to be used during the meeting, what can be done to aid the participants in locating a particular item?

22. What is an agenda?

23. List the order of the agenda items for most formal meetings conducted under parliamentary law.

24. Why is a printed agenda not needed for all meetings?

25. Explain the use of courtesy and position titles for individuals listed in a printed program.

26. Explain the French-fold arrangement of a program.

27. Why should margins of at least one-half inch be left on all pages of a program?

28. How may items in the program be highlighted?

29. Discuss what can be done to minimize or avoid interruptions in meetings.

30. List the follow-up duties that frequently must be performed.

———————————————— Projects ————————————————

1. Look through several professional magazines for announcements of conferences or meetings. Prepare a list of the good features of each one.

2. Attend a meeting for which a formal agenda has not been prepared. Prepare the agenda as the meeting progresses.

108
Secretarial
Procedures:
Office
Administration and
Automated Systems

3. Make a list of the advantages of following a formal agenda for all meetings.

4. Assume that you have been given the following information and asked to prepare a one-fold program for a Professional Development Seminar for Executive Secretaries:

"Assertiveness Training"—to be discussed by Kathy Kitzinger, psychologist at California State University, Los Angeles

"Understanding the Team Approach"—to be discussed by Dr. Alice Skornia, professor of management at Pasadena City College

"Decision Making"—to be discussed by Ralph Speer, President of the Justin Company in Arcadia

"Interpersonal Skills"—to be discussed by James Spencer, associated with Eastland Management Consultants, Los Angeles

Make a list of the additional information needed before the program can be prepared.

5. Use hypothetical data for the information missing in project 4 and prepare an attractive program.

 Cases

1. Assume that you made the arrangements for equipment required for a meeting. About an hour before the meeting, you check the room and find that the movie projector you requested has not been delivered. You telephone the rental office and are assured that the projector is on the way. The projector has not been delivered by the time the meeting is to begin. What should you do?

2. Lynnette Klopper was expected to write the minutes for an important meeting. She decided to make a tape recording of the proceedings and prior to the meeting checked the equipment to make sure it was working properly. An electrical power failure occurred during the meeting. The committee members decided to continue the meeting. How should Lynnette have prepared for a contingency of this type?

3. The members of a committee decided to extend the meeting longer than originally planned. The chairman asked the secretary to go to a vending machine to get refreshments for the 15 members. He did not give her the money for the refreshments and she did not have access to a petty cash fund that could be used for this purpose. How should the secretary handle the situation?

4. Material accompanied the announcement of the meeting sent to the executives. The executives were asked to bring the material to the meeting. Several of the executives failed to bring the material and appeared annoyed that the secretary did not have an adequate supply of duplicates. What should be the secretary's reaction?

CHAPTER 6

Travel Arrangements

The travel arrangements the secretary must make vary considerably. In companies where the personnel travel extensively, a traffic or transportation department may make all the arrangements. When the company does not have a traffic department, the secretary is expected to make the arrangements through a travel agency or directly with the airlines, motels and hotels, and car rental agencies.

TRAVEL AGENCIES

Since travel knowledge gained through study or first-hand experience may become obsolete, the secretary should probably make most arrangements through a travel agent. Furthermore, time can be saved by using the services of a travel agent.

Selecting a Travel Agency

Be careful when selecting a travel agency. Experienced agents who have up-to-date knowledge about the many aspects of the travel industry can ensure the trip is well-planned and often can make money-saving suggestions.

When the company for which you work does not already use the services of an agency, you may ask business acquaintances for the names of agencies with which they have had good experiences. You may want to

112
Secretarial
Procedures:
Office
Administration and
Automated Systems

select an agency that has personnel who have completed continuing education programs offered by the Institute of Certified Travel Agents and those who have been awarded the Certified Travel Counselor designation.

Using a Travel Agency

Travel agencies operate as independent businesses, and they receive the commissions from the companies for which they sell travel services. The agency deducts the commission from the quoted price of an airline ticket or room or car rental rate. The traveler pays the same price regardless of whether the reservation is made through a travel agent or directly with the company involved. Since the travel agents are in business to make a profit by selling services, you should never have a travel agent do the preliminary work and then purchase a ticket or make a reservation on your own.

Even though the secretary should make the reservations through a travel agent most of the time, she will have to provide the agent with information concerning dates and times of travel and the preferences of the executive. By occasionally contacting the airlines, motels, and car rental agencies directly, the secretary can be sure the travel agent is providing the best service possible.

MAKING RESERVATIONS

If you elect to make the appropriate reservations, major airlines, car rental agencies, and chain hotels and motels have toll-free numbers you may call to make reservations. You may call toll-free information, 1-800-555-1212, to obtain the numbers of those you are interested in contacting if the number is not listed in the telephone directory.

Most of the airlines and car rental agencies issue credit cards and accept those issued by the major credit card companies. Your company may establish credit with a travel agency. When you make reservations over the telephone or through a travel agent and intend to pay by using a credit card, you need to supply the name of the card, the number, and the expiration date.

AIR TRAVEL

When your employer or other personnel travel frequently, management may want to subscribe to one or more of the guides published by Reuben

H. Donnelly Publications, 2000 Clearwater Drive, Oak Brook, IL 60521. Subscribers to the *Official Airline Guide,* the *OAG Pocket Flight Guide,* and the *OAG Travel Planner & Hotel/Motel Guide* receive updated materials automatically.

OAG Travel Planner & Hotel/Motel Guide

Perhaps the single most useful source of information for the secretary to use when making travel arrangements is the *OAG Travel Planner & Hotel/Motel Guide.* An abundance of information, including a destination index, is given in the guide. Note that the section of the destination index shown in figure 6-1 gives the following useful information relating to Knoxville, Tennessee:

- Name of the airport.
- Distance of the airport from the city.
- Car rental agencies.
- Bus/limousine service, including the time to the airport, the fare, and the pickup points.
- Airlines serving the city, the reservation phone numbers, and the locations of the ticket offices.
- Selected hotels/motels and the address, range of rates, Mobil rating, and telephone number.

Another important feature of the *OAG Travel Planner & Hotel/Motel Guide* is the diagram of airports. The diagram of the Kansas City International Airport shown in figure 6-2 identifies the airlines using the airport, shows the arrangement of the different buildings, gives parking locations and rates, and gives the location of several hotels/motels in the area.

Airline Timetables

All airlines provide free printed timetables showing flight information for the cities they serve. Since the timetables become outdated in a relatively short time, you should be sure that the timetables you are using are correct. You can ask the airline to add your employer's name to a mailing list to receive new schedules as they are published.

Although the information varies slightly, the timetables published by the different airlines are essentially the same and usually include the following:

- Departure cities and the airports.
- Destination cities and the airports.

KNOXVILLE, TN. ✈ AC 615

AIRPORT: MCGEE-TYSON, TYS, 13 MI. S OF CITY.
CAR RENTAL: AGENCY, AVIS, BUDGET (SEARS), DOLLAR, GENWAY, HERTZ, NATIONAL, THRIFTY.
AIRPORT BUS/LIMO INFORMATION: TIME TO AIRPORT, 20 MIN.; FARE, $10.00. PICK-UP POINTS: ALL MAJOR HOTELS/MOTELS. OPERATOR: AIRPORT LIMO.

Arpt. Bus/Limo Svcs.	Phone	Svc.	Area Served
AIRPORT LIMO	970-2797	S	DOWNTOWN; OAKRIDGE
CAREY LIMO	524-0755	NS	DOWNTOWN & SUBURBS

Airlines	Res. Phone	Ticket Offices
DELTA	690-9696	FIRST TENNESSEE BLDG.; 9000 EXECUTIVE PARK DR.
EASTERN	523-9590	AIRPORT TERMINAL
REPUBLIC	577-7561	AIRPORT TERMINAL
SCHEDULED SKYWAYS >	521-7468	AIRPORT TERMINAL (HANDLED BY UNITED)
TENNESSEE AIRWAYS >	970-3100	AIRPORT TERMINAL
UNITED	637-4411	AIRPORT TERMINAL
USAIR	SEE DIAL 800	AIRPORT TERMINAL
WRIGHT	SEE DIAL 800	AIRPORT TERMINAL

Charter Air Taxi Operators	Res. Phone	Ticket Offices
EXECUTIVE EXPRESS	313/569 -6699	
SKYCAR	834-4202	AIR TAXI LOCATION

HOTEL/MOTEL (near Airport)

FAMILY INNS OF AMERICA, 2450 AIRPORT HWY. (ALCOA)				
NP	$18-69 ® ■ ℗	970-2006	ⓉFAM	ZIP: 37701
HILTON-THE KNOXVILLE AIRPORT, ALCOA HWY. (ALCOA)				
NP	■		ⓉHIL	ZIP: 37701
HOLIDAY INN-ALCOA-MARYVILLE, HWY. 129, BOX 120 (ALCOA)				
★★★	$40-50 ®	983-8111	ⓉHOL	ZIP: 37701
QUALITY INN-AIRPORT, HWYS. 73 & 129 (ALCOA)				
★★★	$36-45 ®	970-3140	ⓉQUA	ZIP: 37701

HOTEL/MOTEL (Downtown and other)

AMERICAN HERITAGE INN, I-40				
★★	$23-28	637-3511		ZIP: 37914
BEST WESTERN-CHERRY TREE INN, 1500 CHERRY ST.				
★★	$28 UP ®	546-7110	ⓉBWI	ZIP: 37917
BEST WESTERN-COUNTRY SQUIRE MOTEL, 7304 KINGSTON PIKE				
★★★	$35-50 ®	584-4674	ⓉBWI	ZIP: 37919
BEST WESTERN MOTEL, MERCHANTS RD. & I-75				
★★★	$28 UP ®	688-9110	ⓉBWI	ZIP: 37912
BLACK OAK MOTEL, 6417 MAYNARDVILLE PIKE				
★	$20-26	687-9131		ZIP: 37918
CAPRI MOTEL, 2801 E. MAGNOLIA AVE.				
	$17-26	524-2755		ZIP: 37914
FAMILY INNS OF AMERICA, 4300 RUTLEDGE PIKE				
★★	$25-70 +	546-3910	ⓉFAM	ZIP: 37914
FAMILY INNS OF AMERICA, INC.-MERCHANTS RD., 300 MERCHANTS RD.				
NP	$30-69 ■	971-5810	ⓉFAM	ZIP: 37912
FAMILY INNS-WESTSIDE, 8167 KINGSTON PIKE				
NP	$15-79 ■	693-1811	ⓉFAM	ZIP: 37919
HILTOP INN, 4001 CHAPMAN HWY.				
★	$34-72 + ■	577-1616		ZIP: 37920
HILTON-THE KNOXVILLE, 501 W. CHURCH ST.				
NP	$42-68 ■	523-2300	ⓉHIL	ZIP: 37902
HOLIDAY INN-NORTHEAST, 4625 ASHEVILLE HWY.				
★★	$29-35 ® +	637-0440	ⓉHOL	ZIP: 37914
HOLIDAY INN-UNIVERSITY CENTER, 621 DALE AVE.				
★★★	$29-37 ® +	525-5371	ⓉHOL	ZIP: 37921
HOLIDAY INN-WEST, 1315 KIRBY RD.				
★★★	$31-41 ®	584-3911	ⓉHOL	ZIP: 37919
HOLIDAY INN-WORLD'S FAIR, 525 HENLEY ST.				
NP	$54-69 ® + ■	522-2800	ⓉHOL	ZIP: 37902
HOWARD JOHNSON'S MOTOR LODGE-IN-TOWN, 3400 CHAPMAN HWY.				
★★★	$34-49 ®	577-4451	ⓉHJO	ZIP: 37920
HOWARD JOHNSON'S MOTOR LODGE-NORTH, 118 NW MERCHANTS DR.				
★★★	$35-65 ®	688-3141	ⓉHJO	ZIP: 37912
HOWARD JOHNSON'S MOTOR LODGE-WEST TOWN, 7723 KINGSTON PIKE				
★★★	$35-65 ®	693-6111	ⓉHJO	ZIP: 37919
HYATT REGENCY KNOXVILLE, 500 SE HILL AVE.				
★★★	$54-82 + ■	637-1234	ⓉHYA	ZIP: 37901
PRIMEWAY INN, 9340 PARKWEST BLVD.				
★★	$24-29	693-6061		ZIP: 37923
PRINCE & PAUPER MOTEL, 5334 CENTRAL AVE. PIKE				
★★	$28-30	688-1010		ZIP: 37912
QUALITY INN-DOWNTOWN, 401 SUMMIT HILL DR.				
NP	**$37-91 ® + ■**	**522-2600**	ⓉQUA	**ZIP: 37902**
CENTRAL WALKING LOCATION ACROSS ST. FROM TVA, 3/4 MI. UT, INDOOR POOL & GARAGE, 12 FLOORS, NEW 1982.				
RAMADA INN, 7621 KINGSTON PIKE				
★★★	$39 UP ■	693-8111	ⓉRAM	ZIP: 37919
RANCH HOUSE MOTEL, 3207 E. MAGNOLIA AVE.				
★	$65-75 DWB	523-1700		ZIP: 37914
RODEWAY INN, 323 CEDAR BLUFF RD.				
★★	$35-41 + ■	693-7330	ⓉRDY	ZIP: 37919

REPS: UT Ⓣ

FIGURE 6-1. Destination index. (Reprinted by special permission from the *OAG Travel Planner & Hotel/Motel Guide*—North American Edition—Winter 1982. Copyright © 1982, Official Airline Guides, Inc. All rights reserved.)

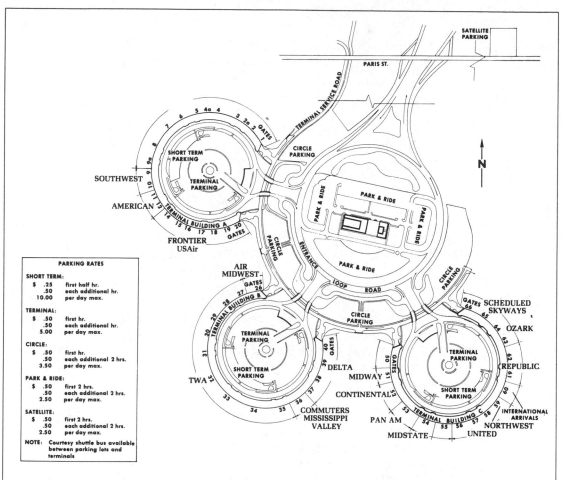

KANSAS CITY INTERNATIONAL AIRPORT

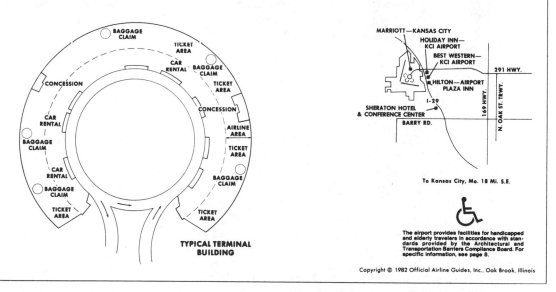

FIGURE 6-2. Airport map. (Reprinted by special permission from the Winter, 1982 issue of the *OAG Travel Planner & Hotel/Motel Guide.* All rights reserved.)

116
Secretarial
Procedures:
Office
Administration and
Automated Systems

- Departure times given in the local time for the city of origin.
- Arrival times given in the local time for the destination city.
- Time zones of the cities.
- Meals served.
- Type of flight: number of stops, nonstop, connecting.
- Flight numbers.
- Codes identifying the cities.
- Types of aircraft.

Let's assume someone wants to fly from Kansas City to Los Angeles. By looking at the portion of the timetable shown in figure 6-3, we find this airline has several flights leaving Kansas City. A person can leave from Kansas City daily on Flight 37 at 10:57 a.m. Central Daylight Time and arrive at Los Angeles International airport at 1:59 p.m. Pacific Daylight Time. The traveler would have to change to Flight 925 in Denver. When we look at the information concerning the flight from Kansas City to Denver, we find that Flight 37 arrives in Denver at 11:30 a.m. Mountain Daylight Time. A snack is served on the flight. The information for flights from Denver to Los Angeles shows that Flight 925 leaves Denver at 12:50 p.m. Mountain Daylight Time and arrives at Los Angeles International Airport at 1:59 p.m. Pacific Daylight Time. Lunch is served on the flight. By looking at the legend, we note that the BOLD STAR indicates a wide body golden jet is the aircraft used for Flight 925.

Some cities have more than one airport. The Los Angeles area, for example, has three airports that are widely separated. When making reservations to cities with more than one airport, you should attempt to plan the arrival and departure from the airport the person prefers. If the person planning to make the trip has not been to the city and does not know which airport is preferable, you may need to make the decision by looking at a map.

Classes of Airline Service

On most domestic flights, the airlines offer first-class and coach service. The first-class fare is considerably more expensive, but the passengers have many benefits not afforded those in the coach section. They are served free alcoholic beverages and meals superior to those served in the coach section, have more seat space and legroom, and receive constant attention. Some airlines have separate check-in counters at the airport for the first-class passengers. The first-class section is always at the front of the plane, and on the 747 aircraft the first-class passengers have access to the upper deck lounge. Many companies permit only the senior executives to travel first class.

FROM DENVER (MDT) (Cont'd)

To: COLORADO SPRINGS (MDT)

Leave	Arrive	Flight	Operates	Meal	Via
710a	740a	18$			0
905a	935a	407			0
1050a	1120a	30			0
1250p	120p	12			0
355p	425p	910			0
700p	730p	405			0
958p	1028p	234$			0

To: EL PASO/JUAREZ (MDT)

Leave	Arrive	Flight	Operates	Meal	Via
815a	1032a	241		B	1
910a	1040a	21		S	0
1250p	307p	435		S	1
750p	1007p	247		S	1
815p	945p	43			0
1000p	1130p	25$			0

To: FORT LAUDERDALE (EDT)

Leave	Arrive	Flight	Operates	Meal	Via
650p	112a+1	402		D	1

To: GRAND JUNCTION (MDT)

Leave	Arrive	Flight	Operates	Meal	Via
1250p	135p	17			0
355p	440p	16			0

To: HONOLULU (HST)

Leave	Arrive	Flight	Operates	Meal	Via
1000a	303p	★607		BL	1
405p	853p	★917		SD	1

To: HOUSTON (CDT)
Airports: I-Houston intercont'l H-Hobby

Leave	Arrive	Flight	Operates	Meal	Via
355a I	852a	430$		B	2
700a I	1006a	440		B	0
1050a I	249p	420			1
1124a I	230p	404		L	0
100p I	405p	★984		L	0
410p I	715p	★986		D	0
415p I	814p	452		S	1
650p I	956p	774		D	0
650p I	1059p	32		D	1

To: KANSAS CITY (CDT)

Leave	Arrive	Flight	Operates	Meal	Via
745a	1008a	38		B	0
1104a	127p	86		S	0
225p	448p	282		S	0
410p	633p	426		S	0
655p	918p	42		D	0
1000p	1223a+1	302$			0

To: LA PAZ (MST)

Leave	Arrive	Flight	Operates	Meal	Via
815a	122p	241	14	BL	3
910a	122p	21/241	14	SL	ELP

To: LAS VEGAS (PDT)

Leave	Arrive	Flight	Operates	Meal	Via
930a	1008a	81		S	0
432p	510p	29		D	0
745p	833p	443$		D	0

To: LOS ANGELES (PDT)
Airports: L-Los Angeles int'l O-Ontario

Leave	Arrive	Flight	Operates	Meal	Via
910a L	1102a	419		B	1
1000a L	1113a	★607		B	0
1250p L	159p	★925		L	0
250p L	359p	401		S	0
305p L	513p	417		S	1
405p L	515p	★917		S	0
615p L	723p	31		D	0
735p L	845p	★941		D	0
750p L	1006p	205			1
900p L	1008p	447$		$	0
1217a L	209a	11$			1

To: LUBBOCK (CDT)

Leave	Arrive	Flight	Operates	Meal	Via
910a	111p	21/226▲		S	ELP

To: TOKYO (GMT +9)
Airports: H-Haneda N-Narita

Leave	Arrive	Flight	Operates	Meal	Via
930a N	745p+1	635	2	LD	6
1020a N	745p+1	655	4	LD	6
1020a N	745p+1	675	6	LD	6

To: TRUK (GMT +10)

Leave	Arrive	Flight	Operates	Meal	Via
930a	128p+1	635	2	L	3
1020a	218p+1	655	4	L	3
1020a	218p+1	675	6	L	3

FROM KANSAS CITY (CDT)

Passenger 816-471-3700 Air Freight 816-243-6000

To: ACAPULCO (CST)

Leave	Arrive	Flight	Operates	Meal	Via
802a	142p	81/21/241	36	BL	DEN/ELP

To: ALBUQUERQUE (MDT)

Leave	Arrive	Flight	Operates	Meal	Via
802a	1015a	81/83		B	DEN
1057a	155p	37/435		S	DEN
202p	417p	417/445		S	DEN
523p	855p	35/247		DS	DEN

To: ANCHORAGE (ADT)

Leave	Arrive	Flight	Operates	Meal	Via
802a	237p	★81/983/WA729		B	DEN/SEA
523p	1113p	★35/989		D	DEN

Service Via CO-WA Interchange

To: BURBANK (PDT)
Airport: B-Burbank/Glendale/Pasadena

Leave	Arrive	Flight	Operates	Meal	Via
1057a B	148p	37/85		SL	DEN
523p B	828p	35		D	2

To: CALGARY (MDT)

Leave	Arrive	Flight	Operates	Meal	Via
1057a	300p	37/WA773		S	DEN

To: CASPER (MDT)

Leave	Arrive	Flight	Operates	Meal	Via
202p	440p	417/23		S	DEN
523p	547p	35/47		D	DEN

To: COLORADO SPRINGS (MDT)

Leave	Arrive	Flight	Operates	Meal	Via
802a	935a	81/407		B	DEN
1057a	120p	37/12		S	DEN
202p	425p	417/910		S	DEN
523p	730p	35/405		D	DEN
708p	1028p	43/234		D	DEN

To: DENVER (MDT)

Leave	Arrive	Flight	Operates	Meal	Via
802a	835a	81		B	0
1057a	1130a	37		S	0
202p	235p	417		S	0
523p	556p	35		D	0
708p	740p	43		D	0
953p	1026p	39$			0

To: EL PASO/JUAREZ (MDT)

Leave	Arrive	Flight	Operates	Meal	Via
802a	1040a	81/21		BS	DEN
1057a	307p	37/435		S	DEN
708p	945p	43		D	1

To: GRAND JUNCTION (MDT)

Leave	Arrive	Flight	Operates	Meal	Via
1057a	135p	37/17		S	DEN
202p	440p	417/16		S	DEN

To: HONOLULU (HST)

Leave	Arrive	Flight	Operates	Meal	Via
802a	303p	★81/607		BL	DEN
202p	853p	★417/917		SD	DEN

To: LA PAZ (MST)

Leave	Arrive	Flight	Operates	Meal	Via
802a	122p	81/21/241	14	BL	DEN/ELP

To: LOS ANGELES (PDT)
Airports: L-Los Angeles int'l O-Ontario

Leave	Arrive	Flight	Operates	Meal	Via
802a L	1102a	81/419		B	DEN
1057a L	159p	★37/925		SL	DEN
202p L	513p	417		S	2
523p L	845p	★35/941		D	DEN
708p L	1008p	43/447		DS	DEN
953p L	209a+1	39/11$			DEN

To: MANZANILLO (CST)

Leave	Arrive	Flight	Operates	Meal	Via
802a	223p	81/21/241	257	BL	DEN/ELP

To: ONTARIO (PDT)
Airport: O-Ontario

Leave	Arrive	Flight	Operates	Meal	Via
802a O	1009a	81/419		B	DEN
1057a O	1259p	37/85		SL	DEN
523p O	739p	35		D	1
953p O	116a+1	39/11$			DEN

To: PHOENIX (MST)

Leave	Arrive	Flight	Operates	Meal	Via
802a	1229p	81/461		BL	DEN
202p	342p	417		S	1
523p	827p	35/205		D	DEN

To: PORTLAND (PDT)

Leave	Arrive	Flight	Operates	Meal	Via
802a	1125a	81/255		B	DEN
1057a	158p	37		SL	1
202p	523p	417/411		S	DEN
523p	903p	35/465		DS	DEN
708p	1048p	43/425		DS	DEN

To: PUERTO VALLARTA (CST)

Leave	Arrive	Flight	Operates	Meal	Via
802a	120p	81/21/241	257	BL	DEN/ELP

To: SAN DIEGO (PDT)

Leave	Arrive	Flight	Operates	Meal	Via
802a	1030a	81/409		B	DEN
202p	410p	417/467		S	DEN
523p	845p	35/45		D	DEN

To: SAN FRANCISCO (PDT)
Airport: S-San Francisco

Leave	Arrive	Flight	Operates	Meal	Via
802a S	1100a	81/263		B	DEN
1057a S	215p	37/235		SL	DEN
202p S	530p	417/233		S	DEN
523p S	910p	35/427		D	DEN

To: SAN JOSE (PDT)
Airport: J-San Jose

Leave	Arrive	Flight	Operates	Meal	Via
802a J	1052a	81/451		B	DEN
523p J	905p	35/415		D	DEN

To: SAN JOSE DEL CABO (MST)

Leave	Arrive	Flight	Operates	Meal	Via
802a	1210p	81/21/241	14	BL	DEN/ELP

To: SEATTLE/TACOMA (PDT)

Leave	Arrive	Flight	Operates	Meal	Via
802a	1105a	★81/983		B	DEN
1057a	202p	37/403		SL	DEN
202p	527p	417/441		S	DEN
523p	905p	★35/989		D	DEN
708p	1052p	43/240		DS	DEN
953p	122a+1	39$			1

FROM KOROR (GMT +9)

Passenger 248

To: DENVER (MDT)

Leave	Arrive	Flight	Operates	Meal	Via
1110a	858p	★645/644/600	4	D	GUM/HNL
1110a	858p	★665/664/600	6	D	GUM/HNL

To: GUAM (GMT +10)

Leave	Arrive	Flight	Operates	Meal	Via
1110a	238p	645	4	L	1
1110a	238p	665	6	L	1
1140a	314p	615	1	L	1
520p	810p	639	3	S	0

B—Breakfast
L—Lunch
D—Dinner
S—Snack
$—Lower Fares Applicable
▲—Higher Fare Routing Applies

+1—Arrives next calendar day after origin date.
-1—Arrives calendar day immediately preceding origin date.
★—**BOLD STAR** represents itineraries incorporating Wide Body Golden Jets on at least one segment.
WA—Interchange flights operated in conjunction with Western Airlines.

x-except	4-Thursday	
1-Monday	5-Friday	
2-Tuesday	6-Saturday	
3-Wednesday	7-Sunday	

CONNECTING CITY CODES

ABQ-Albuquerque	DFW-Dallas/Ft. Worth	IAH-Houston	MCI-Kansas City	ORD-Chicago	SFO-San Francisco
ANC-Anchorage	ELP-El Paso	LAS-Las Vegas	MIA-Miami	PDX-Portland	SJC-San Jose
COS-Colorado Springs	FLL-Ft. Lauderdale	LAX-Los Angeles	MSY-New Orleans	PHX-Phoenix	SPN-Saipan
DEN-Denver	GUM-Guam	LBB-Lubbock	OKC-Oklahoma City	SAT-San Antonio	TUL-Tulsa
	IAD-Washington, D.C	MAF-Midland	ONT-Ontario	SEA-Seattle	

FOR COMPLETE FARE INFORMATION TO CONTINENTAL CITIES INCLUDING **SPECIAL DISCOUNT FARES** CONTACT CONTINENTAL. YOUR COMPANY TRAVEL DEPARTMENT OR TRAVEL AGENT

FIGURE 6-3. Airline timetable. (Source: Continental Airlines)

118
Secretarial
Procedures:
Office
Administration and
Automated Systems

In the coach section, the seats are narrow and the legroom is limited. The passengers in the coach section are usually served complimentary meals and soft drinks and have the opportunity to purchase alcoholic beverages.

In addition to the first-class and coach service, some airlines offer the business class, which is designed to give the passenger more room than coach. The fares in this section are more than those in the coach section, but considerably less than first class. Passengers in this section are also served complimentary alcoholic beverages and are frequently given a choice of entrees when meals are served on the flight. Because of the extra space and the fact that children are not permitted in this section, some executives find the business class particularly desirable.

Many airlines have a limited number of discount fares for coach passengers; however, most of the discount fares involve restrictions that prevent a business person from taking advantage of them. Some requirements, such as staying over a weekend night or purchasing the ticket a certain number of days in advance, may not interfere with the executive's travel plans and may result in considerable savings. When those who are traveling on a discount fare must change their plans or violate a condition applicable to the fare, they lose the discount and must pay the normal fare for the entire trip.

The price of the ticket has nothing to do with the seat assignment in the coach section. People may sit side by side in the section, and they may have paid different prices for the tickets between the same cities. Most executives are pleased when they are able to save the company money if the savings does not involve inferior service or an inconvenience.

Airline Reservations

If your boss is not entitled to fly first class and if your company is cost-conscious and eager to save whenever possible, you should ask for the least expensive fares to the cities the executive will be visiting when you contact the airlines or a travel agent for flight information. Fares charged by the different airlines are not necessarily the same; therefore, unless the person for whom you are making reservations prefers a particular airline or type of aircraft, all the airlines flying between your city and the cities to be visited should be contacted. Some executives prefer a particular type of aircraft. You can learn what aircraft is being used on the different flights by looking at the timetable or by calling the airline.

Most airlines permit seat selection at the time the reservation is made and guarantee that once the ticket is purchased an additional charge will not be assessed if fares increase before the date the ticket is used.

When placing a call to inquire about a flight, you might start the conversation by asking "What is the least expensive round-trip fare between St. Louis and Los Angeles, leaving St. Louis after 8 on Thursday morning, September 1, and Los Angeles between 1 and 6 on Monday afternoon, September 5?" After the airline and flight have been selected, you will need to provide the reservation clerk with the following information:

- Name of the person traveling.
- Whether you want the ticket mailed or picked up at an airline or travel office or at the airport the day of the trip. Most travelers prefer to have the ticket in hand before they depart for the airport. By having the ticket mailed or picked up in advance, you can check it to make sure it is correct.
- Method of payment.
- Telephone number of the person purchasing the ticket.
- Seat desired. The person may prefer a window or aisle seat in the smoking or nonsmoking section. Tall people often prefer the front seats or those near the exits in the coach section since the seats in these locations provide more legroom.

The airlines and the vast majority of the travel agencies use computerized ticketing systems. Even though the three largest computerized ticketing systems are owned and operated by airlines, all systems contain flight information for virtually all major airlines so that when information is requested about flights to a particular city, the agent can instantly offer detailed information about the flights of all the airlines serving that city. When you make your selection, the agent can reserve your seat and have the ticket printed within seconds.

When the travel involves more than one airline, the airline with which the trip originates provides the complete ticket and collects the fare for the entire trip. An open ticket may be purchased when the traveler is uncertain of the date of return. If an open return ticket is purchased, the traveler must, of course, contact the airline and reserve space on a particular flight. The possiblity exists that the flight desired may be booked to capacity, especially during the peak travel periods; thus, the reservation should be made as soon as the time of travel is known.

Although it is not required for domestic flights, you should telephone the airline and confirm the reservation a day or two before the date of departure. The times of the flight may have changed after the ticket was purchased, and you may not have been notified.

Airport Services

Limousine service is available at most airports to provide transportation between airports in the same city and between the airport and downtown locations. The vehicle may be an automobile, van, or bus. The service

120
Secretarial
Procedures:
Office
Administration and
Automated Systems

operates on a regular schedule. The rate is usually lower than that charged for taxi service.

In metropolitan areas, helicopter service may be available between airports and between the airport and the downtown business area. This service is expensive, but it may well be worth the cost when time is extremely important to the executive. The *Official Airline Guide* gives information on helicopter service at the beginning of the listing for each destination city.

RAIL, BUS, AND AUTOMOBILE TRAVEL

Executives seldom travel by train or bus when air transportation is available. Occasionally no commercial airport is in the proximity of the place the person needs to travel and sometimes the weather forces the airlines to cancel flights. Also, a few executives do not like to fly and prefer using some type of ground transportation.

If your employer intends to travel by train or bus, you should obtain the schedules and rates by calling a travel agent or the railway or bus line. When traveling by automobile, your employer may expect you to provide maps. Car rental agencies always provide a map of the city in which the car is rented. However, should your employer want a map prior to the date of departure, you may obtain one by contacting the Chamber of Commerce of the city to be visited or by using travel services such as the AAA Travel Club.

ROOM RESERVATIONS

Your employer may have a preference concerning the hotel or motel, as well as the type of accommodations. Also, you should check with the accounting department to see whether any hotel or motel gives discounts to representatives of your company. In addition to offering discounts to representatives of certain businesses, many hotels offer reduced rates to those who are attending conventions held at the hotel.

The person for whom you are planning a trip may not be familiar with the hotels and motels in the city to be visited. Information on hotels and motels can be obtained from numerous sources, such as the OAG *Travel Planner & Hotel/Motel Guide;* the *Hotel & Motel Red Book;* the *Hotel & Travel Index;* the AAA *TourBooks; Leahy's Hotel-Motel Guide and Travel Atlas of the United States, Canada, Mexico, and Puerto Rico;* and travel guides published by major oil companies. These sources give the number of rooms, the rates, and the type of service plan under which the hotels and motels operate. Most commercial hotels operate under the European plan where the rate covers the room only. The cost of the accommodations includes breakfast, lunch, and dinner when the hotel operates under the American plan.

The reservation can be made by contacting the hotel or motel or by calling a travel agent. If the motel or hotel does not have a toll-free number, you can avoid the unnecessary expense of long-distance telephone calls by having a travel agent make the reservation for you. As part of their membership benefits, oil company travel clubs and the AAA Travel Club offer the same services as a travel agency.

Before placing a call to reserve a room, you should determine several items of information that may be needed. You will need to supply the date of arrival and the approximate length of the stay. Your employer may prefer certain accommodations, such as a room or a suite; a full-, queen-, or king-size bed; or a room in a certain location. If the slightest possibility exists that the person will be arriving at the hotel or motel after 6 p.m., the arrival should be guaranteed. Most hotels will permit you to make a deposit by using a credit card. Even though a deposit has been made, most hotels will permit you to cancel the reservation prior to 6 p.m.

When your employer does not plan to use a rental car, you should ask whether the hotel or motel offers complimentary transportation from the airport. If courtesy pickups are provided, you may need to provide the hotel with the name of the airline, flight number, and time of arrival.

If possible, the reservation should be made far enough in advance so that a written confirmation can be received. The confirmation should be checked for accuracy and should be included with the other material to be taken on the trip.

CAR RENTAL

You may have a travel agent reserve the car, or you may call the rental agency. Several companies have arrangements with car rental agencies whereby their employees receive a discount; therefore, before reserving a car, you should ask your supervisor or contact the accounting office to determine whether your company receives a discount.

At the time you reserve a car, you need to know the date and time the car will be picked up, the flight on which the person will be arriving, the make and/or type of car desired, how long the car will be needed, where the car will be returned, and the credit card that will be used. When a credit card is not used, rental agencies usually require a deposit of several hundred dollars.

Since most major car rental agencies have offices at the airport, all the person should have to do is present his or her driver's license and credit

122
Secretarial
Procedures:
Office
Administration and
Automated Systems

card and sign the rental agreement. When the agency's parking lot is not in the immediate vicinity of the terminal, courtesy shuttle bus service is available to take the person to the rental car lot. No prior arrangements are needed for this service.

FOREIGN TRAVEL

When an executive is planning a trip outside the country, you should seek the assistance of a travel agent if your company does not have a traffic department. As a well-qualified secretary, however, you should be familiar with some aspects of international travel.

Passports

A passport is an official document issued by the country of which the person is a citizen. It grants the holder permission to leave and reenter the country and entitles the holder to the protection of his or her country and that of the countries visited. A citizen of the United States needs a passport to enter most countries. Even though a passport is not required to enter Mexico, Canada, Bermuda, the West Indies, and Central American countries, proof of citizenship may be required.

Passports are issued by the Department of State; however, application is usually made locally. When applying for a passport for the first time, the person must complete Form DSP-11 and then appear in person before an acceptance agent. The form may be obtained from and presented to one of the following: a clerk of any federal or state court of record or a judge or clerk of any probate court accepting applications; a designated postal employee at a selected post office; or an agent at a passport agency. The address and telephone number of the passport agencies are listed in the telephone directories of the cities in which they are located and can be found by looking in the white pages section under United States Government; State, Department of; or Passport Office.

Along with the completed application, the person pays a fee and provides proof of United States citizenship, an official birth certificate, and two special-size photographs. The instructions on the form are easy to understand and thoroughly explain all the steps in the application process.

The passport is valid for ten years, unless expressly limited to a shorter period. Passports may be renewed by completing Form DSP-82. The completed form and the required attachments, including the old passport, may be mailed or presented to a passport agency office. The application for a passport should be submitted several weeks prior to the expected date of departure.

When the passport is received, the person to whom it is issued should sign it and supply the information requested on the inside cover. A record of the passport number and the expiration date should be kept on file.

Visa

A visa is issued by the government of the country in which one plans to travel. A visa is usually a stamp on a page in the traveler's passport, as shown in figure 6-4. Occasionally, a visa may be a separate document.

Although many countries do not require visas for citizens of the United States, the only way to be certain is to check with the embassy or a consular office of the foreign government. Embassies are located in Washington, DC, and many countries have consular offices in large cities. The addresses of foreign embassies and consular offices are listed in the telephone directory and in the *OAG Travel Planner & Hotel/Motel Guide*.

If a visa is needed, the passport must be submitted to the embassy or consular office of each of the foreign countries involved. Obviously, this can be a time-consuming process and should be started several weeks prior to the date of travel.

FIGURE 6-4. Passport and visa.

124
Secretarial
Procedures:
Office
Administration and
Automated Systems

Health Certificate

Information about vaccinations or inoculations required by the country to be visited can be obtained from a travel agent or the consulate of the country to be visited. If one is needed, the International Certificate of Vaccination can be obtained from a passport office, the local health department, or a travel agent.

CANCELING RESERVATIONS

Since many flights are booked to capacity you should show consideration for others by canceling reservations as soon as the executive's travel plans change. If the ticket has been purchased through a travel agency, you can obtain a refund by presenting the ticket to the agency. When the ticket has been purchased from the airline, you may present the unused ticket to the ticket office of the issuing airline in any city or mail it to the refund department of the airline. The ticket should be sent by registered mail. If the ticket was charged, the account number and the name of the account holder should be given.

Motel and hotel reservations should be canceled when travel plans change, even when the arrival has not been guaranteed. If the arrival has been guaranteed, the deposit will not be refunded unless the reservation is canceled before 6 p.m. A few hotels and motels will not refund the deposit once the reservation has been confirmed.

ITINERARY

The itinerary is a necessity for the traveling executive. The details you include in the itinerary depend on the preferences of the person for whom it is being prepared. Some executives like to have all aspects of the trip incorporated into one document; others prefer to have the information concerning meetings and appointments listed on a separate schedule. Regardless of where the information is shown, you need to consider in chronological order all the data the executive may need.

If the person is traveling by air, you should indicate the airline and flight number, the airport for the departure and arrival should the cities have more than one airport, the dates and times of arrival and departure, whether the flight is nonstop or connecting, and whether meals are served. Always give the local times. If the trip involves different time zones and the executive does not travel extensively, indicate the zones on the itinerary. When connecting flights are involved, you should indicate the time of arrival and departure in the connecting city.

For the ground travel, you need to give information concerning the agency, as well as the credit card you indicated would be used, when a car is being rented. You may also need to indicate where you have placed maps for the various cities.

Information concerning the motel and hotel accommodations should include the name, address, and telephone number and whether or not the arrival has been guaranteed.

You should include the address and room and telephone numbers of the places for meetings and the names and telephone numbers of those participating in the meetings.

At least two copies of the itinerary should be prepared, one for the person doing the traveling and one for your file. Executives frequently want to leave a copy with their superiors and with their family. If last-minute changes are made and if changes are made after the trip has begun, you should notify those who have copies of the original plan. The file copy of the itinerary can be useful when you plan other trips for the executive and can be used as a guide when you complete the forms so that the executive can be reimbursed for the expenses involved.

The complete schedule should be typed on paper 8-1/2 inches by 11 inches. In addition, some executives like to have the information typed on separate cards or sheets for each day. All confirmations, tickets, and material needed for each day of the trip should be placed in clearly labeled folders or envelopes; and they should be arranged chronologically. Errors made in preparing the itinerary can be annoying and costly; therefore, you must confirm everything in the itinerary to be certain that all the information is correct.

A detailed itinerary is shown in figure 6-5.

Some executives prefer to have a separate envelope for each day of the trip. An itinerary, tickets, and other material relating to a particular day should be included in the envelope, as shown in figure 6-6.

FINANCIAL ARRANGEMENTS

You should follow the policy manual or talk with someone in the accounting department concerning the procedures to be followed when arranging for the executive to obtain a cash advance and reimbursement for expenses.

ITINERARY FOR JACK GOODSON

November 6-10, 1984

TUESDAY, NOVEMBER 6 (Kansas City to Denver)

6:32 p.m. Leave Kansas City on Continental Flight 43. No meal served.

7:05 p.m. Arrive in Denver. Map in Folder 1. Hertz car. Use MasterCard.
MST   Holiday Inn, 1475 South Colorado Boulevard, Denver, (303) 747-7731.
           Guaranteed arrival.

8:00 p.m. Dinner reservations for four (Eric Teter, Scott McMillin, Bryce
           Pepper, and you) at the Colorado Mine Company, 4490 East Virginia
           Avenue, Denver, (303) 321-6555.

WEDNESDAY, NOVEMBER 7 (Denver to Phoenix)

9:00 a.m. Meeting with Herb Callas, 400 South Glen, Denver, (303) 685-2076.

12:10 p.m. Leave Denver on Continental Flight 461. Lunch served.

1:47 p.m. Arrive in Phoenix. Map in Folder 2. Avis car. Use MasterCard.
MST

3:00 p.m. Meeting with Fred Pierce, 2400 Yale, Phoenix, (604) 798-7011.
           Holiday Inn, 915 East Apache Boulevard, Tempe, (602) 968-3451.
           Guaranteed arrival.

THURSDAY, NOVEMBER 8 (Phoenix to Los Angeles)

9:30 a.m. Leave Phoenix on Continental Flight 417. Snack served.

10:40 a.m. Arrive at LAX in Los Angeles. Map in Folder 3. Hertz car.
PST   Use Mastercard.

1:15 p.m. Meeting with Mary O'Hern, 1500 Colorado, Pasadena, (213) 446-3920.
           Huntington-Sheraton, 1401 South Oak Knoll Avenue, Pasadena,
           (213) 792-0266. Guaranteed arrival.

8:00 p.m. Dinner reservations for four (Sue Scott, Melanie Smith, Rhonda
           Snyder, and you) at Perkins, 510 South Arroya Parkway,
           Pasadena, (213) 795-8000.

FRIDAY, NOVEMBER 9 (Los Angeles to Santa Barbara)

9:30 a.m. Meeting with Dr. Wilmer Stone, 51515 State University Drive,
           California State University, Los Angeles, (213) 224-3887.

           Drive rental car to Santa Barbara. Map in Folder 4.
           Santa Barbara Biltmore, 1260 Channel Drive, Santa Barbara,
           (805) 969-2261. Guaranteed arrival.

5:30 p.m. Dinner reservations for you and Leon Brady at Chuck's Steak House
           of Hawaii, 3888 State Street, Santa Barbara, (805) 687-4417.

8:15 p.m. Reserved seats for four (Leon Brady, Cathy Henry, Mary Schroeck,
           and you) for Annie Get Your Gun at Lobero Theater, 33 East Canon
           Persido Street, Santa Barbara, (805) 665-3201.

SATURDAY, NOVEMBER 10 (Santa Barbara to Kansas City)

           Drive to Los Angeles.

11:30 a.m. Leave Los Angeles on Continental Flight 12. Lunch served.

2:33 p.m. Arrive in Denver.

3:15 p.m. Leave Denver on Continental Flight 42. Dinner served.

6:12 p.m. Arrive in Kansas City.

FIGURE 6-5. Itinerary.

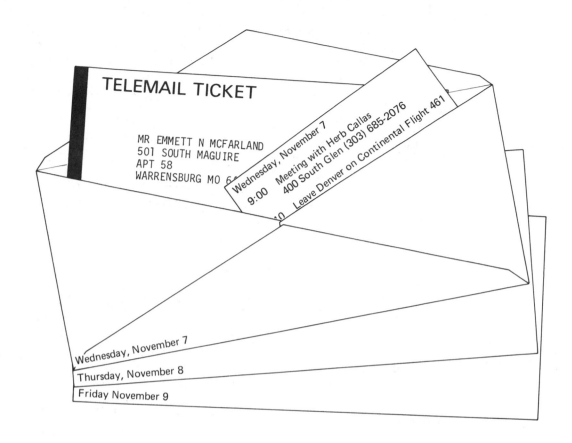

FIGURE 6-6. The itinerary, tickets, and other material for each day of the trip may be placed in separate envelopes.

Cash Advances

Many companies permit the executive to obtain a cash advance for at least a portion of the anticipated cost of the trip. Sometimes the cash advance cannot be obtained immediately; therefore, you should check with your boss several days prior to the date of departure.

Reimbursement

After the trip has been completed, you should obtain from the executive all of the information you need to complete the travel reimbursement form. Some companies require that receipts be submitted along with the reimbursement form; others require supporting documents only when the

128
Secretarial
Procedures:
Office
Administration and
Automated Systems

expenses exceed a stipulated amount. To help you accurately complete the form, the executive should either obtain receipts or list the expenditures on the itinerary. The travel expense form usually provides space for a breakdown of expenditures relating to transportation, meals, lodging, telephone calls, and tips. A detailed expense report form is shown in figure 6-7.

You should make sure that the expense report is accurately and completely prepared so that the accounting department will not have to contact you for additional information and thus delay the reimbursement.

Summary

Most secretaries are expected to know how to make travel arrangements; however, much time can be saved by using the services of a travel agent or the traffic department of the company. The secretary needs to know the questions that should be asked and the types of information that must be provided when airline, motel, and car rental reservations are made.

When the company personnel travel extensively, the company should subscribe to one or more of the airline and hotel/motel travel guides. The secretary should be thoroughly familiar with the types of information included in the guides.

A travel agent may prepare the transportation portion of the itinerary, but the secretary is responsible for checking the accuracy and for preparing the other parts of the itinerary. Errors in the itinerary are always noticed and can result in confusion that may not be resolved easily; therefore, the secretary should check the itinerary several times to be sure all of the data included are accurate. The secretary is also expected to notify all interested parties when the travel plans change before or during the trip.

The secretary may be responsible for obtaining a cash advance for the executive and almost always is expected to prepare the travel reimbursement form after the trip is completed.

Questions

1. How are business travel arrangements normally made?

2. Since all travel agencies sell travel services, why should care be exercised when selecting an agency?

3. How can one determine the toll-free number of a business?

4. If a person purchases a $300 airline ticket through a travel agent and the agent is entitled to a 10 percent commission, how much will the traveler have to pay the agent?

EXPENSE REPORT

NAME _____

LOCATION _____ FROM _____

PURPOSE OF TRIP _____

DATE AUTHORIZED _____ AUTHORIZED BY _____ TO _____

DATE	CITY	BREAKFAST	LUNCH	DINNER	HOTEL	Pub. Trans.	Car Rental	TOLLS	PHONE	1 ENTERTAINMENT	2 AUTO	3 MISC.	TOTAL
TOTALS (Including Tips)													

PURPOSE OF TRIP:

AUTHORIZED BY _____ DATE _____

EXPENSE REPORT SUMMARY

TOTAL EXPENSES	
LESS CHARGES TO COMPANY	
LESS CASH ADVANCES	
BALANCE DUE	$
☐ COMPANY ☐ EMPLOYEE	
COMPLETED BY	DATE
AUDITED BY	DATE
APPROVED FOR PAYMENT BY	DATE

1 ENTERTAINMENT — ENTER ALL REIMBURSEABLE ENTERTAINMENT EXPENSES. LIST EACH OCCASION SEPARATELY. GIVE THE COMPLETE DETAILS OF WHO, WHERE, AND WHY. ENTER DAILY AMOUNTS UNDER #1 ABOVE.

DATE	EXPLANATION	AMOUNT
		XXXXXXXXXXXXXXXXXXXXXXXXXXXXXXXXXXXXXXXXX TOTAL

2 AUTOMOBILE — ALL AUTOMOBILE EXPENSES SHOULD BE ENTERED BELOW BY DATE INCURRED-SHOW MILEAGE FOR COMPANY GAS-ENTER TOTAL UNDER #2 ABOVE.

DATE	EXPLANATION	AMOUNT
	XXXXXXXXXXXXXX TOTAL	

3 MISCELLANEOUS — ANY ADDITIONAL EXPENSE SHOULD BE ENTERED HERE WITH APPROPRIATE RECEIPTS BY DATE-ENTER TOTAL UNDER #3 ABOVE.

DATE	EXPLANATION	AMOUNT
	XXXXXXXXXXXXXXX TOTAL	

ATTACH RECEIPTS FOR ANY EXPENSES OVER $10.00. FILE EXPENSE REPORT WITHIN 2 WEEKS OF BUSINESS TRIP.

FIGURE 6-7. Detailed expense form.

130
Secretarial
Procedures:
Office
Administration and
Automated Systems

5. Look at figure 6-2 and answer the following questions:

   a. What airlines use the Kansas City International airport?

   b. Does the Kansas City International airport have a centralized baggage claim area for passengers on all airlines?

   c. How far is the airport located from Kansas City, Missouri?

   d. What is the least expensive parking rate per day?

   e. What is the cost of riding a bus between terminals and between the terminals and parking lots?

6. Look at the timetable in figure 6-3 and answer the following questions:

   a. How many nonstop flights does the airline have from Kansas City to Los Angeles each day?

   b. How many direct flights does the airline have from Kansas City to Los Angeles each day?

   c. What is the flying time between Denver and Houston on Flight 440?

   d. What is the actual flying time between Kansas City and Los Angeles if one leaves Kansas City at 8:02 a.m.?

7. What are the disadvantages of discount fares?

8. Does the price paid for the ticket determine the seat the passenger is assigned in the coach section?

9. Explain the advantages of the use of the computer when a travel agent is making an airline reservation.

10. Assume the executive must travel on three different airlines to reach the destination. Will three separate payments be made when purchasing the ticket?

11. What is a major disadvantage of purchasing an open airline ticket?

12. Should the reservation for the car rental be made before or after the airline reservation? Why?

13. Some companies expect their employees to stay in certain hotels and motels. Why?

14. Do you agree that when one expects to arrive at the hotel before 6 p.m. a guaranteed arrival reservation is not necessary?

15. Why are written confirmations always desirable?

16. What is domestic travel?

17. Are passports needed to enter all foreign countries?

18. Which must be obtained first, the passport or the visa? Why?

19. If a citizen of the United States plans to travel in Germany, would a passport be obtained from the German or the United States government?

20. What is the purpose of an itinerary?

21. Why should the itinerary be checked several times to make certain it is accurate?

22. When receipts are not obtained, what can an executive do to make sure no reimbursable expenditures are overlooked?

23. Why should reservations be canceled when the executive's travel plans change, even when the ticket has not been purchased and a deposit has not been made?

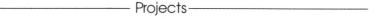 Projects

1. Plan a trip for an executive. The trip should involve overnight stops and meetings in at least three cities. Type a detailed itinerary.

2. Type in dialogue form what would be said in making airline, motel, and car reservations for an executive.

3. Visit a travel agency or an airline office and observe the use of the computer in the reservation process.

4. Obtain the customer's copy of a used airline ticket from a friend or acquaintance and make copies for everyone in the class. Discuss the information shown on the ticket.

5. Obtain schedules from several airlines. Plan trips between cities. The trips should involve the person traveling on more than one airline.

6. Obtain copies of the *OAG Travel Planner & Hotel/Motel Guide* and the *Official Airline Guide*. Outdated copies may be obtained from a travel agency or from Reuben H. Donnelly Publications, 2000 Clearwater Drive, Oak Brook, IL 60521. Study the indexes and content carefully. Discuss the types of information contained in each of the guides.

7. Ask a travel agent to visit the class and discuss the services provided by the agency.

132
Secretarial
Procedures:
Office
Administration and
Automated Systems

8. Obtain copies of reimbursement forms from several companies and discuss the similarities and differences in the forms.

9. Call an airline and ask for the first-class, business-class, coach, and discount fares between New York and Los Angeles or two other cities. Discuss the differences.

10. Study the travel section of the Sunday edition of a metropolitan newspaper. Discuss the differences in the fares quoted by the airlines and travel agencies for flights between the same cities.

--- Cases ---

1. Assume that your boss took several file folders with him on a trip to the branch offices in different cities. When he returns to the office, he cannot find one of the folders. He assumes he left it on a plane. Although the folder did not contain confidential information, the only copy of some important data was in the folder. What should you do? What can you do to prevent this from happening on other trips your boss may take?

2. You made the travel arrangements for Mrs. Jordan. The day before she left, you reserved a room for her at the Elegant Hotel in Albany. When she arrived at the hotel, she was told that they had no record of the reservation; furthermore, they were booked to capacity. Was Mrs. Jordan justified in being irritated with you? What can you do to avoid this type of situation?

3. Your company requires executives to submit receipts for transportation and lodging, but it does not require receipts for meals under $20. The person for whom you work asks you to list amounts slightly under $20 on the reimbursement form. You know that he eats only one big meal a day. What should you do?

4. You prepared the itinerary for your supervisor, Cynthia Ince. Her flight arrived in Dallas at 2 p.m., the scheduled time; however, she was late for her 3:30 appointment with an important client. You had not allowed sufficient time for her to rent a car and travel from the airport to the client's office. Since you have never been in Dallas, you explain to Ms. Ince that you had no way of knowing how much time to allow. How could you have prevented this problem?

5. The executive for whom you work consistently fails to obtain and provide you with the receipts you need to submit with the travel reimbursement form. What can you do to help her remember to obtain receipts?

CHAPTER 7

Telephone Use

INTRODUCTION

Even though various forms of communication are used in offices, the telephone is used more often than any other because of the convenience and speed with which the message may be conveyed and the opportunity for immediate feedback. Furthermore, the cost of using the telephone to send a message is often much less than that of a letter, memorandum, or some other type of communication.

The efficient secretary must be aware of the techniques involved in placing and receiving calls and of the impression she is making each time she uses the telephone.

TELEPHONE PERSONALITY

When using the telephone, remember that you are creating an image of you and the company in the mind of the other person. You should answer each call as if the president or chief executive officer of the company were calling; in fact, that may be the person who is calling. Always display interest and give the call personal attention. Never treat any call as if it were unimportant. Each telephone conversation provides you with the opportunity to increase goodwill and business relations.

Enthusiastically answer the telephone and give the caller the impression you are glad he or she called. Your company may have a standard greeting, such as "Good Morning" or "Thank you for calling XYZ Company." Such expressions can be effective when said with meaning, but they are meaningless and possibly create a negative impression when

136
Secretarial
Procedures:
Office
Administration and
Automated Systems

FIGURE 7-1. Convey a "voice with a smile" to the caller.

said in a monotone or mechanical way. To say "Good Morning" when the time is actually afternoon indicates a total lack of concern and always gives the caller the impression you are not efficient.

The person with whom you are talking over the telephone cannot see you; nevertheless, your attitude is conveyed. The secretary shown in figure 7-1 is undoubtedly conveying a "voice with a smile" to the caller.

Visualize the person and talk and act as if he or she were sitting in the room with you. Use simple, straightforward language you are sure the caller will understand. Avoid using technical words that may confuse the caller.

Give the caller the impression you are wide awake and alert. Talk in a natural and pleasant manner. Enunciate clearly and distinctly. A well-modulated voice carries best over the telephone. Talk at a moderate rate, neither too fast nor too slow. Vary the tone of your voice to help bring out the meaning and add vitality to what you say.

The telephone is designed to carry a normal tone of voice; therefore, use a normal tone when you talk and hold the transmitter about one-half inch from the mouth.

If you are often asked to repeat what you say, ask some friends or coworkers to consider the following questions as you talk with them over the telephone:

- Are you speaking too softly or too loudly?
- Are you speaking too rapidly?
- Are you enunciating clearly?
- Are you speaking in a well-modulated tone?

Those who call your office often will assume you recognize their voice; therefore, you should attempt to learn to recognize voices just as you learn to recognize faces. Listen closely and try to associate the voice with the name. When you know the caller's name, try to use it in a natural way during the conversation. If you are in doubt about the identity of someone, you should ask rather than offend the person by mistakenly identifying him or her.

Always observe business etiquette and show consideration for the caller. *Please, thank you,* and *you're welcome* are positive, powerful words that can be used to help the caller develop a good image of you and your company.

LISTENING

Listen closely while the other person is talking and concentrate on what is being said. Treat callers over the telephone as you would in a face-to-face conversation. Do not interrupt or make the callers feel they are in competition with someone else in your office.

If excessive noise in your work area makes hearing difficult, briefly explain the situation to the caller. That way he or she will know that lack of attentiveness on your part is not the reason why something may need to be repeated.

PLANNING THE CALL

Effectively planning telephone conversations is as essential as planning other office activities. Planning creates a businesslike impression and results in the following:

- Shows consideration for the person you are calling.
- Saves time for you and the other person.
- Saves money on long-distance calls.
- Avoids tying up telephone equipment unnecessarily.
- Eliminates follow-up calls.

138
Secretarial
Procedures:
Office
Administration and
Automated Systems

Before placing a call, you should plan your message just as you would if you were writing a letter or memorandum. Jot down what you believe to be the relevant points and have available all the data you anticipate you will need during the conversation. For extremely important calls, you may need to silently rehearse what you expect to be your part of the conversation.

Consider also whether the time you are placing the call will be convenient for the other person. Is the person you are calling apt to be on a midmorning coffee break, at lunch, or preparing to leave the office for the day? When calling long distance, have you considered the different time zones?

Unless the telephone number is known, check the telephone directory or your list of numbers. Jot down the number so you will have it handy if the call is not completed on the first attempt.

PREFERENCES OF YOUR BOSS

Thoroughly understand the preferences of your boss in regard to the following:

- Whether or not you are to screen calls (determine the name of the caller and the purpose of the call).
- Whether or not you are to tell your boss the identity of the caller before making the connection.
- What you should say and the action you should take if the caller refuses to identify himself or herself.
- What the caller should be told when your boss does not want to be disturbed at the time of the call.
- What the caller should be told when your boss does not want to talk with him or her at any time.
- Whether collect long-distance calls are to be accepted.
- When you should make long-distance calls.
- Whether your boss will accept calls while away from the office, either in some other office or at home.

PLACING CALLS

Some executives believe that the secretary should place all of the calls, but the trend seems to be for executives to place their own calls, especially when the person being called is likely to be in the office. By placing their own calls, executives do not interrupt the work of the secretary and time is not wasted once the called party has been reached. Furthermore, an expression such as "One moment please, Mr. Watt is calling" is very irritating to some executives and frequently is interpreted to mean that the time of the called person is not nearly as important as the time of the caller.

Many executives place their own calls, as shown in figure 7-2. You may encourage your boss to place his or her calls by providing an up-to-date list of the frequently called numbers or suggesting that a Touch-A-Matic Dialer be used.

If you are placing the call for your boss, be sure he or she is ready to talk before you dial. When the call is internal, the higher-ranking person should never be kept waiting for the lower-ranking person, unless the executive has placed the call. Therefore, if you are secretary to a vice president and are placing a call to the president, you should ask the vice president to pick up the telephone before the secretary has the president come on the line. If you are placing a call to another vice president of equal rank, the vice president for whom you work should be on the line before the other one picks up the telephone.

FIGURE 7-2. Most executives place their own telephone calls.

140
Secretarial
Procedures:
Office
Administration and
Automated Systems

How you identify yourself when the party answers depends on whom you are calling. Frequently, you will need to give complete identification, such as "This is Mary Harkness, secretary to Miss Hemphill at Lake Shores Manufacturing." If you recognize the person who answers, you may call the person by name and then tell who you are, such as "Ms. Simpson, this is Mary Harkness at Lake Shores."

For internal calls and those people with whom you talk often, an expression similar to the following is generally appropriate:

"This is Mary Harkness in Purchasing."

"This is Mary Harkness in Miss Hemphill's office."

"Susan, this is Mary Harkness."

Always identify yourself unless you are certain the other person will recognize your voice. Never initiate a guessing game by asking "Do you know who this is?," either in a business or a social situation.

After you have properly identified yourself, either explain the reason for calling or ask to speak with a particular person. If you anticipate the conversation will be lengthy, show consideration for the other person by asking whether he or she has time to talk. If the person prefers to talk with you later, ask in a courteous way what would be the best time to call.

ANSWERING CALLS

Demonstrate efficiency by answering the telephone on the first or second ring. Even though you may be talking with someone or working on an important project when the telephone rings, the caller does not know this and should not be kept waiting. If the caller is a customer or client, he or she may become impatient and decide to give the business to some other company if the telephone is not answered promptly and courteously.

When you answer the telephone, be ready to talk. Never lift the handset to stop the ringing and then continue carrying on a conversation. By doing this, you are being discourteous and, furthermore, the caller may hear what is being said. Never try to talk with an office visitor and a telephone visitor at the same time.

Calls from Within the Organization

When the call is from within the organization, you should answer the telephone by saying something such as "Mrs. Tate's office, Sharon speaking," "Provost's office, Sharon speaking," or "Sharon." Do not answer by saying "hello" or "yes."

Calls from Outside the Organization

Callers like to know to whom they are talking. Properly identifying yourself and the office saves time, is businesslike, and helps to gain the confidence of the caller.

The way you identify your office depends on the preference of your employer and on the type of telephone system used by the company. If calls do not come through a switchboard, you usually should answer by identifying the company and yourself in one of the following ways:

"Good morning, Wright and Associates, Miss Markley speaking."

"Smith Manufacturing Company, Comptroller's office, this is Bettie Hensley."

"Budget Department, Elaine Hanks speaking. May I help you?"

By identifying yourself by name, you are prompting the caller to give you his or her name. Generally, executives and professional people use their first and last names in answering and do not use courtesy and professional titles, such as Mr., Ms., president, dean, and professor, when answering the telephone.

A secretary may use the first and last name or a courtesy title and the last name. Neither the secretary nor the executive should use only the first or the last name.

When the company has a switchboard, the operator will answer by identifying the company; therefore, you need to identify only the office and yourself as follows:

"Vice President Wilson's office, Miss Ellis speaking."

"Personnel office, Ms. Fuller speaking."

The term *office* is preferable to *desk, telephone,* or *line.*

Since you do not know who is calling, you cannot assume that the caller will recognize your voice; therefore, "hello" is an inadequate and time-wasting response. A "yes" or "last name" response is brusque and gives the caller the impression you did not want to be disturbed. The caller is entitled to know the identity of the person with whom he or she is talking; therefore, do not answer by giving your telephone number, such as "This is 729-2303."

142
Secretarial
Procedures:
Office
Administration and
Automated Systems

If the company has a Centrex system, the caller had to know your number or place the call through the Centrex operator; thus, you answer the telephone by identifying the office and yourself.

Long-Distance Calls

When a station-to-station long-distance call is received, you should provide the necessary assistance as rapidly as possible so that costly time will not be wasted. If the caller wants to talk with someone who is not available, offer the assistance you believe to be appropriate. Remember to follow the company policy regarding the return of toll calls.

If the call is person-to-person and the executive is not available, the telephone operator will probably ask where or when the executive can be reached or ask that the call be returned. If your employer is not to pay for the return call, the operator should give you the following information:

- Name of the city.
- Operator number.
- Name and telephone number of the calling party.

Answering a Second Telephone

When you work in an office that has more than one telephone, you may be talking with someone when you receive another call or two telephones may ring simultaneously. Unless the first caller is a very important client, you should not let the second telephone continue to ring even though the first caller may be involved in a lengthy explanation and may not pause long enough for you to tactfully interrupt.

The following procedures should usually be followed when you must interrupt a conversation to answer another telephone:

Local Calls

Tell the first caller "The other telephone is ringing. Please excuse me for a second while I answer it." Indicate to the second caller "I have a call on the other line. Do you prefer to hold or shall I return the call?" If you are to return the call, be sure you know the name and telephone number of the caller.

Long-Distance Calls

Tell the first caller "I have a call on another line. Please excuse me for a second while I answer it." If the first call is local, tell the second caller "I have a call on another line. Please excuse me for a second while I tell him I have this long-distance call." You should then tell the first caller "The other call is long-distance. May I call you back, or do you prefer to hold?" When both calls are long-distance, you should offer to return the second call, if at all possible.

Answering for Someone Else

When you are responsible for answering the telephone for coworkers who are away from the office, identify the office and yourself by using an expression such as "Miss Conley's office, Janet Willis." When you cannot provide the assistance that is needed, offer to take a message or indicate when the coworker will be back.

Leaving Your Telephone

Never leave your telephone unattended. When you must leave the office, let the person who will answer your telephone know where you are going and when you expect to return. In this way, the person can answer your calls knowledgeably, courteously, and in a businesslike manner.

SCREENING CALLS

Courteous callers always identify themselves or are confident their voice will be recognized. Unfortunately, not all callers are courteous and you may need to screen the calls; that is, find out the name of the caller and the purpose of the call. Screening calls often irritates callers; therefore, screening is recommended only when you frequently need to direct the caller to another person who can better provide the assistance that is needed or when your boss does not have the time to talk with all of these who may call.

If you are expected to screen calls and the caller does not give his or her name and volunteer to tell you what the call is about, you must not give the caller the idea that he or she is not worthy of your employer's time. Here are some helpful suggestions for screening calls effectively:

"May I tell Mr. Morgan who is calling?"

"Ms. Toler is not available at the moment. Perhaps I can help you."

"May I give Ms. Harvey your name?"

"May I ask who is calling, please?"

144
Secretarial
Procedures:
Office
Administration and
Automated Systems

If your boss refuses to accept calls without first knowing the caller's identity, you probably should make a statement such as "I'm sorry Mr. Creighton is not available at the moment. May I tell him who called?" Obviously, Mr. Creighton may become available if you know that the caller is someone with whom he wants to talk. Goodwill is difficult to maintain when you ask the caller's name and then indicate your boss is not available.

You and your boss should have clearly established procedures to be followed if a caller refuses to give you any information and continues to insist on talking with your boss.

When the person for whom you are answering the telephone is out of the office or otherwise unavailable, you should offer to take a message, ask if someone else can help, or give information concerning when the person will be available. One of the following statements is usually appropriate:

"Ms. Cowger is in a meeting, but she is expected back by 2:30. May I help you?"

"Mr. Tuttle is out of the office. I expect him back within 15 minutes. May I help you or take a message?"

"Mr. Hoffman will be out of the office until Monday morning. Could someone else help you, or may I take a message?"

Indicating someone is in a "meeting" is more believable than saying the person is in a "conference."

When you know that the executive wants to talk with the caller, you may offer to have the call returned as soon as he or she returns to the office. However, if the call is long-distance, do not offer to return the call unless you are sure you should do so. Some organizations operate on budgets that restrict the amount of money that may be spent on telephone calls.

Never tell the caller anything that may be embarrassing to your employer or reflect unfavorably on your company. Avoid expressions such as the following:

"He hasn't come in this morning."

"She left for lunch at 11:30 and hasn't returned."

"He's in conference with the president and cannot be disturbed."

"She's meeting with her attorney and won't be back in the office until tomorrow."

"He left the office and didn't tell me where he was going."

"He's busy and won't be able to talk to you today. Why don't you try calling back tomorrow?"

"She's out to lunch."

"She is playing golf this afternoon."

"He went home sick."

PLACING A CALLER ON HOLD

You may need to delay the conversation while you search for information, answer another telephone, locate someone, or when the person with whom the caller wants to talk is temporarily unavailable. Always ask the caller for permission to place the call on hold by saying something such as "May I place you on hold while I locate what you need?" Do not say "Hang on a minute," "Hold on," "Jissa' minute," or leave the line without saying anything. Placing the caller on hold without asking is inconsiderate and may lead the caller to believe the call has been terminated.

The telephone is a sensitive instrument. Conversations and noise in the office may be picked up even though the transmitter is covered by cupping it in your hand, placing it against your chest, or laying the handset face down on the desk. Therefore, to avoid discourtesy to the caller or possible embarrassment, always place the caller on hold when the conversation is to be delayed. After the call has been placed on hold, leave the handset on the desk as a reminder that the call is not completed. If your telephone is not equipped with a hold button, lay the handset down gently on a book or papers to help reduce the noise level.

Time passes slowly for the person who has been placed on hold. Since the person waiting cannot see what you are doing, after a short time (approximately 30 seconds) you should report your progress to assure the caller that the call is receiving attention and to give the waiting person the opportunity to continue to wait, call back, or leave a message. If the party prefers to remain on hold, continue to offer an apology or an explanation every 30 or 40 seconds so that he or she will realize you are doing all that is possible to assist. If you offer to return the call, state the approximate time you will call. Be sure you know the caller's name and telephone number.

On returning to the line, attract the caller's attention by using his or her name or by using a courteous expression, such as the following:

"Thank you for waiting, Mr. Runyon. I have the information you need."

146
Secretarial
Procedures:
Office
Administration and
Automated Systems

"I can connect you with Ms. Hilyard now. Thank you for waiting."

By getting the caller's attention first, you will eliminate having to repeat all or part of the information.

TAKING MESSAGES

When the caller cannot be provided the assistance needed at the time the call is received, often you will need to take a message. Always have a notebook, a pencil or pen, and a pad of message forms beside the telephone. Record the details accurately and completely while they are being given by the caller. Making a mental note may result in the message being incomplete, inaccurate, or forgotten.

By using a message form similar to the one shown in figure 7-3, you will be reminded of the information you need to record.

FIGURE 7-3. Telephone message form.

If the caller's name is an unusual one, verify the spelling; you may also need to give the called party a clue regarding the pronunciation (Ms. Schoenley—pronounced "Shaneley"). For names such as "Smith" or "Jones," the first name or initial may be needed. The telephone number should include the area code when the call is long distance.

The message should be recorded carefully, but not necessarily verbatim. Some people will give lengthy explanations, but you may need to record only a few words. Ask that the message and other information be repeated rather than record something that will be incorrect or misunderstood.

Be courteous when you ask for information to be repeated. "May I have your name again, please?" or "Will you spell your name, please?" is better than "What did you say your name is?" or "Repeat your name; I didn't get it."

Indicate the date and time of the call and sign or initial the message form.

Your boss should not be expected to return all calls. For example, an applicant should not expect a personnel director to return his or her call. High-level executives should not be asked to return calls to lower-level executives in the same company; however, in companies where good working relationships prevail, the secretary will often offer to return the call, especially when she may not know when the executive will be available.

When you believe you should not offer to have your boss return the call, you should do all that is possible to help the caller. You may be able to indicate a time when you believe your boss will be available.

Your final responsibility is to make certain the person for whom the message is intended gets it. Messages should always be left at the same prearranged place so that they will not be overlooked. Never toss the message on a desk and hope the person will find it.

TRANSFERRING CALLS

A call should be transferred only when you cannot provide the assistance needed and you are reasonably sure the person to whom the call is being transferred will be able to help. If you are not sure the person can help, ask the caller to call later or offer to return the call. By offering to assist in locating someone who can help, you are letting the caller know you are concerned.

Transfers can irritate the caller, especially if he or she has already called another number or two; therefore, always ask the caller for permission to transfer the call. If the caller seems annoyed, suggest a call-back rather than a transfer.

148
Secretarial
Procedures:
Office
Administration and
Automated Systems

If the caller tells you the purpose of the call and you know that he or she should talk with someone else, you may respond in one of the following ways:

"Mr. Wilson in the Credit Department handles all account inquiries. May I transfer the call to him at Extension 4401?"

"Ms. Tray in Public Relations will be able to provide the information you need. May I transfer your call to her office? The extension is 3001."

"All employee records are kept in the Personnel Department. Would you like for me to transfer you to that department?"

Never say "You have called the wrong office. You should have called the XYZ Department."

When the caller agrees to the transfer and the extension is answered, indicate that you want to transfer the call, identify the caller, and possibly explain the nature of the call. As soon as the person to whom you are transferring the call agrees to talk to the caller, return to the caller and excuse yourself by saying something such as "Ms. McGuire is on the line, and she will be glad to help you."

ENDING CONVERSATIONS

End the conversation with a simple "Good-bye" or an appropriate expression such as the following:

"Thank you for calling, Mrs. Adams. Good-bye."

"I appreciate your help, Mr. Stone. Good-bye."

"You're welcome, Mr. Henry. Good-bye."

"Okay," "Bye-bye," "Thanks a bunch," and other unprofessional expressions should be avoided. "Have a good day" may sound friendly to you, but the expression is overused and some people may not appreciate your using it.

The called party should follow good business etiquette and remain on the line until the caller terminates the conversation and hangs up. Since the caller initiated the call to give or get information, the caller is the one who should know when the purpose of the call has been accomplished.

Always replace the handset gently.

Long-distance telephone charges represent a major operating expense in many companies; therefore, you should be thoroughly familiar with the different types of long-distance calls that can be made. The long-distance charge is based on the type of call, the place called, the time when the call is made, and the number of minutes talked.

Station-to-Station

A station-to-station call is not placed to any one individual; therefore, where Direct Distance Dialing (DDD) is available the call can be made without operator assistance.

When DDD is available, a station-to-station long-distance call can be made by dialing an access code (usually 1), the area code (if it is different from your area code), and the number of the party being called. Although in a few localities the operator may come on the line to obtain the number from which you are calling, you are still billed the station-to-station rate.

The initial rate period is one minute any time of the day or night. Charges are based on rates in effect at the time of connection at the calling point. Charges for additional minutes change if the call continues into a new time period.

The evening rate is less than the weekday full rate, and the night and weekend rate is less than the evening rate. The days and times when the different rates apply are shown in figure 7-4.

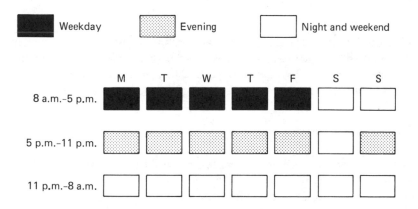

FIGURE 7-4. Discount rates apply to calls placed during evenings, nights, and weekends.

150
Secretarial
Procedures:
Office
Administration and
Automated Systems

Operator-Assisted

All long-distance calls may be placed by dialing "O" and giving the operator the necessary information; however, operator-assisted calls can be dialed direct from most cities through the use of Extended Direct Distance Dialing (EDDD). An EDDD call is placed by dialing "O" and then immediately dialing the seven-digit number desired. If the call is outside your area, dial "O," the area code, and the number.

When the operator comes on the line, you need to supply information such as the following:

"Person-to-person. I want to talk with Ms. Velma Hall."

"Collect call to Mr. Harry Wiggins. My name is John Duston."

"Calling card call. My card number is _____ ."

"Charge this call to (area code plus telephone number)."

Charges for the call do not begin until you are connected with the party you are calling. The charge for operator assistance is in addition to the dial-direct charge.

Person-to-Person

A person-to-person call should be placed when the caller wants to talk with a particular person. The caller is not charged for the call unless it is completed.

Collect

With collect calls, the person you are calling agrees to pay the charges. The request that the charges be reversed must be made at the time the call is placed. When collect calls are placed to your company, you should not accept charges unless you have been given proper authority.

Time and Charges

When placing a long-distance call, you may ask the operator to tell you the length of time you talked and the amount of the call. After the call is completed, the operator will call your number to report the information.

Unless the charges are needed immediately, this type of operator assistance should not be requested. Instead, a record of the toll calls should be maintained and the cost of each call can be obtained from the information shown on the monthly statement.

Calling Card

Those who have a telephone calling (charge) card can have both domestic and international long-distance calls charged to the regular monthly telephone statement. Calling cards are free and are obtained from the business office of the telephone company.

Executives who travel frequently appreciate the convenience of the calling card. Calling card calls can be made from any telephone. When made from some pay telephones, the call is completed without operator assistance by dialing "O," the area code (if different from that on the calling card), the number of the party called, and then the number printed on the calling card.

Third-Number Charge

A long-distance call may be charged to a third telephone number only when someone is at the number to authorize the call. This service is useful if a long-distance personal telephone call must be made from the office and the person making the call does not have a calling card.

Conference

The conference call can be used to talk with several people in different places at the same time. If the company has a switchboard, the operator can place the calls; otherwise, the calls can be placed by the telephone company operator. The operator must be given the names and telephone numbers of the people to be called. The arrangements for the conference call may be made in advance.

Toll Call Records

To control the cost of toll calls and to ensure that only authorized personnel make the calls, many companies require employees to complete a form similar to the one shown in figure 7-5 each time a toll call is made from the office or a calling card is used.

Since the small forms may be easily lost, those who are authorized to make long-distance calls may be asked to record the calls in a book similar to the one shown in figure 7-6.

152
Secretarial
Procedures:
Office
Administration and
Automated Systems

RECORD OF LONG DISTANCE CALL

DATE _____ TIME _____ A.M.
P.M.

CITY CALLED _____

PHONE _____
AREA CODE   NUMBER

Station ☐
FIRM CALLED _____ Person ☐

TALKED WITH _____

CALLED BY _____

SUBJECT MATTER OF CALL _____

_____

_____

_____

RESULT _____

_____

_____

CHARGES _____

TAX _____

TOTAL
_____ MINUTES   COST $ _____

TOPS ⬥ FORM 1209   LITHO IN U.S.A.

FIGURE 7-5. Long-distance call record form. (Courtesy of Tops Business Forms)

INTERNATIONAL CALLS

Overseas calls to many countries can be made from many cities by using International Direct Distance Dialing (IDDD). To dial a station-to-station international call, dial the international access code, the country code, the city code, and, finally, the local number. For example, to place a call to Munich, Germany, to telephone number 7779201, you would dial 011 (international access code), 49 (country code), 89 (city code), and 7779201 (local number of the party called).

International calls can be placed on either dial or Touch-Tone telephones. The call will go through several seconds faster if the "#" button is pushed on the Touch-Tone telephone. The ringing for international calls

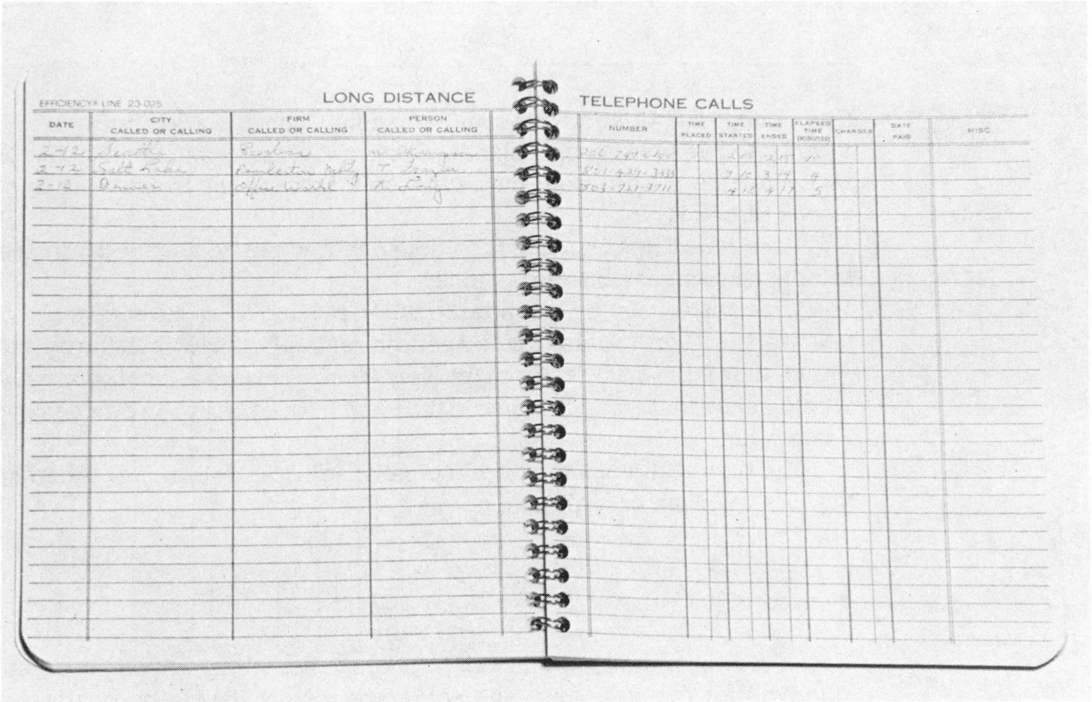

FIGURE 7-6. Long-distance call log. (Courtesy of Ampad Corporation)

does not start immediately (allow at least 45 seconds) after the dialing is completed. The ringing tone may be quite different from the tone you hear on domestic calls.

To place a person-to-person, collect, calling card, or any other operator-assisted call, follow the instructions for a station-to-station call, except dial "01" instead of "011" for the international access code. After the call is dialed, the operator will come on the line to request information, such as the calling card number or the name of the person with whom you want to talk.

Calls to the Bahamas, Bermuda, Canada, Puerto Rico, and the Virgin Islands can be dialed in the same way as long-distance calls within the United States. Most locations in Mexico can be reached by using the international dialing instructions. When you must frequently make international calls, you should obtain a brochure on international calling from the telephone company business office.

Assistance in obtaining an international telephone number, completing a call, or receiving credit on a call to a wrong number can be obtained by dialing "O."

Reduced night and weekend rates apply on calls to some, but not all, countries.

153

154
Secretarial
Procedures:
Office
Administration and
Automated Systems

TIME ZONES

The continental United States and adjacent Canadian provinces are divided into five time zones: Atlantic, Eastern, Central, Mountain, Pacific. A map showing the different time zones is located in the front of the telephone directory.

Time zone maps or charts for other countries can be obtained from the telephone company business office.

Time zones must be considered when placing long-distance calls. A secretary in a Los Angeles office needs to remember that when the time is 4 p.m. there, the time is 7 p.m. in New York; therefore, a call normally would not be placed after 2 p.m. in the Pacific time zone to an office in the Eastern time zone.

The time at the place where the call originates determines whether the day, evening, or night rate applies.

Summary

Each time a secretary uses the telephone, she has an opportunity to create goodwill for the company. The secretary should always be courteous, pleasant, and tactful and should always show concern for the one with whom she is talking.

Although the fundamentals of telephoning are familiar to almost everyone, many situations arise in business that make using the telephone somewhat complex. The secretary needs to know the appropriate action to take when the person the caller wants to talk with is not available, when the caller must be placed on hold, when the call is to be transferred to another extension, and when numerous other situations may arise. In addition, a secretary should be familiar with the classes of service and when each should be used to help control office operating costs.

Good telephone manners and habits are essential if good business relationships are to be established and maintained.

Questions

1. Why is the telephone used more frequently than other forms of communication media?

2. Is "Good morning" or "Good afternoon" always a good greeting to use when answering the telephone?

3. Since the other person cannot see you, how can interest be shown when talking on the telephone?

4. What is meant by a "Voice with a smile"?

5. Tell how planning the call can help create a businesslike impression.

6. When should calls be screened?

7. List the employer's telephone call preferences you need to consider.

8. How can you encourage the executive to place his or her own calls?

9. What are the advantages of the executive placing his or her own calls?

10. When should the name of the company be mentioned when answering the telephone?

11. Why should "hello" not be used when answering the telephone?

12. What should you do when the caller wants to talk with someone who is not in the office?

13. Should you offer to return all telephone calls when the person with whom the caller wants to talk is not available? Discuss.

14. What is meant by being ready to talk when you answer the telephone?

15. Why should you be ready to talk when you answer the telephone?

16. Explain the procedures to follow when placing a caller on hold.

17. List the information that should be recorded on a message form and explain why each item of information is needed.

18. If the caller does not give his or her identity, should you ask who is calling before or after you indicate whether the executive is in? Why?

19. When should a call be transferred?

20. Who should normally end the telephone conversation? Why?

21. Discuss effective ways of ending a telephone conversation.

22. How can you tactfully terminate a call that is not resulting in the desired action?

23. If you want to talk with Mr. Stone and you dial direct a station-to-station call, when do the charges begin?

24. Do you agree that a person-to-person call should always be made when the executive wants to talk with a particular person? Discuss.

25. When the time is noon in Miami, Florida, what is the time in Dallas, Texas?

26. Must the operator dial all of the operator-assisted calls?

27. What factors affect the charge for a long-distance call?

28. If you want to place the least expensive long-distance call possible, when and how should the call be placed?

29. When is operator assistance needed when making station-to-station calls?

30. What is the difference between dialing long-distance calls within your area and outside your area?

156
Secretarial
Procedures:
Office
Administration and
Automated Systems

31. Describe how to place international calls.

32. How can you avoid being charged when the connection is poor and when a wrong long-distance number is reached?

33. When, if ever, should personal long-distance telephone calls be made from an office telephone? Discuss.

-- Projects --

1. Assume that you work for Terrance Harden, president of the Community Leaders Association. You must call 25 members of the Association and tell them that the meeting that had been scheduled for 7 p.m. on February 28 at the Arrow Hotel has been canceled because the speaker, Stacy Zuroweste, is ill. The meeting has been rescheduled for 7:30 on March 27 at the West End Hotel, Kliethermes Drive. Prepare a typewritten copy of what you expect to say when you call each of the members.

2. Arrange to call two or three of your friends and convey the message you prepared in project 1. Ask your friends to consider the following questions as you talk with them:

   a. Do you speak too softly or too loudly?

   b. Do you speak too rapidly?

   c. Do you sound natural?

   d. Do you enunciate clearly?

   e. Do you speak in a well-modulated tone?

   f. Do you convey a "voice with a smile" as you talk?

3. Keep a record of the telephone calls you place to businesses during a two-week period. Record the following information regarding each of the calls:

   a. How many times did the telephone ring before it was answered?

   b. What type of greeting was used in answering the telephone?

   c. Did the person answering appear interested?

   d. How could the person have been more effective?

   e. Did the person appear ready to talk when he or she answered the phone?

   f. Did you have to ask for anything to be repeated?

   g. Were you asked to repeat anything you said?

4. Write the dialogue for both parties for each of the following situations:

    a. Placing a caller on hold.

    b. Transferring a call.

    c. Answering a telephone for a secretary in another office.

    d. Screening a call.

    e. Placing a person-to-person call.

    f. Checking the accuracy of a message you have taken.

    g. Placing a call for your boss to a lower-level executive.

    h. Placing a call for your boss to a higher-level executive.

─────────────────── Cases ───────────────────

1. Assume that you are private secretary to Stephen Young, president of the company. A secretary who has just begun working for Gary Wooten, a low-level executive, calls and says "Mr. Wooten wants to talk to Mr. Young. Put him on please." When you tell her that "Mr. Young will be out of the office until late in the afternoon," she responds by saying "Tell him to call Mr. Wooten when he returns." Which of the following actions should you take?

    a. Tell her that a secretary to a low-level executive does not tell the president to return a call.

    b. Call the low-level executive and tell him that he needs to instruct his secretary on business protocol.

    c. Report the incident to the president.

    d. Return the call when the president returns to the office.

    e. Take some other action.

2. Occasionally someone calls your office and says "Do you know who this is?" Although you are not sure, you usually believe you recognize the voice. How should you respond?

3. Ms. Woods and Ms. Golding sound very much alike over the telephone. Since they call your office frequently, they assume you recognize their voice and do not identify themselves. You are sometimes embarrassed when you fail to correctly recognize the one to whom you are talking. What should you do?

4. Mr. Gentry insists that all of his long-distance calls be placed person-to-person so that the party being called will always be on the line first

158
Secretarial
Procedures:
Office
Administration and
Automated Systems

and he will not have to waste time. Do you believe this practice is logical?

5. Assume that you place a call for your boss, Ms. Glover, to a client who has owed her a considerable amount of money for accounting services for several months. When the client's secretary answers and you say "Ms. Glover would like to talk with Mr. Gould," she responds by saying "Just a moment, please." Apparently she forgot to place the call on hold and you hear Mr. Gould say "Tell her I just left the office for a business trip out of town and won't be back for a week." What should be your response when Mr. Gould's secretary conveys the message?

6. An important client called to talk with Mr. Arwood while he was out of the office. The client asked you to have Mr. Arwood call him as soon as he returned to the office. You completed the message form and left it on Mr. Arwood's desk. Apparently he forgot to call the client. When the client called later in the day, you overheard Mr. Arwood say "I'm sorry, Mary must have forgotten to tell me you wanted me to call." What should you do?

PART IV

CHAPTER 8

Communication Services

The telephone directory is a reference that is used daily by most secretaries to determine the names, addresses, and telephone numbers of individuals and businesses. The directory is frequently used to locate emergency numbers, government offices, and information relating to the services provided by the telephone company.

No one type of telephone is found in all offices. The telephone found in small offices may have only a few lines. Complex systems are needed to satisfy the telecommunication requirements of many large organizations. Many computer controlled systems have discriminatory ringing, call forwarding, call pickup, call transfer, automatic callback, trunk queuing, account coding, and numerous other features. Wide Area Telecommunications Service (WATS) lines and other long-distance services are often used to lower the cost of toll calls.

The Telex network and other services provided by Western Union continue to be used by many businesses in the United States and foreign countries. If you work for a company that uses the services of Western Union, you need to study the equipment manuals so that the services can be used efficiently.

This chapter discusses the telephone directory, the types of telephones frequently found in offices, long-distance services, and telegraph services.

162
Secretarial
Procedures:
Office
Administration and
Automated Systems

TELEPHONE DIRECTORIES

The telephone directories in major cities usually have a white pages section, a blue pages section, an alphabetical listing of businesses in the white pages section, and a yellow pages section.

White Pages

The white pages contain the telephone numbers and addresses of residence listings. Listings in the white pages are arranged alphabetically according to the surnames of the individuals. The surname is printed in all capital letters the first time it is listed at the top of each column, but it is not repeated for other listings with the same surname.

Listings for surnames such as "Jones" and "Smith" may involve several directory pages. When the surname may be spelled several ways, alternate spellings are suggested with a notation, such as "AARON—See also Ahren, Aren, Arend, Arends, Aron."

Professional people often have separate listings for their residence, office, and answering service and indicate their professions, such as "MD," or "attorney."

Blue Pages

The blue pages of the directory provide easy reference to government offices and some other agencies and organizations. The government offices may be listed under four headings in the blue pages section: city, county, state, and United States.

If the directory includes more than one city, the cities are listed alphabetically and the government offices are then listed under the appropriate city heading. The same procedure is followed if listings are included for more than one county or state.

The departments are listed alphabetically in the United States government offices section, and the offices within the different departments are then listed alphabetically.

Business Listings in White Pages

The directories for major cities include in the white pages section an alphabetical listing of businesses. The pages are located at the back of the directory and are marked with a black tab for easy identification.

When the name of the company is known, you can usually find its telephone number more readily by looking at the white pages section than by searching for the number in the yellow pages section.

If you cannot readily find a listing for a business, consider the different ways the name might be listed. For example, "A Cut Above" might be listed with the As, the Cs, or both.

When the name of the company is the full name of an individual, the listing may be under the first name, surname, or both.

Company names beginning with a number are listed as if the number were spelled out. For example, a "7-Eleven Food Store" would be listed in the directory as "Seven-Eleven Food Store" and "8-11 Baseball Inc." would be listed in the directory as if it were spelled out, but might appear in a listing as follows:

Edison's Florist and Bridal Registry

8-11 Baseball Inc.

Eight Eleven Cafeteria

Several businesses have promotional listings in the telephone directories of cities in which they do not have offices. These listings are usually one of the three following types. (This example is from the Kansas City telephone directory.)

- Toll-free number listing:
  TAP AIR PORTUGAL—
    Reservations & Information
      New York NY
    Toll-Free—Dial "1" &
    Then————————————800 221-7370
- Listing of a local number to dial to talk toll-free to an office located in another city:
  Precisionaire Inc 1601 E Cholla
    Phoenix AZ Kansas City KS Tel No——281-0818
- Listing that would require the caller to pay for the call:
  Public Relations International LTD
    Franklin Building Tulsa OK ————918 583-5816

Yellow Pages

The yellow pages are especially helpful in finding the name and telephone number of a company engaged in a particular type of business. The yellow pages listings are arranged alphabetically by product or service and the businesses are then arranged alphabetically under the appropriate heading.

When using the yellow pages, consider all relevant headings. For example, if you are looking for the name of a company from which to rent a car, you may need to consider several headings, such as Automobile Rental, Car Rental, and Rental Agencies.

164
Secretarial
Procedures:
Office
Administration and
Automated Systems

Frequently, the advertisements included in the yellow pages section give useful information, such as directions regarding the location, the hours of operation, and the brand names stocked.

Some cities have two yellow pages books: consumer yellow pages and business to business yellow pages. The residential telephone customers get the consumer book and commercial enterprises get the business directory. Some companies list in both directories, but the business directory usually omits listings for consumer-oriented establishments, such as beauty salons, that businesses do not normally patronize. The consumer directory does not list establishments that cater mainly to businesses, such as heavy equipment.

Other Directory Information

In addition to telephone numbers and street addresses of businesses and individuals, the telephone directory contains much valuable information, including the following:

- *Rate information.* The directory includes comparative data concerning the cost of calls made during the day, the evening, at night, and on weekends, as well as for calls dialed direct and those placed with operator assistance.

- *Emergency numbers.* The telephone numbers for the fire and police departments, highway patrol, and ambulance service for the area are usually given inside the front cover of the directory. Write the emergency numbers for your particular location in the space provided.

- *Dialing instructions.* Easy-to-follow instructions for placing station-to-station and operator-assisted domestic and international long-distance calls are outlined.

- *Maps and charts.* Directories for metropolitan areas normally include a chart listing the first three digits assigned to telephone numbers in the area, as well as a map showing the locations for each prefix. The time zones, as well as the area codes, for the different areas are shown on a map of the United States, which is included in the front of the directory. In addition, the area codes for some areas and cities in the United States and parts of Canada are listed in a chart. A map showing the major streets in the area is also included in most telephone directories.

DIRECTORY ASSISTANCE

Call directory assistance only when numbers are not readily available from another source. When you are responding to a letter, you can usually find the telephone number on the letterhead. Local numbers should be obtained by looking at the telephone directory. New listings may not be included in the directory and the number must be obtained by dialing the directory assistance number listed in the directory. If a number has recently changed, a recorded new number reference is generally provided when the old number is dialed.

When you must call directory assistance, spell the name of the party you want, give the first name or initial, and volunteer the street address if it is known.

Directory assistance for other cities within the area of the caller can be obtained by dialing 1-555-1212 and for cities in other areas by calling 1, the area code, and 555-1212. When calling directory assistance in another city, give the city name first and then the information about the party you want.

The party you want to reach may have a nonpublished or unlisted number. Unlisted numbers are not available through directory assistance. In emergency situations, however, the directory assistance supervisor will call the party with the unlisted number if you can provide the name and complete address and will relay the message that you want him or her to call. This does not, of course, assure you that the call will be returned.

When calls are frequently made to parties in a particular city, you may want to obtain a directory for that city by calling your telephone company business office.

Always write down the number obtained from directory assistance so that you will be able to locate it if you need to call the party again.

TELEPHONES

The telephones and the telephone systems found in offices vary considerably, depending on the needs of the particular company.

Rotary Dial and Touch-Tone® Telephones

The rotary-dial and Touch-Tone telephones are the regular types found in homes and offices. The rotary-dial is seldom found in offices since it can handle only one call at a time and can be used only for regular telephone service.

The Touch-Tone telephone has buttons for the same ten number and letter combinations found on the rotary-dial telephone, plus two additional buttons. The Touch-Tone telephone provides for tone transmission of data, as well as for the regular telephone service. The two additional buttons can be used to reach a dictating center, a computing center, or some other service center.

166
Secretarial
Procedures:
Office
Administration and
Automated Systems

The rotary-dial telephone requires that you let the dial return freely to the original position after dialing each of the numbers; the buttons on the Touch-Tone telephone can be pressed successively and no delay is involved. Therefore, you can place a call on the Touch-Tone telephone much more rapidly than on the rotary-dial telephone.

Key Telephones

Key telephones have more than the 12 buttons found on the regular Touch-Tone so that a person can make or receive several calls simultaneously. Key telephones may have enough buttons to provide for only a few lines, as shown in figure 8-1, or as many as 59 lines.

All key telephones work in essentially the same way. The telephone rings and a flashing light for the line to be answered indicates an incoming call. The light burns continuously while the line is in use and flashes when on hold.

A call is answered on a key telephone by depressing the button, lifting the receiver, and talking to the caller. A call is placed by selecting a line

FIGURE 8-1. Key telephone. (Courtesy of Honeywell Inc.)

that is not in use, depressing the button for that line, removing the receiver, and dialing the number desired.

To place a call on hold, you should explain the reason that you need to leave the line and then depress the hold button for two or three seconds to automatically place the call on hold. The button for the line being held returns to normal position, but the light of the line on which the call is being held continues to flash. While the call is on hold, you can place or answer a call on another line without the caller placed on hold being able to overhear the conversation. If necessary, all of the lines can be placed on hold at the same time.

Simply depress the lighted button of the line being held to return to the caller you placed on hold.

Automatic Dialing

Frequently called numbers can be stored in the electronic memory of a Touch-A-Matic telephone so that calls to those numbers can be made by pressing a single button. A Touch-A-Matic telephone retains the last number dialed and will redial that number when the "Last Number Dialed" button is depressed.

A Card Dialer can also save the user time in dialing. Frequently called numbers can be recorded on cards or tapes that can be inserted into the automatic dialing device when a call is made to one of the numbers.

Speakerphones

The speakerphone provides a hands-free approach to using the telephone. The speakerphone frequently is used when several people are participating in a conference call. Both sides of the conversation can be amplified so that all participants can hear the comments that are made.

The speakerphone is also useful when the secretary must frequently leave the desk to obtain material that is needed to complete the call. By using the speakerphone, she can complete the call without returning to her desk.

Mobile Phones

Local and long-distance calls can be made to and from automobiles, trucks, aircraft, boats, and ships that have telephones. All of the standard services, such as person-to-person, station-to-station, collect, calling card, and so forth, can be used. In some cases, the calls can be dialed direct, but in others the calls must be placed through the mobile operator.

168
Secretarial
Procedures:
Office
Administration and
Automated Systems

CUSTOM CALLING SERVICES

When a company does not have a switchboard, the following Custom Calling services, which can be used with all styles of rotary dial and push-button telephones, are available in some localities.

Call Waiting

With the call waiting service, a tone signals that someone is trying to call while you are talking on the telephone. The person with whom you are talking can be placed on hold while the second call is answered. After the call is answered, the second caller can be placed on hold. You may alternate between the two calls. Neither call is terminated until the caller hangs up.

Call Forwarding

The call forwarding service permits you to transfer local and long-distance calls to another telephone number. While call forwarding is in effect, your telephone will ring once when someone calls; however, calls can be answered only at the telephone where the call has been forwarded. Outgoing calls can continue to be placed from your telephone while call forwarding is in effect.

Three-Way Calling

Three-way calling enables you to add a third party, local or long-distance, to your conversation. With this service, you may talk privately with either party or talk simultaneously with both parties.

Speed-Calling

With speed-calling, the subscriber may code frequently called numbers. Calls can then be placed to these numbers by dialing a one- or two-digit code rather than the entire telephone number.

PRIVATE BRANCH EXCHANGE

Various types of switchboards or Private Branch Exchange (PBX) systems are available. The system used depends to a considerable extent on the organization's telephone traffic volume and its specific needs. A small PBX is shown in figure 8-2.

The nondial PBX requires an operator to connect all calls. Dial PBX systems permit interoffice calls to be made without operator assistance and are frequently equipped so that outside calls can be made by dialing 9 to get an outside line and then dialing the telephone number desired.

CENTRAL EXCHANGE

The Central Exchange (Centrex) system does not require switchboard operator assistance to complete incoming or outgoing calls. Each telephone in the organization is assigned a seven-digit number; thus, if the number of the individual desired is known, the caller can dial the number direct and avoid the possible delay caused by the call being answered by a switchboard operator. Calls can be made to extensions within the company by dialing only the last four digits of the number.

All individual Centrex numbers are not listed in the public telephone directory, therefore an operator is usually needed to provide directory assistance.

Since toll charges for outgoing calls made from the different telephone numbers are itemized and shown individually on the monthly bill prepared by the telephone company, the accounting department can allocate the cost of the service to the different departments.

COMPUTER CONTROLLED PBX FEATURES

Computer controlled PBX systems are flexible and have custom-tailored features to meet the company's individual requirements. Users of the system should carefully study the instruction manual so that they will understand the various features. Many systems include some or all of the following features:

- *Discriminating ringing.* The ringing pattern, such as a succession of long rings or double-interrupted ringing, indicates whether the call is made from an internal extension or an outside phone.
- *Call transfer.* An incoming call can be transferred to another extension.
- *Call pickup.* When you want to continue your conversation at another location, you can "park" (transfer and hold) the call at the new location.

FIGURE 8-2. PBX.

- *Speed call.* Frequently called business numbers can be listed in the system.

- *Call forwarding.* This feature enables a call to be diverted to another extension after a preset number of rings. Call forwarding may be continued to additional extensions when you leave one forwarded extension and move to a different one.

- *Call hold.* A caller may be placed on hold while a call is made to another party.

- *Camp-on call.* A short "beep" tone indicates that the operator has a caller waiting to talk to you or that someone has parked a call on your extension.

- *Automatic callback.* If an internal call is placed to a busy number, you will be called back when the extension you desire is free. When you lift your handset, the previously busy extension will ring.

- *Trunk queuing.* The queuing feature enables you to assume a waiting position for a busy trunk, such as a busy WATS line. Your telephone will ring when the trunk is free.

- *Account coding.* The calling extension, the external number dialed, and the duration of the call may be recorded automatically.

- *Automatic hold of calls.* With this feature, a person may push a button or enter a code and anyone who calls you will receive a high-pitched busy signal or the call will be diverted to someone else.

- *Conference calls.* Several parties may be added on one call, and some of the parties may be external.

WIDE AREA TELECOMMUNICATIONS SERVICE

Wide Area Telecommunications Service (WATS) is used by many companies to substantially reduce long-distance telephone costs. A company may have inward and/or outward service on a full- or measured-time basis.

When a WATS line is rented on a full-time basis, the subscriber pays a flat monthly rate and the line can be used as often and as long as desired. If the line is rented on a measured-time basis, the subscriber is charged a flat rate for a stated amount of talking per month—usually ten hours—and an additional amount for the excess time.

Since all companies do not necessarily need the service to all areas, the subscriber may purchase the service to include as many as seven zones. The continental United States is divided into five zones. Zone 6 includes Hawaii and Alaska, and Zone 7 includes Puerto Rico and the Virgin Islands.

Outward WATS lines can be used only for placing calls from the company premises to people outside the organization. To control use of the lines, many companies require the calls to be placed from certain telephones or through the company switchboard operator. Some companies assign access codes to authorized personnel.

Inward WATS lines can be used to call the organization that rents the line; the party is reached by dialing 1-800 plus the number. Many toll-free (800 numbers) are listed in the local telephone directory. If a number is not listed and you want to determine whether the company has a toll-free number, you may call toll-free information by dialing 1-800-555-1212. You will need to give the operator your area code since the company's toll-free coverage may not extend to your area.

ALTERNATIVE LONG-DISTANCE SERVICES

The company for which you work may use one of the alternative long-distance telephone services.

172
Secretarial
Procedures:
Office
Administration and
Automated Systems

In addition to major telephone companies, such as Southwestern Bell, common carrier companies normally serve metropolitan areas. The common carriers use their own microwaves and satellites and often buy some circuits from major telephone companies. MCI Telecommunications Corporation, United States Transmission Systems (Division of International Telephone and Telegraph), Southern Pacific Communication (SPRINT), and Western Union (Micro) are well-known carriers.

Resellers, such as Combined Network's All-net, do not own their own circuits. Instead, they buy WATS lines from major companies, along with some lines from common carriers, and rent or buy a switch to transfer customers' calls into those lines.

A Touch-Tone telephone must be used with the alternative long-distance services. A subscriber calls the service's access number and after the computer has answered with a dial tone, the subscriber punches in a code number with five to eight digits. When the computer answers again, the subscriber dials the area code and seven-digit local number of the party.

Calls placed over an alternative service usually require 22 to 25 digits, compared with 11 for a call placed through a telephone company. To eliminate part of the long process, at least one company providing the alternative service provides three-digit codes for frequently dialed numbers.

Calls made through alternative long-distance service companies are billed in varying time increments, such as one minute, 30 seconds, and so forth. Generally, the smaller the increments, the more customers may be able to save because they do not pay for time that is not used. For example, if a company bills in one-minute increments, but a call lasts only three minutes and ten seconds, the customer will be billed for four full minutes. If, however, a company bills in ten-second increments, the customer would be billed for only the time used.

FEDERAL TELECOMMUNICATIONS SYSTEM

Federal Telecommunications System (FTS) is a private communications service that permits direct dialing between federal government offices. Major government contractors also have the service. Frequently numbers outside the system can be dialed and some FTS lines can be dialed into from non-FTS numbers.

The system provides for regular telephone conversations, as well as facsimile, high-speed data, and teletype transmissions. Confidential messages may be sent when attachments are used to encrypt the data.

Tie-lines are private lines that are leased by a company or organization to provide unlimited service between two or more locations. For example, a state government may lease lines to directly connect specific state agencies located in several cities. Tie-lines are economical for organizations and companies that need to communicate frequently between the same locations. Calls can be made between the locations by dialing an access code and the tie-line extension number desired.

Tie-lines can be used for all types of telecommunication, such as facsimile and teletypewriter messages.

FACSIMILE

Many businesses use facsimile (also called fax) equipment similar to that shown in figure 8-3 to transmit material over regular telephone lines. The material to be transmitted must not exceed the maximum size that can be handled by the equipment at the sending and receiving stations, but it may be of almost any type, including pictures and figures, as well as typewritten and handwritten documents.

Facsimile equipment is especially useful when error-free documents must be transmitted immediately to another office within a facility or complex or to an office located a long distance from the sending station. The time required for the transmission depends on the type of fax equipment used, but with some equipment a standard letter can be transmitted in about a minute. The cost for fax transmissions includes the long-distance toll charge, if the transmission is not local, and the use of the machine.

All fax equipment is operated in a similar way. Usually, the operator places the document in the transceiver (the transceiver receives as well as sends copy), dials the number to which the message is to be sent, places the telephone handset into a coupler cradle, and presses the send button. With some types of fax equipment, the operator can load several copies in the transceiver at one time and each sheet is fed automatically, leaving the operator free to do other things. Also, some types of equipment will automatically reproduce incoming documents if no one is in when the call is received.

The sending and receiving stations must, however, have compatible equipment before fax messages can be sent and received.

174
Secretarial
Procedures:
Office
Administration and
Automated Systems

FIGURE 8-3. Facsimile machine and operator. (Courtesy of The Mutual Benefit Life Insurance Co.)

TELEGRAPH SERVICES

Since many businesses use the services offered by Western Union, you should be familiar with the services described in the following sections.

Telegrams

A Western Union telegram is a fast way to send a message. It provides a written record of the message and almost always attracts the attention of the person receiving it.

The telegram may be delivered by messenger or by telephone. With messenger service, the Western Union courier will make delivery within five hours during the open hours of the receiving office. If no one is at home, a notice will be left and a reminder will be mailed if the person does not call for the telegram that day. For telephone delivery of regular telegrams, Western Union guarantees a first attempt at telephone delivery within two hours and will continue to make repeated calls for several hours if the telephone attempts are unsuccessful. The recipient will be contacted by mail if the message cannot be delivered by telephone.

Prepare the message before you telephone it to Western Union and be sure it is complete, clear, and accurate. Be sure you know the correct spelling of the addressee's name, the correct address, and the correct telephone number. Speak slowly and distinctly when dictating the message and spell words that are pronounced alike, such as *Allyn-Allen* and *Berk-Burke,* and technical or foreign language terms. When you have completed dictating the message, have the operator read the message back to you.

The operator can tell you whether you are requesting the most appropriate service. The cost, speed, and delivery method vary according to the type, length, and destination of the message. A message placed by telephone can be billed to your telephone, MasterCard, or VISA.

The minimum charge for a regular telegram is based on 15 words, exclusive of the address and signature; therefore, the message should be brief, but always make sure it is clear and complete.

Mailgrams

A Mailgram® is a form of electronic mail involving Western Union and the Postal Service. Voice originated Mailgram messages can be telephoned or filed in person with Western Union; terminal originated messages may be sent over the Telex networks; and high-volume users may initiate messages through a communicating computer or other interfacing equipment. The messages are transmitted to post offices near the addressee and are delivered with the regular mail.

Many companies and individuals use the Mailgram because they believe the Mailgram envelope, shown in figure 8-4, attracts the addressee's attention more readily than an ordinary envelope.

Businesses use the Mailgram to promote sales, to announce price and schedule changes, to collect overdue accounts, to follow up on sales calls, and in numerous other ways where the recipient's prompt attention is important.

TELEX AND TELEX II (TWX)

The Telex and Telex II (TWX®) network of Western Union can be interconnected through Teleprinter Computer Service to provide terminal-to-terminal electronic written communication among businesses located within the United States, Canada, Mexico, and overseas.

FIGURE 8-4. Mailgram® envelope.

In addition to over 140,000 terminals in the United States, over 1.5 million terminals are a part of the Telex network in overseas countries. Most companies that subscribe to the service have the Telex number printed on the letterhead. *Western Union's Telex Directory and Buyers Guide* has a complete listing of subscribers in America, as well as other information concerning using the terminal and sending messages.

A teletypewriter with a keyboard similar to a typewriter keyboard is provided by Western Union to subscribers of Telex and TWX. Telex and TWX are similar in many respects. TWX uses an eight-level code perforated tape; Telex uses a five-level code tape. Telex messages are transmitted at the rate of 66 words per minute and the TWX messages are transmitted at the rate of 100 words per minute. A Telex II (TWX) machine is shown in figure 8-5.

To prepare a message to be sent, the operator types a perforated paper tape message. The accuracy of the message can be checked since the message is not sent as it is typed. To send the message, the operator inserts the tape in the machine and dials the receiver's number. As the message is sent, identical copies are printed at both the sending and the receiving terminals.

Teletypewriter messages can be sent even though the receiving office may be closed; therefore, the service is especially useful when messages that do not require an immediate response need to be sent to offices located in another time zone.

In addition to the convenience of being able to send and receive messages 24 hours a day, the teletypewriter provides the sender and the receiver with an accurate written record of the message.

When a business needs to frequently send a message to the same list of customers or some other group of people, the company can use West-

FIGURE 8-5. Telex II (TWX) machine. (Courtesy of Western Union)

ern Union's InfoMaster® computer system. An address list can be stored in the system. When a message is to be sent, the operator simply dials InfoMaster, enters the list access code, and types the text. The computer then automatically merges the addresses and the text. The message is delivered through a Telex terminal or by telegram or Mailgram. Businesses often use this service to keep their customers informed about price changes, special promotions, and so forth.

Telex subscribers can offer customers 24-hour collect service through the InfoMaster system. The subscriber can arrange for customers, dealers, and distributors to use Telex to send orders, make reservations, and give shipping instructions at any time.

Summary

The telephone directory contains a considerable amount of information the secretary may need in carrying out her duties in the office; therefore, the directory should be studied carefully in advance so that time will not be wasted when it is used as a reference.

Although most telephones and telephone systems are simple to use, the secretary should study the manual for each so that all of the features of the system can be used efficiently. The secretary should also study the Telex manual and receive instruction when she is expected to use that network.

178
Secretarial
Procedures:
Office
Administration and
Automated Systems

———————————— Questions ————————————

1. What listings are often found in the white pages section of the telephone directory?

2. Describe the arrangement of the listings in the yellow pages section.

3. Are toll-free numbers ever listed in the telephone directory?

4. Discuss the information that may be found in the telephone directory in addition to telephone numbers.

5. What is the primary advantage of a speakerphone?

6. Can only station-to-station calls be made from a mobile phone?

7. Discuss the "call forwarding" feature.

8. Do all PBX systems require the services of an operator to complete the calls? Discuss.

9. Discuss features frequently found on PBX systems.

10. What is the difference between "call forwarding" and "call pickup"?

11. Explain trunk queuing.

12. How do some companies control the use of WATS lines?

13. How can a toll-free number not listed in the directory be determined?

14. Discuss the advantages and disadvantages of using alternative long-distance services.

15. Can facsimile messages be sent to both local and remote locations?

16. What are the primary advantages of a telegram?

17. Must a message to be sent by telegram be hand delivered to Western Union? Explain.

18. Discuss the differences between telegrams and Mailgrams.

19. Discuss the advantages of using Telex equipment.

1. Look at the telephone directory for your city and list the office name, telephone number, and directory page number for the following:

   a. Local police

   b. County sheriff

   c. Army recruiting office

   d. Post office

   e. City park department

   f. Public library

   g. Veterans Administration

   h. Federal Bureau of Investigation

   i. County treasurer

   j. Fire department

   k. Internal Revenue Service

   l. State highway patrol

   m. City street department

   n. County prosecuting attorney

   o. Ambulance service

   p. Social Security Administration

   q. City manager

   r. Environmental Protection Agency

   s. Federal Information Center

   t. State employment office

180
Secretarial
Procedures:
Office
Administration and
Automated Systems

2. Look at the yellow pages of the telephone directory and identify two individuals or companies for each of the following categories. List the names, telephone numbers, and heading under which each was found.

   a. Surgeons

   b. Car rental agencies

   c. Airlines

   d. New car dealerships

   e. Oral surgeons

   f. Office cleaning services

   g. Druggists

   h. Psychiatrists

   i. Car leasing agencies

   j. Elementary schools

   k. Household goods movers

   l. Life insurance companies

   m. Lawyers

   n. Copying machine companies

   o. Apothecary shops

3. Use the white business pages section of the directory as you prepare a list of two businesses that give toll-free numbers, two that do not have a local office but give a local number that may be called, and two that do not have a local office but give the address and telephone number of an office located in another city.

1. When Sally cannot readily find a telephone number in the directory, she calls information. Frequently, the information operator is not able to locate the number because Sally does not have the full name of the individual or business, the correct spelling, or the address. What steps should Sally take to be able to obtain the number she needs?

2. One of your coworkers cannot find the telephone number of The Downtowner Restaurant. What suggestions should be made to help her locate the number?

3. Assume that your boss calls toll-free information and the operator asks him for his area code. He tells the operator that he knows his area code and that what he needs is the number of the party he is trying to reach; but he gives the operator his area code. You overhear his comment. After he has obtained the number, you believe you should tell him why the operator asked for his area code. What should you say?

CHAPTER 9

Postal Services

Where in the organization the outgoing mail is processed usually depends to a considerable extent on the volume of mail. In most companies, postal costs represent a major operating cost. Unnecessary postal expenditures can be avoided when those who are responsible for processing the outgoing mail thoroughly understand the different services offered by the U.S. Postal Service and know when each type of service should be used.

Even in large companies where mailroom personnel have the primary responsibility for processing outgoing mail, the efficient secretary needs to be aware of the different classes of mail and the frequently used special services discussed in this chapter.

Secretaries who have full responsibility for processing the mail should have access to the *Domestic Mail Manual,* which may be purchased for a nominal price from the Superintendent of Documents, U.S. Government Printing Office, Washington, DC 20402. The cost of the manual includes free copies of revisions for an indefinite period. The manual completely covers all domestic mail regulations. Most of the information in this chapter is based on the description and regulations contained in the manual.

CLASSES OF DOMESTIC MAIL

Domestic mail is mail transmitted within, among, and between the United States; its territories and possessions; the areas constituting the former canal zone; Army-Air Force (APO) and Navy (FPO) post offices; and mail for delivery for the United Nations, New York.

184
Secretarial
Procedures:
Office
Administration and
Automated Systems

First-Class Mail

In general, all mailable matter may be sent as first-class mail, and some things may be mailed only as first-class or Express Mail. The material for which the first-class postage rate is charged includes all typewritten, handwritten, and computer prepared matter that has the character of actual and personal correspondence; printed forms, such as checks and statements, filled out in writing; and matter sealed against postal inspection or wrapped in such a way that it cannot be examined easily. Other examples of first-class mail include postal cards, greeting cards, personal notes, and money orders.

When mail is sent at the first-class rate, it is transported the fastest way possible. Although airmail is no longer offered as a class of domestic service by the Postal Service, first-class mail is sent by air when it is available and when it would result in the mail being delivered faster than by surface transportation.

The postage for first-class mail weighing 12 ounces or less is computed per ounce or fraction of an ounce. The postage for the first ounce is slightly more than that for each additional ounce or fraction of an ounce.

Letter-size first-class mail that is not rectangular and not at least 5 in. long, 3.5 in. high, and .007 in. thick does not meet the minimum size standards and is prohibited from the mails. Letters or cards weighing one ounce or less and exceeding 11.5 in. in length, 6.125 in. in height, and .25 in. in thickness are considered nonstandard. A surcharge is assessed on each piece of nonstandard first-class mail since it cannot be machine processed.

The standards for flat-size mail and machinable, irregular, and outside parcels sent as first-class mail are explained in the *Domestic Postal Manual.*

Priority Mail

First-class mail weighing more than 12 ounces but no more than 70 pounds is known as priority mail. It is principally used for parcels and flat items larger than letters when delivery faster than that provided by parcel post is desired.

The priority mail rate is based on the weight and the zone to which the material is being sent. The maximum weight for each piece of priority mail is 70 pounds, and the maximum combined length and girth of a piece may not exceed 108 inches.

Express Mail

The fastest service provided by the Postal Service is Express Mail. When the required surface and scheduled airline transportation is available between designated postal facilities, several options are offered to both private and business customers.

Where Express Mail Next Day Service is available, a letter or package left at a designated Express Mail post office by 5 p.m. will be delivered to the addressee by 3 p.m. the next day (weekends and holidays included). It can also be picked up at a designated destination post office by the addressee as early as 10 a.m. of the next day the office is open for regular business. Additional Express Mail services available include Same Day Airport Service and Custom Designed Service.

The Express Mail postage rates are based on the weight of the matter and on the zones measured by air miles between the airports serving the origin postal facility and the destination postal facility. The Express Mail charge includes a service guarantee and insurance against loss, damage, or rifling.

Second-Class Mail

Second-class mail is generally used by publishers and registered news agents who have been authorized second-class mailing privileges for publications mailed in bulk lots. Publications issued by and in the interest of some organizations qualify for the second-class rate if the organization does not operate for profit and meets other conditions. A special rate authorization must be obtained before a publication may be mailed by an organization at the special nonprofit rate.

Complete copies of the regular issues of a second-class publication may be mailed at the transient rate by individuals. Copies that are not complete because pages or portions of pages are missing will be charged with postage at the applicable third- or fourth-class rate. Since the publication must be prepared so that it can be easily examined, a slit envelope is often wrapped around the publication, as shown in figure 9-1. Attention may be called to an article in the publication by using a symbol and writing "Marked Copy" on the wrapper; however, any writing on the publication will result in it being classified as first-class mail. "Second Class" should be written above the address on the wrapper.

Third-Class Mail

Third-class mail consists of matter that is not mailed or required to be mailed as first-class mail, is not entered as second-class mail, and weighs less than 16 ounces. Circulars, printed matter, pamphlets, and merchandise parcels are examples of third-class mail.

Individuals and businesses may send items at the single-piece third-class rate, and many organizations and businesses use the economical third-class bulk rate. Businesses and organizations using the third-class

186
Secretarial
Procedures:
Office
Administration and
Automated Systems

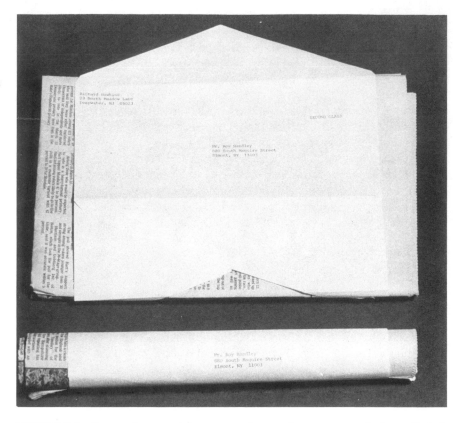

FIGURE 9-1. An envelope may be wrapped around a newspaper to be mailed at second-class rate.

bulk mailing rate must obtain a permit and pay an application fee and an annual bulk mailing fee. The bulk rate applies when identical pieces are sent to at least 200 different addresses, the mailing weighs at least 50 pounds, and the mailing is properly prepared. Certain nonprofit organizations qualify for special third-class bulk rate postage.

Single pieces sent as third-class mail must be prepared so that they can be easily examined, but they should be sealed or secured so that they may be handled by machines. Each piece should be legibly marked with the words "Third Class" below the postage and above the name of the addressee.

Third-class mail may receive deferred service; thus, the Postal Service does not guarantee the delivery of third-class mail within a specified time.

Fourth-Class (Parcel Post) Mail

Fourth-class mail, often called parcel post, consists of printed matter, merchandise, and other items that are not mailed or required to be mailed as first-class mail, are not entered as second-class mail, and weigh 16 ounces or more.

The rates for fourth-class mail are based on the parcel's weight and the zone to which it is being mailed. The United States is divided into eight postal zones, based on the radial distance from the center of a given unit of area. For example, all units of area outside the local area lying in whole or part within a radius of approximately 50 miles are considered Zone 1 and those units outside Zone 6 and within a radius of approximately 1,800 miles are considered Zone 7. The postage for parcels of the same weight is the same to all addresses within the same zone. Zone charts may be obtained free from the post office.

Certain types of material may be sent at a special fourth-class rate or a library rate. Books of 24 pages or more and containing no advertising, 16mm or narrower width films, printed music, printed objective test materials, sound recordings, and printed educational reference charts are examples of the educational material that may be sent at the special fourth-class rate.

Schools, libraries, and some nonprofit organizations may mail specific types of material, such as books, printed music, bound volumes of academic theses, and sound recordings, at the fourth-class library rate. An individual may use this rate when returning qualifying material, but the name of the school, library, or nonprofit organization must always appear in the address or the return address.

"Special Fourth-Class Mail Rate" or "Library Rate" must be legibly marked on each piece mailed at the respective rate.

Fourth-class mail must be wrapped or packaged so that it can be examined easily. When mailing a parcel at the fourth-class rate, the sender is giving consent to postal inspection even though the parcel may be sealed.

Fourth-class parcels mailed for delivery in the domestic mail service generally may not weigh more than 70 pounds and may not exceed 108 inches in length and girth combined. The size of a parcel is computed by measuring the longest side, measuring the distance around the parcel at its thickest part (girth), as shown in figure 9-2, and then adding both measurements.

Mixed Classes of Mail

Sometimes higher-class mail needs to be sent with lower-class mail to ensure delivery at the same time. When first-class mail accompanies a piece of lower-class mail, the message may be enclosed and the parcel labeled "First-Class Mail Enclosed" or the letter may be placed in an envelope and securely attached to the address side of the parcel. Postage must be paid on the separate classes of mail, but the parcel will be sent at the lower class.

Incidental first-class matter closely associated with or related to the piece to which it is attached or in which it is enclosed may be sent at the applicable postage rate of the piece being sent at the lower rate. The inci-

188
Secretarial
Procedures:
Office
Administration and
Automated Systems

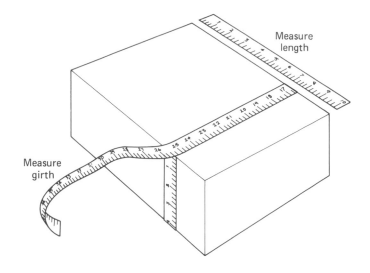

FIGURE 9-2. How to measure a parcel. (Source: *Domestic Mail Manual,* Washington D.C.: U.S. Government Printing Office)

dental first-class matter must be secondary and must not encumber postal processing. A packing slip or bill for the products or publications, assembling or operating instructions, and a standard greeting are examples of incidental enclosures for which first-class postage need not be paid.

The preferred method of affixing a first-class letter to a parcel is shown in figure 9-3.

Official Mail

Two types of official mail, franked and penalty, may be sent without prepayment of postage.

The Vice President of the United States, members and members-elect of Congress, the Secretary of the Senate, the Resident Commissioner or Resident Commissioner-elect from Puerto Rico, Sergeant at Arms of the Senate, each of the elected officers of the House of Representatives, and a few other officials are entitled to send franked mail. Each piece of franked mail must bear a written facsimile signature instead of a postage stamp.

Official government correspondence and publications sent without prepayment of postage is known as penalty mail. Penalty mail must be sent in envelopes or under labels with "Official Business" and "Penalty for Private Use" clearly indicated, along with the address of the agency sending the mail. Franked and penalty envelopes are shown in figure 9-4.

Electronic Computer-Originated Mail (E-COM)

In 1982, the Postal Service introduced Electronic Computer-Originated Mail (E-COM), which allows companies that have computers to transmit

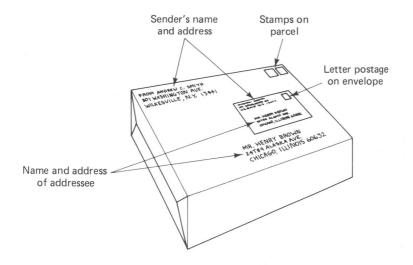

FIGURE 9-3. First-class mail may be attached to a parcel. (Source: *Domestic Mail Manual,* Washington, D.C.: U.S. Government Printing Office)

the text of messages via telephone lines to computers in specially equipped post offices located in 25 cities. At the destination post office, the message is reproduced the required number of times, inserted into distinctive blue-and-white envelopes, and delivered as first-class mail within two business days.

E-COM users must send the same message to at least 200 addressees; thus, much of the mail is promotions and advertisements. The cost of E-COM includes an annual fee of $50, 26 cents for each one-page letter, and, of course, the company's computer and transmission costs. An additional 5 cents is charged for each two-page message.

SPECIAL SERVICES

Those who are involved in processing outgoing mail should be familiar with the special services offered by the Postal Service.

Registered Mail

The most secure service offered by the Postal Service is registered mail, and it should be used when mailing negotiable instruments, jewelry, and other items that would be difficult or impossible to replace. Receipts are used to monitor the registered mail from points of acceptance to delivery and a Registered Mail sticker is placed on the envelope as shown in figure 9-5.

190
Secretarial
Procedures:
Office
Administration and
Automated Systems

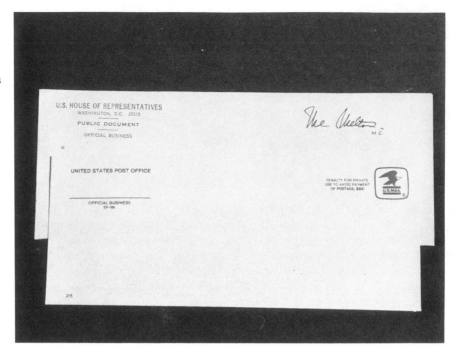

FIGURE 9-4. Official franked envelope and penalty envelope.

Only securely sealed envelopes and packages sent as first-class or priority mail may be registered. The sender must indicate the full value of the mail matter presented for registration, but no indemnity will be paid for articles for which no fee has been paid for postal insurance. Postmasters at only the main office or large branches and stations will accept mail of unusually high value.

Registered mail must bear the complete names and addresses of both the sender and addressee. A receipt, such as the one shown in figure 9-6, is accepted for registration. If requested to do so by the sender, the accepting postal employee will show on the mailing receipt and post office record the time the registered article was accepted for mailing.

A registry fee, which is based on the declared value of the item, must be paid in addition to the regular first-class postage. Registered mail may be sent COD and certified. Delivery may be restricted and a return receipt may be obtained by paying the required fees.

Insured Mail

Third- and fourth-class mail, as well as first-class mail containing third- and fourth-class matter, may be insured to provide indemnity coverage of up to $400 for an article that is lost, rifled, or damaged.

An "Insured" stamp is placed on the insured parcel by the postal clerk and a receipt, such as that shown in figure 9-7, is given to the person

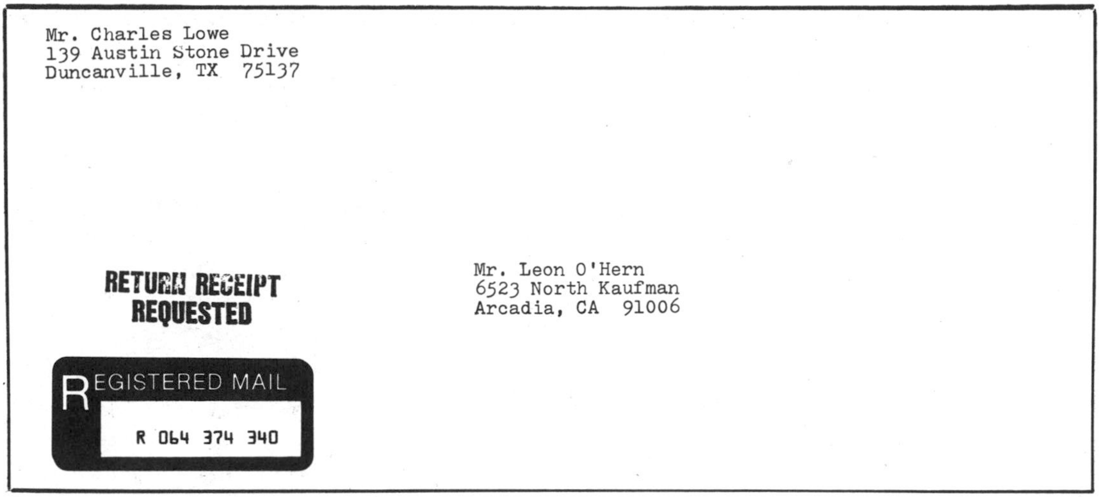
Mr. Charles Lowe
139 Austin Stone Drive
Duncanville, TX 75137

RETURN RECEIPT
REQUESTED

REGISTERED MAIL
R 064 374 340

Mr. Leon O'Hern
6523 North Kaufman
Arcadia, CA 91006

FIGURE 9-5. Envelope with a registered mail sticker attached.

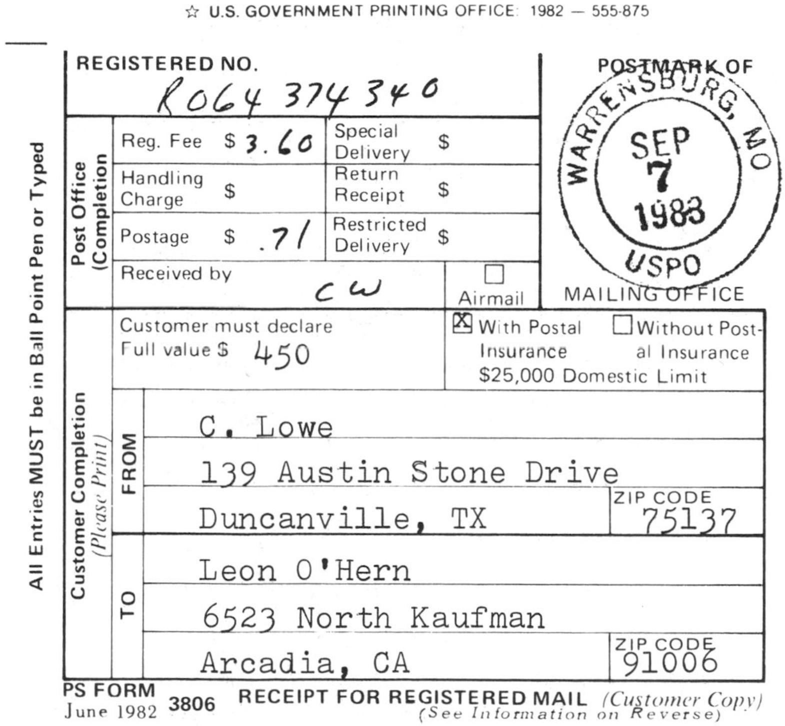
☆ U.S. GOVERNMENT PRINTING OFFICE: 1982 — 555-875

All Entries MUST be in Ball Point Pen or Typed

REGISTERED NO. R064 374 340

POSTMARK OF MAILING OFFICE: WARRENSBURG, MO SEP 7 1983 USPO

Post Office (Completion)

Reg. Fee	$ 3.60	Special Delivery	$
Handling Charge	$	Return Receipt	$
Postage	$ .71	Restricted Delivery	$
Received by	CW	☐ Airmail	

Customer Completion (Please Print)

Customer must declare Full value $ 450

☒ With Postal Insurance ☐ Without Postal Insurance
$25,000 Domestic Limit

FROM
C. Lowe
139 Austin Stone Drive
Duncanville, TX ZIP CODE 75137

TO
Leon O'Hern
6523 North Kaufman
Arcadia, CA ZIP CODE 91006

PS FORM 3806 June 1982 RECEIPT FOR REGISTERED MAIL (Customer Copy)
(See Information on Reverse)

FIGURE 9-6. Receipt for registered mail.

192
Secretarial
Procedures:
Office
Administration and
Automated Systems

mailing the parcel. The receipts are numbered when the package is insured for more than $20.

The post office does not keep a record of insured packages; therefore, the mailer should enter the name and address of the addressee on the receipt and retain it until certain the package has been delivered in acceptable condition.

The insurance fee, which is based on the amount for which the package is insured, is in addition to the regular postage.

Mailing books are more convenient than receipts, and they are furnished by the Postal Service without charge to customers who frequently insure an average of three or more parcels at one time. Spaces are provided for entering the description of parcels to be insured, and the books must be presented with the parcels to be mailed.

Collect on Delivery

Merchandise valued at $400 or less for which the seller has not been paid may be sent collect on delivery (COD). The goods shipped must have been ordered by the addressee and the sender must guarantee to pay any return postage unless otherwise specified on the mail.

First-, third-, and fourth-class matter may be sent as COD mail. The COD fee is based on the amount to be collected, which may include the amount for the item, insurance, the COD fee, and postage. The fees and postage must be prepaid. The amount collected is returned to the mailer by a postal money order.

Certified Mail

Mailable matter of no intrinsic value and on which first-class postage has been paid may be sent as certified mail. Since certified mail has no intrinsic value, no insurance is provided. No record is kept at the post office at which certified mail is sent. However, the mailer is provided with a receipt, as shown in figure 9-8, as evidence of having mailed the material and a record of delivery is maintained at the addressee's post office. The "Certified Mail" stamp on the envelope gives it an important appearance and can be effective in attracting the addressee's attention.

When the prescribed fees are paid, certified mail may be sent special delivery, a return receipt may be requested, and delivery may be restricted.

Return Receipt

A return receipt, as shown in figure 9-9, provides the mailer with proof of delivery. The postal employee delivering the mail must obtain the signa-

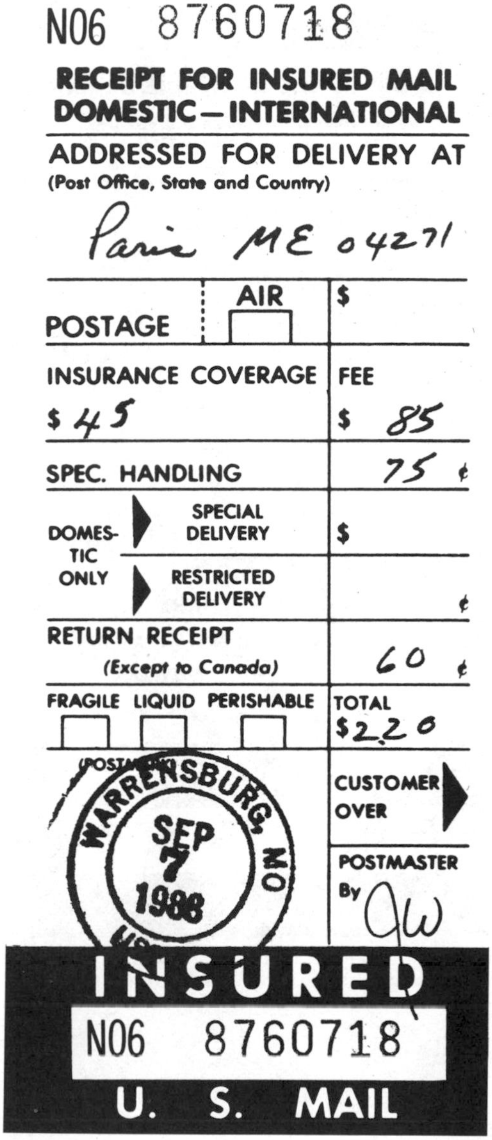

N06 8760718

RECEIPT FOR INSURED MAIL
DOMESTIC — INTERNATIONAL

ADDRESSED FOR DELIVERY AT
(Post Office, State and Country)

Paris ME 04271

	AIR	$
POSTAGE	☐	

INSURANCE COVERAGE	FEE
$ 45	$ 85

SPEC. HANDLING	75 ¢

DOMES-TIC ONLY ▶ SPECIAL DELIVERY	$
▶ RESTRICTED DELIVERY	¢

RETURN RECEIPT (Except to Canada)	60 ¢

FRAGILE LIQUID PERISHABLE ☐☐☐	TOTAL $220

(POSTMARK) WARRENSBURG, MO SEP 7 1988

CUSTOMER OVER ▶

POSTMASTER By *Qw*

INSURED
N06 8760718
U. S. MAIL

FIGURE 9-7. Serially numbered insured mail receipt.

ture of the person receiving the mail when the fee for the return receipt has been paid by the mailer. The receipt is returned by mail by the Postal Service to the mailer after the article is delivered to the addressee.

Return receipts may be obtained for mail that is sent Express Mail, COD, registered, certified, or insured for more than $20.

194
Secretarial
Procedures:
Office
Administration and
Automated Systems

P 263 675 497

RECEIPT FOR CERTIFIED MAIL

**NO INSURANCE COVERAGE PROVIDED—
NOT FOR INTERNATIONAL MAIL**
(See Reverse)

SENT TO	
Ms. J. Sutton	
STREET AND NO.	
792 Southwest Blvd.	
P.O., STATE AND ZIP CODE	
Fairfax, MN 55332	
POSTAGE	$1.22
CERTIFIED FEE	75¢
SPECIAL DELIVERY	¢
RESTRICTED DELIVERY	1.00¢
ADDRESS OF DELIVERY WITH RESTRICTED DELIVERY	
TOTAL POSTAGE AND FEES	$2.97
POSTMARK OR DATE	

PS Form 3800, Apr. 1976

WARRENSBURG MO
SEP 7 1986

CERTIFIED
P 263 675 497
MAIL

FIGURE 9-8. Receipt for certified mail.

Certificate of Mailing

A certificate of mailing may be obtained for a small fee when evidence is needed to prove that something has been mailed. The certificate is prepared by the mailer by using a typewriter, ink, or ballpoint pen and must include the name and address of both the sender and the addressee, as shown in figure 9-10.

The fee paid for a certificate of mailing does not insure the article against loss or damage and does not provide for a receipt to be obtained upon delivery of the mail to the addressee.

Restricted Delivery

A mailer may use restricted delivery to ensure that delivery is made only to the addressee or to an agent of the addressee who has been specifically

U.S. MAIL

PENALTY FOR PRIVATE
USE TO AVOID PAYMENT
OF POSTAGE, $300

UNITED STATES POSTAL SERVICE
OFFICIAL BUSINESS

SENDER INSTRUCTIONS
Print your name, address, and ZIP Code in the space below.
- Complete items 1, 2, 3, and 4 on the reverse.
- Attach to front of article if space permits, otherwise affix to back of article.
- Endorse article "Return Receipt Requested" adjacent to number.

RETURN TO

Mr. Alan Fuerbourne
(Name of Sender)

111 Noland Road
(Street or P.O. Box)

Las Vegas, NV   89101
(City, State, and ZIP Code)

PS Form 3811, Dec. 1980

RETURN RECEIPT, REGISTERED, INSURED AND CERTIFIED MAIL

● SENDER: Complete items 1, 2, 3, and 4.
Add your address in the "RETURN TO" space on reverse.

(CONSULT POSTMASTER FOR FEES)

1. The following service is requested (check one).
☐ Show to whom and date delivered .... __¢
☒ Show to whom, date, and address of delivery.. 70¢
2. ☒ RESTRICTED DELIVERY 1.00¢
   (*The restricted delivery fee is charged in addition to the return receipt fee.*)

TOTAL $1.70

3. ARTICLE ADDRESSED TO:

Alma Chambers

4. TYPE OF SERVICE:		ARTICLE NUMBER
☐ REGISTERED ☐ INSURED		
☐ CERTIFIED ☐ COD		
☐ EXPRESS MAIL		

(Always obtain signature of addressee or agent)
I have received the article described above.
SIGNATURE ☐ Addressee   ☐ Authorized agent

5.
DATE OF DELIVERY | POSTMARK

6. ADDRESSEE'S ADDRESS (*Only if requested*)

7. UNABLE TO DELIVER BECAUSE:	7a. EMPLOYEE'S INITIALS

FIGURE 9-9. Return receipt.

authorized in writing by the addressee to receive the mail. Restricted delivery is available only for mail addressed to natural persons specified by name.

Restricted delivery may be obtained for mail that is registered, certified, COD, or insured for more than $20.

Special Delivery

Mail should be sent special delivery when delivery is desired as soon as the item mailed reaches the destination post office. Special delivery mail is given immediate delivery during prescribed hours every day of the week to customers served by city carriers and to most other customers within a one-mile radius of the delivery post office.

The special delivery fee is in addition to the regular postage and is based on the weight of the item and the class of mail. "Special Delivery"

196
Secretarial
Procedures:
Office
Administration and
Automated Systems

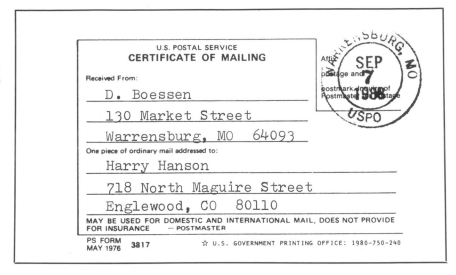

FIGURE 9-10. Certificate of mailing.

should be marked below the postage and above the name of the addressee on the mail, as shown in figure 9-11.

Since payment of a special delivery fee does not ensure safe delivery of an article or provide for the payment of indemnity, valuables sent special delivery should also be registered or insured.

Special Handling

The special handling service provides for third- and fourth-class mail to be handled as first-class mail. Special handling provides for preferential handling to the extent practical in dispatch and transport, but it does not provide for special care of fragile items or special delivery. Special handling parcels are delivered as parcel post is ordinarily delivered.

The special handling fee is based on the weight of the parcel and is in addition to the regular postage. "Special Handling" should be marked below the stamps and above the name of the addressee on the parcel.

Mail that is sent special handling may also be insured or sent COD. Special handling is required for parcels containing baby poultry or honey bees.

ANCILLARY SERVICES

Some mail may need to be forwarded or returned to the sender.

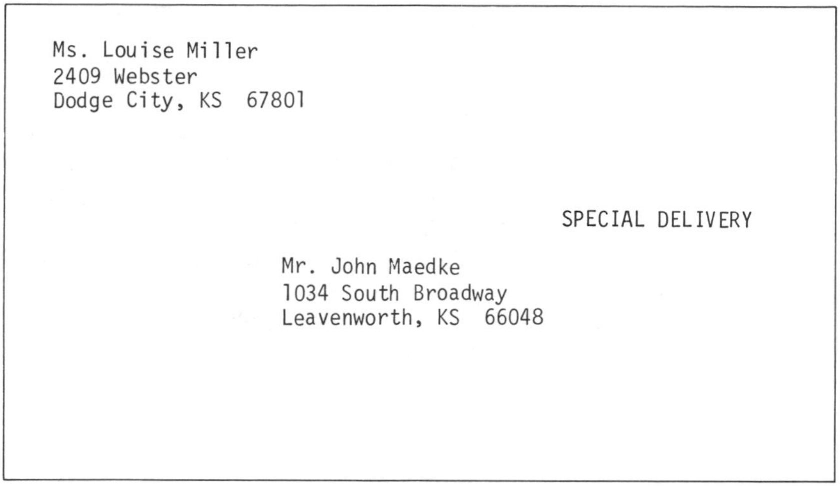

```
Ms. Louise Miller
2409 Webster
Dodge City, KS  67801


                                    SPECIAL DELIVERY

              Mr. John Maedke
              1034 South Broadway
              Leavenworth, KS  66048
```

FIGURE 9-11. Special delivery mail.

Forwarding

The following classes of mail will be forwarded without additional postage:

- First-class mail.
- Second-, third-, and fourth-class mail when specifically requested by the order.
- Third- and fourth-class mail for which the sender has guaranteed to pay the forwarding postage.
- Express Mail.

Some mail forwarded to another post office is subject to additional postage, but no additional postage is required for first-class mail weighing 12 ounces or less, except postal and postcards, or for Express Mail.

Registered, certified, insured, COD, and special handling mail is forwarded without the payment of additional fees, but additional forwarding postage may be charged.

Return of Undeliverable Mail

Undeliverable-as-addressed Express Mail and first-class mail is returned to the sender at no additional charge. Mail of other classes that is marked "Return Postage Guaranteed" may be returned to the sender, but the sender must pay the return postage. Any piece of mail marked "Return to Sender" must be put in another envelope and the proper amount of postage must be affixed before it is remailed.

198
Secretarial
Procedures:
Office
Administration and
Automated Systems

EQUIPMENT

The equipment used in most companies to process mail usually depends on whether or not the cost of performing the functions is reduced and the overall efficiency of the operation is improved by using the equipment.

In many companies, electric letter openers, time and date stamping machines, and numerous sorting devices are used in processing incoming mail and addressing machines, folding and inserting machines, and weighing and metering machines are used in handling outgoing mail. A few of the most common types of equipment used in processing mail are described in the following sections.

Scales

Accurately weighing mail helps eliminate postage overpayment and delays caused by mail being returned because of insufficient postage. In offices where most of the mail is letters and other small pieces, a scale capable of weighing only a few pounds may be adequate; but when the volume of mail is large and of different classes and sizes, more sophisticated equipment can often be justified.

Electronic desktop scales using solid-state electronic circuitry automatically compute the exact amount of postage required to send any mailing piece weighing 70 pounds or less to any destination. When postage rates change, the scale can easily be updated by replacing the appropriate electronic memory unit.

Many of the scales can be interfaced with a variety of peripherals. For example, some may be interfaced with postage meters to automatically set the correct postage and stamp the mail or with computers to provide shipping charges and data needed for invoicing and maintaining other types of records.

Postage Meters

Rather than affix the postage on mail by hand, most companies obtain a license to use a postage meter that is made to print single, several, or all postage denominations. The meter contains in one sealed unit the printing die or dies, a recording counter that adds and keeps a total of all postage printed by the meter, and a counter that subtracts and shows the balance of postage remaining in the meter.

Postage meters may be leased from authorized manufacturers who are responsible to the Postal Service for controlling, operating, maintaining, and replacing the meters.

After obtaining a license, the customer must have the meter set at the post office at which it is licensed. A customer may not possess a postage meter until it has been set, sealed, and checked into service by the Postal Service. The one to whom the license is issued must maintain custody of the meter until it is returned to the authorized manufacturer or to the post office. Metered mail, other than reply mail, must be dispatched through the post office shown in the metered stamp.

Postage for the meter must always be purchased in advance, just as when buying postage stamps. The meter may be taken to the post office where the counter is set by a postal employee, or it may be set through a Remote Meter Resetting System (RMRS) when the meter is a computerized resetting type.

If computer resettings are involved, the customer must deposit and maintain funds in an account to cover the desired postage increment prior to each resetting transaction. At the time the resetting is requested, the customer places a telephone-to-computer call to the manufacturer's data center and provides the meter serial number, the account number, and the ascending and descending register readings on the meter. After the data center verifies the data and checks the status of the customer's advance deposit account balance, the customer is then provided with the combination needed to add postage to the meter.

The types, sizes, and styles of meter stamps are fixed when meters are approved by the Postal Service, and only approved designs may be used. Postal Service regulations must be followed concerning the legibility, position, and content of the stamp; date of mailing; and so forth. Approved advertising matter, slogans, and other approved markings may be printed with the meter stamps.

Since properly prepared metered mail can be sent directly to distribution, mailings of five or more letter-type pieces must be packaged with the addresses facing in one direction to prevent them from becoming mixed with other mail that has to be faced, canceled, and postmarked at the post office. Although metered mail other than bulk third-class mail may be deposited in street collection boxes and other places where mail is accepted, it should be deposited at the main post office or at a station or branch to ensure the fastest possible dispatch.

The functions performed by many postage meter mailing machines include automatic feeding, postage imprinting, postmarking, sealing, counting, stacking, and postage accounting. Tape for oversized envelopes and parcels is meter-imprinted in the desired denominations.

Folding and Inserting Machines

When large numbers of identical mailing pieces are prepared, such as promotional material, paychecks, announcements, and invoices, folding and inserting machines can be used to increase productivity. Some systems can fold and insert into envelopes up to 3,500 pieces in an hour.

200
Secretarial
Procedures:
Office
Administration and
Automated Systems

ZIP CODE SYSTEM

The ZIP (Zone Improvement Plan) Code System is a numbered coding system that enables the Postal Service to accurately, quickly, and economically process and deliver the mail.

The most complete ZIP Code is a nine-digit number divided by a hyphen between the fifth and sixth digits, such as 70885-5868. The Postal Service has adopted the term *ZIP + 4* as the trademark for the nine-digit ZIP Code.

The first three digits of any ZIP Code number represent a particular sectional center area or a major city post office serving the area in which the address is located. The fourth and fifth digits identify the delivery area of the associate post office or branch station serving the address. The final four digits of the ZIP + 4 code identify specific geographic units, such as a side of a street between intersections and individual buildings.

The ZIP + 4 code should be used whenever possible. The address of each piece of mail sent as part of a bulk mailing or second- and third-class mail, presorted special fourth-class mail, and presorted first-class mail must include either the ZIP + 4 code or the 5-digit ZIP Code or carrier route code if presorted directly to carriers.

Five-digit ZIP codes for all post offices in the United States are given in the *National ZIP Code and Post Office Directory,* which can be purchased from all main post offices, classified stations, and branches.

INTERNAL PICKUP AND DELIVERY

Although clerks pick up and deliver mail to the separate work stations and offices in many companies, large companies often find a mechanical system to be more efficient and economical. Conveyors and automated mail vehicles are common types of mechanical devices used to deliver incoming mail, pick up outgoing mail, and transport internal correspondence.

Conveyor Systems

Some type of conveyor system is often used in companies where documents need to be transported frequently or on a continuing basis to the work stations.

A horizontal conveyor has a belt with a separate channel for each station to be served. Documents for a particular station are placed in the appropriate channel, and when they reach the destination they fall into a receiving tray. The conveyor is fast and allows people to remain at their stations; however, the conveyor can only be used for stations located on the same floor and the number of stations that can use the conveyor is limited to the number of channels available in the system.

Vertical conveyors are used in many companies where offices are located on several floors. Mailroom personnel place the mail for the various floors in separate containers that are then placed on a vertical conveyor housed in a space that resembles a small elevator shaft. The containers are automatically ejected on the appropriate floors. Someone on each floor is then responsible for picking up and distributing the mail to the work stations. The vertical conveyor provides for mail to be delivered on a continuous basis and in consecutive order.

Automated Mail Vehicles

A self-propelled mail cart that uses a photoelectric guidance system to follow an invisible chemical path painted on the floor is used by some large organizations to distribute and collect mail.

The chemical path followed by the cart can be easily removed and repainted when the work station arrangement changes. The cart is programmed to automatically stop for a specific period of time at the various work stations so that incoming mail can be removed and outgoing mail can be placed in a tray for another office in the organization or in the mailroom tray. The cart also automatically stops when a person or object is in the path. Some of the self-propelled carts can be programmed to ride elevators without human assistance.

ALTERNATIVE DELIVERY METHODS

Several delivery services are available in addition to those provided by the Postal Service. The companies can be identified by looking at the telephone directory and literature can be obtained by calling the various companies serving the area. The secretary needs to consider the advantages and disadvantages of each.

Some of the well-known services are discussed briefly in this section.

United Parcel Service

United Parcel Service (UPS) operates in all states and offers both pickup and delivery services for individuals and businesses. Rates are based on the weight and delivery zone. Packages are limited to a maximum of 50 pounds and 108 inches in length and girth combined.

A package to be sent by UPS may be taken to a local office, if one is available, or a toll-free number may be called and the package will be picked up for a nominal fee. Delivery is made to the addressee.

202
Secretarial
Procedures:
Office
Administration and
Automated Systems

Next-day delivery service is provided to points up to 150 miles and fourth-day service to points between 900 and 1,500 miles from the shipping point.

The UPS charge includes insurance coverage up to $100 for each package, and additional coverage is available. Packages may be sent COD.

Air Express

Emery Worldwide and Federal Express are two well-known companies that provide a variety of air express services. Although the fees for the services are higher than those charged for many other methods of shipment, many companies use air express because of the speed with which packages are delivered. Next-day service is provided to most points in the United States.

Bus

When air service is not available, same-day service can be provided by bus express to many communities located on regular bus routes. Although pickup and delivery service is not available in many areas, the shipping charge is reasonable and includes insurance of $100. The weight of the package is usually limited to 150 pounds or less and the length to 6 feet or less.

Taxis and Local Delivery Services

When a package or documents need to be delivered rapidly to a local business or individual and no one in the company is available to make the delivery, the material may have to be sent by taxi or a local delivery service. Although the cost may be considerable, it can sometimes be justified when speed is an important consideration.

―――――――――――――――― Summary ――――――――――――――――

Most people who do not process outgoing mail in an office probably think of mail consisting primarily of letters and other first-class pieces, magazines, and parcel post. In many offices, however, the secretary is expected to be familiar with the many other classes of mail and the special services offered by the Postal Service.

A thorough understanding of the *Domestic Mail Manual* is essential when the mail to be processed involves numerous classes and services. The manual gives complete details regarding the mailing of all classes of domestic mail and the many services provided by the Postal Service.

In addition to the services provided by the Postal Service, the secretary needs to be aware of the alternative delivery methods that are available and when each should be used.

———————————————— Questions ————————————————

1. Define "first-class mail."

2. List five different types of things that must be sent as first-class mail.

3. Is the first-class rate the same for each ounce or fraction of an ounce? Explain.

4. Should Express Mail always be used to send something that must reach the destination by the next day? Discuss.

5. Describe the minimum and maximum size requirements for letter-size first-class mail.

6. Why is a surcharge assessed for nonstandard first-class mail?

7. Is priority mail the same as special handling?

8. On what is the rate for priority mail based?

9. Is the second-class mail rate based on the weight and the zone to which the publication is being sent?

10. What is the maximum weight for third-class mail?

11. Would a zone chart obtained at a post office in New York be the same as one obtained at a post office in Seattle? Explain.

12. Explain what an individual must do to be able to return a book to the library when using the library rate.

13. The four sides of an irregularly-shaped parcel measure 30 in. by 12 in. by 25 in. by 10 in. The parcel is 15 inches thick all around. What is the combined length and girth?

14. When first-class mail accompanies a piece of lower-class mail, at which class will the combined mail be sent?

15. Explain the difference between franked mail and penalty mail.

16. May certified mail be insured?

17. What is the purpose of a return receipt?

18. Why is registered mail considered the most secure service offered by the Postal Service?

19. Is special delivery mail always given immediate delivery when it reaches the destination post office? Discuss.

20. Assume your boss hands you a report late Friday afternoon and asks you to send it by Express Mail to an executive whose office is located in a city 500 miles away. You know that the executive's office will not be open on Saturday and Sunday. Should you comply with the request of your boss or send the report some other way? Discuss.

204
Secretarial
Procedures:
Office
Administration and
Automated Systems

———————————————— Projects ————————————————

1. Either obtain a rate leaflet or look at the rate chart posted in the lobby of the post office and determine the cost to send each of the following:

   a. A 12-ounce first-class letter to another address in your city.

   b. A 12-ounce first-class letter to an address in a city in Zone 5.

   c. A one-ounce letter to a local address.

   d. A two-ounce letter to an address in a city in Zone 8.

   e. A 10-ounce newspaper mailed for an individual at the second-class rate.

   f. Priority mail weighing 14 ounces to Zone 4.

   g. Priority mail weighing 14 ounces to Zone 8.

   h. A 10-ounce handwritten document to Zone 6.

   i. A 5-pound box of candy insured for $25 and sent to Zone 3.

   j. A registered one-ounce letter.

   k. A 2-pound package sent to Zone 3 by parcel post and special handling.

   l. A 2-ounce first-class letter sent special delivery.

2. Recommend the class of service that should be used to send each of the following. If more than one class of service could be used, explain why you selected a particular class.

   a. An unsealed carton of food weighing 10 pounds and sent to an address 500 miles away.

   b. A newspaper on which a message has been written.

   c. Stock certificates.

   d. A sealed parcel of tulip bulbs weighing 14 ounces and sent to an address in Zone 7.

   e. Jewelry weighing 6 ounces and valued at $300.

   f. A book weighing 2 pounds and containing 500 pages to be sent by an individual to a friend.

   g. A cashier's check for $500.

   h. A statement showing $600 due on account.

   i. A term paper mailed to a professor by a student who is enrolled in an internship with a business located in another town.

   j. A document that has no intrinsic value but one for which you want to have evidence of delivery.

k. A package weighing 20 ounces that must be delivered to a rural address as soon as possible.

l. A package weighing 20 ounces that must be delivered to an address in a city 100 miles away as soon as possible.

m. A book weighing 3 pounds being returned by an individual to a public library.

3. For each of the items listed in project 2, indicate the types of charges that would have to be paid in addition to the regular postage.

4. Have a committee obtain two or three boxes of different shapes and demonstrate for the class how to measure the boxes to determine whether they could be sent through the Postal Service.

———————————————— Cases ————————————————

1. Occasionally a letter or other document must be mailed at the end of the day after the company mailroom is closed. Sometimes, but not always, you know the amount of postage required. You are willing to take the mail to the post office; however, your company uses a postage meter and you do not have access to it. What should be done to cope with this situation?

2. As a service, you are expected to keep a supply of stamps on hand to sell to workers in the company. Frequently, a coworker asks you for a few stamps and always offers to pay with a large bill that you cannot change. Sometimes she remembers to bring the money the next day, but you usually have to remind her. What should you do?

3. Mary Long is secretary to Jack Wilson, president of Smith Tool Company. Mr. Wilson regularly brings personal mail, including Christmas cards in December, and asks Mary to process them through the company postage meter. What should Mary do?

CHAPTER 10

Processing Mail

Mail delivered to the office must be processed, and the secretary almost always has this responsibility. In many offices, the work to be performed throughout the day depends to a considerable extent on the actions that need to be taken as a result of the incoming mail; therefore, most executives want to see their mail soon after it arrives. This chapter explains procedures you may need to follow to process the mail efficiently as soon as possible after it arrives in your office. It also covers procedures for preparing outgoing mail.

INCOMING MAIL

Sorting

When the mail arrives, first sort it into groups according to the degree of importance. The following groups are appropriate in most instances:

1. Telegrams, Mailgrams, telex and TWX messages, computer printouts of correspondence, and mail for which special fees have been paid.
2. First-class mail, which includes letters, invoices, checks, and other important documents.
3. Mail from other departments or offices of the company.
4. Personal and confidential mail.

208
Secretarial
Procedures:
Office
Administration and
Automated Systems

5. Newspapers and periodicals.

6. Catalogs, booklets, and advertising material.

7. Packages.

The desk should be reasonably clear except for the stacks of incoming mail.

The degree of importance of the mail in regular envelopes is usually easily determined by looking at the markings on the envelopes (e.g., "Registered," "Certified") or by the amount of postage paid. Large envelopes used for first-class mail will be clearly marked "First-Class."

Personal Mail

Unless you have been asked by your boss to open all mail, you should not open mail addressed to him or her when the envelope is marked "Personal" or "Confidential." Even though the envelope may not be marked, you should send it to your boss unopened if you believe it contains personal correspondence. The name and return address on the envelope, as well as an address written in longhand, may provide a clue that the letter is personal.

Should you open a letter and then find that it is personal, you should immediately put it in the envelope and write "Sorry, opened by mistake" and your initials on the envelope. Obviously, anything you may have read before learning the letter was personal should be considered confidential and should never be discussed with anyone.

Envelopes

All of the envelopes in the group to be opened should be turned the same way and tapped on the desk so that the contents will fall to the bottom and will not be damaged when the envelope is opened at the top.

Envelopes may be opened manually by using an envelope opener; however, an electrically operated opener is used in many offices to speed the process, especially when the volume of mail is heavy.

To open an envelope manually, have the flaps of the envelope facing up and in the same direction. Remove an envelope from the stack, place it flat on the desk, and slip the letter opener approximately halfway under the flap. Hold the bottom of the envelope flat on the desk as you cut the envelope open with a quick forward and outward motion. If the cut is jagged, practice using different opening techniques or different openers until you are able to consistently open envelopes without tearing them. Jagged edges are unattractive and can be a nuisance when the envelope must be attached to the letter that is sent to the boss or placed in the file.

When the envelopes are opened by using a machine, you should have the address side of the envelope facing up. The envelopes are fed by hand or automatically and the machine cuts a thin edge off the envelope. The possibility of damaging the contents of the envelope is reduced when a machine is used.

The mail should be kept in the same stacks and in the same order into which it was originally sorted. Open all of the envelopes in a particular stack before removing the contents.

Remove the contents and then look inside the envelope or hold it to the light to make sure all enclosures have been removed. Check the following each time you remove the contents from an envelope:

- *Is the address on the letterhead the same as that on the envelope?* When the addresses are different and the letter must be answered, you should write or type on the letter the address shown on the envelope or attach the envelope to the letter.

- *Is the writer's name typed or legibly written on the letter?* When the name is on the envelope but not on the letter, type or write the name on the letter.

- *Was the letter received a reasonable time from the date of the letter?* If an unusual amount of time has elapsed, note the date so that if necessary a logical explanation for the delay in responding can be offered when your boss answers the letter. The letter may not have been mailed soon after it was written, or the delay may have been caused by the Postal Service.

- *Are the enclosures mentioned in the letter or noted in the enclosure notation included?* If some enclosures are not included, write "Enc. missing" on the letter and keep the envelope. If the enclosures are included and are not to be submitted to the boss along with the letter, indicate on the letter what was included by placing a check mark by the items listed in the notation or by listing the items on the letter.

  When a negotiable instrument (e.g., check, money order) is enclosed with the letter, write "Rec." by the amount mentioned in the letter when the amounts are the same. If the amounts are not the same, note the discrepancy on the letter in a way that will attract the attention of your boss.

  If several negotiable instruments are received, prepare a list before sending them to the cashier. The list should include the dates of the instruments, from whom they were received, and the amounts. Your boss may be interested in seeing the list, especially if the payments are for services rendered by him or her.

- *Is the time and date the letter was postmarked or received important?* When the customer's payment of an invoice reflects a cash discount and the check was mailed several days after the end of the discount period,

210
Secretarial
Procedures:
Office
Administration and
Automated Systems

you should keep the envelope so the date of the postmark can be used as evidence. When you believe an envelope may be needed, you should stamp or write the date of receipt on it. Unless your boss requests you to do so, you should not attach the envelope to the letter; instead, you should file it by the date of receipt and keep it until you are confident it will not be needed.

Packages

A knife should be used to slit open cartons and a staple remover should be used for cartons sealed with staples. An opener that can be used for all types of packages can be purchased at office supplies stores. It should be used to avoid cuts and other injuries.

When opening packages, check to see whether a first-class letter or document, such as an invoice, is attached or enclosed. If first-class mail is enclosed, the package should be marked "Letter Enclosed" or "First-Class Mail Enclosed." Use the purchase order form or order letter as you check the contents of packages containing things that you have ordered. Prepare a receiving report or other form to let the accounting department know that the order has been received and checked.

Publications

Find out what your boss wants you to do with periodicals. Some executives like the secretary to look through the periodical and attach a slip of paper indicating articles or advertisements she believes to be of particular interest. The title of the article and page number should be typed on the slip. If the article is written by someone your boss will recognize, you should include his or her name on the slip of paper. Use removable adhesive tape to attach the slip to the front of the periodical.

With experience, you may be expected to read the article and underline the important parts, prepare an outline, or write a summary. Note advertisements of equipment, supplies, and so forth on the slip if you believe your boss should consider them for use in your office.

Incorrectly Delivered Mail

When mail is incorrectly delivered to your office, you should return it to the mail room or post office. Sometimes mail addressed to someone who no longer works for the organization may be delivered to your office. If the letter appears to be personal and you know the person's current address, you should write the forwarding address on the envelope and include it with your outgoing mail. Additional postage is not required on first-class mail that is forwarded. If the address on the envelope includes the individual's title and appears to be a business letter, you should deliver it unopened to the person who currently has the title unless you have the responsibility of opening his or her mail.

Dating the Mail

The date and perhaps the time should be written or stamped on the mail. The date should be placed at the top of the letter in approximately the same position each time unless it interferes with printing on the letter-head or for some other reason it should be placed in another position. In a few instances, you may need to place the date on the back of the letter or document.

The date is especially important when a letter is received too late for your boss to take the action desired. If you believe that the time and date of receipt may be important from a legal standpoint, you may want to have a coworker or your boss initial the letter or document to prove that it was received at the time indicated.

Mail Register

A mail register, such as the one shown in figure 10-1, is maintained in many offices. The register may be used to record the receipt of important documents and mail for which a special fee has been paid, such as registered, insured, and certified. The entry in the register usually includes a description of the mail and the date it was received.

The mail register may also be used to record the disposition of some incoming mail. Your boss may send mail to other executives for information or action. An entry in the register giving a description of the correspondence, the date it was received, and the name of the person to whom it was sent can be useful if you need to follow through to see that the desired action was taken.

You may be told in a telephone conversation or observe in a letter that mail has been sent under separate cover or will be sent at a later time. So that you will be reminded to follow up, you should maintain a "mail expected" register similar to the one shown in figure 10-2. Make an entry at the time you learn of the mail you should anticipate receiving and then draw a line through the entry when the mail arrives.

Mail Digest

Prepare a digest of the mail received while your boss is away from the office. You should keep the digest in chronological order, indicate from whom the mail is received, and give a brief summary of the message, as shown in figure 10-3.

MAIL REGISTER

Date	From/Description	Disposition To	Date	Date of follow-up
10/12	Quimby — Contract for roof	Attorney	10/12	
10/14	Sylwester — Request for speaker	Pub. Rel.	10/15	
10/16	Request for employment record Adams — of T. Jones	Personnel	10/16	
10/17	Request for interview for Hickley — newspaper article	Pub. Rel.	10/18	
10/19	Tulle — Complaint about late shipment	Boessen	10/19	
10/19	Creighton — Question about account	Accounting	10/19	

FIGURE 10-1. Mail register.

When returning to the office, the executive can more readily see what mail has been received by looking at the digest than by looking through the stack of correspondence. The digest can be used by the executive when deciding the sequence to be followed in responding to the mail.

Some executives want the digest sent to them if they are away from the office for several days. Others telephone the office and expect the secretary to use the digest when discussing the mail that has been received.

Routing Mail

When correspondence must frequently be sent to someone else in the organization for information or action, you can save time by using a duplicated form similar to the one shown in figure 10-4.

Keep the form small and list only those messages you may need to check. When the person to whom the correspondence is being sent will need additional information from your office to take the action requested, you may need to attach previous correspondence or supply dates, figures, and so forth.

MAIL EXPECTED

Date	From whom	Description	Date of receipt	Date of follow-up
11/9	~~Mayfield~~	~~Contract~~	11/12	
11/10	Wilson	Annual reports		
11/12	Cooley	Check for Oct. statement		
11/13	Beardsley	Pictures		
11/15	Walker	Registration forms		

FIGURE 10-2. Mail expected register.

DIGEST OF MAIL

Date	From	Summary	Action Taken
9/9	Dr. Riley	Time for annual physical.	Scheduled for 9 a.m., Thurs., Sept. 27
9/9	Chamber of Commerce	Want you to talk on your trip to China; suggested 7 p.m., Sat., Sept. 22.	
9/10	Home Office	Want the audit report by Sept. 20.	Sent copy of letter to Accounting Dept.
9/11	Prestige University	Endowment Committee meeting; 2 p.m., Fri., Oct. 19, in Pittsburg.	
9/11	W. W. Wilson	Cannot meet as scheduled on Sept. 15; out-of-town business trip.	
9/13	T. S. Scott	Wants to discuss shipping contract.	Scheduled for 1 p.m., Thurs., Oct. 25

FIGURE 10-3. Mail digest.

214
Secretarial
Procedures:
Office
Administration and
Automated Systems

In some companies, the person forwarding the correspondence to some other executive for reply wants to receive an information copy of the response. A copy of the response is usually filed in the office of the one who wrote the letter; therefore, the copy sent to your boss is usually destroyed after it has been read.

Your boss may want to share with others some correspondence, documents, and other materials received in your office. When the material is not the type others will want to retain, you can save the cost of making multiple copies by using a routing slip such as the one shown in figure 10-5.

Sometimes material routed to others is misplaced or follow-up action is required; therefore, you should make a copy of the correspondence and material you send to others and indicate where and when the material was sent.

The names of those to whom material is frequently circulated are usually listed alphabetically. The order in which material is to be circulated is indicated by placing numbers in the sequence column.

Date_____

To_____

From _____

_____ For your information; return to me.

_____ For your information; do not return.

_____ Read and make an appointment to
          discuss this with me.

_____ Please supply me with the information
          needed for the reply.

_____ Please answer and send me a copy.

_____ Please indicate your comments.

Comments:

FIGURE 10-4. Mail routing form.

```
┌─────────────────────────────────────────────┐
│              ROUTING SLIP                     │
│                                               │
│              Date    8/12/84                  │
│                                               │
│   Sequence        Sent To:        Date Sent On│
│                                               │
│      2         D. Duessenberry                │
│                                               │
│      4         R. Ferguson                    │
│                                               │
│                B. Franke                      │
│                                               │
│      1         S. Hargadine                   │
│                                               │
│                M. Howard                      │
│                                               │
│                P. Kirk                        │
│                                               │
│      3         C. Skogen                      │
│                                               │
│                M. Thompson                    │
│                                               │
│                H. Whitlock                    │
│                Return to:                     │
│                                               │
│                M. McCann                      │
└─────────────────────────────────────────────┘
```

FIGURE 10-5. Mail routing slip.

Presenting the Mail

Before giving the mail to your boss, you should read each letter. You may need to obtain additional information, material, and so forth to submit along with the letter. You may decide that you should answer the letter, send the letter to someone other than your boss, or take some other action. You should do all that you possibly can to enable your boss to be able to read the letter one time and immediately take the required action.

Your boss may want you to make relevant notations in the margin of the letter. Some executives want the secretary to underline important points in the letters; others do not. Therefore, you should not underline parts of the letter unless you are asked to do so. Use caution when you underline. The person who wrote the letter must have considered everything in the letter important; otherwise, it would not have been included. As you read the letter, you, too, may consider essentially everything important and find that you are underlining almost everything in the letter.

Always use a ruler or straightedge when drawing the lines. Colored ink helps to highlight what you believe to be important. A letter on which a

216
Secretarial
Procedures:
Office
Administration and
Automated Systems

notation has been made and lines have been drawn is shown in figure 10-6. If you believe that the letter will need to be copied and sent to others, you may want to place your comments on the back of the letter or write them on removable adhesive slips.

The mail should be presented to your boss arranged according to his or her preferences. The procedures to be followed may vary according to the time the mail is delivered, the schedule of your boss, the type of work you are performing at the time the mail is delivered, as well as other factors.

Priority mail is usually placed in one stack and includes mail that provides important information that your boss needs to know as soon as possible, as well as mail that requires immediate action. The most urgent mail is placed on top. Some executives prefer to keep the interoffice mail in a separate stack.

Routine mail may be placed in another stack. It, too, may include mail providing information and requiring action. Reports and lengthy documents may be placed in a separate stack unless they should be attached to a letter or other correspondence that is placed in another stack.

Publications, advertisements, and similar types of mail may be placed in another stack and may or may not be presented to your boss along with the mail that requires action.

The boss may want the mail in the separate categories placed in different folders or arranged in one stack with the priority items on top. You should place the mail the same place on the desk each time, preferably in a space where it cannot be confused with other documents that may be on the desk. The periodicals may be placed on the desk or on a credenza or shelf.

When your boss is not in the office at the time you place the mail on the desk and other people may have an opportunity to glance at material on the desk, you should reverse the top letter of the stack.

Handling Mail During Executive's Absence

You should know the action your boss expects you to take regarding the mail received while he or she is away from the office on a business trip, vacation, or for some other reason.

Except for matters that require immediate attention, you may process the mail in the usual way and have it ready to present to him or her when returning to the office if the absence is for only a short period.

You may be asked to send all correspondence requiring decisions you are not authorized to make to his or her superior or an associate. Before sending the original to another executive, make a copy and indicate on it the action you have taken.

```
                              Finance Club
                              Western University
                              1010 Hill Top Road
                              Denver, CO  80201
                              September 19, 1984


Mr. Raymond West
West Securities Incorporated
841 North Mountain Drive
Aurora, CO  80010

Dear Mr. West:
```

Return from Hawaii at 3p.m. on that day

Dr. Milton Turner, our faculty adviser, frequently comments on the many articles you have published and recognizes you as an expert in the financial area. He recommended that we ask you to talk with our group at 7 p.m. on Thursday, October 18.

We would like for you to give a 45-minute talk on "Starting Your Investment Portfolio." The 50 members in the Finance Club have all had at least one course in finance, and a few have had at least one investment course.

We will appreciate your agreeing to meet with our group.

Where is the meeting?

```
                              Sincerely,

                              Ruth Wilson

                              Ruth Wilson
                              Secretary
```

FIGURE 10-6. Annotated letter.

Your boss may expect you to answer some letters and take routine actions. When this is the case, you must exercise good judgment in deciding what needs to be done. If you write a letter, attach a copy of your reply to the letter that was received and include both with the other mail you are accumulating. When a written reply is not required, you may write on the letter you received the action you have taken.

When your boss is to be away from the office for an extended time, you may need to forward some of the mail. Except for the personal mail that you are not to open, you should always make a copy of the letters and other mail you forward. Although first-class mail can be forwarded without paying additional postage, to avoid the possibility of the mail being returned to the sender you should place the mail in a business envelope and type the name of your boss and the address to which it is to be sent.

218
Secretarial
Procedures:
Office
Administration and
Automated Systems

Sometimes the boss will call and dictate replies or tell you the action you are to take. Occasionally you may need to call your boss and discuss the action that should be taken concerning an urgent matter.

If your boss will be away from the office for several days, you may be expected to acknowledge receipt of the correspondence and indicate when your boss is expected to return. The following type of message is often appropriate:

Mr. Wilson is out of town until October 15. I am sure he will contact you soon after that date concerning the proposal presented in your October 10 letter.

OUTGOING MAIL

Addressing Mail

The Postal Service is using sophisticated optical character readers (OCRs) and bar code sorters to increase postal efficiency. These machines can process five-digit ZIP coded mail, but they are even more cost effective when the ZIP + 4 code is used since the mail can be sorted automatically to the carrier route level.

The automated postal equipment can process 10,000 pieces of mail per hour; however, the items to be processed must meet Postal Service physical dimension guidelines. Envelopes must be rectangular, at least 3 ½ inches high by 5 inches long, no larger than 6 ⅛ inches by 11 ½ inches, and at least .007 of an inch thick.

For the electronic eye of the automated equipment to scan the address information and translate it into a bar code that is printed on the envelope, you should follow certain guidelines to ensure readability.

Placement of Address

The address must be visible to the electronic eye in the OCR; otherwise, the OCR may reject the piece of mail and it will have to be sorted by another method. The guidelines to be followed in placing the address are shown in figure 10-7 and are as follows:

- The address should be parallel to the bottom of the envelope. The line slant relative to the bottom edge should not exceed five degrees.

- The top of the last line of the address should be no higher than 2 ¼ inches from the bottom of the envelope.

- A margin of at least 1 inch should be left on either end of the envelope.

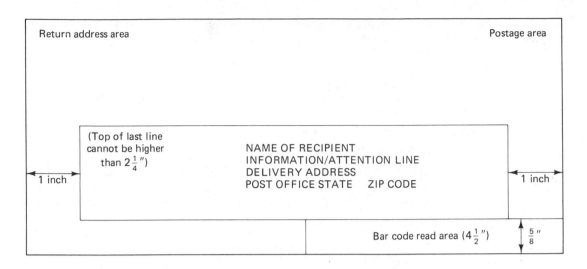

FIGURE 10-7. Properly placed address.

- A space ⅝ inch high and 4 ½ inches wide should be clear for bar code printing at the lower right portion of the envelope.

- The entire address must be visible when window envelopes are used.

- The return address should be blocked and started two or three lines from the top edge and three spaces from the left edge of the envelope.

To save time in addressing envelopes and to have the address positioned so that it can be read by the OCR, you should determine an acceptable line and space on which to begin the address on the various sizes of envelopes used in your office and consistently type the addresses in those positions.

You can place the address appropriately on a No. 10 (large size) envelope by starting the address on line 14 from the top edge and about 4 inches from the left edge. When using No. 6 ¾ (small size) envelopes, start the address on line 12 from the top edge and about 2 ½ inches from the left edge. The address must be typed in a position where it will be visible when window envelopes are used.

Arrangement of Address

The following guidelines should be followed to ensure the information in the address is arranged in the proper sequence:

1. Place the receiver's name on the top line.

2. Give identifying information on the following lines. If both the department and company names are used in the address, the department

219

220
Secretarial
Procedures:
Office
Administration and
Automated Systems

name should be placed on line two and the company name on line three. The following example illustrates the correct arrangement of the address lines:

MISS TERESA LONG
INDUSTRIAL MARKETING DEPT
A B LONG CO
90 W BURNETT RD
HOUSTON TX   77251-2201

3. Type the street address or the post office box number on the next to last line. When both a post office box number and a street address are used, the one appearing on the line immediately above the bottom line is the one to which the mail is delivered. Observe the following examples:

MOUNTAIN BROKERAGE SERVICES
PO BOX 2040
26 BROADWAY   (Will be delivered to 26 Broadway)
DENVER CO   80201

MOUNTAIN BROKERAGE SERVICES
26 BROADWAY
PO BOX 2040   (Will be delivered to Post Office Box 2040)
DENVER CO   80201

4. If the address includes an apartment number, place the number at the end of the delivery address line or on the line preceding the delivery address, as follows:

MS CYNTHIA LEBACH
1520 VIKING LANE APT 202
BELLEVILLE IL   62220-8653

MR DENNIS WOOTEN
APT 101
801 S MAGUIRE ST
DRUMMOND OK   74735-1220

5. Place the city, state, and ZIP code on the bottom line. No extraneous material should appear on or below the city, state, and ZIP code line.

A properly addressed No. 6 ¾ envelope is shown in figure 10-8.

Typing the Address

To ensure that the address can be properly read by OCR, the following guidelines should be followed when typing the address:

```
EDWARD GILMORE
956 WINDSOR AVE
WEBSTER CITY IA    50595-0767




              MS KATHLEEN HAMMOND
              403 FITZGERALD RD
              SHAWNEE KS    66203-0302
```

FIGURE 10-8. Properly addressed envelope.

- Black ink on a white background is best, but any print that contrasts well with the background is acceptable.
- Standard-size and individual letter and number type styles should be used. Script and italic type styles cannot be processed by OCR.
- Do not place extraneous printing, such as logos, on or below the delivery address line.
- The address should be blocked and single spaced.
- All capital letters should be used and all punctuation should be omitted.
- One or two character spaces should be left between words in the address.
- Two to five character spaces should be left between the last character of the two-letter state name and the first digit of the ZIP code.
- Mail notations, such as SPECIAL DELIVERY and REGISTERED, should be typed in all capital letters below the stamp position. The notations should be at least three line spaces above the address block.
- Notations, such as PLEASE FORWARD and HOLD FOR ARRIVAL, should be typed in all capital letters a triple space below the return address near the left edge of the envelope.

222
Secretarial
Procedures:
Office
Administration and
Automated Systems

Folding and Inserting Letters

Before folding the letter, consider the following questions:

- Is each part of the address on both the letter and envelope correct and identical?
- Is the letter signed?
- Are enclosures involved?
- Is the appearance of the letter as attractive as you would want it to be if you had signed it?

You can make the fold straight more easily when you place the letter on a flat surface than when holding the page in your hand. Fold the letter correctly the first time so that it will have no more creases than are necessary.

When one-page or two-page enclosures are to be sent along with the letter, place the letter on top and fold the enclosures along with the letter. When enclosures are involved, you should use a No. 10 or larger envelope. Here are the steps to follow in folding and inserting a letter in a No. 10 envelope (see figure 10-9):

1. Place the letter face up on your desk or some other flat surface. Fold approximately one third of the page toward the top. Make sure the fold is straight and then crease the page.

2. Fold down the top of the page to approximately one-half inch of the first fold. Again, make sure the fold is straight and then make a second crease.

3. Insert the letter into the envelope with the second crease toward the bottom of the envelope.

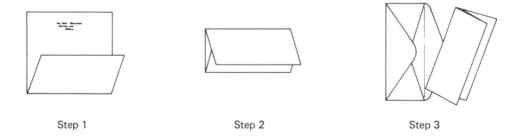

Step 1   Step 2   Step 3

FIGURE 10-9. Steps for folding and inserting a letter in a No. 10 envelope.

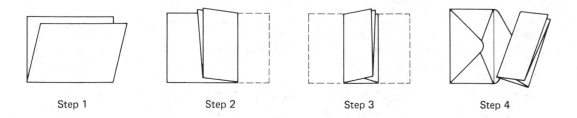

| Step 1 | Step 2 | Step 3 | Step 4 |

FIGURE 10-10. Steps for folding and inserting a letter in a No. 6 3/4 envelope.

The following steps are involved in folding a single page to be mailed in a No. 6 ¾ envelope (see figure 10-10):

1. Place the letter face up on your desk and fold the bottom part of the sheet to approximately one-half inch of the top edge. Make sure the fold is straight and then crease the sheet.

2. Fold the right-hand third of the page toward the left. Make sure the fold is straight and then crease the page.

3. Fold the left-hand third toward the center to within one-half inch of the other crease.

4. Insert the letter into the envelope with the second crease toward the bottom of the envelope.

The following steps are involved in folding a letter for a window envelope (see figure 10-11):

1. Place the letter face down on your desk and fold the upper third of the page toward the bottom. Make sure the fold is straight and then crease the sheet.

2. Fold the lower third toward the top so that the address is showing.

3. Insert the sheet into the envelope with the last crease at the bottom.

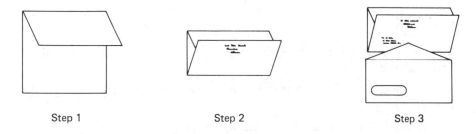

| Step 1 | Step 2 | Step 3 |

FIGURE 10-11. Steps for folding and inserting a letter in a window envelope.

224
Secretarial
Procedures:
Office
Administration and
Automated Systems

Interoffice Mail

Chain envelopes are frequently used for interoffice mail. They are usually not sealed and the envelopes can be used repeatedly, thus reducing the cost of stationery. The envelopes frequently are perforated so that enclosures remaining in the envelopes are easily observed.

--- Summary ---

Processing the mail involves much more than opening envelopes and removing the contents. The process usually involves first sorting the mail into stacks according to the degree of importance. After the contents have been removed and stamped, the secretary frequently needs to record the receipt of some documents in a mail register and after reading the mail may need to make entries in the mail expected register. Executives have preferences concerning how they want mail arranged and placed on their desk.

The secretary needs to know how to handle the mail during the executive's absence and may need to prepare a mail register so that the executive will be able to readily see what mail was received during his or her absence without having to sort through stacks of correspondence. The secretary needs to know when and how to route mail to other offices.

The placement, arrangement, and typing of the addresses are important considerations when preparing outgoing mail so that the pieces can be processed accurately and efficiently by the Postal Service. The secretary needs to know how to properly address mail for all sizes of envelopes and how to properly fold and insert the letters.

--- Questions ---

1. Why should incoming mail be sorted?

2. Name some ways to determine the importance of the mail before opening the envelope.

3. What can usually be done to avoid mistakenly opening a confidential letter?

4. Should all envelopes be kept for a few days? Discuss.

5. What should be done if the return address on the envelope and the address on the letterhead are not the same?

6. Should all incoming mail be recorded in a mail register? Explain.

7. Explain the types of information usually recorded in a mail register.

8. Discuss the importance of a mail digest.

9. Why should you usually read each letter before submitting the mail to your boss?

10. Should the secretary always highlight the important points in a letter before submitting it to the boss? Explain.

11. Discuss different ways of presenting mail to the boss.

12. How should mail be handled when the boss is away from the office?

13. If a letter is delivered to your office for someone who no longer works for your company, should you always forward the letter to the current address of the individual? Explain.

14. Can the Postal Service use OCR in processing all mail properly addressed?

15. Should all addresses be double spaced on the envelope?

16. When the name of the company, department, and individual are included in the address, in what sequence should they appear?

17. Where should a REGISTERED notation appear on the envelope?

18. Explain the steps to follow in folding and inserting a letter in a No. 10 envelope.

19. What questions should be considered before folding and inserting a letter in an envelope?

20. What is an advantage of using window envelopes?

——————————— Projects ———————————

1. Arrange and type the following names, addresses, and notations on No. 10 and No. 6 ¾ envelopes according to the guidelines discussed in this chapter:

   a. Douglas Sparks, Manager, 605 West 47, Business Rentals Department, Southern Real Estate Agency, New Orleans, Louisiana 70062. (The letter is to be registered.)

   b. Pamela Thompson, 301 Southwest Boulevard, Apartment 5, P.O. Box 330, Hammond, Indiana 46320. (The letter is to be sent special delivery.)

   c. Mary S. Sterline, 46 Thunderbird Court, Gurnee, Illinois 60031. (The letter is to be forwarded to her new address.)

226
Secretarial
Procedures:
Office
Administration and
Automated Systems

2. Fold 8 ½-inch by 11-inch sheets of paper and insert them in one of the No. 10 and one of the No. 6 ¾ envelopes addressed in project 1.

3. Prepare a summary of an article appearing in a magazine or professional journal. The summary should be prepared in a form appropriate to submit to an executive who does not have time to read the entire article.

4. Visit an office supplies store and examine the different items that could be used when processing mail. Pay particular attention to openers, staple removers, and forms. Make a list of the items.

———————————————— Cases ————————————————

1. A letter was received from Mona Straub and the material she requested was sent. A few days later, Ms. Straub telephoned your office and asked why the material had not been sent. You assured her it had been mailed to her at the Milwaukee address shown on the letterhead. She replied that it should have been sent to the Rochester address shown on the envelope. What should have been done to avoid this confusing situation?

2. A customer states that he mailed your company a check for $9,800 within 10 days from March 3, the date of the $10,000 invoice, and that since the terms were 2/10, n/30, he was entitled to the $200 discount. The accounting department records show that the payment was received on March 21. What can be done to convince the customer he was not entitled to the cash discount?

3. Edna Thames works as private secretary to Ted Tennison, president of the company. A letter addressed to Mr. Tennison is received from an irate customer complaining about Eric Stafford, a salesman Edna respects very much. Should Edna show the letter to Eric so that he can be prepared to discuss the situation when the letter is given to Mr. Tennison?

PART V

CHAPTER 11

Writing Principles

INTRODUCTION

Since your letters, memorandums, and reports will affect the reader, you must make sure that what you write affects the reader the way you intend. If your correspondence does not inform or get desired action, you have wasted your time and effort. Time is a scarce commodity in business offices. Thus, the secretary who can save time by presenting ideas clearly, succinctly, and persuasively will be able to contribute to the efficiency of the organization and promote her career as well.

You should express yourself in writing the way you would if you were talking directly to the person. This conversational style is not a license to use slang or other language inappropriate in the business environment, but it will help you make your writing appear natural. Many people express themselves naturally and persuasively when they speak, but sound mechanical, stereotypical, and unoriginal when they write.

Many of the things you need to consider concerning the tone and the technical aspects of your written message will be discussed in this chapter.

TONE

Many words can be used to describe letters and memorandums with proper tone, but most of them relate to the way the message sounds to the reader. The tone of the message expresses the writer's attitude toward the reader.

230
Secretarial
Procedures:
Office
Administration and
Automated Systems

To make a favorable impression on the reader, you must make a conscious effort to control the tone of the message by being courteous, personal, and considerate. The tone of what you write is influenced by your attitude toward the reader, by your choice of words, and by the way you express yourself.

"You Attitude"

All of us are tempted to assume that everyone is interested in our problems and in what we want. But we must constantly keep in mind that we can most effectively create goodwill and persuade others to do what we want them to do by showing them how they will benefit by doing it. This point of view is known as the "you attitude." You must visualize the reader and write from his or her point of view. By looking at the situation from the reader's point of view, you will not write in terms of "how much I need you to do this" but of "how you will profit by doing this."

Courtesy

The person who writes courteous messages takes the reader's feelings into consideration. Courtesy involves using common sense in getting along with others by showing respect and understanding. Your written messages should treat people with the same courtesy and respect you would show in face-to-face communication.

When used naturally and sincerely, polite words like "please" and "thank you" can make the message sound courteous. For example, "Please send the report by March 1" is much more courteous and less demanding than "Send the report by March 1." A good way to determine whether the message is courteous is to ask yourself "How would I feel and react if I were to receive this communication?"

Personal

An effective message lets the reader know that you think of him or her as an individual rather than as a statistic. You need to show, too, that you are an individual and not some inanimate part of the organization for which you work. Since you and the reader are the two people directly involved, you can make your writing sound personal by using the pronoun "I" to refer to yourself and "you" to refer to the reader, just as you would do if you were talking to the person.

Negative words contribute to poor letter tone by creating unpleasant images in the reader's mind. Unpleasant news must sometimes be discussed by those in business, but the excessive use of negative words and ideas usually can be avoided by making a positive statement. Even if a negative word must be used occasionally, the negative thought should not be reinforced through repetition. Observe how the following negative thoughts might have been written in a positive way:

Negative: We close at four.

Positive: We stay open until four.

Negative: Your account is delinquent.

Positive: Please send us a $200 check so that we can mark your account paid in full.

Negative: I will not make this mistake again.

Positive: I will check the figures carefully.

Negative: You failed to complete the credit application form; therefore, we cannot process it.

Positive: Please complete the reference section of the application form so that we can process it immediately.

Negative: Unfortunately, our magazine is not published in November and December.

Positive: *Viewpoint* is published January through October.

Negative: I cannot have the report completed before November 5.

Positive: I will have the report completed by November 5.

Negative: We regret that you are one of the few Wilson customers to experience a problem with our product.
                 or
While we are delighted to hear from one of our customers, we are distressed to hear that you have experienced such dissatisfaction.

Positive: We appreciate your taking the time to explain the experience you have had with your radio.

232
Secretarial
Procedures:
Office
Administration and
Automated Systems

Negative: When there is a disappointing experience with Tarless, we want to know because Tarless cigarettes normally sell at too great a volume to allow customers to get those that are stale or aged.

Positive: The turnover of Tarless cigarettes is normally so great that only fresh cigarettes are found on the shelves.

Negative: We regret we are unable to process your order because you failed to tell us the kind of trombone mouthpieces you wanted.

Positive: Please let us know whether you want the solid or screw rim model trombone mouthpieces.

Negative: We have your complaint regarding nondelivery on the order you placed with one of our representatives a long time ago.

Positive: Thank you for your letter concerning the subscription you placed with one of our representatives.

When a negative message must be sent, many people believe that involved explanations and the repetition of "I'm sorry" make the message sound sincere. Although the message should not be blunt, a verbose message wastes the time of the reader and frequently creates an unfavorable impression by needlessly reinforcing the negative response. The letter in figure 11-1 was made considerably more effective by eliminating the repetition of the refusal, by omitting the things that were known by the reader, and by changing only a few words.

A member of a record club received the following letter concerning her account. Can you identify all of the negative words and expressions in the letter?

Please accept my personal apology for our negligence in complying with your previous correspondence. No discourtesy was intended, I assure you. Our files now show your address correctly and you will again receive your monthly club material on schedule.

At this time, your account is active, clear of charges, and in good standing. It is not our desire to have members keep and pay for recordings not ordered or not suited to their musical tastes. Should you prefer to return "Kenny Rogers and the First Edition's Greatest Hits" for credit or replacement, you may certainly do so. I have enclosed sufficient postage and a mailing label for your convenience. If you wish, you may order an alternate record of your choice on the order form I have included. Also enclosed is a current magazine for you.

> Thank you for your letter ~~of July 24, 1983,~~ telling us about the mass media-politics symposium ~~being sponsored by Sigma Delta Chi, Alpha Epsilon Rho and the Public Relations Student Society of America~~. The topic you have chosen is certainly timely, and I am sure the symposium ~~could~~ *Can* serve a useful purpose in educating students and the public about the mass media and its influences on voters. ~~I am afraid, however, that it will not be possible for us to provide the financial support you require~~. Although we are interested in all aspects of mass communications, we are a small foundation, ~~and this means we must restrict our grant making in many ways~~. ~~In particular, we generally do not~~ *and* provide funds for *only* meetings or conferences ~~unless they are~~ related to a larger project we are supporting. ~~Unfortunately, this means we are unable to be of help with many interesting requests such as yours.~~
>
> ~~I am sorry to have to send a disappointing reply, and~~ I very much hope you will be able to find the necessary funds to carry out your plans ~~from other sources.~~

FIGURE 11-1. Letter containing unnecessary information.

Your membership is valued and I am certain you will find your future association with us to be thoroughly enjoyable.

The letter could have reflected a much more positive tone had the writer omitted the use of the negative words and ideas, as shown in the following example:

Our files now show your correct address and you will again receive your monthly club material on schedule. Your account is active, clear of charges, and in good standing.

We want our members to keep only those recordings suited to their musical tastes. Should you prefer to return "Kenny Rogers and the First Edition's Greatest Hits" for credit or replacement, you may certainly do so. I have enclosed sufficient postage and a mailing label for your convenience. You may prefer to order an alternate on the order form I am enclosing.

We will do all that we can to make sure your association with us is thoroughly enjoyable.

Here is a list of some negative words you should attempt to avoid using in your business correspondence:

234
Secretarial
Procedures:
Office
Administration and
Automated Systems

blame	inability
blunder	inadequate
cannot	inconvenience
careless	inferior
claim	mistake
complaint	negligence
conflict	overdue
criticism	poor
damage	problem
defective	prohibit
delay	refuse
delinquent	regret
disagree	selfish
disappoint	sorry
dislike	trouble
displeasure	unable
dissatisfied	unacceptable
distress	uncomfortable
error	unfair
expired	unfavorable
failure	unfortunately
fault	unsatisfactory
hesitant	wrong

Archaic Expressions

Archaic and inflated words and phrases contribute to unclear and unnatural writing. The following words and phrases were considered acceptable several years ago and are found in much business correspondence today even though authors of business writing textbooks have been discouraging their use for many years:

attached hereto
awaiting your reply
duly noted
enclosed herewith
for your information

I have received your report

in accordance with your request

in compliance with your request

in lieu of

in receipt of

in reference to

in regard to

in reply to

inasmuch as

kindly

our records indicate

permit me to say

pursuant to your request

take the liberty of

take this opportunity

thank you in advance

thank you kindly

the undersigned

the writer

this will acknowledge receipt of

trust

up to this writing

upon receipt of

we are in receipt of

we deem it advisable

with reference to

would like to

you will herewith find

Active and Passive Voice

A sentence is in the *active voice* when the subject of the sentence acts; it is in the *passive voice* when the subject is acted upon. As a general rule, sentences written in the active voice have more impact than sentences written in the passive voice because they state who is doing what and give the information quickly and forcefully. Sentences written in the passive voice usually are wordy, vague, and impersonal.

236
Secretarial
Procedures:
Office
Administration and
Automated Systems

"The secretary wrote the letter" conveys the message more directly than "The letter was written by the secretary" because the *secretary* is the *doer* of the action. The passive sentence downplays the role of the secretary and places the focus of the sentence on the *letter* as the *receiver* of the action.

The following examples illustrate how the passive voice can be changed to the active voice to make the writing more emphatic:

Passive: This instruction manual will be of interest to all our office personnel.

Active: All of our office personnel will be interested in this instruction manual.

Passive: The report was completed yesterday.

Active: The auditor completed the report yesterday.

Passive: The package was mailed to you on Monday, December 15.

Active: We mailed your package on Monday, December 15.

Passive: The report will be prepared by the accountant.

Active: The accountant will prepare the report.

Passive: It is suggested by Miss Wilson that your consideration be given to enrolling for night classes.

Active: Miss Wilson suggests that you consider enrolling for night classes.

Passive: The meeting was convened by the president.

Active: The president convened the meeting.

Passive: Your address has been changed on our records.

Active: We have changed your address on our mailing list.

Expletives

An expletive is a meaningless word. Even though expletives are not considered grammatical errors, *there are* and *it is* and their variants delay the real idea of the sentence and make the writing unnecessarily wordy, weak, and passive. Observe that *there* is a meaningless word in the following sentence:

There is no charge for the use of the film.

The same idea can be presented in a positive way and in fewer words:

The film is free.

Expletives, such as *there is, there are,* and others, can be eliminated and the sentence can be improved upon by presenting the words in the normal sequence: subject, verb, complement.

Weak:	There are many styles from which to choose.
Revised:	You may choose from many styles.
Weak:	There are 50 students in the class.
Revised:	Fifty students are in the class.
Weak:	There are several plans you may consider.
Revised:	You may consider several plans.
Weak:	There is an increase in the sales for November.
Revised:	Sales increased in November.
Weak:	There must be a proper foundation of gravel and sand in order for us to guarantee our concrete driveways.
Revised:	We guarantee our concrete driveways when a gravel and sand foundation is used.
Weak:	There is a need for you to sign the form.
Revised:	You need to sign the form.

Sentences that begin with *it* can also be improved upon unless *it* refers to an antecedent. In the following message, *it* clearly refers to the report and is not an expletive:

The typist will complete the report today. It will be mailed in the morning.

In the following sentences, *it* is an expletive. The sentences are more vivid when the subject is doing the acting and the expletives are eliminated.

Weak:	It is believed that we will realize a profit in the fourth quarter.

238
Secretarial
Procedures:
Office
Administration and
Automated Systems

Revised: I believe we will realize a profit in the fourth quarter.

Weak: It should take the typist only a few minutes to complete the report.

Revised: The typist should complete the report in only a few minutes.

Weak: It is certain that the position will be accepted by Mary.

Revised: Mary will accept the position.

Weak: It is important for me to hear from the voters in my district.

Revised: I need to hear from the voters in my district.

Weak: It is our policy to offer the lowest rates possible.

Revised: We offer the lowest rates possible.

CONCISENESS

Conciseness means that the message should be expressed in the fewest words possible without sacrificing completeness, courtesy, clarity, and the other qualities necessary for the message to be effective. Conciseness and brevity should not be confused. Messages that are too short may be incomplete, blunt, and unclear. The effectiveness of the message must not be diminished merely to accomplish an economy of words.

Wordiness wastes the time of the reader, makes ideas difficult to understand, and usually indicates the writer does not think logically and clearly.

Many messages can be shortened simply by eliminating redundant expressions and unnecessary words and phrases and by using one word rather than several to express an idea.

Redundancy

Some expressions are wordy simply because they repeat an idea contained in an accompanying word; they are redundant. For example, in the sentence, "The box is large in size," the phrase *in size* is redundant. By studying the following list of redundant expressions, you will be able to increase your ability to identify this kind of wordiness:

Revise this:	To this:
accurate facts	facts
at a price of $70	at $70
at the hour of 6:30	at 6:30
basic fundamentals	fundamentals (or basics)
consensus of opinion	consensus
costs the sum of $10	costs $10
dated September 15	September 15
during the year of 1984	during 1984
exact same	same
exactly identical	identical
extremely unique	unique
has not arrived yet	has not arrived
I personally	I
in the amount of $20	for $20
in the state of Alaska	in Alaska
my personal opinion	I believe
near proximity	proximity
necessary essentials	essentials
nine in number	nine
square in shape	square
start over again	start over
the color of the car is blue	the car is blue
three different firms	three firms
to cooperate together	to cooperate
to order in the future	to order
true facts	facts
visible to the eye	visible

Substitution

By substituting one word for several words that have a similar meaning, you can make your writing more concise, as indicated in the following:

240
Secretarial
Procedures:
Office
Administration and
Automated Systems

Instead of:	*Use:*
along the lines of	like
at all times	always
at the present time	now
due to the fact that	because
first of all	first
for the purpose of	for
for the reason that	because
give consideration to	consider
in order to	to
in the amount of	for
in the event that	should (if)
in the nature of	like
in the near future	soon
in view of the fact that	since (because)
is at this time	is
is of the opinion that	believes
made the announcement that	announced
on the occasion of	when
prior to	before
subsequent to	after
under the date of	on
until such time as	until
we would ask that	please
with regard to	about

An honor student received the following letter from a law firm. Do you agree that the verbosity tends to confuse and tire the reader?

As a result of the interviews of Mr. Smith and myself of some 33 law students, we are in the process of interviewing six or seven during the Christmas vacation who will come up to see us and see our office and discuss further the possibility of employment.

You are one of three others in whom John and I have a strong interest. All three of you are in somewhat the same situation, which is that you have hopefully a three-month obligation of active duty which may come at any time within a year after your graduation from law school. As you know, we need someone now and if we find someone in the group interviewed who could be available on or before June 1, and who likes us and whom we like, we will presumably make an offer to such young man. On the other hand, we would not be telling you the truth if we indicated that we did not have a continuing interest in you and the possibility of your employment. We would appreciate it if you would not find it unduly taxing to come over and see us during the Christmas vacation. You might in fact want to bring your wife so that she could see something about the city as well. If you can give us some advance notice of the time you might be able to come, we will try to have several of our partners here to see you.

Personally, I hope that you can come and will come as nothing is certain in this world, and we might in fact decide on someone who in the last analysis cannot or does not wish to join us.

We realize that this is not giving you quite an unequivocal answer as we would like but trust you understand the circumstances.

Looking forward to seeing you and with best regards, we are

The same student received the following letter from another law firm. The writer of this letter showed consideration for the reader by using the conversational approach and by expressing the message succinctly.

Cliff Henry and I certainly enjoyed having the opportunity to meet and talk with you.

We would like you to visit us in Kansas City before Thanksgiving so you can see our offices and meet the other members of our firm.

Please write or call to let me know when we may expect you. Plan to arrive about 10:30 and stay until midafternoon.

I look forward to hearing from you soon.

CONCRETE WORDS

You can add to the clarity and precision of what you write by using specific rather than general words. Concrete language gives the reader vivid mental pictures. Vague language often gives the reader only hazy ideas, causes confusion, and requires follow-ups, which are an additional

242
Secretarial
Procedures:
Office
Administration and
Automated Systems

expense for the business. "We want you to talk to our group" is not nearly as clear and meaningful as "We invite you to give a 60-minute talk on 'Effective Communication' at the June 15 meeting of the Legal Secretaries Association."

The messages you write as a secretary should be well thought out and should be written in concrete language that can be readily understood by the reader. The following examples illustrate how vague ideas can be expressed in meaningful terms.

Vague: We are sending your book.

Clear: We mailed *Happy Days* today.

Vague: The meeting will be held at a local motel.

Clear: The meeting will be held in the Eastover Room at the Restful Inn.

Vague: There will be about 35 people in your audience.

Clear: Ten administrators and 25 clerks will attend the communications workshop.

Vague: Mary is an excellent shorthand student.

Clear: Mary earned an A in the Advanced Shorthand class.

Vague: She is an excellent woman in her field.

Clear: Ruth Delaney is a Certified Professional Secretary.

GRAMMAR

Knowledgeable readers of business messages expect grammatical correctness. The efficient secretary must have a working knowledge of the rules of grammar and must always consult up-to-date references when uncertain of the correct usage. Although the purpose of this section is not to cover the theory of grammar, the following grammar functions are used and misused frequently enough in business correspondence to warrant review.

Subject-Verb Agreement

The subject and verb must agree in number. A singular subject requires a singular verb and a plural subject requires a plural verb. Deciding whether the subject is singular or plural is generally easy, but many people have difficulty remembering that the following words are singular. When used alone as the subject, they require a singular verb.

anybody	neither
anyone	nobody
each	none
either	nothing
everybody	somebody
everyone	someone
everything	

Examples: *Neither* of the machines *is* operable.

Everyone is eligible to compete for the award.

Either Doris or Velma *has* the file folder.

Each of the workers *is* expected to arrive by 8 a.m.

When the parts of a subject are joined by combinations, such as *either ...or, neither ...nor,* and *not only ...but also,* the verb is singular if both parts are singular.

Examples: Neither the *executive* nor the *secretary is* aware of the change in the meeting date.

Either this *file* or that *one contains* the information you need.

If both parts of the subject are plural, the verb is plural.

Examples: Neither the line *workers* nor the *supervisors were* aware of the malfunctioning machines.

Neither *credit unions* nor *banks* are open on Saturday morning.

Not only *Republicans* but also *Democrats support* a strong national defense program.

If one part of the subject is singular and the other part is plural, the verb agrees with the part of the subject nearer the verb.

244
Secretarial
Procedures:
Office
Administration and
Automated Systems

Examples: Neither the executive nor the *secretaries were* in the office.

Neither the secretaries nor the *executive was* in the office.

Either I or *they are* to plan the activities.

Either they or *I am* to plan the activities.

Pronouns

A pronoun is a word that stands for another word or group of words. The noun for which a pronoun stands is the antecedent of that pronoun. When the connection between the pronoun and the antecedent is unclear, an error in pronoun reference exists. For example, two possible antecedents are contained in "The executive and the secretary talked, and then she left the room." Who left the room? The executive or the secretary? The above sentence might read: "The executive and the secretary talked, and then the secretary left the room." When a sentence contains more than one possible antecedent, you ordinarily can make the meaning clear by replacing the pronoun with the correct antecedent. The following sentences illustrate how the meaning can be clarified by replacing the pronoun.

Unclear: Mary and Jane made plans to go to the convention, but she could not get a plane reservation.

Clear: Mary and Jane made plans to go to the convention, but Jane could not get a plane reservation.

Unclear: Frazier could not talk to Watson until he had a telephone installed.

Clear: Frazier could not talk to Watson until Watson had a telephone installed.

Unclear: The nurse took the secretary to her office.

Clear: The nurse took the secretary to the secretary's office.

Unclear: Place the container by the office door and leave it open.

Clear: Place the container by the office door and leave the door open.

The pronoun and the antecedent must agree in *number.* A singular antecedent requires a singular pronoun. A singular antecedent and its pronoun may be in the same or in different sentences.

Examples: The *comptroller* expressed *his* satisfaction with the audit report.

An efficient *secretary* always checks *her* work.

An efficient *secretary* is accurate. *She* always checks *her* work.

A word that comes between an antecedent and its pronoun should not be mistaken for an antecedent. You usually can avoid errors in pronoun-antecedent agreement by answering the question: To what does this pronoun refer?

Examples: Your *shipment* of books is on *its* way.

Our new *design* for offices is popular because of *its* versatility.

Here are hints to help you make every pronoun agree with its antecedent in number:

1. Use a singular pronoun to refer to such antecedents as *anyone, each, everyone, somebody,* and *someone.*

Examples: *Each* of the executives has *his* desk computer.

Every secretary expects to advance on *her* merit.

When you believe the reader may be sensitive to sexual bias if *he* or *she* is used alone, you may rewrite the sentence in the plural, use *his or her* instead of a single pronoun, or possibly omit the pronoun completely.

Examples: All *executives* have *their* desk computers.

Everyone has *his* or *her* idea concerning the office arrangement.

Executives have desk computers.

2. Use plural pronouns to refer to two or more antecedents connected by *and.*

> *Examples:*   *John* and *Virginia* are planning *their* trip.
>
> *Betty* and *Ruth* took *their* shorthand pads to the meeting.

3. Use singular pronouns to refer to two or more singular antecedents connected by *or* or *nor.* When one is singular and one plural, make the pronoun agree with the nearer of the two.

> *Examples:*   Neither John nor *Steve* can locate *his* report.
>
> Either the executive or the *secretaries* will have *their* pictures taken.

4. Use either a singular or plural pronoun for referring to a collective noun, depending upon whether the collective noun is considered singular or plural in its meaning.

> *Examples:*   The *committee* has been asked for *its* recommendation. (Here the *committee* is thought of as *a unit.*)
>
> The research *staff* have been asked for *their* suggestions. (Here the *staff* is thought of as *more than one individual.*)

Modifiers

A modifier is any word or group of words that describes or qualifies another word or group of words. When properly used, modifiers add to the clarity of sentences. Modifiers that do not apply to the specific word or words you want them to modify make the meaning of the sentence ambiguous. Sometimes misplaced modifiers can be humorous (the following captions appeared in newspapers); but in business correspondence, misplaced modifiers annoy the reader and frequently embarrass the writer.

Board Decides Against Sex Education Behind Closed Doors

Police Officer Shot the Man with the Motorcycle

Landon Skips Speech with the Flu

Mismodification may be avoided by placing the modifier as close as possible to the word, phrase, or clause that it modifies. The misused modifier can be *dangling, squinting,* or *misplaced.*

Dangling Modifiers

A modifier "dangles" when it cannot logically modify any word in the sentence and is forced to hang on to the nearest word. Since most dangling modifiers are verbal phrases, the problem can be corrected either by adding the appropriate noun or pronoun for the phrase to modify or by making the phrase into a clause. Observe how the following sentences can be changed to eliminate the dangling modifiers:

Dangling: Knowing that you want it today, your package is being delivered by courier. (Did the package know you wanted it today?)

Correct: Knowing that you want the package today, we are sending it by courier.

or

We are sending the package by courier since we know you want it today.

Dangling: Rushing to complete the annual report, many errors were made. (Did the errors rush to complete the annual report?)

Correct: Rushing to complete the annual report, the typist made many errors.

or

The typist made many errors while rushing to complete the annual report.

Dangling: Flying at about 2,000 feet, the accident on Interstate 435 was reported by the traffic reporter. (Was the accident flying at about 2,000 feet?)

Correct: Flying at about 2,000 feet, the traffic reporter observed an accident on Interstate 435.

or

The traffic reporter, while flying at about 2,000 feet, observed an accident on Interstate 435.

248
Secretarial
Procedures:
Office
Administration and
Automated Systems

Squinting Modifiers

A modifier "squints" when it can be interpreted as modifying something that precedes it in the sentence or something that follows it. You may use punctuation, move the modifier, or revise the sentence to correct the problem, as shown in the following examples:

Squinting: As the president entered suddenly the workers stopped talking. (Did the president enter suddenly or did the workers suddenly stop talking?)

Correct: As the president entered suddenly, the workers stopped talking.

or

As the president entered, suddenly the workers stopped talking.

Squinting: The executive took the stand reluctantly answering the attorney's questions. (Did the executive reluctantly take the stand or did the executive reluctantly answer the attorney's questions?)

Correct: The executive reluctantly took the stand and answered the attorney's questions.

or

The executive took the stand, reluctantly answering the attorney's questions.

Squinting: The president walked around the office nervously rehearsing his speech. (Was the president walking nervously or was the president nervously rehearsing?)

Correct: The president walked around the office nervously, rehearsing his speech.

or

The president walked around the office, nervously rehearsing his speech.

Squinting: The football players agreed during the last week in October to return to work. (Did the players agree in the last week or did the players return to work in the last week?)

Correct: During the last week in October, the football players agreed to return to work.

or

The players agreed to return to work during the last week in October.

A modifier is "misplaced" when it refers, or appears to refer, to the wrong word or phrase. This problem can be avoided by placing the modifier as close as possible to the words it modifies, as shown in the following sentences:

Misplaced:	He almost earns $300 a week. (Does he earn $299 or does he receive $300 and almost earns that amount?)
Correct:	He earns almost $300 a week.
Misplaced:	We have examined the report you sent in great detail. (Was the report in great detail or was the report examined thoroughly?)
Correct:	We examined the detailed report.
	or
	We have examined in great detail the report you sent.
Misplaced:	Your reports will be sent the day you call by Emery Express. (Will the call be made by using Emery Express?)
Correct:	The day you call, we will send the report by Emery Express.
Misplaced:	Secretaries can accomplish more work when sitting in chairs with erect spines. (Do the chairs have erect spines?)
Correct:	Secretaries can accomplish more work when sitting with erect spines.

Parallelism

Parallelism is used to indicate equality of ideas and of words that represent those ideas. Parallelism is accomplished by using the same kind of grammatical structure for expressing ideas that are used coordinately, as in pairs, series, comparisons, and outlines. The ideas in a series should have something in common, and that relationship should be readily evident to the reader. Consider this list:

airplane

car

train

typewriter

250
Secretarial
Procedures:
Office
Administration and
Automated Systems

Even though train, airplane, car, and typewriter are all nouns and are thus stated in parallel grammatical form, they should not be used in a series since *typewriter* is a discordant item.

Parallel ideas should be expressed in parallel grammatical form. Consider this list:

> to bowl
>
> to ski
>
> to jog
>
> hiking

The idea expressed by the dissimilar form (hiking) is in the same category as the other three, but it would have to be *to hike* to be in a grammatical form consistent with the others.

Parallel structure usually achieves an economy of words, clarifies meaning, and enables the reader to go from one idea to another quickly because the direction of a sentence can be determined easily, as shown in the following examples:

Faulty parallelism:	You may contact Henry Hart by calling 747-6111 or write to 1010 West South, Milwaukee.
Parallel:	You may contact Henry Hart by *calling* 747-6111 or *writing* to 1010 West South, Milwaukee.
Faulty parallelism:	Secretaries are expected to greet visitors, to compose letters, and miscellaneous office work must be done.
Parallel:	Secretaries are expected to *greet* visitors, *compose* letters, and *perform* miscellaneous office work.
Faulty parallelism:	The correspondence secretary's duties included composing, editing, typing, and to watch for errors.
Parallel:	The correspondence secretary's duties included *composing, editing, typing,* and *proofreading.*
Faulty parallelism:	The success of a person in this position of responsibility is determined by her ability to relate effectively with adolescent boys, modeling appropriate kinds of behavior, to cooperate willingly with other treatment personnel, and maintaining sound judgment under pressure.
Parallel:	The success of a person in this position of responsibility is determined by her ability *to relate* effectively with adolescent boys, *to model* appropriate

kinds of behavior, *to cooperate* willingly with other treatment personnel, and *to maintain* sound judgment under pressure.

In outlining and writing that involves enumerating several ideas or actions, you should be consistent in the way the items are listed. The use of parallelism helps the reader realize the relative value of each item. In the following example, *college* is not listed along with elementary and secondary as being part of education.

Nonparallel:
I. Education
   A. Elementary
   B. Secondary
II. College
III. Experience
   A. Part time
   B. Full time

Parallel:
I. Education
   A. Elementary
   B. Secondary
   C. College
II. Experience
   A. Part time
   B. Full time

Not only should the ideas be parallel, but all items at a particular level should begin with the same part of speech:

Nonparallel:
I. Analyses of Display Techniques
   A. Colors are coordinated
   B. Appropriate locations for displays
   C. Themes are innovative
II. Stock Management is Evaluated
   A. Quantity is adequate
   B. Reasonable turnover
   C. The variety is appropriate

Parallel:
I. Analyses of Display Techniques
   A. Colors are coordinated
   B. Locations are appropriate
   C. Themes are innovative
II. Evaluation of Stock Management
   A. Quantity is adequate
   B. Turnover is reasonable
   C. Variety is appropriate

252
Secretarial
Procedures:
Office
Administration and
Automated Systems

PROOFREADING

Since the finished letter, memorandum, or report is your representative, take care to make it correct in every detail. The final responsibility for every aspect of a letter or memorandum rests on the person who signs or initials it, but the most effective correspondence results from the writer and transcriber working as a team. The person who types the document should proofread carefully for errors in spelling, punctuation, grammar, and typing. All names, dates, figures, and addresses should be checked. The writer should then read the letter or memorandum carefully for the same purposes and see that it effectively accomplishes what was intended. Those who sign documents without reading them are evading their responsibility to see that everything that leaves the office is accurate.

Summary

Letters, reports, and memorandums are a major business expense. Business writing that does not inform, get action, or make a good impression represents wasted time and effort. As a secretary, you can help reduce the cost of communication and help yourself professionally by making sure that everything you write accomplishes the desired objectives.

The conversational test will help you write messages that appear natural and readily understood by the reader. Ask yourself, "Would I say it this way if I were talking instead of writing?" Your writing should reflect the proper tone by being natural, courteous, and personal. It must convey the "you attitude." The choice of words and phrases you use and the way you express yourself are important in achieving a tone that shows concern for the reader. Negative, archaic, and meaningless words and expressions may distract the reader. In addition to the tone, your writing should be concise, forceful, clear, and correct.

As a conscientious secretary, you are responsible for ensuring that all messages leaving your office reflect favorably on you and on the company.

1. Why is the secretary's writing ability important?

2. What is the "conversational test"?

3. Define tone.

4. What factors contribute to the proper tone of a letter or memorandum?

5. What is meant by writing from the reader's point of view?

6. Negative words contribute to poor letter tone. Why?

7. What approach can be used to eliminate negative words from the messages you write?

8. Must a concise message be brief? Explain.

9. What techniques may be used to make your writing forceful?

10. Define an expletive.

11. Expletives are not considered grammatical errors. Why, then, should the writer avoid using them?

12. What is the best way to eliminate expletives from your messages?

13. When is *it* not an expletive?

14. Name two common errors in using pronouns.

15. Why should the following expressions not be used?

    a. basic fundamentals

    b. near proximity

    c. consensus of opinion

    d. true facts

16. Must an efficient secretary know all the rules of grammar? Discuss.

17. Does the pronoun *everybody* require a singular or a plural verb?

18. When the subject of the sentence is made up of two parts, what determines whether the verb is singular or plural?

19. How may sexual bias be avoided when using pronouns?

20. What is a modifier?

21. What are the three types of mismodification?

254
Secretarial
Procedures:
Office
Administration and
Automated Systems

22. What is the result of using modifiers incorrectly?

23. Why is parallelism important?

24. Ideas in a series should be parallel. In what other way should the items in the series be parallel?

--- Projects  ---

1. Make a transparency of an actual letter or memorandum and lead a class discussion concerning the strengths and weaknesses of the correspondence.

2. Without changing the meaning, make these sentences concise by omitting the clauses and phrases:

   a. All items that were on the agenda were discussed.

   b. The sales manager discussed the project with great enthusiasm.

   c. The car has a price that is reasonable.

   d. The production manager hired the workers who have the most skill.

   e. We will be glad to send you more copies that are free of charge.

   f. The secretary gave a report that was up to the minute.

   g. The applicant, who is 25 years old, was hired.

   h. We will employ in the neighborhood of 75 clerical workers.

   i. The lady, who is beautiful, is a model for several major department stores.

3. Make the following sentences positive:

   a. We carefully wrapped each gift to prevent damage.

   b. Your order will be delayed four weeks.

   c. The broken dish will be replaced.

   d. You mailed your order too late for us to get the coat to you by September 1.

   e. Do not fail to take advantage of this money-saving offer.

f.   We have looked for the check you claim you sent on April 15.

g.   We can allow you a trade-in of only $100.

h.   We cannot accept the return of damaged merchandise.

i.   We regret that you are one of the few customers to experience a problem with our product.

j.   I deeply regret that you did not advise us of the disturbance during the evening so that we could have moved you to a different location.

k.   I am enclosing a copy of the report so that you can plainly see where you made the error.

l.   Please accept my apology for our negligence in not complying with your previous correspondence.

m.   Mrs. Smith states she attended your school from September 1980 to February 1983.

n.   As you may understand now, and certainly will understand when you ultimately find employment, this material is of a highly confidential nature and cannot be divulged.

4.   Rewrite these sentences to make them more forceful by omitting the expletives:

a.   Please let me know if there are any special instructions.

b.   It would be helpful if you would use the enclosed reference form.

c.   Each year there are many new businesses started in the United States.

d.   It is believed that Weston Electronics will realize a savings and conserve energy by insulating the buildings.

e.   It was a profitable investment.

f.   Our company finds it is a good business decision to buy the building.

g.   Before the house was finished, there was a strike of construction workers.

h.   Please indicate on the enclosed card when it will be possible for you to submit the report.

i.   Without inspection, it is impossible for us to know the action that should be taken.

256
Secretarial
Procedures:
Office
Administration and
Automated Systems

5. Rewrite these sentences to make them concise and correct.

    a. In reply to your memorandum of inquiry, we are attaching a copy of our 1985 sales figures.

    b. A reply at your earliest convenience will be very much appreciated.

    c. I am in receipt of your letter dated March 31.

    d. For your information, your enrollment certification was sent to the office in Muskogee on October 3.

    e. Reference is had to your letter regarding your stay with us the night of August 25.

    f. As you can see, you are to sign the form that is enclosed.

    g. Regarding your memo request of April 17 requesting local traffic statistics, we were able to obtain the latest issue of the Montana Vital Statistics booklet, which gives the vital statistics you asked about for the year 1984.

    h. You may charge your account or you may pay cash for the $10 balance, whichever you choose.

    i. Referring to your communication of recent date, we wish to take this opportunity to state that the items about which you inquired were shipped on March 1 as per your instructions.

    j. In order to obtain absolutely accurate facts that will be agreeable and satisfactory to you, it is the consensus of our staff's opinion that we should conduct an audit and notify you of the results.

    k. Acknowledging receipt of your order of June 1, your merchandise will be shipped within the next week. As per your instructions, shipment will be by express collect.

6. Rewrite the following sentences to make them grammatically correct:

    a. I am looking forward to becoming a delegate and to attendance at the convention.

    b. Our company is devoting most of their resources to research and development.

    c. When it arrived, the dish was broken and the stand was bent.

d. To be fair to all our customers, only one gift certificate may be used per person.

e. The Prestige Company has a reputation of complying with the terms of their agreement.

f. Neither of the applicants you recommended were qualified for the administrative position.

g. The secretaries were given in-house training in handling incoming calls and how to log in the mail.

h. No textbook will be distributed to a student that is out of date.

i. The executive dictated a letter, finished the report, and phones his wife.

j. The education and experience of the candidate was evaluated.

k. None of the accountants are more competent than John.

l. Every member of the department has to do their share of the work.

m. Why should those who are employed periodically look at the help wanted section of the newspaper?

n. He likes to ride his horse, to drive his boat, and racing his car.

o. Each of the customers are sent a $5 gift certificate.

p. To establish credit, three references must be submitted.

q. She typed a letter, a memo, and report.

r. The teacher told us eventually tests would be returned.

s. Everyone will be happy to learn that neither the fire nor water have damaged their records.

t. We hope you will be able to find the necessary funds to carry out your plans from other sources.

u. The executive gave the secretary instructions for checking the work and how to revise it.

v. While driving to the office, the car stalled.

w. We need a person to supervise the project with management experience.

x. Advertisers have the American consumers in their hands. They can persuade him to buy about anything.

258
Secretarial
Procedures:
Office
Administration and
Automated Systems

y. To qualify for the secretarial position, a shorthand test must be passed.

z. We will wrap each piece and put them in corrugated boxes for shipping.

7. Rewrite the sentence, "Only Ruby typed letters between semesters," to give different meanings by changing the placement of "only."

8. Rewrite the following letter so that it will reflect the qualities discussed in this chapter:

Dear Mr. Squires:

I am writing in response to your letter of December 27, 1983, which indicated that you had sent your application letter and resume to our bank. We did receive this letter and resume in the month of November and presently had it filed with similar resumes that would indicate individuals qualified for a management position.

You mentioned in your letter that you would like to obtain a management trainee position with our bank. At the present time we do not have a formal management program, but as I am sure you are aware banks of our size do not have individuals that fall into this type of position even though we do not have a formal program.

To say that we have an opening at this time would not be totally honest, but I would rather indicate that we are always looking for potential members of management even when we don't have a specific need.

I am not sure whether I should encourage you to come to Springfield at this particular time for a personal interview but I am sure if you are in the area I will be able to make myself available to visit with you and I am also sure Mr. Turner will also make his presents available if you so desire.

Thank you for your resume and continued interest.

Sincerely,

1. Your supervisor asks you to write letters and memorandums for her signature. You enjoy writing, and you believe you write well; however, your supervisor often makes changes in what you present for her signature. Should you interpret this to be a criticism of your writing ability? What should you do or say?

2. Assume that you have just had your first six-month evaluation. Your employer complimented you on the way you perform most of your duties, but he suggested that you enroll in a night course to improve your writing skills. How should you have responded to his suggestion?

3. Your supervisor uses archaic expressions and wordy phrases and clauses in his letters and memorandums. You believe the correspondence reflects unfavorably on the company. What should you do?

4. Your supervisor told you to make the messages she dictates technically correct. Although you check the dictionary and references when you are unsure of a technical aspect of the message, the supervisor frequently disagrees with the way you have punctuated the sentences and questions the spelling. How should you handle this situation?

5. Mary Ellis and Bettie Baker share an office. Mary repeatedly asks Bettie questions concerning grammar and punctuation. Bettie believes she should not have to take time from her duties to answer Mary's questions. What do you think?

CHAPTER 12

Writing Procedures

One of your duties as a secretary will be to write routine letters. Some of the letters you will write for the signature of your boss; others you will be expected to sign. Regardless of who signs the letters, you want them to be effective. For letters to be effective, they not only should be technically correct but they must accomplish the desired purpose. Letters may have three basic objectives: to inform, to get action, and to create goodwill. Some letters may involve only one of the objectives, but others may involve all three.

The first step in the letter-writing process is deciding on the overall objective or objectives of the letter. The next step is preparing the letter. To prepare the letter, identify all the points to be covered. Then collect and verify all the pertinent data. Finally, prepare an outline of the logical sequence to be used in covering the points. When only one or two things are involved, a mental outline is usually sufficient. But when several points are to be covered, you'll find that a written outline can help you tremendously when you start actually writing the letter.

ORDER LETTERS

Order letters are not written as often today as they once were. Many orders are placed orally with sales representatives or are made on standard purchase order forms or order blanks. In large companies, orders are placed through the purchasing department. But when an order letter is written, you must specify the exact information that will be needed for the order to be filled correctly.

261

262
Secretarial
Procedures:
Office
Administration and
Automated Systems

Products

When something is ordered for personal use, the writer's address is given in the return address section and the name is given in the closing section.

The order letter is started by making a definite offer to buy since it represents one-half of a contract. To assure the seller of your desire to buy, you may start the letter courteously and succinctly by saying "Please ship ..." or "Please send...." Avoid wordy openings, such as "I would like to place an order for..." or "I'm interested in your sending the following merchandise to my home address." You want to place the order; otherwise, you would not be writing. The seller will assume the order will be sent to the address given in the letterhead or in the return address section unless some other address is given. Never tell the reader the obvious by using an expression such as "Please assemble, pack, wrap, and ship ...."

After you have established the offer to buy, state all essential data definitely and completely. For example, "Ten reams of Colorite paper, Cat. No. 12, $5 per ream" gives an adequate description of what is wanted by identifying the quantity, item, brand, catalog number, and price. Even though the seller desires to fill the order, he would have difficulty if the buyer indicated only "Ten reams of paper." Use a separate, single-spaced sentence for each type of item ordered and leave a double space between the sentences. When several items are ordered, you usually place the data in easy-to-read column form.

End the letter by clearly stating the method of payment and by giving relevant special instructions. Payment for orders may be made in several ways. When a business or an individual has established credit with the seller, the order often is charged. When a credit card is used, specify the name of the card, the number, and the expiration date. If the order is not charged, enclose a check or money order unless you want the shipment sent collect on delivery (COD). Some companies will not ship orders COD, those who do charge a fee for the service. The method of payment or the request that the order be charged should be clearly and concisely stated in the body of the letter.

"Please charge my account No. 502" and "Enclosed is a $29.10 money order" specifically identify the method of payment. Simply asking the seller to "Charge my account" may cause confusion, especially if several people with the same name have charge accounts with the seller or if the buyer's name on the account is different from the one given in the letter.

Sometimes special instructions are required. For example, you may say "I need the equipment by June 15" or "Please send the supplies by Speedy Express." Expressions such as "Send the equipment as soon as possible" and "Please ship by the best method" are not needed and may suggest that you believe the reader has to be told how to perform the job. When you want to indicate that a substitution is desired if an item is out of stock or discontinued, clearly state what you want done.

The following questions provide a helpful checklist for evaluating the order letters illustrated in figures 12-1 and 12-2. Look at the letters and determine whether each question can be answered with a "yes."

1. Does the return address section or letterhead contain the complete address of the writer?

2. Is the inside address complete?

3. Is the method of shipment indicated?

4. Is the quantity indicated?

5. Is the catalog number, model number, or model name given?

6. Is the price or price range stated?

7. Is the description complete?

8. Are the brand names capitalized?

9. Is the form of payment indicated?

10. Is the writer's name given in the closing section?

11. Was the enclosure notation used when payment accompanied the order?

12. Is the letter easy to read?

13. Is the letter courteous?

14. Is the letter concise?

Service

When orders for service are not made by telephone, they are usually written as letters rather than on order blanks or purchase order forms. Whether the order is placed by writing a letter or by telephoning, the information required is essentially the same. Be sure you supply all the instructions or information the reader will need to take the action desired. Frequently, you may need to ask specific questions concerning dates, times, and costs of the services to be performed.

The writer of the letter illustrated in figure 12-3 probably would not get the action desired because of some of the following weaknesses:

- The exact date of the move was not given.

- The type of service was not indicated.

- The business office will not remain open until after 6 p.m.

- The date service is desired is vague; perhaps some dates should have been suggested.

264
Secretarial
Procedures:
Office
Administration and
Automated Systems

The Wilson Company
12121 West Main
Ashbury Park, NJ 07712

August 13, 1984

Office Supply Company
115 Main Street
Absecon, NJ   08201

Gentlemen:

Please ship the following by Speedo Express:

Quantity	Cat. No.	Description	Price
1	AB100	File box, 12½" x 10" x 10"	$ 22.00
1	B2020	Horizontal tray, 5 tier	20.50
2	3K70Z	Calculators, Exacto, 12 digits, fully addressable 4-key memory, S98.99 each	197.98
		Subtotal	$240.48
		Shipping	5.50
		Total	$245.98

I need the file accessories and calculators by August 30.

Enclosed is a check for $245.98.

Sincerely,

B. C. Dent
Office Manager

ms

Enclosure

FIGURE 12-1. Business order for a product.

- The company representative cannot correspond with the writer before the move is made because a current address is not given.
- The handwritten signature is almost illegible; the name should have been typewritten.

```
                              1515 West Street
                              Wichita, KS  67201
                              August 15, 1984


Structo Division
King-Seeley Thermos Co.
Route 74
Freeport, IL  61032

Gentlemen:

Please ship me a Model 9340 Structo gas grill, $139.50.

Charge my Visa account No. 100 100 111.  The expiration
date is March 1986.

                    Sincerely,



                    John W. Myers
```

FIGURE 12-2. Personal order for a product.

The following questions should be asked concerning the effective order for service letter in figure 12-4. You should be able to give a positive answer to each question.

1. Is the writer's current address given?

2. Is the approximate date for the service indicated?

3. Is the type of service indicated?

4. Would the reader know the action desired?

5. Were sufficient data given for the reader to be able to answer the questions asked?

6. Is the writer's name given in clear form?

7. Is the letter complete?

8. Is the letter courteous?

9. Is the letter concise?

REQUEST LETTERS

As a secretary, you will often need to write request letters. The letters are written to acquire specific information about goods, prices, services, or a

266
Secretarial
Procedures:
Office
Administration and
Automated Systems

```
867 East Front Street
Atlanta, GA   30302
August 29, 1984



Manager
Ace Plumbing Company
1157 Peachtree Avenue
Atlanta, GA   30301

Dear Sir:

I am going to move to the above address soon.  I
would like to have some plumbing done.

Please let me know what day you can do the work
and what you charge.  You can now call me at 786-3345
any evening after 6 p.m.

Yours truly,

Brent Elliott
```

FIGURE 12-3. Personal order for service.

number of other subjects. The solicited request letter is usually written in response to an advertisement inviting the reader to write for information. Since the solicited letter is written as a result of a specific suggestion, it should be brief. For example, you might write "Please send me the brochure describing the ABC collator you advertised in the June 15 issue of *The Wall Street Journal.*"

The writer of an unsolicited letter of request must make certain the letter contains all the specific details the reader will need to provide the information or take the action desired. The letter must be courteous; however, it need not be persuasive when a response may result in a sale or at least create goodwill for the person to whom you are writing.

The beginning of the request letter should tell the reader what is desired. A direct opening, such as "The members of the Dollars and Sense Investment Club would like for you to meet with them on Wednesday, October 15," lets the reader know immediately what the letter is about. The opening "You are an expert in the investment field..." may appear to be flattery and delays letting the reader know the real purpose of the letter. Avoid wordy and meaningless beginnings like "I would like to...," "I am writing in regard to...," and "It would be appreciated...." You should also avoid starting the letter by telling the reader who you are ("I am secretary to...") since the statement does not give the reader a clue as to

```
                          1186 Van Deventer Avenue
                          St. Louis, MO  64101
                          November 10, 1984



Southwest Telephone Company
1145 Ward Parkway
Alhambra, CA  91067

Gentlemen:

On December 15, I will be moving to a private dwelling
at 9976 Golden West Boulevard, Alhambra.  I would like
to have telephone service as soon as possible after
that date.

I will have three telephones and would like to have
a private line with unlimited service.

Let me know the regular monthly charge and whether
or not a deposit is required.  I now have telephone
service in St. Louis and my number is 221-0011.

I will also appreciate your letting me know on what
date I may expect to have telephone service.

                          Sincerely,



                          Susan McKindrick
```

FIGURE 12-4. Personal order for service.

what the letter is about; furthermore, if the reader is interested in knowing the writer's position, he can look at the closing section of the letter.

After the request has been made, you should continue the letter by giving the specific details the reader needs to comply. "The two-hour meeting will begin at 7 p.m. and will be held in Room 10 of the Executive Building" gives the reader specific information. "The meeting will be held in the main office building" is vague. The details should be arranged logically, and all of them should be relevant to the request.

You should never apologize for making the request. "I realize you are a busy person..." and "Even though I know you are called upon often..." may suggest to the reader that he should not comply with your request.

You should end the request letter by being positive and by making the response easy for the reader. When the reader will realize no apparent benefits by responding, you should send along an addressed, stamped envelope or offer to pay the cost involved. "Please call me collect at (212) 747-6200 by June 30 to let me know you will serve on the panel" is positive

268
Secretarial
Procedures:
Office
Administration and
Automated Systems

and makes a response easy. "If you will be our speaker..." and "We hope..." do not express confidence. And ending the letter with "If you need additional information..." indicates you believe you may not have planned your request carefully.

At the time you are writing the letter, the reader has not complied with the request; therefore, you should never say "Thank you in advance." After the person has responded favorably, you should write a letter of appreciation.

See if you can give a positive answer to each of the following questions as you evaluate the request letter in figure 12-5.

1. Does the letter start by letting the reader know what the letter is about and by asking the key question?

2. Are specific dates and times given?

3. Is the reader given information about the participants and what is of particular interest to them?

4. Does the writer ask specific questions?

5. Did the writer avoid making a definite commitment to engage the services of the reader since the writer first needs to know the answers to the questions?

6. Does the writer express confidence the response will be positive?

7. Is the letter complete?

8. Is the letter concise?

RESPONSES TO REQUESTS AND INQUIRIES

All companies interested in creating and maintaining goodwill will respond promptly to all reasonable requests and inquiries. If a delay is involved, one should offer an explanation so that the person making the request will know that the letter was received and will know approximately when to expect compliance.

Some companies receive numerous requests of the same type, such as for catalogs and literature. When you need to respond the same way frequently, you should consider merely sending what was requested or using a form letter typed individually. Replies with sales possibilities should be written by those who are thoroughly knowledgeable about the

```
                    ABC Company

                                    10 West Prestige Lane
                                    St. Charles, MO  63301
                                    March 9, 1984


Dr. Henry Schmidt
Professor of Communications
XYZ University
2500 West Willow Lane
Monterey, CA  93940

Dear Dr. Schmidt:

Are you interested in conducting a two-day communications
workshop for 25 of our managers?

We would like to schedule the workshop for 8 to 5 on Thursday
and Friday, June 14 and 15.  All of the participating managers
have completed at least four years of college and have been
managers at least two years; some of them have been managers
for ten years.  They are particularly interested in learning
about the use of technologies in the communication area.

I will appreciate your letting me know you are interested in
conducting the workshop.  Please send along an outline of the
topics you would like to cover and tell me what you would
charge to conduct the workshop.

                    Sincerely,



                    H. B. Handley
                    Director of Training


ms
```

FIGURE 12-5. Request letter.

product or the service. The secretary is usually not expected to have the expertise necessary to compose letters of this type; therefore, the letters should be written by someone in the marketing area. However, when paragraphs have been written to answer specific questions or to give complete information about a product or service, the secretary may be expected to write the opening of the letter, incorporate the appropriate paragraph or paragraphs, and then write the ending of the letter.

270
Secretarial
Procedures:
Office
Administration and
Automated Systems

Favorable Responses

A favorable response to a request should tell the reader you are doing what was asked. For example, an appropriate response to a letter from a student requesting information needed for a class project might be "Here are the booklets concerning franchising. I am confident you will find much of the information helpful as you complete your project in your retailing class." A letter of this type tells the reader the action that has been taken, reflects a positive tone, and personalizes it by mentioning the type of class. A favorable reply to a request letter should not be so concise that it is blunt; however, expressions such as "We have received your request...," "Thank you for your letter of July 6...," and "Please accept with our compliments..." simply add to the length of the letter and do not increase the effectiveness. Above all, never grudgingly comply with a request or hint that the request should not have been made. "Even though it involves considerable time and expense, we are sending you information on our flextime program..." tells the reader you are complying with the request but negates goodwill that might have been generated.

You must make certain that all specific questions have been answered completely; otherwise, the reader will presume you are indifferent or careless. Furthermore, additional correspondence will involve more time and expense. If a purchasing agent had written to a company asking a representative to call on him at 9 or 10 a.m. on Friday, May 15, he would expect an answer similar to the following: "Velma Knotts will be in Weston on Friday, May 15, and looks forward to calling on you at 9 a.m."

When compliance with a request involves many details, you should start by indicating that you are doing what was asked, continue by completely and specifically answering all questions and supplying all relevant data, and end graciously. Look at the letter granting a request shown in figure 12-6 as you consider the following questions. Can each question be answered with a "yes"?

1. Does the letter begin by answering the question that must have been asked?

2. Is the professor given all the details needed to make plans for the entire day?

3. Does the letter convey the idea the writer will be pleased to have the group visit?

4. Is the letter sincere?

5. Does the letter have a pleasant tone?

Refusing to Comply

When you must refuse to comply with a request, use tact and try to maintain the goodwill of the person making the request. Frequently, when

```
                    ABC Company

                                10 West Prestige Lane
                                St. Charles, MO  63301
                                January 3, 1984


Professor J. S. Landon
Elite University
Mission, KS  66222

Dear Professor Landon:

We will be pleased to have your Advanced Management
class visit us on Wednesday, January 25.

The tour will leave from the main lobby at
1010 West Broadway at 10 a.m. and will proceed to
the interviewing room and testing center.  Following
an examination of sample tests and a 15-minute film
illustrating our interviewing procedure, we will visit
the production area.  The students will be able to
observe our assembly line in operation and will be
able to ask questions of either the tour guide or the
employees on the job.

We will serve you and the 25 students a complimentary
lunch in our executive dining room at approximately
12:15.  After lunch we will meet in the conference
room for a question-and-answer period.

I look forward to meeting you and your group on
January 25.

                        Sincerely,



                        Elizabeth Benton
                        Director of Tours


ms
```

FIGURE 12-6. Granting a request.

you cannot comply, you can offer some alternative. When that is not possible or practical, you should try to give convincing reasons for not being able to comply.

Use an indirect approach in responding to a request that cannot be granted. Try to create a favorable impression before telling the bad news. "We appreciate your interest in touring our plant" would be a positive way to start the letter and would avoid misleading the reader. Do not start

272
Secretarial
Procedures:
Office
Administration and
Automated Systems

by using negative or wordy expressions like "I am sorry I cannot meet with you at..." or "I have your request asking me to speak at the football banquet." The opening, "My company and I feel very privileged to be requested to contribute to the banquet for the winning football team," could lead the reader to believe you are intending to contribute. A misleading approach may antagonize the reader.

Continue the letter by offering an alternative or giving logical reasons for not being able to comply. Here are some responses that should convince the reader you are doing all you can to be helpful:

I can meet you at 9 a.m. on Friday, March 15.

Our collection letters are prepared for us by experts in the field of written communication. This approach makes our letters unique, and we believe that is the reason our letters are effective.

I am enclosing an article written by one of the experts. I am confident you will find her suggestions helpful.

Only our employees have access to the figures relating to the composition of our share of the hair coloring market. We are, however, enclosing a list of trade publications that provide general data.

When the company policy prohibits your responding favorably to the request, give the reasons for the policy rather than simply saying "Our policy is...." In some cases, the person should not have made the request, but you cannot maintain goodwill by making statements such as the following:

The high cost of manufacturing and our policy of never distributing samples obviously prevents us from giving you what you want.

Since you failed the Secretarial Procedures class you had with me, obviously I cannot recommend you.

As you may understand now, and certainly will understand when you ultimately find employment, material you requested is of a highly confidential nature and cannot be divulged.

"Best wishes for a successful MSA convention" could be an effective way to end a letter in response to a request asking you to donate samples of your products. When you have not complied, never say "Please contact us when we can be of service" or any other expression that will encourage the reader to make other requests to which you will not be able to respond favorably.

When the response may have considerable impact on the company image, you should let someone in a high position of authority write the letter or at least suggest the approach you should use. The response to some requests may have legal implications. Obviously, the secretary should not be expected to compose the letters in these instances.

Look at the letter in figure 12-7 as you consider the following questions. Can you give a positive answer to each question?

1. Did the letter begin without giving bad news?

2. Will the reader know that his request for an evening tour is not being granted?

3. Are logical reasons given in a positive way?

4. Will the reader have a favorable impression of the company and believe that the company sincerely wants to be helpful?

5. Did the writer make the response easy?

6. Did the writer avoid using negative words and ideas?

7. Is the letter concise?

8. Is the letter courteous?

CLAIM LETTERS

"To err is human," according to Alexander Pope. Fortunately, in the business world, most errors can be corrected. However, much correspondence is often involved before all parties are completely satisfied. The error may be made by the buyer when he or she places an order or asks for a service to be performed, or the error may be made by the seller.

Buyer Error

When the error has been made by the buyer in specifying exactly what is wanted, the seller is not legally obligated to make an adjustment; however, since most businesses are eager to maintain goodwill, they usually do what is necessary to satisfy the customer. When you need to request some type of adjustment as a result of your actions, you should admit that the need for the adjustment was created by you and should be reasonable regarding the extent you expect the seller to assume the costs involved.

When you have erred and an adjustment is required, the claim letter should contain a statement that you assume the responsibility for having created the need for the adjustment, the necessary details, and a request for the adjustment desired.

274
Secretarial
Procedures:
Office
Administration and
Automated Systems

ABC Company

10 West Prestige Lane
St. Charles, MO   63301
March 13, 1984

Dr. George Hilton, Professor
College of Business and Economics
Elite University
1000 Knowledge Hill
Las Cruces, NM   88001

Dear Dr. Hilton:

We appreciate the interest your class has in touring our
plant.

We provide tours only during our regular visiting hours
from 1 to 4 p.m. when guides are on duty to make the
tour meaningful. Also, during the afternoon hours your
group will be able to observe the assembly line in
operation and ask questions of either the tour guide or
the employees on the job.

Should you be interested in touring our plant during the
afternoon, please call me collect at 215-7777 and let me
know the date you would like to visit us.

                    Sincerely,

                    Harlan B. Stone,
                    Director Public Relations

ms

FIGURE 12-7. Refusing to comply with a request.

Start the letter by identifying the order by date or invoice number. The
opening, "Today we received goods shipped under invoice No. 111D,"
gives the reader information needed to identify the order. Vague expressions, such as "We recently received goods we ordered from you" or
"Today we received goods we ordered on purchase order No. 1010,"
would not help the reader locate the order in his files.

Continue the letter by giving specific data. For example, you might
say "I should have ordered the Model Z241 paper shredder rather than the
Model Z240." The statement would let the reader know that you accept
responsibility for the error and also let him or her know what you should
have ordered. Even though you should admit the error, you should not

```
                    ABC Company

                              10 West Prestige Lane
                              St. Charles, MO  63301
                              April 9, 1984


        Globe-Wells Office Equipment Co.
        863 Seneca Avenue
        Buffalo, NY  14283

        Gentlemen:

        Today we received the 25 metal letter trays for
        legal-size paper that we ordered on April 2.

        We now realize we should have indicated trays
        for letter-size (Cat. No. 229) instead of legal-size
        paper.  We will appreciate your giving us
        permission to exchange the trays.

                              Sincerely,



                              Joe E. Ross
                              Purchasing Agent


        ms

        Enclosure:  Invoice No. 220.
```

FIGURE 12-8. Claim letter; buyer at fault.

apologize excessively. Expressions such as "I am deeply sorry to have inconvenienced you" or "Please forgive me for making this terrible error" should be avoided.

The letter should end with a specific request. If you want to return an item, you should ask for permission. For example, you could say "May I return the black briefcase and exchange it for a brown one?" Let the reader know precisely what you want, but remember that when you create the problem you do not have the right to demand a certain type of action.

Look at the claim letter in figure 12-8. Can you give a positive answer to each of the following questions?

1. Does the writer identify the order?

2. Does the writer assume the responsibility for having created the need for the adjustment?

276
Secretarial
Procedures:
Office
Administration and
Automated Systems

3. Is the action desired clearly specified?

4. Is the letter courteous?

5. Is the letter concise?

Seller Error

When the error is the fault of the seller and you request that an adjustment be made, you should use the same degree of consideration you would like from others if you were at fault. The adjustment request should be made calmly, courteously, and objectively. The facts should be given. And, even though the temptation is sometimes great, little can be accomplished by griping or "bawling out" someone. Lengthy explanations are usually unnecessary, irritating, and confusing.

Use the same type of opening in this letter as used when the buyer is at fault. Continue the letter by telling what is wrong. For example, you might say "The watermark on the letterhead is not in reading position" or "Only 10 of the 20 file cabinets were received." Avoid pointing an accusing finger or second-guessing what happened. Do not say "You made a mistake" or "Someone in your shipping department did not send 10 of the 20 file cabinets." The person who will be reading the letter may not be the one who made the mistake, and possibly all 20 file cabinets were shipped and some of them were misplaced by the transportation company. When registering a complaint, you should use the passive sentence structure; that is, "A mistake was made" rather than "You made a mistake."

The letter should end with a specific adjustment request. If you are entitled to a refund, you may ask for it. If you want other action taken, let the reader know precisely what you desire. Unless you are willing to let the seller make the decision, do not use the expression "Please make a suitable adjustment."

Consider the following questions concerning the claim letter shown in figure 12-9. Can each question be answered with a "yes"?

1. Does the writer identify the order?

2. Are specific details given?

3. Is the reader told in a subtle way the damage must have been caused before the item was shipped?

4. Is the action desired clearly specified?

5. Is the letter courteous?

6. Is the letter concise?

7. Did the writer avoid pointing an accusing finger and second-guessing what happened?

```
                    ABC Company

                              10 West Prestige Lane
                              St. Charles, MO  63301
                              February 1, 1984

Bristol Manufacturing Company
3188 East Street
Cincinnati, OH  45201

Gentlemen:

Today we received goods shipped under invoice No. 747.

Two Model A10 pencil sharpeners and three Model B2
staplers are missing.  Even though the box containing
the shipment arrived in good condition, the cash box
is bent.

Please send the two sharpeners and three staplers and
a replacement for the cash box.

                    Sincerely,



                    Theresa Jones
                    Office Manager


Enclosure:  Order Letter
```

FIGURE 12-9. Claim letter; seller at fault.

GOODWILL LETTERS

Executives are often so occupied with the business-related tasks that must be completed that they fail to take advantage of the opportunity to build goodwill by writing congratulatory and appreciation letters. As a secretary, you may remind the executive of the promotions or other significant achievements of colleagues or acquaintances. In many instances, you may write the letter for his or her signature.

Congratulatory

The timeliness of the congratulatory letter is important. And the letter should sound sincere and personal. For example, "Congratulations on

278
Secretarial
Procedures:
Office
Administration and
Automated Systems

ABC Company

10 West Prestige Lane
St. Charles, MO 63301
February 10, 1984

Dear Mary:

I just learned of your election as
President of the Merrymakers Club. Congratulations!
Those of us who have worked with you in other
organizations know the club is fortunate to have
you at the helm.

Best wishes for a successful year.

Cordially,

Beth Holland

Ms. Mary Lowell
1010 Meadow Lane
Clawson, MI 48017

FIGURE 12-10. Congratulatory letter.

your promotion to Vice President of Operations" is more meaningful than
"Congratulations on your promotion." The congratulatory letter may have
only one or two sentences.

A letter of congratulations on the occasion of an acquaintance's election to a position in a service organization is shown in figure 12-10. The
letter is personal and sincere. Note, too, that the double spacing, the
ten-space paragraph indention, and the executive letter format give the
letter a less businesslike appearance. Messages of this type may, of
course, be handwritten; but the typewritten letter is acceptable.

Appreciation

In many companies, executives are expected to be actively involved in
activities outside the business. When a business person has held a high
office in an organization or has chaired an important committee, he or she

```
┌─────────────────────────────────────────────────────────────┐
│                      DO GOOD CLUB                             │
│                                                              │
│                           10 West Prestige Lane              │
│                           St. Charles, MO  63301             │
│                           March 10, 1984                     │
│                                                              │
│   Mr. Bob Morgan                                             │
│   25 Morningside Drive                                       │
│   Bloomsburg, PA  17815                                      │
│                                                              │
│   Dear Bob:                                                  │
│                                                              │
│        The many comments I have heard from the elderly       │
│   residents at the Sunset Rest Home indicate your weekly     │
│   Happy Hours were deeply appreciated.  I'm sure you         │
│   have been compensated for your hard work as Social         │
│   Chair of the Do Good Club by experiencing a sense of       │
│   personal pride in knowing that you did each job well.      │
│                                                              │
│        Thank you, Bob, for performing the duties of your     │
│   office so competently.                                     │
│                                                              │
│                   Sincerely,                                 │
│                                                              │
│                                                              │
│                                                              │
│                   Ralph Henderson                            │
│                   President                                  │
│                                                              │
│                                                              │
│   ms                                                         │
│                                                              │
└─────────────────────────────────────────────────────────────┘
```

FIGURE 12-11. Letter of appreciation.

should write a letter of appreciation after someone has done an especially nice job and when he or she leaves office. Expressing appreciation orally is important, but a written expression can be more meaningful. When a letter of this type is written, one must take the letter out of the form letter category and make the letter personal by mentioning specifics. "You did a fine job," "You are a hard worker," and "You did much to help the organization" do not suggest to the reader that the letter was written with only him or her in mind.

The letter of appreciation shown in figure 12-11 conveys the idea that the letter was written with Bob in mind by including the position he held and by mentioning an activity that was particularly successful.

Thank-You

When someone has done a favor for your company, a thank-you letter should be written. For example, if someone recommended an applicant

280
Secretarial
Procedures:
Office
Administration and
Automated Systems

for a position within your firm, a thank-you letter shows appreciation and also lets the reader know that you received the recommendation. This type of letter usually has only one or two sentences. Here is an example:

Thank you for your letter in support of Ms. Harriette Benton's application for an accounting position with our company.

We appreciate your cooperation and assure you Ms. Benton will receive our careful consideration.

INVITATIONS

In many companies, the secretary is responsible for preparing and sending invitations. The informal invitation may be handwritten or typewritten. Commercial invitations, which require pertinent data to be added, are available; but they are usually not used in business. Formal invitations may be handwritten, typewritten, or engraved; but they are always written in the third person. The printer will have samples of the proper form; how-

Mutual Benefit Life's Annual Open House
Thursday, September 30, 3:30 PM

_____ *Yes, I plan to attend.*
Guests who will be attending with me are:

_____

_____

_____ *Sorry, I will be unable to attend.*

Signed, _____
Please return by September 24

FIGURE 12-12. RSVP card.

```
Central Bank

We are pleased to announce the opening of our
new bank building at 25 West Washington Avenue
in Pasadena.

You are cordially invited to attend our Ribbon
Cutting Ceremony at 1:30 p.m. on Sunday, June 17.
The ceremony will be followed by a reception in
the lobby.

We look forward to seeing you.
```

FIGURE 12-13. Informal typewritten invitation.

ever, the secretary is responsible for selecting the appropriate paper and style of type, supplying the data, and checking the accuracy of the proofs.

When you prepare an invitation, you need to consider *who, what, when, where,* and *why,* and you may need to specify the attire. When you want a response prior to the event, ask for an RSVP. You may make the response easy by including a printed card for the person to complete and return, as illustrated in figure 12-12.

```
You and your spouse-guest

are invited to the

First Annual

Byler Award Reception

in honor of the nominees.

Announcement of the awards

will be made at this time.

4 to 5 p.m.              Faculty Lounge

May 15, 1984            University Union
```

FIGURE 12-14. Informal engraved invitation.

282
Secretarial
Procedures:
Office
Administration and
Automated Systems

The Board of Directors

ABC Company

request the honor of your presence

at dinner

in honor of

President and Mrs. William Hendrix

on Friday, the fifth of August

One thousand nine hundred and eighty-three

at six-thirty o'clock

Elegant Hotel

10 Devonshire Drive

Kansas City, Missouri

RSVP
10 West Avenue
Black Tie   Kansas City, Missouri

FIGURE 12-15. Formal engraved invitation.

When you mail an invitation to a business address, clearly indicate that the spouse or a guest is also invited. Formal invitations are addressed by hand and should carry a postage stamp rather than metered postage. The courtesy titles used for other types of business correspondence should be used for invitations.

Observe that the following invitations tell *who, what, when, where,* and *why.* An invitation written in informal style is shown in figure 12-13.

A slightly more formal invitation in printed form is shown in figure 12-14.

A formal invitation in printed form is shown in figure 12-15.

When a written response is expected by the one extending the invitation, use the same formal or informal style used in the invitation.

A handwritten acceptance of a formal invitation is shown in figure 12-16.

NEWS RELEASES

If you work for a company that does not have a public relations department, you may occasionally be asked to write news and publicity re-

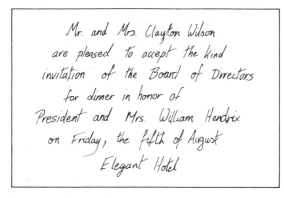

Mr. and Mrs. Clayton Wilson
are pleased to accept the kind
invitation of the Board of Directors
for dinner in honor of
President and Mrs. William Hendrix
on Friday, the fifth of August
Elegant Hotel

FIGURE 12-16. Handwritten acceptance of a formal invitation.

leases. When the event is of major interest to the public, most media will be pleased to send reporters. However, for routine events, such as promotions and personnel changes, you may be expected to prepare the release and send it to the media.

Although the media staff may edit what you write, they are more likely to use it when you have included all relevant information and prepared it in appropriate format. When writing the release, you should consider the five W's of journalism—who, why, what, where, and when. You must be certain that all dates, names, spellings, addresses, and other important data are correct. Errors in information disseminated to the public can cause much confusion and can sometimes result in embarrassing situations.

Observe the following technical aspects of the news release illustrated in figure 12-17:

- The title (news release) is typed as a spread heading and is typed approximately 1½ inches from the top of the page.

- The company name and address are given.

- The time of release is indicated. When a later date of release is desired, the line should be stated as follows: For Release on Friday, March 16, 1984.

- The release title is active rather than passive and is typed in all capital letters.

- The city, state, and date precede the text.

- The text is double spaced.

- The first line of each paragraph is indented five spaces.

- The end of the release is indicated by using number symbols.

When more than one page is needed for the release, you should leave a bottom margin of approximately 1½ inches and type MORE a double space below the last line of text on each page except the last.

284
Secretarial
Procedures:
Office
Administration and
Automated Systems

```
          N E W S     R E L E A S E


Southwest Electronics, Inc.
999 East Expressway
Albuquerque, NM  87101

         FOR IMMEDIATE RELEASE


  SOUTHWEST ELECTRONICS ANNOUNCES PERSONNEL CHANGES

     Albuquerque, NM, March 15, 1984--Southwest Electronics has
announced the appointment of David D. Hickman as director of
marketing for the land mobile radio division.  Mr. Hickman
was formerly vice president of marketing for Malmack's radio
products division and served as vice president of its ARS
division.  He has also been associated with Electron, Inc.,
Arcadia, California, and Perfection Electronics, Ogden, Utah.
     J. R. Ralston has been promoted from director of special
projects to director of engineering and manufacturing.


                    #    #    #
```

FIGURE 12-17. News release.

Summary

The extent to which a secretary is expected to compose letters depends on her ability, on the types of letters that originate in the office, and on the preferences of the boss. Most experienced secretaries are expected to write at least some of the routine letters that do not require management-level decisions.

The secretary can save the supervisor valuable time by writing orders, requests, replies to requests, and some goodwill letters. And even when the secretary is not expected to compose the letters, she can often collect and verify the data needed to assist the one who actually composes the letters. Regardless of who writes the letters, the secretary is, of course, expected to make sure all technical aspects are correct.

Questions

1. What is a routine letter?

2. When is a letter effective?

3. Can a letter that contains spelling and punctuation errors be effective?

4. Name the three basic objectives of letters.

5. Why should personal order letters not be written on business stationery?

6. Explain why an order letter should be started by making a definite offer to buy.

7. Discuss the methods of paying for orders and when each may appropriately be used.

8. Why do some companies not ship items COD?

9. Why might you not want something shipped COD?

10. Discuss the difference between solicited and unsolicited request letters.

11. Why are businesses often eager to comply with all reasonable requests even when no immediate benefits are apparent?

12. You should not apologize for making a request. Why?

13. When should you send along an envelope or offer to pay for the cost of complying with your request?

14. Give two reasons why you should never thank a person in advance.

15. The secretary should not be expected to write the responses to all request and inquiry letters. Explain.

16. When you cannot comply with a request or offer an alternative, what approach should you use?

17. How should the adjustment request letter end?

18. What is the primary objective of congratulatory and appreciation letters?

19. What style is used when responding to an invitation?

20. Why is the executive letter style frequently used for congratulatory letters?

21. How can you make a letter of appreciation appear personal?

—————————————— Projects ——————————————

Make logical assumptions in each of the following cases; however, when possible use the library to find addresses and other relevant information.

1. Write a letter to order a two-year subscription to a professional magazine.

2. Assume that you received your college degree two years ago. You are now planning to change positions and want to use as a reference the name of a professor you expecially liked. You have not corresponded

286
Secretarial
Procedures:
Office
Administration and
Automated Systems

with the professor since you left college. Write an appropriate request letter.

3. You spent last weekend as a guest in the home of the parents of a friend. Write an appropriate letter of appreciation.

4. Before you buy an expensive item, you are interested in learning the opinions of someone who owns a similar item. Write an appropriate letter of inquiry.

5. Your boss, Ms. Beth Hickman, is planning a two-week vacation in La Jolla. She has asked you to write to the La Jolla Cove Motel and ask for a reservation. Assume Ms. Hickman has supplied you with all of the information you need except the address.

6. Your boss is moving and asked you to notify *Fortune* of his new address. Write the letter.

7. Your boss asked you to write to a word-processing company and ask for a movie that would be appropriate to show to all of the management personnel. He indicated that any day about a month from now will be acceptable.

8. Your boss is a member of the board of directors of the Excelo Company. She has asked you to write a letter to the chief executive officer and tell him that she will not be able to attend the regular meeting in July. She did not tell you why, but you know that she has been asked to meet with the IRS on the day of the meeting. Write the letter.

9. A local service club has requested that your company donate something that can be auctioned at an annual fund-raising function. Your boss is willing to donate a country-cured ham this year; however, he does not believe the goodwill created will be sufficient to justify donating each year. Thus, you want to discourage them from asking next year.

Cases

---

1. Your boss dictates all of the letters that are sent from your office. You earned an A in your college business letter writing class and you are confident you can write effective routine letters. How can you tactfully ask to be given the responsibility of writing routine letters?

2. Assume that in your office you are expected to answer all request and inquiry letters. Occasionally, those receiving your letters are not satisfied and call either your boss or other executives in your organization seeking additional information or action. What should you do to keep this from happening?

3. Your supervisor frequently uses archaic, trite, and wordy expressions. You believe his poor writing causes others to have a bad impression of your company. What should you do?

4. In your office you frequently do not receive requests in time to comply in writing by the date indicated by the one making the request. When the request involves things to be mailed, what should you do?

5. You are the supervisor of a junior secretary who recently graduated from college. She has many good qualities, but you observe that she is extremely weak in using the English language and she frequently makes technical errors when typing letters and reports. You believe she has the ability to be a good secretary. How should you handle the situation?

CHAPTER 13

Preparing Reports

The secretary is frequently expected to help collect, analyze, organize, and present the data for a report in a meaningful form. The data used in the report may be obtained from many different sources that may be classified as either secondary or primary.

Data obtained from primary sources are usually "raw"; that is, they are data that have not been analyzed or interpreted previously and are often in the form of computer printouts, microform, handwritten facts and figures, reports, and so forth. Sales, production, personnel, merchandising, accounting and other internal records of the company are sources of much of the primary data needed for business reports. Computer technology has drastically increased the quantity of data readily available. As a secretary, you are often responsible for providing these data in easy-to-understand form.

Secondary data are gleaned from printed material that someone else has compiled, analyzed, and made available to the general public. Secondary sources of information are available in libraries and include periodicals, newspapers, directories, government documents, and many other published sources. All information taken directly from secondary sources should be treated as quoted material, and the source should be referenced.

Many companies have desk-top terminals that not only process words but also have the capacity to produce computer graphics. The data for both the words and the graphics for the report can be keyed in and all necessary changes can be made before it is printed on paper. Even though the use of electronics has eliminated much of the time-consuming

290
Secretarial
Procedures:
Office
Administration and
Automated Systems

work previously required, someone must still possess thinking, organizing, and communication skills for the finished product to present the desired message.

The secretary who is involved with preparing a report will find the following discussion of graphics and the presentation of data helpful.

GRAPHIC AIDS

Graphic aids, or illustrations, can often be used to save time for the reader by presenting visually many of the important aspects of the information contained in the report.

An illustration is any kind of visual presentation of data. When tables, figures or charts, and exhibits are integrated with the text of a report, the reader should be able to understand the message more easily and readily than by sorting out the information presented in textual form only.

A table is a columnar display of numbers and words. An exhibit is an actual copy of something, such as a drawing or a document, that is included as part of the report. All other kinds of illustrations that are not tables or exhibits may be referred to as figures or charts and include circles, bars, and lines.

A random number of illustrations should not be arbitrarily selected. Illustrations should be used only when they are needed to help communicate the message. If an illustration is to add to the effectiveness of a report, the writer must consider the reason for using the illustration, review the possibilities available, and select the one most appropriate for the type of information to be presented.

Illustrations not only must be accurately compiled but must also be systematically arranged so that they can be read and interpreted easily. Spacing, ruling, headings, and the placement of the illustration within the text all contribute to the effectiveness of the visual presentation.

The illustration should be self-explanatory; that is, the reader must be able to understand the data presented in the illustration without having to look at the textual material. The paramount question you should ask as you prepare a graphic aid is "Can the illustration stand alone?" If the reader must look at the textual material to completely understand the data presented in the illustration, the illustration is not complete.

All illustrations should have a title caption that, along with other headings, completely describes the contents. Although they may not all be required for the caption to be complete, you should consider the journalist's five W's—who, what, where, when, and why. Sometimes you may need to include *how* (the classification principle). The caption of an illustration comparing the annual sales volume of Districts I and II of the Warner Company, Minneapolis, for the 1983 calendar year should include the following:

Who—Warner Company

What—annual sales

Where—Districts I and II, Minneapolis

When—1983

Why—comparison

The caption may be "Comparison of Sales of Districts I and II of the Warner Company, Minneapolis, 1983."

The size of the illustration should be justified by the content. Since illustrations are used in reports to aid the reader in understanding the message, simplicity is important. When the amount of data placed in the illustration is so extensive that the reader has difficulty readily grasping the meaning, the illustration has not served a useful purpose. On the other hand, the illustration should not be so large or simple that the reader will think you have placed an undue emphasis on that part of the report. The illustration must never extend into the margins.

Tables

Tables can contribute to the readability and appearance of a report and are especially effective when used to present precise quantitative data in an orderly form.

General purpose tables include a broad area of primary or secondary data. If general purpose tables are included as part of the report, they are usually placed in the appendix. Special purpose tables include data (obtained from the general purpose tables) that are pertinent to the report and are included in the body of the report to visually show the relevant data. A general purpose table might include scores made by 1,000 students on a series of tests. The table showing the individual scores could be included in the appendix; and the analysis, such as the mean, mode, median, and range, could be included in the body of the report in a special purpose table.

Before preparing a table, you should thoroughly understand the following procedures involved in typing the title and number, column heads, stubs (side titles), dollar amounts, percentages, and footnotes.

Number and Title

If more than one table is to be used in the document, type the word TABLE in all capital letters and center it and the number on a line by itself. Arabic numerals should be used for the number, and the tables should be numbered consecutively throughout the report.

Center the table title, also typed in all capital letters, a double space below the table number line. The table title must not extend beyond the

292
Secretarial
Procedures:
Office
Administration and
Automated Systems

width of the table. Titles requiring more than one line should be arranged in inverted pyramid form and single spaced.

When the titles of most of the tables in the report are more than two lines, you may save time and space by placing the table number and title at the edge of the table rather than in the center. You may capitalize the first letter of all words except articles, prepositions, and coordinate conjunctions or only the first word and all proper nouns. Type all titles of tables in a consistent style throughout the report.

Different methods of arranging the table number and title are as follows:

```
                          TABLE 1

         BEST-REMEMBERED AND BEST-LIKED TELEVISION
              COMMERCIALS IN THE UNITED STATES IN
                            1984

   TABLE 1.--Best-remembered and best-liked television commercials
              in the United States in 1984

   TABLE 1.--Best-Remembered and Best-Liked Television Commercials
   in the United States in 1984
```

Column Heads

Each column heading is centered above the data in the column it identifies. Capitalize all words except articles, prepositions, and coordinate conjunctions. When the table is ruled, the column headings are never underlined.

Stubs

The titles to the rows of data are known as stubs and are listed in the left-hand column of a table. The column heading should accurately and clearly identify the items listed.

The stubs should be arranged in a logical order, such as alphabetical, chronological, geographical, or frequency. Stubs should be consistent in grammatical form and only the first letter of the title and of proper nouns and adjectives should be capitalized. If an item is entitled "others," it should be listed last in the column. When stubs are in the form of ranges, be sure that the intervals do not overlap and that all intervals within the range are accounted for.

If the individual items require more than one line, the carryover lines should be indented two or three spaces. Although they usually are not needed, the stub may be followed by leader periods. The following illustrates how to type stubs requiring more than one line and how to use leaders:

Estimated value of
   machinery and equipment ...
Value of land and
   buildings ....

The stubs are single spaced; however, if the table is long, a blank line should be left after groups of three, four, or five items unless the majority of the stubs are more than one line in length.

Dollar Amounts

Several things must be considered when using dollar amounts in a table. The dollar sign must be used at the top of each dollar amount column and at every break, such as subtotals and totals. The dollar signs must be aligned vertically. For dollar amounts of one thousand or more, the thousands are marked off with commas. The rule preceding the total is drawn under the longest line, including the dollar sign.

Amount
$ 500
100,000
1,000
73,000
150,000
175,000
500,000
600,000
$1,599,500

If the decimal and cents are used with at least one amount in one or more columns in the table, the decimal and digits must be used with all amounts. If the following columns were to appear in the same table, the correct and incorrect ways of typing the amounts are as shown:

Correct:

Amount	Amount
$ 1.50	$ 7.00
2.00	9.00
10.00	15.00
25.00	20.00
$38.50	$51.00

294
Secretarial
Procedures:
Office
Administration and
Automated Systems

Incorrect:

Amount	*Amount*
$ 1.50	$ 7
2.00	9
10.00	15
25.00	20
$38.50	$51

When the amounts in a table are large, space may be saved by omitting the relevant zeroes and noting the following in the heading to the table:

SALES OF THE SPRITE COMPANY FOR A FOUR-YEAR PERIOD
1980-1984
(Money Amounts in Millions of Dollars)

Percentages

The percent sign should not be used when the column heading clearly indicates that the figures are percentages:

Percentage of Total
5.0
10.2
12.8
30.0
42.0
100.0

When the column heading does not clearly indicate that the figures are percentages, the percent sign must be used with each figure:

Increase
10.0%
17.0%
25.5%
70.0%
100.0%
110.5%

Percentages of less than a whole number should be preceded by a zero if the column is not totaled. Three spaced period leaders should be left for each entry for which no percentage is to be recorded. The decimals in percentages are always aligned vertically.

Change
0.8%

. . .

22.2%
33.5%
110.5%

. . .

17.4%
0.4%

Footnotes

The source must be identified when secondary data are used in a table. No reference is made to the footnote in the table, but the footnote is typed one and one-half spaces below the line at the bottom of the table. The word *SOURCE* is typed in all capital letters and is indented five spaces from the left edge of the table. The footnote must not extend beyond the width of the table. The carryover lines are started at the left edge of a table.

The data in the footnote should be arranged according to the instructions in an acceptable reference manual.

Either superior letters ($^{a,\ b}$) or asterisks (*, **) are used in the table and in the footnote when referring to a specific part of a table. Notes referring to specific parts of a table are typed one and one-half spaces below the source reference:

SOURCE: U.S. Department of Commerce, Bureau of the Census, Census of Agriculture: 1978, vol. 1, part 10, State and County Data (Washington, D.C.: Government Printing Office, 1981), pp. 263-64.

*Percentages are rounded to the nearest whole number.

Format

The format of the table should be consistent with the complexity of the data to be presented. Some data may be presented in a simple unruled table and other data may require the use of a ruled table with several braced headings.

296
Secretarial
Procedures:
Office
Administration and
Automated Systems

TABLE 1

AVERAGE YEARLY EXPENDITURES OF 5,000 UNDERGRADUATE
STUDENTS AT EXCELSIOR UNIVERSITY
1984

Expenditure	Amount	Percentage of Total*
Supplies	$ 200	2.3
Books	300	3.4
Food	1,500	17.0
Housing	1,800	20.5
Personal	2,000	22.7
Tuition	3,000	34.1
Totals	$8,800	100.0

*Percentages are rounded to the nearest tenth.

FIGURE 13-1. Unruled table.

Unruled Tables

Both horizontal and vertical rules may be omitted when the table is simple and uncrowded. When rules are not used, the table may appear as shown in figure 13-1.

Observe that the column headings are underlined, a line is drawn immediately after the last figures in the amount and percentage columns, and a one-inch line separates the footnote from the body of the table.

Ruled Tables

When several types of data are presented in a table, the appearance may be improved and the information may be easier to read if rules are used. All or none of the tables in a report should be ruled.

The data presented in the previous table could have been presented in a table with horizontal rules, as shown in figure 13-2. Observe the following about the rules, spacing and headings:

TABLE 1

AVERAGE YEARLY EXPENDITURES OF 5,000 UNDERGRADUATE
STUDENTS AT EXCELSIOR UNIVERSITY
1984

Expenditure	Amount	Percentage of Total*
Supplies	$ 200	2.3
Books	300	3.4
Food	1,500	17.0
Housing	1,800	20.5
Personal	2,000	22.7
Tuition	3,000	34.1
Totals	$8,800	100.0

*Percentages are rounded to the nearest tenth.

FIGURE 13-2. Table with horizontal rules.

Horizontal Rules

A double rule is used before the column headings; single rules are used elsewhere. Lines begin and end with the longest items in the left- and right-hand columns.

Vertical Spacing

Single spacing is used before and double spacing is used after the horizontal lines, except one and one-half spacing is used before the footnote. Items in the table are single or double spaced.

Column Headings

Headings are centered over the longest item in the column. The last item in all headings is placed on the same line. The first letter only is capitalized.

298
Secretarial
Procedures:
Office
Administration and
Automated Systems

Boxed Tables

The columns in boxed tables are separated by vertical lines, but vertical lines are not used along the sides of the table. To allow for the vertical rules, leave at least two spaces at either end of the longest line in each column. The vertical rules are made by hand by using black ink. Obviously, the rules must be straight and evenly spaced between the columns. Horizontal rules are extended the same number of spaces on either side of the table as the number left between the vertical rules and the column, as indicated in the following:

Catalog Number	Description	Amount Sold	Percentage of Total

A boxed table may have one or more braced headings. Be sure headings are centered above the columns to which they apply. The same vertical spacing should be used before and after the braced headings as is used with other column headings. The stub heading should be centered between the double horizontal rule at the top of the table and the single rule following the headings.

Observe in the illustrations below that vertical lines may be used between some but not all of the columns. Rules are important for ease of reading when the data in the columns are extremely close together.

Appliances Owned	Respondents	
	Males	Females

District	Quarterly Earnings		Total
	First	Second	

Boxed headings may be typed vertically, if necessary, to save space. They should be typed so that they may be read up from the bottom of the page. When more than one line is needed in the boxed heading, the lines should be single spaced, as shown in the following illustration:

Grades Earned	Major							
	Accounting		Business Education		Management		Marketing	
	No.	Per-cent	No.	Per-cent	No.	Per-cent	No.	Per-cent
A	5	10	7	15	8	30	6	12

Wide Tables

If a full-page table is too large for the page in a study being typewritten in pica type but can be kept within the margins if elite type is used, you may use elite type for the table as long as no other typing appears on the page.

When a table is too wide for the page, the paper should be placed in the typewriter sideways and the table typed so that the table title and number are at the binding side of the page. The table must not extend into the margins and no text should be typed on a page containing a broadside table.

Continued Tables

The second and succeeding pages of a table that is continued should begin with the word *TABLE,* in capital letters, and the number followed by the word *Continued* in parentheses with only the first letter capitalized:

TABLE 5 (Continued)

The heading should be centered over the table and should be followed by a double rule and the column headings.

Charts

All illustrations, other than tables, have the following common features:

- The entire chart is framed.
- The title is placed at the bottom of the chart.

300
Secretarial
Procedures:
Office
Administration and
Automated Systems

- A horizontal line separates the data portion of the chart and the title.

- The title is preceded by the word *Chart* or *Figure* and an Arabic numeral.

- The title is single spaced.

- The charts are numbered consecutively throughout the paper.

- The first letter of the first word in the title and all proper nouns are capitalized.

- The carryover lines are started at the point where the first line begins.

- The secondary source reference is single spaced and typed a double space below the title.

```
Chart 1.   Consumer credit in the United States
           in 1982.

Source:    New York Times Almanac, 1983, p. 90.
```

Pie Charts

The pie chart, sometimes called a circle chart, is a circular illustration that can be used to effectively compare the percentages of the variables that comprise the whole. For example, a pie chart may be used to show the total number of students enrolled at a university, as well as the percentage of that number in each of the classes. Or it may show the total revenue of a company and the percentage generated by the different divisions. Pie charts are easy to read; therefore, they are useful in written reports as well as in oral presentations of a report if they can be enlarged or projected on a screen.

When preparing a pie chart, you should consider the following:

- The entire pie represents the whole of something; therefore, the segments that comprise the whole must be presented in percentage form and the total of the segments must equal 100 percent.

- A good rule to follow is to begin the largest segment at the 12 o'clock position and present the other segments in descending order of magnitude, moving in a clockwise direction. However, another sequence may sometimes be more logical. For example, the divisions of a company may be shown in numerical order. In other instances, the segments may be appropriately arranged in a time sequence.

- The size of each segment must be accurate. If you don't use a protractor, draw the rough copy of the pie on graph paper, divide the circle into quarters and then divide each quarter into halves. You will now have eight equal segments with each representing 12½ percent of the whole

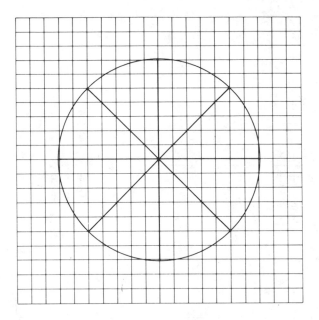

FIGURE 13-3. Pie chart drawn on graph paper.

pie, as shown in figure 13-3. The smaller slices enable you to allot the correct amount of space for each item.

- The whole pie should not have more than six segments so that the reader may easily identify all parts.

- The segments of the pie must be identified. The captions should be typed horizontally. If space permits, place the captions inside the segments; otherwise, place some or all of the captions outside the circle.

- The total quantity represented by the segments of the pie must be included in the chart.

A simple pie chart is illustrated in figure 13-4.

Shading, coloring, and crosshatching are often used to differentiate the various segments. The segment may be moved slightly away from the remainder of the pie to highlight it, as shown in figure 13-5.

Bar Charts

The bar chart is made up of a series of vertical or horizontal bars used to show data according to the relative size or importance of each item.

When preparing any type of bar chart, you should consider the following:

- The bars must be labeled.

- The bars should be the same width.

- The quantity scale must be labeled.

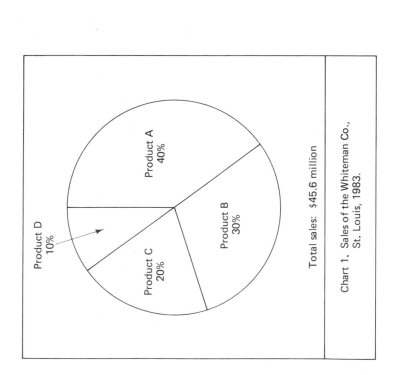

Materials
50%

Overhead
21%

Labor
29%

Total cost: $1,450,000

Chart 2. Production costs of the
E. E. Whinney Company,
Cincinnati, in 1983.

FIGURE 13-5. Pie chart with one segment removed.

Product A
40%

Product B
30%

Product C
20%

Product D
10%

Total sales: $45.6 million

Chart 1. Sales of the Whiteman Co.,
St. Louis, 1983.

FIGURE 13-4. Simple pie chart.

- The quantity scale must begin at zero.

- The quantity intervals must be of equal magnitude and go only as high as needed to record the data.

A simple bar chart is shown in figure 13-6.

The bars may be divided into sections representing the different factors of which they are comprised. When this is done, the factors must be presented in the same order in each bar. The segments of the bars may be colored or striped in different ways to indicate the various types of data represented. The segments must be identified. The bar should not have more than six segments.

A subdivided bar chart is shown in figure 13-7.

A multiple bar chart can be used to compare two or three different kinds of quantities in one chart. As with the segmented bars, you may use colors or stripes to indicate the different types of data.   You must include somewhere in the chart a legend identifying the different bars.

A multiple bar chart showing the comparison of three items is illustrated in figure 13-8.

Line Charts

Line charts are particularly valuable in showing the trend of one or more factors. For example, the line chart can be used effectively to show the sales over a period of months, quarters, or years.

When preparing the line chart, you should consider the following:

- The scale intervals must be equal.

- The time periods must be equal.

- The scale values and the time periods should be clearly indicated.

- The chart must have a zero point of origin; however, when data to be plotted have high values, you may start at zero and show a scale break.

- A legend must be given when more than one line is shown in the chart. Different colors or types of lines (---, —, ...) may be used to indicate the types of data shown.

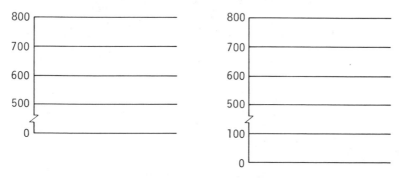

A line graph showing two trend lines is illustrated in figure 13-9.

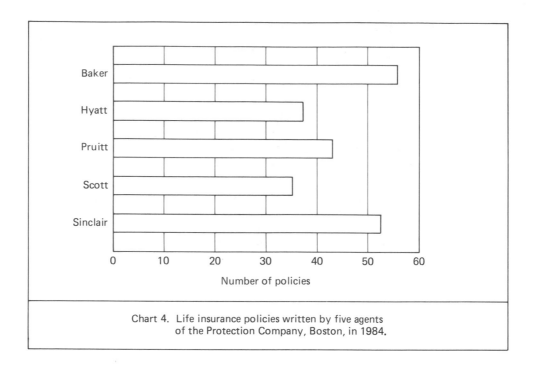

Chart 4. Life insurance policies written by five agents
of the Protection Company, Boston, in 1984.

FIGURE 13-6. Simple bar chart.

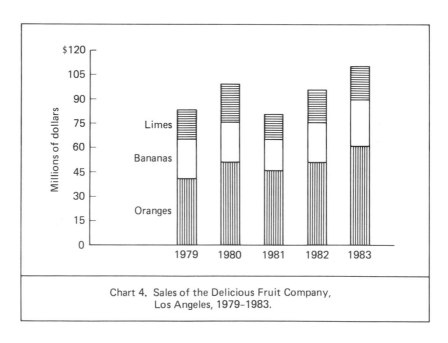

Chart 4. Sales of the Delicious Fruit Company,
Los Angeles, 1979–1983.

FIGURE 13-7. Subdivided bar chart.

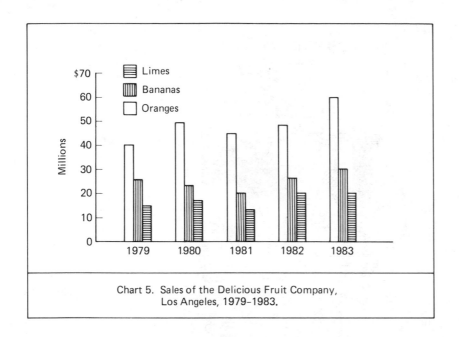

Chart 5. Sales of the Delicious Fruit Company,
Los Angeles, 1979-1983.

FIGURE 13-8. Multiple bar chart.

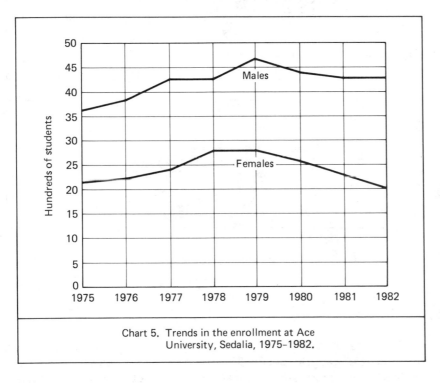

Chart 5. Trends in the enrollment at Ace
University, Sedalia, 1975-1982.

FIGURE 13-9. Line graph.

306
Secretarial
Procedures:
Office
Administration and
Automated Systems

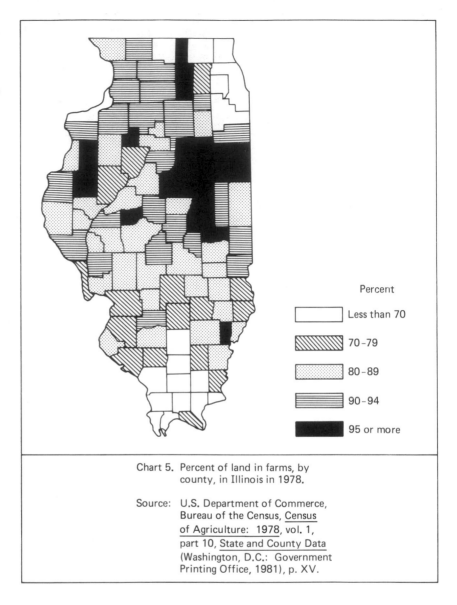

Chart 5. Percent of land in farms, by
county, in Illinois in 1978.

Source: U.S. Department of Commerce,
Bureau of the Census, Census
of Agriculture: 1978, vol. 1,
part 10, State and County Data
(Washington, D.C.: Government
Printing Office, 1981), p. XV.

FIGURE 13-10. Map.

Maps

Maps may be used to communicate quantitative information that is to
be compared geographically. The geographical areas must be clearly
outlined. Color, crosshatching, shading, or some other graphic technique,
along with a legend, must be used to explain the quantitative meanings.

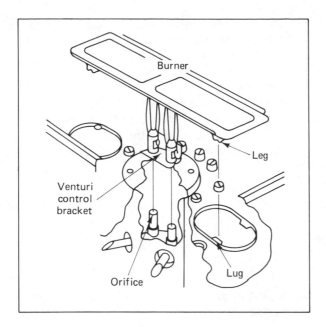

FIGURE 13-11. Exhibit.

The entire map should be enclosed and the title and source placed at the bottom, as shown in figure 13-10.

Exhibits

Exhibits are illustrations used to explain or clarify the text of the report. They are frequently included in highly technical reports. Many reports prepared to explain the use of equipment include exhibits with the various parts clearly identified.

A check, letter, form, or other document included in the report is considered an exhibit. Since exhibits vary widely, no specific format is required; however, they must be numbered and referred to in the text. The number may be placed at the top or bottom of the exhibit and is usually not placed within the frame enclosing the exhibit.

An exhibit is shown in figure 13-11.

Placement of Illustrations

An illustration must be introduced, presented, and interpreted. The illustration must be introduced before it is presented. Ideally, the illustration should be presented immediately after the introduction and then be followed by the interpretation; however, the exact placement of the illus-

308
Secretarial
Procedures:
Office
Administration and
Automated Systems

tration on the page depends on the size of the illustration and the space available on the page. If space does not permit the illustration to be placed on the page on which it is introduced but some space is available on the page, the interpretation may follow the introduction and the illustration may be placed on the following page. Everything relating to an illustration must be included in the report before another illustration is introduced.

The introduction to an illustration should emphasize what the reader may expect to find when referring to the illustration. The number of the illustration should be included but should be given a secondary position in the introduction:

Correct: The ratings assigned to three car rental agencies are shown in Table 2.

Incorrect: Table 2 shows the ratings assigned to three car rental agencies.

An acceptable introduction, presentation, and interpretation section of a report is illustrated in figure 13-12.

The charges for rental of full-size cars by the Highland Company in September 1983 are shown in Table 1.

TABLE 1

CHARGES FOR RENTAL OF FULL-SIZE CARS AS QUOTED
BY THREE CAR RENTAL AGENCIES
SEPTEMBER 10, 1983

Agency	Daily rate	Mileage rate	Daily rate plus mileage charge*
Wilson	$28.50	None	$28.50
O'Hern	29.00	$0.10	36.50
Simmons	30.00	0.15	41.25

*Assumed the car is to be driven 75 miles.

The charges for rental are $28.50 for the Wilson cars, $36.50 for the O'Hern cars, and $41.25 for the Simmons cars.

FIGURE 13-12. Introduction, presentation, and interpretation section.

Margins

A margin of at least one inch must be left on all four sides of all pages. If the report is to be stapled or bound at the left, the left margin should be one and one-half inches.

The first page of every chapter or other major division of the paper should have a two-inch top margin. Although a bottom margin of one inch is desired on the pages of the text, except the last page of a chapter, you should have at least two lines of a paragraph on a page.

Indentions

Paragraphs of double-spaced reports are usually indented five spaces. Paragraphs of single-spaced reports do not need to be indented.

Spacing

Although lengthy reports may sometimes be single spaced to reduce reproduction and distribution costs, either double or one and one-half spacing is normally used for the text. Double spacing is always used between paragraphs.

Footnotes

A one and one-half inch line should be preceded by a single space and followed by a double space. The first line of each footnote should be indented the same number of spaces as the paragraphs. The following lines should begin even with the margin. Use single spacing for the footnotes and double spacing between the footnotes, as shown below:

---

[1]Craig Zarley, "Making Mailing Lists More Personal, "Personal Computing, July 1983, pp. 85-93.

[2]David Pomerant, "Electronic Mail: A New Medium for the Message," Today's Office, August 1982, pp. 41-47.

[3]S. Vincent Wilking, "Your Mailroom Is A Business: Why Not Run It Like One?" The Office, April 1983, pp. 56-58.

310
Secretarial
Procedures:
Office
Administration and
Automated Systems

Page Numbers

The title page is not numbered, but the page is counted in the pagination. The numbers for the other preliminary pages are centered one-half inch from the bottom of the page. Small Roman numerals are used for the preliminary pages; Arabic numerals are used for all other pages. Since the title page counts as page i, the numbering of the preliminary pages begins with ii.

The number for the first page of each major division of the text, the appendix, and the bibliography is centered and typed one-half inch from the bottom of the page. The numbers of other pages are typed at the right margin on line four from the top of the page. The first line of the text is typed on line seven.

Major Headings

Each new chapter and all preliminary and supplementary sections should be started on a new page. The heading should be centered and typed in all capital letters on the 13th line from the top of the page.

If the paper is divided into chapters, the word *CHAPTER* and the number appear alone on the 13th line and triple spacing is used between it and the chapter title, which is also centered and typed in all capitals. When the word *CHAPTER* is not used, the title of the section is typed on the 13th line. No punctuation is used at the end of the line. If the title is more than five inches, use more than one line. Use double spacing and type the lines in inverted pyramid form. Triple spacing is used between the major heading and the text or the first entry of a list, such as the table of contents.

Subheadings

The first letter of major words in all subheadings is capitalized and all subheadings are underlined. Centered headings of more than five inches should be typed on more than one line. The lines should be single spaced and typed in inverted pyramid form.

Side headings that are longer than half the line of writing should be divided, and the carryover lines should be single spaced and started at the left margin.

No punctuation is used after centered and side headings. Paragraph headings end with a period. Triple spacing is used before and double spacing is used after all subheadings, except paragraph subheadings.

A page involving major, centered, side, and paragraph headings, as well as a footnote, is shown in figure 13-13.

MAJOR HEADING

XXXXXXXXXXXXXXXXXXXXXXXXXXXXXXXXXXXXXXXXXXXXXXXXXXXXXXXXXXXXXXXX
XXXXXXXXXXXXXXXXXXXXXXXXXXXXXXXXXXXXXXXXXXXXXXXXXXXXXXXXXXXXXXXX
XXXXXXXXXXXXXXXXXXXXXXXXXXXXXXXXXXXXXXXXX.

Centered Heading

XXXXXXXXXXXXXXXXXXXXXXXXXXXXXXXXXXXXXXXXXXXXXXXXXXXXXXXXXXXXXXXX
XXXXXXXXXXXXXXXXXXXXXXXXXXXXXXXXXXXXXXXXXXXXXXXXXXXXXXXXXXXXXXXX
XXXXXXXXXXXXXXXXXXXXXXXXXXXXXXXXXXXXXXXXXXXXXXXXXXXXXXXXXXXXXXXX
XXXXXXXXXXXXXXXXXXXXXXXXXXXXXXXXXXXXXXXXXXXXXXXXXXXXXXXXXXXXXXXX
XXXXXXXXXXXXXXXXXXXXX.

Side Heading

XXXXXXXXXXXXXXXXXXXXXXXXXXXXXXXXXXXXXXXXXXXXXXXXXXXXXXXXXXXXXXXX
XXXXXXXXXXXXXXXXXXXXXXXXXXXXXXXXXXXXXXXXXXXXXXXXXXXXXXXXXXXXXXXX
XXXXXXXXXXXXXXXXXXXXXXXXXXXXXXXXXX.

Paragraph Heading. XXXXXXXXXXXXXXXXXXXXXXXXXXXXXXXXXXXXXXXXXXXXX
XXXXXXXXXXXXXXXXXXXXXXXXXXXXXXXXXXXXXXXXXXXXXXXXXXXXXXXXXXXXXXXX
XXXXXXXXXXXXXXXXXXXXXXXXXXXXXXXXXXXXXXXXXXXXXXXXXXXX.

Paragraph Heading. XXXXXXXXXXXXXXXXXXXXXXXXXXXXXXXXXXXXXXXXXXXXX
XXXXXXXXXXXXXXXXXXXXXXXXXXXXXXXXXXXXXXXXXXXXXXXXXXXXXXXXXXXXXXXX
XXXXXXXXXXXXXXXXXXXXXXXXXXXXXXXXXXXXXXXXXXXXXXXXXXXXXXXXXXXXXXXX
XXXXXXXXXXXXXXXXXXXXXXXXXXXXXXXXXXXXXXXXXXXXXXXXXXXXXXXXXXXXXXXX

---

[1]XXXXXXXXXXXXXXXXXXXXXXXXXXXXXXXXXXXXXXXXXXXXXXXXXXXXXXXXXXXXXX
XXXXXXXXXXXXXXXXXXXXXXXXXXXXXXXXXXXXXXXXXXXXXXXXXXXXXXXXXXXXXXXX
XXXXXXXXXXXXXXXXXXXXXXX.

FIGURE 13-13. Text page format.

312
Secretarial
Procedures:
Office
Administration and
Automated Systems

```
WHAT SKILLS SHOULD BE TAUGHT IN A MANAGEMENT

   TRAINING PROGRAM AT ROLAND ENTERPRISES?




              Prepared
                for
       Mr. James Cohn, President




            August 15, 1984

             Prepared by
             Ruth Petersen
    Director of Research and Development
```

FIGURE 13-14. Title page.

PRELIMINARY PAGES

A formal report may have several pages of front matter. These pages may include the title page, letter of transmittal, table of contents, list of illustrations, and abstract or summary.

Title Page

Although the data on the title page may be arranged in various ways, the page is normally attractive when the title of the report is centered on line 13 from the top of the page and typed in all capital letters. When the title is more than five inches long, it should be divided logically and placed on more than one line. The lines should be double spaced and typed in inverted pyramid form, as shown in figure 13-14.

The author identification (name and title) and date may be treated as a block and typed so that 13 lines are left in the margin at the bottom of the page. Remember that if the report is to be bound at the left, the items typed on the title page, as well as the other pages of the report, must be centered over the line of writing rather than the center of the sheet of paper.

Table of Contents

The table of contents contains a list of the parts of the report, except the title page. The heading should be typed in all capital letters, centered over the line of writing, and placed on line 13 from the top of the page. The side margins used for the table of contents page are the same as those used for the other pages of the report.

Double space after the title and type the word *Page* to end at the right margin. The first entry should be started at the left margin a double space below the line on which *Page* is typed. Double spacing should be used before and after all main headings and before and after each group of subheadings. Single or double spacing may be used between the individual subheadings.

The titles of main sections of the paper should be typed in all capital letters. The subheadings are typed in lowercase letters with the first letter of each main word capitalized. The titles should be followed by spaced leader periods. The leaders must be aligned vertically and at least one blank space must precede the leaders on all lines. Two or three spaces should be left between the last leader in a line and the number of the page.

An acceptable table of contents is illustrated in figure 13-15.

List of Illustrations

When illustrations have been included in the report, they may be listed either at the bottom of the table of contents or on a separate page as shown in figure 13-16.

When tables, charts or figures, and exhibits are included in the report, they are numbered and listed separately.

The format for the list of illustrations should be essentially the same as that used for the table of contents. The titles of the illustrations should be single spaced and listed exactly as they appear in the report. Carryover lines should be indented two or three spaces. Double spacing should be used between the titles.

Letter of Transmittal

A letter of transmittal is often used for long formal reports and, as the name suggests, is used to transmit the report to the organization or person for whom the report was prepared.

TABLE OF CONTENTS

Page

LETTER OF TRANSMITTAL   ii

SUMMARY AND CONCLUSIONS   iii

I. INTRODUCTION   1

    Problem   2

    Scope   3

    Methods   4

II. COMPARISON OF CAR RENTAL AGENCIES   7

    Charges for rental   7

    Condition of cars   8

    Courtesy of personnel   9

    Selection of cars   10

APPENDIX   12

FIGURE 13-15. Table of contents page.

LIST OF ILLUSTRATIONS

Page

1. Information Appropriate for Inclusion in a Letter
    that Accompanies a Job Application Packet 10

2. Specific Information Appropriate for Inclusion in
    a Resume 13

3. Specific Information Appropriate for Inclusion in
    a Job Application Packet 16

FIGURE 13-16. List of illustrations page.

The transmittal letter is typed as an ordinary business letter. The letter may be sent as a separate item or included as part of the report. When the letter is part of a report bound at the left, the left margin must be one-half inch wider than the right margin.

Summary

A summary (also referred to as a synopsis or an abstract) may be given in the preliminary section to give the reader a concise overview of the important points of the report. The title of the summary page should be centered, typed in all capital letters, and placed on line 13 from the top of the page. The margins should be the same as those used for the text of the report. Either single or double spacing may be used. When included in the preliminary section, the summary immediately precedes the first page of the text of the report.

SUPPLEMENTARY SECTIONS

Appendix

Some material may need to be included in the report but does not belong in the text. Detailed supporting data, questionnaires, and letters are examples of items that may need to be included in an appendix at the end of the report. If only one item is included, the word *APPENDIX* should be centered, typed in all capital letters, and placed at least an inch from the top of the page. When more than one item is included, each item should be lettered, such as *APPENDIX A, APPENDIX B,* and so forth.

The appendix follows the text of the report and may precede or follow the bibliography. Each page of the appendix is numbered.

Bibliography

When the data for a report are obtained from secondary sources, the references should be included in the bibliography. A report based entirely on primary data, as most business reports are, does not have a bibliography.

The word *BIBLIOGRAPHY* should be centered, typed in all capital letters, and placed on line 13 of the page. Triple spacing is used before the first entry. Single space each reference, but double space between entries. Begin the first line of each reference at the left margin and indent the following lines five spaces, as shown in figure 13-17.

```
                          BIBLIOGRAPHY


Pomerant, David.  "Electronic Mail:  A New Medium for the Message."  Today's
     Office, August 1982, pp. 41-47.

Wilking, S. Vincent.  "Your Mailroom Is A Business:  Why Not Run It Like One?"
     The Office, April 1983, pp. 56-58.

Zarley, Craig.  "Making Mailing Lists More Personal."  Personal Computing,
     July 1983, pp. 85-93.
```

FIGURE 13-17. Bibliography page.

INFORMAL REPORTS

Informal reports are usually written in letter or memorandum style, but they may be written in manuscript form.

Letter Reports

As the name implies, a letter report is a report written in letter form. Although no rule dictates the maximum length of letter reports, they are generally not more than a few pages. A letter report may be used to present information to people outside the company or organization; a memorandum is normally used to disseminate information internally. A letter report might be used to provide information concerning a product or service or to convey to the members of a civic group information concerning a project.

Any standard business letter format may be used, and the report is typed on letterhead. The report often has a subject line, and headings may be used to separate the sections of the report. When data need to be presented in columns, informal spot tables are usually used. Spot tables do not have titles, are not numbered, and are introduced by a sentence ending with a colon. A double space should precede and follow the table.

A spot table may be introduced and presented in the following way:

The test scores and typing speeds of the three applicants are as follows:

Applicants	Test Scores	Typing Speeds
Arlene Cole	99	75
Joyce Higgins	92	80
Wayne Rollins	95	70

Memorandum Reports

The memorandum format is used extensively to informally transmit information within an organization. Most companies have standardized interoffice memorandum stationery that has *date, to, from,* and *subject* headings printed on it.

Except in large organizations, courtesy titles are usually omitted and the names of the writer and recipient are not followed by position titles.

Three or four blank lines should be left after the last line of the heading. The paragraphs should be single spaced. Double spacing should be used before and after centered or side headings and between paragraphs.

Memorandums never have a salutation or complimentary close and usually do not have a signature line. The writer's initials may precede the typist's initials in the reference section. Sometimes, however, the writer's initials are omitted or are typed at the center or slightly to the right of the center four lines below the message. The writer may initial the memorandum in the space above the typed initials or beside the name in the "From" section of the heading. Routine memorandums often are not initialed.

When memorandums are more than one page, the additional pages should begin with appropriate identification typed on line seven from the top of the page and should be followed by three or four blank lines. The following are examples of appropriate headings for the second page of a memorandum:

Memorandum	2	March 10, 1984
Sales Report for Fairfax District	2	March 10, 1984

A one-page memorandum containing headings and tabulated material is shown in figure 13-18.

```
                    M E M O R A N D U M


TO:       Bettie Smith                  DATE:  March 15, 1984

FROM:     John Hildebrand

SUBJECT:  Annual Banquet
```

As you asked during our meeting on March 1, I collected information concerning arrangements for the annual banquet to be held on July 17.

Coachlight Inn, Fireside Lounge, and Maxine's Gourmet House were considered because they are the only restaurants in Hillside that have rooms large enough for a banquet for 200. I visited with the banquet manager at each restaurant on March 13.

Parking

All three restaurants have adequate free parking space for 150 cars. Only Maxine's Gourmet House has valet parking available.

Seating

The banquet room at Maxine's Gourmet House is large enough to accommodate a head table for 10 and 20 round tables for 10 each. A head table for 10 and four long tables for 50 each would be used at Coachlight Inn and Fireside Lounge.

Cost

The managers quoted prices for meals consisting of an appetizer, lettuce or frozen fruit salad, twice-baked potato, steamed broccoli, and three different entrees. Dessert (pie or sherbet) and soft drinks are included in the prices quoted.

Restaurant	Fillet Steak (12 oz.)	Prime Rib (10 oz.)	Baked Salmon (9 oz.)
Coachlight Inn	$17.50	$16.00	$14.00
Fireside Lounge	18.00	16.50	13.00
Maxine's Gourmet House	18.00	16.50	13.00

Recommendation

Based on the desirable seating arrangement, valet parking option, and competitive prices, I recommend that the banquet be held at Maxine's Gourmet House.

FIGURE 13-18. Memorandum report.

Reports to be used within the organization may be typed in manuscript form. The format for this type of report may be the same as that used for formal reports, except the preliminary parts are not included. A cover letter or memorandum is normally used to transmit this type of report.

———————————————— Summary ————————————————

An interesting and important aspect of a secretary's job can be assisting the executive in collecting, analyzing, organizing, and presenting data in an acceptable report format. The secretary may need to decide whether the data in the report should be presented in textual form or whether illustrations such as tables, graphs, charts, exhibits, and maps can be used to make the data more easily understood by the reader. She must have a thorough understanding of all types of graphic aids to select the most appropriate type for each situation.

The secretary is usually totally responsible for making sure each graphic aid is prepared in an acceptable format and that the entire report is constructed so that it will make a favorable impression on the reader.

———————————————— Questions ————————————————

1. What tasks may the secretary logically be expected to perform in preparing a long formal report?

2. What criteria should be used in deciding whether to include graphic aids in a report?

3. What is meant by the statement, "Illustrations should be self-explanatory"?

4. What questions should be asked to determine whether the caption of a graphic aid is complete?

5. Discuss what should be considered in determining the size of a graphic aid.

6. Explain the difference between general, special purpose, and spot tables.

7. When should a table be numbered?

8. Discuss the two arrangements that may be used for table titles.

9. List the things that should be remembered when dollar amounts are used in a table.

10. Define table stubs.

320
Secretarial
Procedures:
Office
Administration and
Automated Systems

11. List techniques that may be used when typing the table stub to aid the reader in interpreting the data.

12. Are column heads underlined? Explain.

13. Must the percent symbol always be used with each percentage included in the table? Explain.

14. In what order should the data in the footnote to a graphic aid be arranged?

15. Explain braced headings and how they are typed.

16. If a six-inch line of writing is being used for the report and seven inches are needed for the column headings and the spaces between the columns, what should be done?

17. Discuss the considerations that are unique to preparing a pie chart.

18. List four ways of differentiating the various segments of a pie chart.

19. For what type of data is the line chart especially effective?

20. Explain what is meant by the zero point of origin on a line graph.

21. Discuss the introduction, presentation, and interpretation of a graphic aid in a report.

22. Write an interpretation of the pie chart shown in figure 13-4.

23. Write an introduction to the line graph shown in figure 13-9.

24. List the preliminary pages that may be included in a report.

25. What material is often found in the supplementary section of a report?

26. When a memorandum does not have a signature line, how may the writer indicate he or she has seen and approved the typewritten memorandum?

———————————————— Projects ————————————————

1. Assume that a report included secondary data from the following sources:

   Communication in Business, Second Edition, by S. Bernard Rosenblatt, T. Richard Cheatham, and James T. Watt, Copyright 1982, Prentice-Hall, Inc., Englewood Cliffs, New Jersey, pages 149–155

   Business Communication, by Berle Haggblade, West Publishing Company, St. Paul, Minnesota, Copyright 1982, pages 100–102

   "Copiers: Toning Up For the Eighties," by Brian J. Dolley, *Today's Office,* January 1983, Volume 17, Number 8, pages 55–57

"New Directions in Telecommunications," by Lou Pilla, *Management World,* March 1982, Volume 11, Number 3, pages 11–12

"Hewlett-Packard Adds New Versions to Its Line of Business Computers," *The Wall Street Journal,* May 25, 1983, Volume LXIII, Number 158, page 50

Use a reference manual suggested by your instructor and prepare the entries in correct footnote form. Prepare a bibliography.

2. The following sales were made by five sales representatives of the Redd Corporation during October 1983:

Christensen—$25,550.00

Donaldson—$117,225.00

Lawrence—$79,800.50

Alwell—$66,750.25

Moore—$33,350.75

Prepare a table and a pie chart according to the guidelines discussed in this chapter. Use dollar amounts and percentages in each of the graphic aids.

3. Prepare a line graph showing the trend in the average monthly salary earned by secretaries in West Plains during the following five-year period:

1979—$925

1980—$950

1981—$1,000

1982—$1,100

1983—$1,225

4. Four sales representatives of the Wheaton Corporation sold the following number of units of Product A during each of the following three years:

	1981	1982	1983
Osborne	25	33	35
Loesch	29	27	38
Mallot	32	39	42
Boehmer	27	40	35

Prepare a bar chart and a segmented bar chart to correctly show the sales data.

322
Secretarial
Procedures:
Office
Administration and
Automated Systems

——————————————— Cases ———————————————

1. Mr. Haley uses only tables in his reports. Ann, his secretary, believes that the data could frequently be presented more effectively by using a pie chart or a line graph. Should Ann discuss her ideas with Mr. Haley?

2. Each time Helen's boss has her include a graphic aid in a report, he asks her to include all of the data in the textual interpretation. Helen believes that only the highlights of the graphic aid should be included in the text. What action should Helen take?

3. Joan spends a considerable amount of time making sure that each section in the pie charts she prepares is precisely the correct size. Ruth believes that the sections need to be only accurate enough to present the desired picture. With whom do you agree?

4. Assume that you followed the guidelines presented in this chapter when you prepared your first report for your boss. When you presented the report to your boss, he suggested that you make several format changes. What should have been your reaction? How can similar situations be avoided?

PART VI

CHAPTER 14

Reference Material

A tremendous amount of information is processed in the typical business office. Although much of the information needed for the business's day-to-day operation is available within the company, sometimes the information must be obtained from other sources. The library is often a logical source to:

- Obtain statistics or data needed for a report.
- Collect information for a presentation.
- Obtain financial information about a company or industry.
- Check names, spellings, and titles of individuals.
- Learn the addresses of companies.
- Obtain or verify biographical data about individuals.
- Identify the individuals with specific responsibilities within a company.
- Stay abreast of the developments in a particular field or area.
- Learn where books, directories, pamphlets, and other materials may be obtained.

A secretary's responsibilities in the area of library research depend on the type of business and the people for whom she is working and to a large extent on her skills in using the library. To effectively and efficiently use the library, you must thoroughly understand the types of resources available, their location, and the procedures to locate them.

326
Secretarial
Procedures:
Office
Administration and
Automated Systems

TYPES OF LIBRARIES

Many businesses and organizations, both large and small, have libraries stocked with books and references pertinent to the particular business, industry, or profession. The libraries frequently are staffed by well-qualified personnel who can perform much of the needed research. In some organizations, however, the library is primarily a depository of books and other reference material. If the organization for which you work has a library, become thoroughly familiar with the material stored in it and the services provided.

The public libraries, as well as some university libraries, may be used to obtain material that is not available in your organization's library. When you need the answer to a question that does not involve an extensive amount of research, you usually can obtain the answer by calling the reference librarian in a public library. If a considerable amount of information is involved and several resources need to be searched, you should go to the library rather than call.

Special libraries usually are limited by subject and are maintained for a particular group. Colleges and universities and large public libraries often have departmental collections that concentrate on one particular subject or area, such as business. Libraries often are maintained by departments and agencies at the different governmental levels. Libraries are also maintained by some nonprofit organizations, such as business, trade, and professional associations.

The *Directory of Special Libraries and Information Centers,* published by the Gale Research Company, Detroit, is an excellent reference to consult should you need to identify a source from which to obtain specialized information.

Private and special libraries may not be open to the public; however, arrangements often can be made to borrow material through the interlibrary loan department of a public library.

When you are not familiar with a particular library you need to use, start by reading brochures or guides that may be available to explain the use of the library and the services offered.

Diagrams showing the different sections of the library usually are available in printed form or are posted near the entrance. By strolling through the library, you can observe the size, placement, and features of the different sections and meet and talk with some of the library personnel.

When you cannot find the material you need or it is not available in the library you are using, always ask the librarian for assistance.

The purpose of this section is to help you become familiar with the types of references that can be used to locate information about people, businesses, places, events, and so forth. Therefore, only a few specific references of each type are discussed.

Card Catalog

The card catalog consists of alphabetically filed cards that give information about books and their locations.

The cards are filed by author, title of the publication, and subject. Author cards are filed under the author's surname; title cards, under the first word in the title (not counting articles); and subject cards, under the subject area covered. Since each book is indexed in three ways, you can find a particular book if you know the name of the author, the title, or the subject.

An author card is illustrated in figure 14-1.

Note the following explanation of the information shown on the card:

- "Healy, Charles C." is the name of the author.
- "HF5381 H338" is the call number and tells where the book is located in the library.
- "Career . . . c1982." gives the title of the book; the author's name, this time written in standard order; the place of publication; the name of the publisher; the copyright date.
- "ix . . . indexes" tells that the book has nine pages numbered in Roman numerals and 662 in Arabic numerals. It has illustrations, is 25 centimeters in height, has a bibliography that can be found on pages 611-649, and has indexes.
- "ISBN 0-205-07557-6" is the International Standard Book Number.
- "1. Vocational . . . Title" tells the subject categories under which the book can be found in the card catalog. This book can be found under "Vocational Guidance" and under its title.
- "81-8056" is the Library of Congress number.

The Dewey decimal system of classifying library materials is used by many public and private libraries because every subject upon which anything has been written is included in ten general classes. Each of the major classes is divided into ten parts, each of which can be further

328
Secretarial
Procedures:
Office
Administration and
Automated Systems

```
HF
5381      Healy, Charles C.
H338        Career development: counseling through
          the life stages / Charles C. Healy. --
          Boston, Mass. : Allyn and Bacon, c1982.
          ix, 662 p. : ill. ; 25 cm.
          Bibliography: p. 611-649.
          Includes indexes.

          ISBN 0-205-07557-6



          1. Vocational guidance.   2. Title


                                             81-8056
```

FIGURE 14-1. Catalog card.

subdivided. Many books about business are filed in the social sciences and technology (applied sciences) groups. The social sciences group is subdivided as follows:

300 The social sciences
   310 Statistics
   320 Political science (politics and government)
   330 Economics
   340 Law
   350 Public administration
      Executive branch of government
      Military art and science
   360 Social problems and services; association
   370 Education
   380 Commerce, communication, transportation
   390 Customs, etiquette, folklore

The Library of Congress classification system is an alphabetic system of subject filing. The system has 24 main divisions and numerous subdivisions. Many books on various business subjects may be found in the social sciences classification.

From the user's standpoint, the main difference between the two classification systems is the call numbers. The Dewey system is numerical; the Library of Congress system is alpha-numeric.

The following table illustrates the two systems. The first part of each call number is given.

Book Title	Classification	
	Dewey	Library of Congress
The Amy Vanderbilt Complete Book of Etiquette	395	BJ1853
Legal Secretary's Complete Handbook	651.934	KF319
Economics Explained	330	HB171
The Work Ethic	658.314	HD4905

Indexes

Three approaches may be used to locate articles in periodicals or newspapers. First, you can browse through numerous publications and possibly find the information desired, although this approach is not recommended. Second, when you know that articles concerning a subject have been published in a certain periodical, the indexes of the periodical may be searched; however, this can be a time-consuming process if several issues of the periodical must be searched.

The third approach is to use an index, which is usually the best way to find articles on a particular subject. Indexes provide alphabetical listings of articles by subject and sometimes by author and title. An index can be general in nature, such as the *Readers' Guide to Periodical Literature;* it can relate to a certain publication, such as *The Wall Street Journal Index;* or it can be specialized, such as the *Business Periodicals Index,* and cover periodicals relating to a specific field.

Periodical, magazine, and *journal* all refer to publications that are issued with some regularity, such as weekly, monthly, or quarterly. Although all three terms have essentially the same meaning, *periodical* is frequently used as a general term; *magazine* is used to refer to popular titles; and *journal* is used to refer to scholarly or technical titles.

Periodicals are one of the best sources of current information and often contain articles by various authors on a variety of topics.

The *Business Periodicals Index* is a cumulative index to more than 300 American business periodicals and covers the fields of accounting, advertising, banking and finance, management, marketing, and numerous other aspects of business. The index is extremely useful for locating up-to-date articles concerning business and business-related fields.

Entries in the index are arranged alphabetically by subject and then alphabetically by titles of articles under the subject. An example of an entry in the index is shown in figure 14-2. The article is indexed under the subject of "Secretaries." "Will You be Able to Find a Secretary in 1989?" is the name of the article written by G. W. Heffner. The article appeared on pages 14 through 16 in volume 27 of *Personnel Administration,* which was published in December 1982.

330
Secretarial
Procedures:
Office
Administration and
Automated Systems

Secretaries
See also
Word processing—Employees
Personalized tests tailored for your office. D. Holmquist.
tabs *Pers Adm* 27:12+ N '82
Recruiting
Will you be able to find a secretary in 1989? G. W.
Heffner. *Pers Adm* 27:14-16 D '82

FIGURE 14-2. *Business Periodicals Index* entry. (Copyright © 1983 by The H.W. Wilson Company. Reprinted by permission of the publisher.)

The *Readers' Guide to Periodical Literature* is a useful reference tool to use in locating current articles in nearly 200 periodicals. Although the index is primarily a listing of articles appearing in general magazines, the articles in some business magazines, such as *Business Week, Forbes,* and *Fortune,* are also included.

The index is arranged alphabetically by author and subject. Since many magazine articles are unsigned, the arrangement of entries under a subject heading is alphabetical by title rather than by author. A typical entry is shown in figure 14-3. "Employment" is a subdivision of the subject "Women." "On-the-Job Image Makers: The Big Dos and Don'ts" is the name of the illustrated article that appeared on pages 278 and 279 in volume 80 of *Glamour,* which was published in August 1982.

Most libraries maintain a file of many useful publications—leaflets, booklets, and pamphlets—that are not listed in the indexes for general interest periodicals or those for specific fields. The *Vertical File Index* is published monthly and lists hundreds of these publications. Libraries normally keep these publications in office-type file cabinets and have a subject index of the file.

As shown in figure 14-4, the *Vertical File Index* gives the name of the publication, a brief description of the content, and information concerning where each publication may be obtained.

Newspapers are used extensively as a source of news about current events. Most local newspapers give a concise report of major events and an in-depth coverage of local news items. In addition to the local newspapers, many business people regularly read *The New York Times, The Wall Street Journal,* and other business-oriented newspapers.

In addition to general news events, *The New York Times* comprehensively covers many areas, including business. While *The Wall Street*

```
Women

              Employment
On-the-job  image  makers:  the  big  dos  and  don'ts.
il Glamour 80:278-9 Ag '82
```

FIGURE 14-3. *Readers' Guide to Periodical Literature* entry. (Copyright © 1982 by The H. W. Wilson Company. Reprinted by permission of the publisher.)

Journal covers some general news, it primarily emphasizes national and international business news.

Businesses often subscribe to *The Wall Street Journal* and business magazines. Public and university libraries often subscribe to newspapers published in many of the major cities.

The indexes to the newspapers cover a precise period of time; therefore, to locate a news article, you must know the approximate date of the event. For example, if you were searching for articles concerning the merger of two particular companies, you would need to know the month or year in which the merger took place.

The Wall Street Journal Index is divided into corporate news and general news sections. The names of companies and industries are listed in alphabetical order in the corporate news section. The items in the general news section are listed alphabetically by subject headings. In both sections, the articles under the headings are listed chronologically and the entries contain the same type of information, as shown in figure 14-5.

Note that the headings are in bold-face type and the entries contain a brief annotation and bibliographic information. For example, the first entry under the "Bendix Corp." heading indicates Bendix received an Army contract and the article appeared in column 5 on page 10 in the January 4 issue.

The New York Times Index is issued twice a month, with yearly cumulations. The index consists of bold-face type headings arranged in one alphabetical list by subjects, persons, and organizations. The entries under the heading are arranged chronologically and give a synopsis of the news item and bibliographic information. A letter is placed in parentheses to indicate the length of the article: (S) for articles of less than one-half column; (M) for articles one-half to two columns; and (L) for articles over two columns.

In addition to the information relating to the articles, entries are often cross-referenced as shown in figure 14-6.

Several references that provide information about books which have been published are available at large libraries. If either the title or the author of the book is known, you can find other information about the book.

PERU

Politics and government

Peru's troubled return to democratic government, by James M. Malloy. (1982 Rep no 15 S Am) 11p '82 Am univs field staff Box 150 Hanover N H 03755 $3

The Belaunde government is under increasing economic stress, with political opposition growing proportionally. The response has been creation of a tripartite council that maintains the democratic framework but actually strengthens the executive.

PETROLEUM

Prices

Outlook for world oil prices, prepared by A. David Sandoval & W. Calvin Kilgore. (Stock no 061-003-00260-9) 28p tables figures '82 Supt of docs Gov printing office Washington D C 20402 $4.50 send payment with order.

This paper considers possible trends in the price of world oil on an annual basis from the present through the year 1995 and considers the factors that will influence these trends.

PHOTOENGRAVING

Vocational guidance

Photoengraver (relief printing). (Career summary S-86) 2p '82 Careers Box 136 Largo Fl 33540 65c send payment with order

PHOTOGRAPHY

Handbooks, manuals, etc.

How to take pictures like a pro. (Learn photography ser) 96p col il '82 H.P. bks Box 5367 Tucson Az 85703 $5.95; Canad $7.50

Book gives step-by-step instruction on how to photograph people outdoors or under studio conditions; how to make character studies, glamour shots and candids; how to capture action and movement of athletes, children and pets, or performers on stage; how to improve your landscape and flower photography.

SLR tips & techniques. (Learn photography ser) 96p il col il '82 H.P. bks Box 5367 Tucson Az 85703 $5.95; Canad $7.50

Book explains how the single lens reflex camera and lenses work. It includes information on motion effects, control of depth, use of lenses, flash techniques and closeups.

Processing

Basic guide to b & w darkroom techniques. (Learn photography ser) 94p il col il '82 H.P. bks Box 5367 Tucson Az 85703 $5.95; Canad $7.50

Step-by-step illustrations and explanations show how to process black and white film, how to make a contact sheet and enlarge negatives. The use of sepia and color toning is explained and suggestions are given for selecting the right developer and paper.

Basic guide to creative darkroom techniques (Learn photography ser) 96p il col il '82 H.P. bks Box 5367 Tucson Az 85703 $5.95; Canada $7.50

Book gives directions for achieving texture and grain effects, enlarging methods for diffusion and multiple images, and screen-printing onto fabric.

PHOTOVOLTAIC power generation

Electricity from sunlight: the future of photovoltaics, by Christopher Flavin. (Pa 52) 63p '82 Worldwatch inst 1776 Massachusetts av N W, Washington D C 20036 $2

Solar photovoltaic cells may become one of the most rapidly expanding energy sources—the late twentieth century, according to this study. It reviews the rise of solar cell production from its use in the space program to its spread into over twenty countries. Cost reduction, environmental compatability and uses in developing countries are all discussed as factors in the future growth of the photovoltaics industry

PHYSICALLY handicapped and libraries. See Libraries and the physically handicapped

PICTURE frames and framing

Mounting & framing pictures, by Michael Woods. 96p il '82 Acro pub inc 219 Park av S N Y 10003 $6.95

Starting with methods for making a simple frame, this guide goes on to double mounts, ovals, lining and covering. There are additional sections on restoring old frames, cutting glass and hanging methods.

PILES (disease). See Hemorrhoids

PLASTERERS

Plasterer. (Career summary S-80) 2p '82 Careers Box 135 Largo Fl 33540 65c send payment with order

POLITICAL persecution

Namibia

Detainees' Parents Support committee memorandum on security police abuses of political detainees. 18p '82 Episcopal churchmen for South Africa Room 1005 853 Broadway N Y 10003 $1 send payment with order

Report describes widespread and systematic use being made by security police of assult and torture during interrogation of detainees. It enumerates many of these abuses, and calls for a code of conduct for interrogators and an independent system of monitoring their behavior.

PRINCIPALS, School. See School superintendents and principals

PRINTING, Practical

Vocational guidance

Printing trades, Jobs in the. (Career brief B-83) 7p '82 Careers Box 135 Largo Fl 33540 95c send payment with order

PROBATION officers

Probation officer. (Career summary S-92) 2p '82 Careers Box 135 Largo Fl 33540 65c send payment with order

PRODUCTIVITY. See Labor productivity

PUBLIC relations

Vocational guidance

Public relations director, School. (Career summary S-331) 2p '82 Careers Box 135 Largo Fl 33540 65c send payment with order

PUBLIC services (libraries). See Libraries and readers

PUBLIC works

See also

United States—Public works

RABBIS

Rabbi. (Career brief B-176) 7p '82 Careers Box 135 Largo Fl 33540 95c send payment with order

REFUSE and refuse disposal

See also

Hazardous wastes—Virginia

RETINA

Diseases

Vision Impairment of the later years: macular degeneration, by Irving R. Dickman. (Pam no 610) 28p il '82 Public affairs com 381 Park av S, N Y 10016 50c send payment with order; no stamps

Macular degeneration is caused by damage to the area of central fine vision in the retina of the eye. Pamphlet describes the effects of the disease on the eye, a breakthrough in treatment, rehabilitation for those whose vision is seriously impaired, and self-help groups.

RETIREMENT

Controversy over mandatory retirement policy: pro & con. (Congressional digest v 61 no 11) 32p '82 Congressional digest corp 3231 P st Washington D C 20007 $2.25

Partial contents: The evolution of retirement practices; Action in the Congress; Major provisions of the ADEA; Pros & cons: Should Congress adopt pending measures to prohibit mandatory retirement?

SALES agent

Automobiles—Vocational guidance

Salesperson, Automobile. (Career summary S-82) 2p '82 Careers Box 135 Largo Fl 33540 65c send payment with order

SCHOOL superintendents and principals

Effective principal: a research summary. 40p '82 Nat assn of secondary sch principals 1904 Association dr Reston Va 22091 $4 send payment with order

Summary outlines the skills in program development, management and interpersonal relations needed for an effective principalship. It discusses the role the principal plays in the morale and general climate of the school.

SECRETARIES

Foreign service secretary. (Career brief B-81) 7p '82 Careers Box 135 Largo Fl 33540 95c send payment with order

SENATE (United States). See United States. Congress. Senate

SEX

See also

Girls—Sexual behavior

FIGURE 14-4. *Vertical File Index.* (Copyright © 1983 by The H. W. Wilson Company. Reprinted by permission of the publisher.)

COLLEGES & UNIVERSITIES

College Crunch: To trim faculty, St. Louis University offers to buy out the contracts of about 30 tenured older teachers. (Labor Letter) 1/4-1;5

Harvard students picketed the opening session of a law school course taught by two prominent civil rights attorneys, one black, one white; boycott organized to protest the school's record in recruiting black teachers. 1/6-1;3

Grad schools build prestige with tax institutes for professionals. (Tax Report) 1/12-1;5

Career-oriented courses are chosen by more college students; traditional liberal education loses favor as more students seek specific professional training, not just a broad cultural background. (Business Bulletin) 1/13-1;5

Campus Glitch: Universities in the U.S. are losing ground in computer education; lack of funds leaves schools with too few teachers, inadequate facilities. 1/14-1;1

BENDIX CORP.

Received $5 million Army contract to provide machines to tool 105-mm guns. 1/4-10;5

A Martin Marietta Corp. shareholder sued the firm over its defense against Bendix's takeover offer. 1/11-12;2

Martin Marietta borrowed about $900 million last year to fend off Bendix's takeover attempt; now firm looks for ways to reduce its large debt but shuns 'fire sale' of assets. 1/11-37;4

Received $4.9 million Army contract for classified electronics. 1/17-8;1

Received $3.5 million Air Force contracts to provide weather radar equipment. 1/21-44;6

Bendix Corp. agreed to acquire a 30% stake in Comau S.p.A., a Fiat S.p.A. unit, for $30 million. 1/25-36;6

FIGURE 14-5. Entries from *The Wall Street Journal Index.* (Reprinted by permission of *The Wall Street Journal*, © Dow Jones & Company, Inc., 1983. All rights reserved.)

DATA Processing. See also
Missiles, Ja 21
Misic — Concerts, Ja 16
Oil, Ja 22
Postal Service, Ja 18.23
Robots, Ja 26
Taxation, Ja 28
Weather, Ja 30

Article on word processing programs available for personal computers; illus (M), Ja 18,III,7:1

Apple Computer Inc to introduce its new Lisa computer this spring, which will sell for $10,000; technical characteristics discussed; co will also display Apple IIe, upgraded replacement for its Apple If plus (M), Ja 19,IV,1:3

Xerox Corp introduces new model in its Memorywriter line and telephone hookup that allows electronic typewriters to communicate with one another and with personal computers (S), Ja 19,IV,5:1

Radio Shack Div of Tandy Corp introduces new microcomputer, TRS-80 model 12; characteristics noted (S), Ja 19,IV,5:2

Memorex Corp to market Intel Corp's solid state information storage products directly to users of IBM computers (S), Ja 19,IV5:3

National Science Foundation panel rept warns that there is 'little likelihood' under current conditions that US will lead world in developing and using new 'super computers'; says Amer leadership in field is being seriously undermined by failure to make such computers widely available to scientists and slowdown to develop even more powerful computers (M), Ja 19,IV,6:1

Apple Computer Inc says its Apple Canada Inc unit will sell company's new computer model, Lisa, beginning in April for about $14,000 (Canadian) per basic unit (S), Ja 20,IV,4:4

Eastman Kodak Co announces what it calls 'world's most advanced system yet' for computerized storage of documents on microfilm (S), Ja 20,IV,4:6

FIGURE 14-6. Entry from *The New York Times Index.* (© 1983 by The New York Times Company. Reprinted by permission.)

334
Secretarial
Procedures:
Office
Administration and
Automated Systems

When neither the author nor the title is known, you can use the subject index of the reference to identify the book.

The *Cumulative Book Index* is a worldwide author, title, and subject listing of books published in English. The price, publisher, number of pages, date of publication, and other information is listed for each entry. A directory of publishers is also included.

Books in Print lists by author and by title books published in the United States. The *Subject Guide to Books in Print* is a companion to *Books in Print* and lists books under more than 60,000 subject headings.

Other sources of books, such as *Business Books and Serials in Print* and *Paperbound Books in Print,* are available in most large libraries and in many bookstores.

Fact Books

Almanacs, yearbooks, and other fact books contain the following types of information:

- Important political, sporting, and miscellaneous events.
- Statistical information about numerous topics.
- Brief biographies or information concerning well-known persons, such as those in politics, sports, and entertainment.
- Developments in the scientific and technological areas.
- News items.

An almanac is an easy-to-use reference source for data and statistics on many subjects, including people, places, and events. The *World Almanac and Book of Facts* is the most detailed and most comprehensive almanac published in the United States. It presents up-to-date factual information on literally hundreds of topics in social, industrial, political, financial, and numerous other areas.

The almanac is indexed alphabetically by subject, occupation, and profession. The index is in the front of the book. Although a few famous people, whether living or dead, are indexed by name, most are not. For example, to look up the mayor of a metropolitan city, you would look under "Mayors" rather than under the person's name.

The *Information Please Almanac* also presents facts and statistical data on a wide range of topics. The table of contents gives a list of the subject areas, and a comprehensive alphabetic index is included at the end of the almanac.

Yearbooks differ from almanacs in that they usually give more information about a broad subject area, a country, individuals, or current events.

The *Statesman's Yearbook* is divided into two parts: International Organizations and Countries of the World A-Z. The yearbook provides information about the history, population, government, defense, economy, natural resources, and industry of various organizations and countries.

Another popular yearbook is the *International Yearbook and Statesmen's Who's Who.* It is divided into three parts: International and National Organizations; Organization of Foreign Ministries of Great Powers, Metric Conversion Tables, and States of the World; and Biographical.

A yearbook may also be a tool for updating preexisting works. New information about a subject may be recorded in a yearbook, and the yearbook serves as a continuation for a work until a new edition is published. Encyclopedias often have yearbooks, such as the *Britannica Book of the Year* and the *World Book Year Book.*

Summaries of important facts of news events, as collected from more than 50 metropolitan newspapers in the United States and abroad, are reported in *Facts on File.* The news items in the weekly publication are arranged under the subjects of world affairs, U. S. affairs, other nations, and miscellaneous. The publication provides a good survey of current standard news items.

Facts on File is indexed every two weeks, and the index is made cumulative every month, every three months, and every year.

Encyclopedias

The general encyclopedia usually is a multivolume work that contains a collection of articles on many subjects. The condensed articles are written by specialists and frequently include illustrations and maps as well as bibliographies listing standard works on the topic. The individual articles on the various topics vary in length from only a few lines to several pages. Encyclopedias can be especially helpful in giving an overview of a subject; however, other references should be consulted when in-depth coverage is needed.

Two of the most widely used general encyclopedias are the *Encyclopedia Americana* and *Encyclopedia Britannica.* Each has 30 volumes. The *Americana Annual* and the *Britannica Book of the Year* are supplemental issues and cover significant events of the year.

The articles in the encyclopedias are arranged alphabetically. The *Index Volume* should always be consulted first since the main article on a subject does not necessarily contain all of the available information contained in the encyclopedia.

Atlases

The *Rand McNally Commercial Atlas and Marketing Guide* is the most comprehensive atlas of the United States. The information is up to date

336
Secretarial
Procedures:
Office
Administration and
Automated Systems

since the atlas is revised each year. It is an especially useful reference for the salesperson because it gives the data about the economy in both map and chart forms. In addition to state, regional, and metropolitan area maps, the atlas gives data on transportation, commerce, economy, population, and other areas. Part of the atlas is devoted to Canada and the rest of the world.

Most libraries also have the *New York Times Atlas of the World.* In addition to maps, this atlas has sections covering the solar system and the physiography, oceanography, climatology, vegetation, mankind, politics, and air routes of the world.

Directories

Specialized directories are published by business and reference book publishers; magazines; trade associations; chambers of commerce; and city, state and federal government agencies.

When information is needed and you do not know how to obtain a copy of the directory or whether a directory has been published for the field, refer to the *Directory of Directories* or the *Guide to American Directories.* Both references identify thousands of directories and give the address and telephone number of the publisher, a brief explanation of the coverage, the number of pages, the frequency of publication, the price, and sometimes other information concerning each of the directories.

The *Congressional Staff Directory* is an easy-to-use reference for information about key members of the federal government. The book has sections on state delegations, congressional committees, congressional staffs, and executive department and agency staffs. The directory also has biographies of key staff members. The color-coded index enables the reader to readily locate the name, job title, address, and telephone number of an individual.

In addition to biographies, the *Congressional Directory* includes listings of committee assignments and activities of members of congress. It also lists personnel of the executive and judiciary departments, independent agencies, international organizations, and foreign diplomatic and consular representatives in the United States.

Daily, weekly, semiweekly, and triweekly newspapers are classified by state, town, province, or territory in the *Ayer Directory of Publications.* Magazines are also included in the directory and are grouped according to classification. Circulation data and subscription prices are given for the newspapers and magazines, plus market and economic profiles for each city. The directory also has a map section.

Biographical Dictionaries

When information about a notable person is needed, you probably can find the information in one of the many biographical dictionaries. Some

IACOCCA, LIDO ANTHONY (LEE), automotive mfr.; b. Allentown, Pa., Oct. 15, 1924; s. Nicola and Antoinette (Perrotto) I.; B.S., Lehigh U., 1945; M.E., Princeton, 1946; m. Mary McCleary, Sept. 29, 1956; children—Kathryn Lisa, Lia Antoninette, With Ford Motor Co., Dearborn, Mich., 1946-78, successively mem. field sales staff. various merchandising and tng. activities, asst. dirs. sales mgr., Phila., dist. sales mgr., Washington, 1946-56, truck marketing mgr. div. office, 1956-57, car marketing mgr., 1957-60, vehicle market mgr., 1960, v.p. Ford Motor Co., gen. mgr. Ford div., 1960-65, v.p. car and truck group, 1965-67, exec. v.p. of co., 1967-68, pres. of co., 1970-78, pres., chief operating officer Chrysler Corp., Highland Park, Mich., 1978-79, chmn. bd., chief exec. officer, 1979--. Wallace Meml. fellow Princeton. Mem. Tau Beta Pi. Club: Detroit Athletic. Office: care Chrysler Corp 12000 Lynn Townsend Dr Highland Park MI 48231*

FIGURE 14-7. Entry from *Who's Who in Finance and Industry*. (Copyright © 1981 by Marquis Who's Who, Inc. Reprinted by permission from *Who's Who in Finance and Industry*, 22nd Edition, 1981-1982.)

biographical dictionaries, such as *Who's Who in Finance and Industry*, are restricted to individuals in a particular field or area; others, such as *Current Biography*, are general.

Who's Who in Finance and Industry gives comprehensive biographical data on approximately 18,000 executives and professionals in insurance, banking, real estate, manufacturing, retail trade, and other professions closely related to business and finance.

Each entry provides such information as name, position, vital statistics, and education, as shown in figure 14-7.

Current Biography presents articles on people prominent in national and international affairs, the sciences, the arts, labor, and industry. The article heading includes the person's name, date of birth, and occupation. The article is supplemented by a list of sources of information: newspapers, magazines, books, and sometimes the biographees.

Biography Index is a comprehensive biographical guide that indexes books, periodicals, obituaries, diaries, letter collections, memoirs, and bibliographies. The main entry section is arranged alphabetically by name and each heading gives the name of the biographee, birth and death dates, and the reason for including the individual in the index. A profession/occupation section is located in the back of the reference.

Financial Information

Financial information may be obtained from newspapers, magazines, and numerous other sources. Three of the most widely known publishers of financial information are Standard & Poor's Corporation, Moody's Investment Service, and Dun & Bradstreet, Inc.

Much financial information is presented in concise form in Standard & Poor's *Corporation Records*. The capitalization, corporate background, stock data, earnings and finance, annual report data, and consolidated balance sheets are given for each of the several hundred companies

338
Secretarial
Procedures:
Office
Administration and
Automated Systems

listed. Since the information for most companies covers several years, these reports are especially helpful when data for more than one year are needed.

Another Standard & Poor's reference, *Industry Surveys,* is useful for examining the prospects of a particular industry. The reference provides up-to-date information regarding the industry, the market, and leading companies in the industry.

Standard & Poor's *Register of Corporations, Directors and Executives* is published in three volumes. The Corporations volume lists approximately 40,000 American and Canadian companies and gives the names of the officers, directors, and other principals. The Directors and Executives volume is an alphabetical listing of approximately 70,000 officers and directors. The Indexes volume has seven sections, including a geographical index arranged by states and major cities and an obituary index that lists the deaths which have occurred during the previous year.

The three-volume *Million Dollar Directory,* published by Dun & Bradstreet, lists approximately 115,000 businesses in the United States with an indicated net worth of over $500,000. In addition to the industrial companies, the directory lists wholesalers and retailers, utilities, banks, and insurance companies. The legal name, address and telephone number, line of business, names and titles of principal officers, annual sales, and other types of information is given for each business listed.

Another Dun & Bradstreet publication, *Reference Book of Corporate Managements,* lists more than 50,000 officers and directors in over 3,000 companies. Biographical data covering age, education, experience, and principal business affiliations are given for each principal officer.

Moody's publishes the following five manuals: *Bank and Finance, Industrial, Municipal and Government, Public Utility,* and *Transportation.* The manuals give financial data and information about the companies and officers.

Moody's *Handbook of Common Stocks* provides information on over 900 companies. The handbook covers financial data as well as information about the background of the company, recent developments, prospects, statistics, and officers. The comprehensiveness of the data is shown in the page from the *Handbook of Common Stocks* given in figure 14-8.

Government Publications

The three branches of the federal government—executive, legislative, and judicial—and independent agencies issue thousands of publications. These publications are made available to depository libraries located in all states and congressional districts. Fifty of the more than 1,350 depository libraries have been designated as regional depositories. They are responsible for retaining depository material permanently and for providing interlibrary loan and reference service in their regions.

INTERNATIONAL BUSINESS MACHINES CORPORATION

LISTED	SYM.	LTPS•	STPS•	IND. DIV.	REC. PRICE	RANGE (52-WKS.)	YLD.
NYSE	IBM	95.3	111.2	$3.44•	97	101 - 57	3.5%

HIGH GRADE. AGGRESSIVE RESEARCH AND STRONG MARKETING SUGGEST THAT OUTSTANDING GROWTH WILL CONTINUE OVER THE LONG TERM.

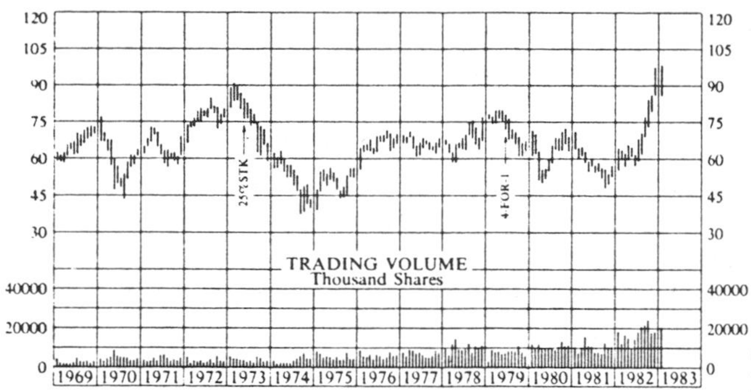

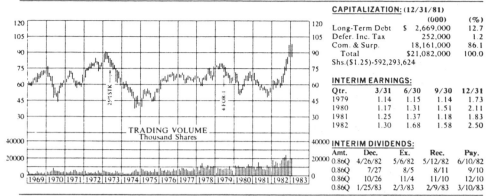

CAPITALIZATION: (12/31/81)

		(000)	(%)
Long-Term Debt	$	2,669,000	12.7
Defer. Inc. Tax		252,000	1.2
Com. & Surp.		18,161,000	86.1
Total		$21,082,000	100.0

Shs.($1.25)-592,293,624

INTERIM EARNINGS:

Qtr.	3/31	6/30	9/30	12/31
1979	1.14	1.15	1.14	1.73
1980	1.17	1.31	1.51	2.11
1981	1.25	1.37	1.18	1.83
1982	1.30	1.68	1.58	2.50

INTERIM DIVIDENDS:

Amt.	Dec.	Ex.	Rec.	Pay.
0.86Q	4/26/82	5/6/82	5/12/82	6/10/82
0.86Q	7/27	8/5	8/11	9/10
0.86Q	10/26	11/4	11/10	12/10
0.86Q	1/25/83	2/3/83	2/9/83	3/10/83

BACKGROUND:

IBM conducts operations throughout the world in the field of information-handling systems, equipment and services. Revenues are derived from the sale of its products, as well as from rentals and services. In 1981 these areas contributed 44%, 37% and 18% of revenues, respectively. A majority of IBM's products are both leased and sold through worldwide marketing organization. Foreign operations contributed 42% of earnings. Growth has been vigorous and dividends have been paid since 1916. In 1/82, the Justice Department agreed to drop its 13-year-old antitrust suit against IBM, which accused the Company of monopolizing markets for computers and peripheral products.

RECENT DEVELOPMENTS:

For the year ended 12/31/82, net income jumped 22% to $4.41 billion, or $7.39 per share, compared with $3.61 billlion, or $6.41 per share, earned in the comparable period a year earlier. Revenues advanced 13% to $34.36 billion. Significant growth for both net orders and net installations contributed to the improvement in results. Comparisons were made with restated prior-year figures to reflect the adoption of FASB No. 52.

PROSPECTS:

Buoyed by successful new products and strong demand for established products, earnings growth will continue, although comparisons will be affected by the strength of the U.S. dollar and unsettled economic conditions. Customers buying rather than leasing new products will further enhance profitability and improve profit margins. Recent price reductions and improvements in several small computer products will further augment sales gains. Gains can be expected as economic conditions improve and business investment accelerates.

STATISTICS:

YEAR	GROSS REVS. ($mill.)	OPER. PROFIT MARGIN %	RET. ON EQUITY %	NET INCOME ($mill.)	WORK CAP. ($mill.)	SENIOR CAPITAL ($mill.)	SHARES (000)	EARN. PER SH.$	DIV. PER SH.$	DIV. PAY. %	PRICE RANGE	P/E RATIO	AVG. YIELD %
73	10,993	25.2	—	1,575.5	3,275	652.2	586,852	2.70	1.12	42	91¼ - 58¾	27.8	1.5
74	12,675	25.0	18.2	1,837.6	3,800	335.8	593,036	3.12	1.39	45	63½ - 37⅝	16.2	2.8
75	14,437	23.7	17.4	1,989.9	4,752	295.1	599,380	3.34	1.63	49	56⅞ - 39⅜	14.4	3.4
76	16,304	25.0	18.8	2,398.1	5,838	275.1	602,780	3.99	2.00	50	72⅛ 55⅞	16.0	3.1
77	18,133	25.7	21.6	2,719.4	4,864	255.8	589,884	4.58	2.50	54	71½ - 61⅛	14.4	3.7
78	21,076	25.8	23.1	3,110.6	4,511	285.5	583,240	5.32	2.88	54	77½ - 58⅜	12.8	4.2
79	22,863	22.9	20.1	3,011.3	4,406	1,589.4	583,594	5.16	3.44	67	80½ - 61⅛	14.1	5.0
80	26,213	21.9	21.6	3,562.0	3,399	2,099.0	583,807	6.10	3.44	56	72¾ - 50⅜	10.1	5.6
81	29,070.0	20.7	18.2	3,308.0	2,983	2,669.0	592,294	5.63	3.44	61	71½ - 48⅜	10.7	6.0
p82	**34,364.0**			**4,409.0**				**7.39**	**3.44**	**47**	**98 - 55⅝**	**10.4**	**4.5**

•Long-Term Price Score — Short-Term Price Score; See page 4a. Adjusted for all stock dividends and splits thru 4-for-1 stock split 5/79.

INCORPORATED:
June 16, 1911 – New York

PRINCIPAL OFFICE:
Armonk, N Y 10504
Tel.: (914) 765-1900

ANNUAL MEETING:
Last Monday in April

NUMBER OF STOCKHOLDERS:
742,162

TRANSFER AGENT(S):
Company Office, New York, N Y
Trust General du Canada
National Trust Co., Ltd.

REGISTRAR(S):
Morgan Guaranty Trust Co., N.Y.
First National Bank, Chicago, Ill.
Montreal Trust Co.

INSTITUTIONAL HOLDINGS:
No. of Institutions: 1,334
Shares Held: 207,482,122

OFFICERS:
Chairman
F. T. Cary
Pres. & Ch. Exec. Off.
J. R. Opel
Vice Pres. - Finance
A.J. Krowe
Treasurer
C. A. Northrop
Secretary
J. H. Grady
Investor Contact
D.P. Otis

FIGURE 14-8. Page from *Handbook of Common Stocks.* (Copyright © 1983 by Moody's Investors Service. Reprinted by permission of the publisher.)

340
Secretarial
Procedures:
Office
Administration and
Automated Systems

The government documents card catalog and the *Monthly Catalog* are the two main approaches to locating government documents. Each issue of the *Monthly Catalog* includes all publications that are ready for distribution at the end of the current month. Each entry appears in fully cataloged form, and detailed instructions concerning the interpretation of the data are given in the front of each catalog.

The *GPO Sales Publications Reference File* (PRF) is a microfiche catalog of publications sold by the Superintendent of Documents. The PRF is arranged in three sequences: Government Printing Office stock numbers; Superintendent of Documents classification numbers; and alphabetical arrangement of subjects, titles, agency series and report numbers, key words and phrases, and individual authors. Each PRF consists of approximately 300 microfiche and is sent to subscribers and depository libraries six times a year.

The *Statistical Abstract of the United States* is published by the Bureau of the Census and gives a summary of statistics on the social, political, and economic organizations of the United States. The data are obtained from government and private publications, and the sources are cited. The emphasis is on national data, but some statistics are given for regions, states, and some metropolitan areas and cities.

The table of contents identifies the 33 sections, which include areas such as population, vital statistics, foreign commerce and aid, as well as labor force, employees, and earnings. The detailed index at the end is arranged by subject, name, and profession.

Copies of government documents may be ordered by mail or telephone, with teletype equipment, or through the DIALOG/DIALORDER computerized reference system available from the Lockheed DIALOG Retrieval Service of Palo Alto, California. A check or money order may accompany the order, or it may be charged to a valid VISA or MasterCard account. Customers who make frequent purchases may open a deposit account.

State Publications

Many bibliographies, legislative manuals, directories, and various other documents are published at the state level. Some of the publications are listed in the *Monthly Checklist of State Publications.* The items listed in the *Checklist* are those sent to the Library of Congress by the state agencies; thus, the completeness of the *Checklist* depends largely on the cooperation of the state agencies.

State Government Reference Publications, published by Libraries Unlimited, Inc., Littleton, Colorado, is an excellent annotated guide to selected representative documents issued by state departments, bureaus, and agencies. The scope of the book is reflected by the titles of the nine chapters: Official State Bibliography; Blue Books; Legislative Manuals and Related References; State Government Finances; Statistical Abstracts and other Data Sources; Directories; Tourist Guides; Audiovisual Guides, Atlases, and Maps; and Bibliographies and General References.

341
Reference Material

other Data Sources; Directories; Tourist Guides; Audiovisual Guides, Atlases, and Maps; and Bibliographies and General References.

Each chapter is arranged alphabetically according to agency, as shown on the page from the Official State Bibliography chapter presented in figure 14-9.

DATA BASES

Many libraries and some businesses subscribe to a computer reference service. When this service is available, a computer can be used to rapidly sort through references to newspaper articles, periodical articles, government documents, published reports, and numerous other publications. The computer search can result in a comprehensive bibliography of research material in only a few minutes. An individual would have to spend hours searching the printed indexes to develop the same bibliography.

The files that the computers scan are stored on magnetic tapes and discs and are referred to as data bases. Many data bases are available as printed indexes and abstracts; others are available on-line only. The data bases contain the same information that appears in printed indexes: author, title, source, and sometimes an abstract.

Using the computer to search for references offers several advantages:

1. *Time Saving.* The equivalent of many index or abstract volumes can be searched in a few minutes.

2. *Current.* The information supplied is often more current than that found in printed sources. New information is loaded into the data base more often than the new editions of the printed index are published.

3. *Access.* On-line data bases can be utilized through key words and word combinations that do not appear in printed indexes. This is particularly useful for new topics for which no printed subject headings have appeared.

4. *Thoroughness.* The results of a computer search will often be more thorough and more accurate than a comparable manual search.

5. *Control.* A search can be limited to information for specific years, to selected types of documents, and in other ways.

To obtain assistance in developing a concise description of the topic and in selecting relevant key words, consult someone within the company or the library who is trained in computer searching and is familiar with the data bases pertinent to the area to be researched.

ALABAMA

AGRICULTURAL EXPERIMENT STATION, Auburn.
Circular, [Auburn]

– 1 –

259. Oasis phalaris: a new cool season perennial
grass [by C. S. Hoveland and others] 1982.
11 p. ill.

– 2 –

260. Triumph: a new winter-productive tall fescue
variety [by C. S. Hoveland and others] 1982.
7 p. ill.

– 3 –

261. Solar radiation and dissolved oxygen concen-
trations in fish ponds [by Claude E. Boyd and
William D. Hollerman] 1982. 12 p. ill.

– 4 –

262. Performance of tall fescue varieties in Alabama [by J. F. Pedersen, C. S. Hoveland, and
R. L. Haaland] 1982. 11 p.

– 5 –

AGRICULTURAL EXPERIMENT STATION, Auburn,
Soil survey of Jefferson County, Alabama [by
Lawson D. Spivey, Jr. Auburn, 1982] vii, 140 p.
ill.

Issued with 24 maps in envelope.
Issued in cooperation with the Dept. of Agriculture and Industries, Surface Mining Reclamation
Commission, U. S. Bureau of Land Management,
and U. S. Soil Conservation Service.

82-603380

– 6 –

BUREAU OF VITAL STATISTICS. Alabama's vital
events. 1981. Montgomery. vii, 259 p. ill.
annual.

74-648227

– 7 –

DEPT. OF EXAMINERS OF PUBLIC ACCOUNTS.
[Report of examination of] Alabama Board of Social
Work Examiners, State of Alabama, Montgomery,
October 1, 1979 through September 30, 1981.
Montgomery [1982] A–B, 14 1.

– 8 –

DEPT. OF EXAMINERS OF PUBLIC ACCOUNTS.
[Report of examination of] Alabama State Council on
the Arts and Humanities, State of Alabama, Montgomery. 1979/81. Montgomery. A–B, 13 1.
Report period ends Sept. 30.

– 9 –

DEPT. OF EXAMINERS OF PUBLIC ACCOUNTS.
[Report of examination of] Chattahoochee Valley
Community College, Phenix City, Alabama.
1977/80. Montgomery. 2 v.
Report period ends Sept. 30.

– 10 –

DEPT. OF EXAMINERS OF PUBLIC ACCOUNTS.
[Report of examination of] Chesebrough Pond's
Scholarship Fund and the Small Business Development Center Fund. Alabama Agricultural and Mechanical University, Normal, Alabama, October 1,
1981 through March 31, 1982. Montgomery [1982]
A–B 1.

– 11 –

DEPT. OF EXAMINERS OF PUBLIC ACCOUNTS.
[Report of examination of] Department of Revenue,
State of Alabama, Montgomery. 1977/80. Mont-
gomery. A–O, 93 p.
Report period ends Sept. 30.

– 12 –

DEPT. OF EXAMINERS OF PUBLIC ACCOUNTS.
[Report of examination of] Stonewall Jackson Memo-
rial Fund Board, State of Alabama, Montgomery,
October 1, 1979 through September 30, 1981.
Montgomery [1982] A, 9 1.

– 13 –

DEPT. OF EXAMINERS OF PUBLIC ACCOUNTS.
State of Alabama financial statement, all counties
(prepared from unaudited data); compilation of indebtedness as of September 30, 1981, revenue and
expenditures for fiscal year 1980-81, comparative
figures – indebtedness and revenue, 1980-81 compared with 1979-80. Montgomery [n. d.] 144 p.

82-623346

– 14 –

[DEPT. OF INDUSTRIAL RELATIONS. Research and
Statistics Division] Alabama civilian labor force
(rounded to hundreds). [Prepared in cooperation
with the U. S. Bureau of Labor Statistics. Montgomery, n. d. 1] 1.

– 15 –

[DEPT. OF INDUSTRIAL RELATIONS. Research and
Statistics Division] Hours and earnings data for
selected nonagricultural industries in Alabama.
1979-81. [Prepared in cooperation with the U. S.
Bureau of Labor Statistics. Montgomery] 3 v.

– 16 –

[DEPT. OF INDUSTRIAL RELATIONS. Research and
Statistics Division] State of Alabama total nonagricultural employment (rounded to hundreds).
1979-81. [Prepared in cooperation with the U. S.
Bureau of Labor Statistics. Montgomery] 3 v.

– 17 –

[DEPT. OF MENTAL HEALTH] A survey of developmental disabilities in Butler, Coffee, Covington,
and Crenshaw Counties [by] Jan Wall [and others.
n. p.] Developmental Disabilities Community Planning and Development Project, South Central Alabama Mental Health Center [n. d.] v, 163 1. ill.

Cover title: Report of the Developmental Disabilities Planning and Development Project for the counties of Butler, Coffee, Covington & Crenshaw.

– 18 –

STATE HIGHWAY DEPT. Bureau of State Planning.
Division of Surveying and Mapping. General highway map[s] ... Alabama. Prepared in cooperation
with the Federal Highway Administration. Montgomery.

7. Butler County. 1982. map on sheet
46 X 57 cm.

15. Cleburne County. 1981. map on sheet
63 X 47 cm.

28. Etowah County. 1982. map on sheet
47 X 57 cm.

49. Mobile County. 1982. map on sheet
102 X 46 cm.

61. Talladega County. 1982. map on sheet
71 X 46 cm.

FIGURE 14-9. Page from *State Government Reference Publications.* (Copyright ©
1981 by Libraries Unlimited, Inc. Reprinted by permission of the publisher.)

If a library charges for the search, the charge will usually include the computer time, telecommunication fees, and cost of printed citations. Because vendors' rates vary greatly and each search differs in complexity, prices differ considerably; however, the cost is normally only a fraction of what it would be if the search were done manually, considering the cost of the researcher's time.

MICROFORM

Many libraries are storing periodicals, newspapers, and other material on microform. The card catalog, indexes, and directories are frequently stored on microform.

The special equipment needed to read or make copies of the microform is always available in the library. The equipment is easy to operate, and the instructions are usually posted near the machine.

SELECTING SPECIFIC SOURCES

Much time can be saved when a systematic approach is used to identify the specific sources to search for the information that is needed. As you search for information in the library, follow these steps:

1. Identify the subject.

2. Know the type and amount of information needed. Are general data, statistics, biographical material, or other types of information needed?

3. List the terms that describe the subject. If the subject is office automation, perhaps electronic data processing, computers, office communication systems, word processing, work stations, and other terms need to be considered.

4. Consider where the information most logically can be found. Are books, periodicals, newspapers, biographies, or other references the most logical sources?

5. Determine whether the library you are using has the reference. Are the listings available in the card catalog, on computer printouts, in microform, or in some other form?

6. Search the card catalog or indexes.

344
Secretarial
Procedures:
Office
Administration and
Automated Systems

7. Copy the information needed to locate the references. Is the information—call numbers for books and volume, dates, and page numbers of periodicals and newspapers—copied completely and accurately?

8. Locate the reference.

LIBRARY ASSISTANCE

When you need assistance in using the library or in locating sources, you should contact the reference librarian. Keep in mind that reference librarians are employed on the assumption that people are not specialists in the use of the library and often need help.

Tell the librarian the purpose of the investigation and state as clearly as possible what you need. If you have already searched for the information, tell the librarian how you proceeded. Time can be saved by telling the librarian where you looked, the indexes and subjects that were searched, and the reference books that were consulted.

Should the librarian suggest a reference with which you are not familiar, ask for assistance in locating and using it. While the librarian may initially suggest only the most logical sources, he or she may be aware of others. If you do not find all of the information you need, ask for additional suggestions.

Summary

Most people have a general understanding of the library and know that books, periodicals, and other resources are stored there. The well-qualified secretary must have more than a cursory knowledge of the library. She needs to know about public libraries and those maintained by businesses, educational institutions, and nonprofit organizations. She must also thoroughly understand the types of resources available and know the steps to follow in locating specific information.

Questions

1. When should the library be used to obtain business information?

2. How may material be obtained from a special library that is not open to the general public?

3. When should the reference librarian be asked to assist in locating information?

4. How are library books indexed?

5. Discuss the types of information shown on a catalog card.

6. Is the Dewey classification system a numerical system of subject filing?

7. What approaches may be used in locating an article in a periodical?

8. What do periodicals, magazines, and journals have in common?

9. List the best sources of current information.

10. What information is given for magazine articles indexed in the *Readers' Guide to Periodical Literature*?

11. Are any business magazine articles indexed in the *Readers' Guide to Periodical Literature*?

12. Is the *Vertical File Index* an index of general magazines?

13. What must be known before a particular news article can be located by using *The New York Times Index*?

14. Which index gives information concerning the length of the newspaper articles?

15. Why do encyclopedias have yearbooks?

16. Where is the information for *Facts on File* obtained?

17. Is an encyclopedia a logical reference to use to find in-depth coverage of a subject?

18. Discuss the types of information that can be found in the *Rand McNally Atlas and Marketing Guide.*

19. Name the two sections of *The Wall Street Journal Index.*

20. Tell how to determine whether a directory has been published for a particular field.

21. Why is color coding used in the *Congressional Staff Directory*?

22. What reference can be used to obtain information about the newspapers published in a certain city?

23. List the types of information normally found in biographies.

24. Name three well-known publishers of financial information.

25. What net worth must a company have in order to be listed in the Dun & Bradstreet *Million Dollar Directory*?

26. How many states have depository libraries for government documents?

27. Are all government documents free to the public?

28. Who may order government documents by telephone?

29. Tell how to determine whether a state agency in Colorado publishes a tourist guide.

30. Discuss the advantages of using a computer to search references.

346
Secretarial
Procedures:
Office
Administration and
Automated Systems

31. Should one look in the card catalog to determine whether a library subscribes to a particular magazine?

32. What should you tell the librarian when you ask him or her for assistance?

Projects

1. Make a list of the publications that are indexed in both the *Readers' Guide to Periodical Literature* and the *Business Periodicals Index.*

2. List the metropolitan newspapers to which your college library subscribes and indicate those for which an index is available.

3. Compare the *Cumulative Book Index* and *Books in Print* and write a short report explaining the differences.

4. Compare the *World Almanac and Book of Facts* with another almanac. Write a short report explaining the differences.

5. Compare two atlases and list the differences.

6. Visit the library and make a list of at least five references that you believe the secretary should be familiar with but that were not discussed in this chapter.

7. Make a list of the types of information your college library has stored in microform that might be valuable to a secretary.

8. Find the answer to the following questions by using only the references discussed in this chapter. List the answer and the name of the reference where the answer was found.

   a. In what magazine did the article, "The Most Essential Office Component Is People," appear in 1983?

   b. What is the home office address of the Bally Manufacturing Company?

   c. How many million dollar businesses are located in Reno, Nevada?

   d. The Ferro Corporation is listed on the New York Stock Exchange. What was the book value of the stock in 1974 and in 1982?

   e. What is the population of Alabama?

   f. Where and when was Robert Goulet, the singer, born?

   g. What language is spoken in Liechtenstein, an independent European principality that lies between Switzerland and Austria?

   h. What is the ZIP Code for Badger, Iowa?

   i. According to the 1980 census, what was the population of the United States?

   j. What is the enrollment of the University of Lisbon, Portugal?

k. What is the International Standard Book Number of *In Search of Excellence,* by Thomas J. Peters and Robert H. Waterman, Jr.?

l. In what magazine did the article, "Letters That Stop Sexual Harassment by Professors," appear in 1983?

m. In what year was Loyola Marymount University founded?

n. What are some of the titles that have been bestowed on Richard Simmons (the physical fitness specialist and television personality) by the media?

———————————— Cases ————————————

1. John Maddox, an executive with the Wright Company, makes numerous talks concerning his particular industry. He uses graphic aids to show trends and comparisons. Frequently, the data he needs must be obtained from references in the public library. He does not want his secretary to be out of the office; therefore, he asks her to obtain the data by calling the reference librarian. When the secretary asked the librarian to provide an unusually large amount of data, the librarian refused to comply. When the secretary told Maddox what happened, he told her to call the director of the library and report the reference librarian for not being cooperative. The secretary believes the librarian should not have been expected to do the research. Should she comply with Maddox's request?

2. Linda Spiro's boss has asked her to go to the public library and prepare a list of the articles in newspapers, periodicals, and other publications that might be valuable to him in preparing a major report. Linda believes she will probably need to spend at least two or three days at the library preparing the bibliography by looking through the indexes. She calls the library and finds that a computer search could be made and the bibliography could be prepared in only a few minutes for approximately $50. Should Linda recommend to her boss that the computer search be made or should she spend the time in the library preparing the bibliography?

3. Doris Rogers asked the reference librarian where information relating to a particular topic could be found. The librarian mentioned two possible sources. Doris could not find the information she needed in either of the sources. Should Doris assume, therefore, that the information is not available in that particular library?

CHAPTER 15

Taking and Preparing Minutes

Almost all secretaries are required to assist with writing minutes. You may be expected to attend the meetings, take notes, and prepare the minutes; or you may be expected to write the minutes by using the notes of someone else or a tape recording.

Understanding the organization and the procedures to be followed during the meeting will enable you to take notes so that minutes can be written that will accurately reflect the proceedings.

The things that should be considered prior to and during the meeting and in preparing the minutes will be discussed in detail in this chapter.

PRIOR PLANNING

You can do several things to simplify the task of recording the minutes. Study the agenda, become familiar with the background relating to the agenda items, and take to the meeting all material that may be needed. Read the minutes of previous meetings to develop an understanding of the types of things you will be expected to include in the minutes and an awareness of the type of meeting to expect.

Another secretary who has attended previous meetings and prepared minutes for the group may be able to offer suggestions that will facilitate your work as recording secretary. The chairperson may be able to give you some insight as to what to expect.

350
Secretarial
Procedures:
Office
Administration and
Automated Systems

RECORDING THE PROCEEDINGS

Most secretaries are not expected to take verbatim notes, except to record motions. When a verbatim transcript is required, a court reporter is normally employed. If a more detailed record is required than the secretary can be expected to write in shorthand, a tape recorder may be used. Many secretaries use a recorder as backup or security when recording the minutes in shorthand.

When a tape recorder is used, several precautions are required. Check in advance to determine the approximate length of the meeting so that you can take an adequate supply of tape. If the meeting cannot be interrupted while the tape is changed, take more than one recorder. Before the meeting starts, set up the recorder and make sure it is functioning properly and that it will pick up what is being said.

People will generally not identify themselves on the tape; therefore, a sheet similar to that illustrated in figure 15-1 can be used to record the names of the individuals and the first few words spoken so that you will be able to identify the speakers when you transcribe the minutes.

Name_____

Identifying words_____

_____

Name_____

Identifying words_____

_____

Name_____

Identifying words_____

_____

FIGURE 15-1. Identification forms to be used when taping meetings.

When a tape recorder is not used, detailed notes should be taken as the discussion occurs. Do not, however, become so concerned with getting every word down that you fail to stay abreast of the proceedings. By waiting until the discussion on a topic is completed and then writing a summary, you may overlook or forget an important point; furthermore, the meeting will continue and you may fail to take adequate notes on the next topic.

A particularly frustrating situation exists when someone has expressed in great detail his or her views regarding a subject and then concludes by saying "I want to put that in the form of a motion." Even when you have taken notes, what the person has said may not have been in a form appropriate for a motion. When this happens, the chairperson should ask the person to restate the motion. If the chairperson does not, you may simply say "Would you mind repeating the motion the way you would like for it to appear in the minutes?"

Taking notes is simplified when an agenda is followed and the meeting is conducted according to parliamentary rules. When parliamentary procedure is to be followed during the meeting, the secretary should become thoroughly familiar with *Robert's Rules of Order* so that she may assist the chairperson if procedural questions arise.

In many meetings held within the company, no motions are made and the minutes merely provide a written summary of what transpired. This summary can be particularly helpful to those who did not attend the meeting and to those who are responsible for taking action on the items discussed. The minutes should be sent to the members who were absent as soon as possible after the meeting.

When you believe you will not be able to recognize the members of the group, you may draw an outline of the seating arrangement prior to the meeting and as the group assembles ask the chairperson or someone else to help you insert the names of those sitting in the different positions. This procedure will help you record the names of those making motions and presenting reports. A sample seating chart is shown in figure 15-2.

You must sit where you can see and hear all of the participants. Ideally, you should sit beside the chairperson so that you can inconspicuously communicate. The chairperson may need to help you by identifying members of the group, restating motions or asking that they be restated, indicating that certain discussion needs to be recorded, and asking for copies of reports and other material that may be needed for the minutes. You may need to help the chairperson by assisting with parliamentary procedures, referring to bylaws or previous actions taken by the group, or reminding him or her of something that needs to be considered.

Prepare an alphabetized list of the members in advance of the meeting and leave a space beside each name to indicate whether the person was present or absent. If you are expected to check attendance by calling the roll, learn how to pronounce the names correctly.

352
Secretarial
Procedures:
Office
Administration and
Automated Systems

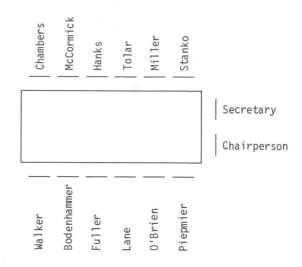

FIGURE 15-2. Seating chart.

CONTENT OF THE MINUTES

Heading

The heading of the minutes should fully identify the meeting. The name of the group is centered and typed in all capital letters. The date is typed a double space below the name of the group:

MINUTES OF THE FRINGE BENEFITS COMMITTEE OF
FARMERS BANK

October 1, 1984

The name of the group and the date should be repeated on all pages of the minutes, and the pages should be numbered:

MINUTES OF THE FRINGE BENEFITS COMMITTEE OF FARMERS
BANK—October 1, 1984—Page 2

Time and Place

Include in the first paragraph the answer to the following questions: Who? What? When? Where?

The regular monthly meeting of the Board of Regents of Elite University was held at 2 p.m. on Wednesday, March 14, 1984, in the Blue Room of the University Union. Chairwoman Joan Morgan presided.

If the group holds special sessions, the purpose of the special or called session should be stated in the minutes.

A special budget-planning session of the City Council was held at 7 p.m. on Monday, December 10, 1984, in Room 12 of the Administration Building. John Tucker, Chairman of the Budget Committee, presided.

When you indicate who presided at the meeting, you can avoid using the sexist expressions, chairman or chairwoman, by referring to the presiding officer as "Chair" or "Chairperson." In some organizations, the presiding officer is referred to as the "Moderator."

Attendance

Indicate in the minutes, in alphabetical order, the names of those who were present and absent and identify those who may have been present for only a portion of the meeting. The attendance must be reported in a way that will let the reader know that a quorum was present and also who was present when motions were voted upon. If some individuals who were not members were present and participated in the meeting, you need to mention their names and the reason for their participation. Courtesy titles are usually omitted. The entire name or the first initial and last name may be given when reporting those who were present and absent; however, only the last name is used in the other sections of the minutes unless two or more of those present have the same last name.

The attendance information may be presented in sentence or column forms as shown in the following examples:

Bruce Jeter, Douglas Kirby, Betty Lemp, Bryce Sloan, and Robert Swearingen were present. Edith Wilson was absent. James Chambers, president of the University, and Becky Hilyard, assistant secretary of the Board, were also present.

Members present:	Members absent:
C. Adams	S. Page
C. Arth	M. Rains
J. Minor	A. Rodgers
J. Quick	
S. Rackers	
S. Wood	

354
Secretarial
Procedures:
Office
Administration and
Automated Systems

When the membership is large and you are not legally required to list the names, you may maintain a separate attendance record and state in the minutes the number present and the number absent, as shown in the following example:

Thirty-three members were present; five were absent.

Minutes of Previous Meetings

The minutes of previous meetings should be read or acted upon as the first item on the agenda. When the minutes are lengthy or involved, they may be duplicated and distributed before the meeting so that the members will have an opportunity to read them carefully.

When the minutes of the previous meeting have not been printed and distributed, the secretary is expected to read the minutes. Read clearly, slowly, and distinctly so that everyone in the room can hear. If the room is large, you may need to stand. The chairperson is responsible for asking for corrections after the minutes have been read.

Regardless of the procedure involved, the minutes should show the action taken, as indicated in the following examples:

Minutes of the February 15 meeting were read and approved.

or

Minutes of the February 15 meeting of the Board of Directors had been mailed to the members. No additions or corrections were made; therefore, Chairwoman Jordan announced the minutes were approved as printed.

or

Minutes of the February 15 meeting were approved as distributed.

Corrections

When errors in the minutes are noted, the secretary must make the corrections so that they can be identified. The errors are not erased and the minutes are not retyped; instead, the corrections are written in ink on the file copy and are always included in the minutes of the meeting during which the error was noted. The copy on which the correction is made should show the date of the meeting in which the change was noted.

Assume that Mary Hart's name was omitted from the list of those present during the February 15 meeting. The minutes of the February 15 meeting and the March 20 meeting, during which the omission was noted, could appear as follows:

Minutes of the February 15 meeting:

Members present were:

Carolyn Adams   Julie Quick

Craig Arth   Susan Rackers
Mary Hart 3/20/84
Jeffrey Minor   Sara Wood

Minutes of the March 20 meeting:

Minutes of the February 15 meeting were approved after the name of Mary Hart was added to the list of members present.

If the correction is extensive, a line may be drawn through the erroneous material and a marginal notation made to indicate that the corrected statement may be found at the end of the minutes or on an attached page.

Main Motions

Motions should be stated verbatim and in the order in which they are made. Motions are always recorded in the minutes, regardless of whether they were passed, defeated, or tabled. The minutes should indicate who made the motion, that it was seconded, and that it carried or failed. The name of the person who seconded the motion is usually not included.

Each motion, and everything relating to the motion, should be presented in a separate paragraph. Underlining or typing the motion in all capitals enables the reader to locate it at a glance. When reporting a motion, always state that "...moved that...." Never use the expressions that "Jones made a motion that..." or "A motion was made that...."

Avalon moved that students must maintain at least a 3.5 grade-point average to be eligible for the John S. Long Scholarship. The motion was seconded.

White moved THAT WILSON REPRESENT THE BETA CHAPTER AT THE NATIONAL CONVENTION OF DELTA PI EPSILON. Hilton seconded the motion.

The presiding officer can tell you how to report the action taken in regard to a motion. The action taken is normally stated in one of the following ways:

The motion carried.

Three affirmative and five negative votes were cast. The motion failed.

356
Secretarial
Procedures:
Office
Administration and
Automated Systems

Six affirmative and six negative votes were cast. The chair broke the tie by voting in the affirmative. The motion carried.

Ten members voted in the affirmative, seven voted in the negative, and two abstained. The motion carried.

The chairperson may direct that the vote on a motion be taken by calling the roll, especially when the members of the deliberative body represent several constituencies. For example, the members of a university curriculum committee may represent the various academic units of the university and the student body. The reader of the minutes may be interested in knowing how his or her representative voted. When the roll is called, the minutes reflect the names of the members and how they voted. Those who may choose not to vote are reported as answering "present." The minutes may be stated in the following way:

Jones, Miller, Nelson, Smythe, and Wilson voted in the affirmative; Hill and Morris voted in the negative; and Norton and Stockman answered present. The motion carried.

Amendments

Amendments may be made to insert, strike out, or strike out and insert a section of a motion. The minutes must state the main motion as well as the motion to amend and should always specify the word before or after which the insertion or deletion is to be made.

Main Motion

Milliard moved that students with at least a 3.5 grade-point average be considered for the John S. Long Scholarship. The motion was seconded.

Amendment

Wilson moved to amend the motion by inserting the words "only upper-division" before students. The amendment was seconded and carried unanimously.

Action on Amended Motion

The motion, as amended, carried.

If the original motion is amended considerably, you should give the entire amended motion in the minutes.

The minutes should state who presented reports, as well as the action taken. The person reading a formal report during the meeting should provide the secretary with a copy. The report should usually be presented as quoted material in the minutes; however, lengthy reports may be copied and attached to the minutes:

> Walker, chair of the Committee for the Development of the General Operating Budget, distributed the report on Resource Allocation (Appendix A). Manlow recommended that questions concerning the report be submitted to the Committee in writing prior to the October 10 meeting.

> Bryant presented the report of the Fringe Benefits Committee and moved that the recommendations be accepted. The motion was seconded and carried. The report was copied and is attached (Appendix B).

When a person gives a short oral report, include a summary of the important points in the minutes. The summary is not presented as quoted material.

> Sampson reported that the Department of Labor had made favorable comments regarding the accessibility of facilities for handicapped persons and that the investigation was closed.

Resolutions

A resolution is always a main motion and should be in writing; therefore, it should be presented as quoted material in the minutes. The person proposing the resolution may give the reasons for the resolution in a preamble with each clause constituting a paragraph beginning with WHEREAS.

WHEREAS and RESOLVED are typed in all capital letters and each clause in both the preamble and resolving portion of the resolution is written as a separate paragraph, as shown in figure 15-3. The first letter of the word following WHEREAS and RESOLVED is capitalized. The paragraphs in the preamble are ended with a semicolon followed by "and" except the last one, which is followed by "therefore, be it." Each of the resolving clauses may be followed by a period.

Discussion

The discussion concerning a motion or topic does not have to be included in the minutes; however, when the membership of the group changes

```
    Welsh moved and Smith seconded the adoption of the following
resolution:

        WHEREAS, An examination of currently used course and
    curriculum proposal forms indicates an inadequacy or in-
    appropriateness for use with semester programs; and

        WHEREAS, The currently used forms were designed
    primarily for proposals relating to the term rather than
    the semester system of instruction; and

        WHEREAS, The University is making a major transition
    involving both courses and curricula; therefore, be it

        RESOLVED, That the Semester Calendar Steering Committee
    recommends the preparation of forms specifically designed to
    give the information needed to evaluate the courses and
    proposals for the semester system of instruction.

        RESOLVED, That this Committee recommends the develop-
    ment of a policy manual to include appropriate instructions
    for the use of the proposed new forms.

        RESOLVED, That this Committee recommends that new forms
    and related material be designated Semester Course Proposal,
    Semester Curriculum Proposal, or such similar identification
    to clarify the designated use of the forms.

    Six members voted that the resolution be adopted; two members abstained.

The motion carried.
```

FIGURE 15-3. Resolution.

frequently, future officers and members may find a summary of the discussion helpful. When someone requests that the minutes show his or her position, you should include the name and the verbatim statement in the minutes. Unless specifically requested to include the names of those making the statements, you should objectively report the relevant points mentioned. Never include anywhere in the minutes words or expressions that reflect your opinion. For example, "well-defined" should be omitted in the following statement:

> Young's argument for the motion was well-defined and centered around the lack of other institutions having a technology requirement, the failure of other institutions to transfer such credits, and the fact that technology was the only area that did not have hours held constant or reduced.

Announcements

Regardless of when the announcements are made during the meeting, those reading the minutes often prefer that all announcements be grouped together and stated near the end of the minutes. This procedure is especially helpful when the announcements involve future meetings, activities, or actions to be taken.

Adjournment

Someone may move that the meeting be adjourned, or the presiding officer may simply state that the meeting is adjourned. Members frequently do not vote on the motion to adjourn. Include in the minutes the time of adjournment and, if announced, the time, date, and place of the next meeting.

Signing

Minutes printed or distributed should be signed by both the secretary and the presiding officer. Minutes that are read at a subsequent meeting are signed by only the secretary. "Respectfully yours" usually is not included in the signature section except in extremely formal situations.

Space should be provided for the date of approval, as shown in figure 15-4.

Signature section for minutes to be read at a subsequent meeting:

_____   _____
Date   Secretary, Faculty Senate

Signature section for minutes to be printed and distributed:

                                 _____
                                 President, Faculty Senate

_____   _____
Date   Secretary, Faculty Senate

FIGURE 15-4. Appropriate ways to sign minutes.

360
Secretarial
Procedures:
Office
Administration and
Automated Systems

ASSISTING OTHERS WITH MINUTES

Executives in many companies are encouraged to become actively involved in professional and community activities, and you may be expected to assist the executive with work relating to the activities. If the executive is the recording secretary, you normally will be expected to prepare the minutes in final form. The executive may take notes in longhand or may use a tape recorder. After the meeting, the executive may write the minutes in longhand, dictate them, or simply supply you with detailed notes or a tape.

You can assist the executive in several ways. Prior to the meetings, you can assemble the materials that will be needed, such as minutes of previous meetings, bylaws, roll of members, and a list of committee assignments.

A list of the members, with a space provided for a check mark to be placed by the names of those present, and motion, report, and announcement forms similar to those illustrated in figure 15-5 can simplify recording the information needed to write the minutes.

A form similar to the one shown in figure 15-6 can be used when recording some of the information needed to write the minutes. Even though the motions, reports, and announcements may be recorded on another form or sheet of paper, the person taking the minutes will be reminded of the need for the information if the items are shown on the checklist.

TYPING THE MINUTES

The minutes should normally be prepared in the form that has been used by the group; however, when you believe the content or appearance of the minutes can be improved, you should discuss your ideas with the chairperson or your supervisor. You should, of course, always observe the principles of effective writing and have the minutes technically correct.

The body of the minutes may be either single- or double-spaced. Although double spacing looks better and the minutes are easier to read, you can conserve filing space and reduce the cost of paper and postage by using single spacing and by using both sides of the paper.

If the minutes are to be bound at the left, the left margin should be one and one-half inches and the top, bottom, and right margins should be one inch. The second and following pages of the minutes should have a one-inch top margin. The paragraphs need not be indented when single spacing is used. Indent the first line of each paragraph five or ten spaces when double spacing is used.

```
┌─────────────────────────────────────────────────┐
│                    Motion                         │
│                                                   │
│  Motion _____  │
│                                                   │
│  _____ │
│                                                   │
│  Made by _____  │
│                                                   │
│  Seconded by _____  │
│                                                   │
│  Affirmative votes: _____    Negative votes: _____ │
│                                                   │
└─────────────────────────────────────────────────┘
```

```
┌─────────────────────────────────────────────────┐
│                Committee Report                   │
│                                                   │
│  Committee _____  │
│                                                   │
│  Reported by _____  │
│                                                   │
│  Summary (or obtain a copy) _____  │
│                                                   │
│  _____ │
│                                                   │
│  _____ │
│                                                   │
└─────────────────────────────────────────────────┘
```

```
┌─────────────────────────────────────────────────┐
│                 Announcements                     │
│                                                   │
│  1. _____  │
│                                                   │
│  _____ │
│                                                   │
│  Made by _____  │
│                                                   │
│  2. _____  │
│                                                   │
│  _____ │
│                                                   │
│  Made by _____  │
│                                                   │
└─────────────────────────────────────────────────┘
```

FIGURE 15-5. Forms the executive may use when recording the minutes.

The rules regarding the typing of quoted material apply when the minutes include resolutions and verbatim reports.

Capitalize the name of the group for which the minutes are written and the titles of officers in the organization.

Write the minutes by using the past tense and complete sentences. The use of "I," "we," and "our" reduces the objectivity of the minutes and should be avoided even though you may have participated in the meeting.

362
Secretarial
Procedures:
Office
Administration and
Automated Systems

```
┌─────────────────────────────────────────────────────────────┐
│                                                              │
│    Time _____ │
│                                                              │
│    Date _____ │
│                                                              │
│    Place _____ │
│                                                              │
│    Regular or Special Meeting _____ │
│                                                              │
│    Person Presiding _____ │
│                                                              │
│    Number Present _____      Absent _____                │
│                                                              │
│    Reports        )                                          │
│                   )                                          │
│    Motions        )       Record on other forms.             │
│                   )                                          │
│    Announcements )                                           │
│                                                              │
│    Next Meeting:          Time _____ │
│                                                              │
│                           Date _____ │
│                                                              │
│                           Place _____ │
│                                                              │
│    Time of Adjournment _____ │
│                                                              │
└─────────────────────────────────────────────────────────────┘
```

FIGURE 15-6. Form to be completed by the executive taking the minutes.

Marginal Headings

Marginal headings, such as those used in figure 15-7, make the minutes easy to read and enable the reader to locate a single item readily. Since the minutes are typed several spaces from the left margin, this format may result in a waste of paper, filing space, and postage if the minutes are to be mailed.

Paragraph Headings

Paragraph or run-in headings, such as those used in figure 15-8, also aid the reader in locating a single item. With this format, the use of the space on the page is maximized.

Headings Not Used

All types of headings frequently are omitted when the minutes are short, as shown in figure 15-9.

```
MINUTES OF THE BUSINESS EDUCATION AND OFFICE ADMINISTRATION
                DEPARTMENTAL MEETING

                    October 10, 1984
```

Time and   The regular meeting of the Business
Place   Education and Office Administration
                    Department of the West Plains Community
                    College was held at 3 p.m. on Wednesday,
                    October 10, in the Rose Room of the
                    University Union. John Burdett, depart-
                    ment head, presided.

Attendance   The following members of the department
                    were present: P. Burden, O. Campbell,
                    L. Clark, E. Moore, A. Williamson,
                    J. Wrigley, M. Wyss, and B. Yager.
                    S. Svacek was absent. M. Wilson, head
                    of the Division of Business, and J.
                    Wright, student representative, were
                    also present.

Minutes of   The minutes of the September 12 depart-
Previous Meeting   mental meeting were read and approved.

Committee Reports   Scholarship Committee. Campbell dis-
                    tributed scholarship application forms
                    that were prepared for use by high
                    school students in the district.

                    Wyss moved that students should have at
                    least a 3.2 grade-point average to be
                    eligible for consideration for a
                    scholarship. The motion was seconded.
                    Six voted in favor of and three voted
                    against the motion. The motion carried.

                    Burden moved that the department head
                    appoint a committee to select the scholar-
                    ship recipients. The motion was seconded
                    and carried unanimously.

                    Business Day Committee. Williamson
                    reported that Ruth Hiland will be the
                    speaker at the noon luncheon on Business
                    Day, Friday, April 12, Hiland is a
                    Certified Professional Secretary and
                    is associated with the Robles, Powell,
                    and Quader consulting firms.

FIGURE 15-7. Minutes with marginal headings.

364
Secretarial
Procedures:
Office
Administration and
Automated Systems

MINUTES OF THE BUSINESS EDUCATION AND OFFICE ADMINISTRATION
DEPARTMENTAL MEETING--October 10, 1984--Page 2

	Placement Committee. Campbell reported on the results of the follow-up study of the 1983 graduates. A copy of the report is attached.
Announcements	Burdett announced that Catherine Woods will attend the departmental meetings as the student representative during the Winter term.
	Burdett appointed Clark, Wrigley, and Yager to serve on the Scholarship Selection Committee.
	The new course proposal, Business Report Writing, has been approved by the University Curriculum Committee.
	The next regular meeting of the department will be held at 3 p.m. on Wednesday, November 14, in the Conference Room of the University Union.
Adjournment	The meeting was adjourned at 3:50 p.m.

_____   _____
          Date   Paul Burden

FIGURE 15-7. Continued

FOLLOW-UP DUTIES

Record on your calendar and that of your employer the date of the next meeting and other important dates. When the minutes indicate action that is to be taken, many members appreciate receiving a reminder. If the minutes are distributed soon after the meeting, you may underline in red the section of the minutes relating specifically to the person to whom you are sending that copy. When the minutes are not distributed, you may write a memorandum or letter to remind the members of important dates and duties.

MINUTES OF THE BUSINESS EDUCATION AND OFFICE ADMINISTRATION
DEPARTMENTAL MEETING

October 10, 1984

The regular monthly meeting of the Business Education
and Office Administration Department of the West Plains
Community College was held at 3 p.m. on Wednesday, October 10,
in the Rose Room of the University Union. John Burdett,
department head, presided.

The following members of the department were present:
P. Burden, O. Campbell, L. Clark, E. Moore, A. Williamson,
J. Wrigley, M. Wyss, and B. Yager. S. Svacek was absent.
M. Wilson, head of the Division of Business, and J. Wright,
student representative, were also present.

The minutes of the September 12 meeting were read and
approved.

Scholarship Committee. Campbell distributed scholarship
application forms that were prepared for use by high school
students in the district.

Wyss moved that students should have at least a 3.2 grade-
point average to be eligible for consideration for a
scholarship. The motion was seconded. Six voted in favor of
and three voted against the motion. The motion carried.

Burden moved that the department head appoint a committee
to select the scholarship recipients. The motion was seconded
and carried unanimously.

Business Day Committee. Williamson reported that Ruth
Hiland will be the speaker at the noon luncheon on Business
Day, Friday, April 12. Hiland is a Certified Professional
Secretary and is associated with the Robles, Powell, and
Quader consulting firm.

Placement Committee. Campbell reported on the results
of the follow-up study of the 1983 graduates. A copy of the
report is attached.

Announcements. Burdett announced that Catherine Woods
will attend the departmental meetings as the student representative during the Winter term.

Burdett appointed Clark, Wrigley, and Yager to serve on
the Scholarship Selection Committee.

FIGURE 15-8. Minutes with paragraph headings.

366
Secretarial
Procedures:
Office
Administration and
Automated Systems

```
MINUTES OF THE BUSINESS EDUCATION AND OFFICE ADMINISTRATION
DEPARTMENTAL MEETING--October 10, 1984--Page 2


     The new course proposal, Business Report Writing, has
been approved by the University Curriculum Committee.

     The next regular meeting of the department will be held
at 3 p.m. on Wednesday, November 14, in the Conference Room of
the University Union.

     The meeting was adjourned at 3:50 p.m.



_____           _____
        Date                        Paul Burden
```

FIGURE 15-8. Continued

You should read through your notes immediately after the meeting to make sure you have recorded all the information and have copies of motions, resolutions, reports, or other material needed to write the minutes. You should obtain copies of distributed material for those who were absent.

If the membership of an organization changes frequently or the organization takes action concerning numerous topics, you should maintain a subject index of the minutes to facilitate locating information readily. A file may be set up by using a separate 3 by 5 card for each topic covered. The dates of the meetings at which the subject was discussed can be noted. Much time involved in looking through the minutes of previous meetings can be saved by taking a few minutes to bring the data on the cards up to date each time you prepare minutes. Cards used by the recording secretary for a university curriculum committee might appear as shown in figure 15-10.

———————————————————— Summary ————————————————————

So that minutes may be written which will accurately and completely reflect the proceedings, adequate information must be recorded during the meeting concerning the time and place, attendance, and what transpired. Often motions are made, reports are presented, and announcements are given that must be reported in the minutes.

Although the secretary may not always be required to attend the meetings, she is usually responsible for preparing the minutes in final form.

MINUTES OF THE ACTIVITIES COMMITTEE MEETING

October 9, 1984

The Activities Committee of The Honor Society of Phi Kappa Phi met at 3 p.m. on Tuesday, October 9, with Chairperson Bettie Willard presiding. William Ackers, Fred Baldwin, Robert Homan, and Katherine Smith were present.

Homan reported that slightly over $500 will be available for the Supplemental Grant Program.

The grant applications received from the Campus Committee on the Holocaust and the German Club, the Department of Music, and the Public Relations Student Society of America were reviewed. Smith expressed the opinion that in the future the applicants should be required to submit full details concerning how the money is to be spent.

Ackers moved that 50 percent of the available funds be allocated to the Committee on the Holocaust and the German Club and 50 percent to the Department of Music. The motion was seconded and carried unanimously.

The Supplemental Grant Program guidelines were discussed. Willard indicated she would make the suggested changes in the wording of the guidelines and submit a revised copy to the Executive Committee.

Baldwin reported that a panel will discuss the article, "A Journey Through Darkness—Vietnam War Films," at the Winter meeting of Phi Kappa Phi.

Speakers or program activities for the Spring meeting will be discussed at the next meeting of the Activities Committee. Willard will notify the members of the time and place of the next meeting.

The meeting was adjourned at 4:15 p.m.

_____   _____
        Date   William Ackers, Recorder

FIGURE 15-9. Minutes without headings.

368
Secretarial
Procedures:
Office
Administration and
Automated Systems

```
General Education

    English

    1/12/83      Test-Out Procedures

    5/5/84       Increase in Hours
```

```
Business Education

    2/5/83       Certification Requirements

    9/25/84      Shorthand Requirements
```

FIGURE 15-10. Index of minutes.

Questions

1. Must a secretary record everything that is said during the meeting to eliminate the possibility of leaving out something important when writing the minutes? Discuss.

2. Discuss the steps that can be taken prior to the meeting that will aid you in taking adequate notes during the meeting.

3. Why is taking notes often easier in a formal meeting than in one that is not conducted according to parliamentary law?

4. What precautions should be taken when a tape recorder is to be used during the meeting?

5. If you are unable to record the motion when it is made, why should you not wait until the end of the meeting to ask the person to repeat it?

6. When parliamentary procedures are not followed and no motions are made, should minutes be prepared? Discuss.

7. Why should the recording secretary normally sit near the chairperson during the meeting?

8. Why is an accurate attendance record important?

9. What can be done to simplify checking the attendance?

10. How can you avoid using the sexist expressions "chairman" and "chairwoman" when writing the minutes?

11. Explain the procedures involved when errors are noted in the minutes of a previous meeting.

12. When reporting a motion, what must be included in the minutes?

13. How may a motion be typed in the minutes to aid the reader in locating it?

14. When the vote on a motion is taken by calling the roll, must each person give an "affirmative" or "negative" response?

15. Why are motions sometimes amended?

16. Since formal reports are to be presented as quoted material in the minutes, must the secretary always be able to write shorthand rapidly enough to record the report verbatim as it is being read?

17. Is a resolution a motion?

18. Why should a summary of the discussion concerning a motion or topics sometimes be included in the minutes?

19. When must a particular individual's comments be included in the minutes?

20. The formal style of writing is used in the minutes. Why?

21. Must announcements be reported in the minutes in the sequence in which they were made?

22. How many people must sign the minutes? Explain.

23. Should the secretary be expected to assist with the minutes when her supervisor is the recording secretary of a professional or community organization? Discuss.

24. Marginal headings assist the reader in readily locating an item; however, they should not always be used. Why?

25. Should an index of the minutes always be maintained? Explain.

370
Secretarial
Procedures:
Office
Administration and
Automated Systems

———————————————— Projects ————————————————

1. Consult a copy of *Robert's Rules of Order* and write a paragraph explaining each of the following motions:

   a. Main

   b. Subsidiary

   c. Incidental

   d. Privileged

2. Attend a meeting of the city council, board of regents of a college or university, or some other governing body at which a formal agenda is followed and the meeting is conducted according to parliamentary law. Take notes and prepare the minutes.

3. Attend a lecture and take notes. Write a summary in sufficient detail so that someone who did not hear the lecture will be able to fully understand what was covered in the lecture.

———————————————— Cases ————————————————

1. During a meeting at which you took notes, John Nolte became very emotional and stated "I want the minutes to show that I vehemently oppose this proposal because...." After the meeting, Mr. Nolte telephoned your office and said that he had decided he did not want his remarks to be quoted in the minutes. How should you respond to Mr. Nolte's request?

2. As you are preparing the minutes of a meeting, you notice that several words in a resolution adopted by the group are misspelled in the copy that was given to you during the meeting. Should the words be spelled correctly in the minutes?

3. Your boss is recording secretary for a civic organization. The notes he gives to you to use in preparing the minutes frequently do not include the names of those who made the motions and often he fails to record the motions verbatim, even though you have suggested that he use forms similar to those discussed in this chapter. Do you believe the members of the organization think the poorly prepared minutes are a result of your inefficiency? What should you do?

4. Vice President West missed an important meeting your boss, President Hickman, had asked all middle- and upper-level executives to attend. President Hickman did not attend the meeting but he asked that you take notes and prepare the minutes. After the meeting, Vice President West called you and asked that you indicate in the minutes that he was present. Should you comply with his request?

CHAPTER 16

Supplies

Making sure that supplies of the proper quality and quantity are available is one of the secretary's responsibilities. In some companies, the secretary simply requisitions supplies from the central storeroom as they are needed in her office. In other organizations, the secretary must determine the types of supplies that are available, identify the sources, place the orders, receive the shipments, and store and issue the supplies.

In addition to having adequate supplies, the secretary must have desk accessories and references readily accessible in order to perform her duties effectively.

SUPPLIES

No organization can operate without supplies. For most offices, maintaining an appropriate level of supplies goes beyond the simple act of going to a supply store and buying what is needed. It includes a wide range of activities:

- Determining the type, quality, quantity, and price.
- Identifying and selecting the sources.
- Deciding when to place the order.
- Preparing the requisition or order.
- Receiving the supplies.
- Storing the supplies.

374
Secretarial
Procedures:
Office
Administration and
Automated Systems

DESCRIPTION OF THE SUPPLIES NEEDED

When supplies are needed, they must be described accurately. As indicated later in this chapter, almost all supplies used in the office vary considerably in characteristics such as color, size, and quality. Time may be lost when the order cannot be filled because of an improper or inadequate description of the items wanted. An improper description is especially unfortunate when the order is filled before the error is observed. The time involved in handling the goods and the freight from and to the supplier can be costly.

QUALITY

Quality refers to the suitability of an item for its intended purpose. The most expensive supplies should not be used for all tasks. Quality must always be judged in terms of how the item will be used. For example, a nylon typewriter ribbon and sulfite paper may be perfectly acceptable for most of the routine work you perform, but the more expensive carbon ribbon and cotton fiber paper may be needed when the appearance of the work is of paramount importance.

Check with your supervisor when you are not sure of the quality of the supplies you should use.

QUANTITY

An adequate stock of supplies must be maintained so that a shortage will not occur and disrupt the flow of work; however, an oversupply sometimes results in an increase in the total cost of supplies.

Some supplies, such as some types of ribbons and carbon, deteriorate after extended periods of time. Other supplies may become obsolete. For example, letterhead becomes obsolete when any of the information printed on it, such as the titles of executives or the address, changes. Typewriter ribbons purchased for a particular type of machine may not be compatible with other types.

The price of supplies often varies with the quantity purchased. The cost of a single ream of paper is considerably more than the cost per ream when ordered in case lots. Use good judgment when deciding on the quantity to purchase. If you anticipate that only two items with a unit price of $5 will be used, do not order a dozen even though the unit price for that quantity might be only $4.50.

The amount of storage space may limit the quantity of some types of supplies that may be obtained at one time and may result in less than optimal-size orders being placed.

DETERMINING THE PRICE

The usual practice is to include the price on the purchase order. However, when you have repeatedly purchased from a supplier or when the items are of small value and do not justify expending much time or effort in determining the price, you may rely on the integrity of the supplier.

Since many inexpensive supplies are purchased locally, the common practice is to telephone the supplier to determine the price when it is not known. If the item has been purchased recently, the price information can be obtained by looking in the file. When the prices are not listed in the catalog, the supplier normally provides periodically updated price lists.

For some supplies that are to be produced according to your specifications, such as letterhead, you may need to seek bids from more than one source and negotiate for the price.

Although you may have the price information you need readily available, you should check periodically to be certain that the supplier's prices are competitive.

WHEN TO ORDER

To have supplies on hand when they are needed but not have an oversupply, you must anticipate the needs and the lead time. Lead time is the length of time between the placement of the order and the actual delivery of the item.

When the supplies are stocked in a central storeroom, often the supplies can be picked up or delivered immediately. When the items are ordered frequently from the same source, through experience you will know the approximate lead time required. However, when the item has never been purchased, you usually have difficulty knowing the lead time involved unless you are able to check with the supplier. Keep in mind that suppliers are sometimes overly optimistic when indicating delivery dates; therefore, you should order the items early enough to ensure delivery by the date needed. Rush orders usually increase the cost of the supplies and with proper planning they can be minimized or eliminated.

You should decide on a system that will result in your maintaining a proper stock of supplies. No one system will work for all offices and for all types of supplies. Perhaps a daily or weekly review of the supplies you

376
Secretarial
Procedures:
Office
Administration and
Automated Systems

have on hand will be adequate. With experience, you may learn that when you start using the last ream of letterhead or the last box of typewriter ribbons, you need to order another supply. A calendar notation may be required as a reminder to order large quantities of supplies that will be needed at certain times. For example, if you were responsible for maintaining supplies for the faculty of a school or college, you should anticipate the need for large quantities of duplicating paper at the end of each semester.

Develop a system that will result in your always having the supplies that are needed but at the same time not waste storage space or increase the cost because of maintaining an oversupply or the supplies deteriorating or becoming obsolete.

PROCEDURES FOR OBTAINING SUPPLIES

Follow the procedures established by your company to obtain the supplies you need for your office.

In large companies, the supplies inventory is stored in a central location and a catalog or listing of the items is maintained. A stock requisition form is completed and sent or taken to the stockroom when supplies are needed. All parts of the stock requisition form should be completed accurately to ensure you receive exactly what is needed.

When the company does not have a central supplies stockroom, you normally must complete a purchase requisition form and submit it to the purchasing department.

Many small service-type companies and professional groups, such as accounting partnerships, do not have a central supplies storeroom or a purchasing department. In these situations, you will be expected to prepare the order in letter form, on a purchase order form or in some cases place the order over the telephone.

RECEIVING SUPPLIES

When supplies have been requisitioned from the stockroom or ordered from a supplier, you should always inspect and check the supplies when they are delivered to your office. The carbon copy of the requisition or purchase order should be used as you identify the items in the shipment and determine whether they are of the quantity and quality ordered. Place a check mark by the item listed on the form when you have determined that it is acceptable.

If you prepared the purchase order, you normally will be expected to prepare and send to the accounting department a report indicating the goods have been received and payment should be made.

When items are received in damaged condition, a claim should be registered immediately with the vendor or carrier. The supplier should be notified when short shipments are received or the order was incorrectly filled.

STORAGE

Once the supplies have been received in the office, they must be stored properly to ensure they will remain in good condition and can be found when they are needed. Consider the following suggestions when storing the supplies:

- Keep the supplies out of the sunlight and away from moisture and excessive heat.
- Place the new supplies at the back or on the bottom; use first the supplies that have been on hand the longest.
- Arrange the supplies so that they will be visible when the door of the cabinet or closet is open or place a list on the door telling where the different supplies are located. People readily become annoyed when they cannot find something because it has been stored in an obscure place.
- Store all small items in boxes; label the boxes clearly.
- Place all types of supplies in separate containers; for example, do not put various types of pencils or pens in the same box.
- Place items that may become warped, such as file folders and paper, flat on a shelf.
- Store heavy items at low levels.
- Keep the storage area neat and orderly.

Maintaining the proper inventory level is greatly simplified when only one person distributes the supplies. When several people have access to the storage area, almost always some will not notify the one responsible when the supply appears low. Furthermore, some people are tempted to take more supplies than they need simply because they see large quantities available.

378
Secretarial
Procedures.
Office
Administration and
Automated Systems

TYPES OF SUPPLIES USED IN MOST OFFICES

Paper

Since paper is the medium for printed communication, it represents a considerable cost factor for many companies; therefore, it should be selected carefully. All paper has numerous peculiar characteristics; but from the user's standpoint, the properties most often considered are the content, substance (weight), and finish.

Content

Bond paper is used in most offices for copying, letterheads, forms, and a variety of documents.

The two predominant types of paper used in the office are cotton fiber (also called rag) and sulfite (wood pulp) bonds. The content of the paper may be all sulfite, all cotton, or a combination. If the paper is 25 percent cotton, it is 75 percent sulfite. Bond paper with cotton content is recognized as the highest quality paper; therefore, it is used when image, permanence, and durability are important. As you can imagine, the higher the cotton content, the more expensive the paper.

Substance

Most paper used in the office is described by a substance number. The substance number refers to the weight of 500 sheets (a ream) of paper that is 17 inches by 22 inches; thus, if a ream of paper that size weighs 24 pounds, the paper is said to be of substance 24, or 24-pound weight. Paper can be cut to various sizes from the 17-inch by 22-inch ream, but it would have the same substance number and the same weight.

Watermarks

When a name or image is impressed on the paper, it is known as a watermark. Good quality bond paper normally has a watermark, and the watermark frequently is the brand name of the paper and the cotton fiber content; however, some users of bond paper often like to have their company logos watermarked in the stationery. Needless to say, a large quantity of paper must be ordered to justify this special procedure.

The watermark, whether on letterhead or ordinary paper, must be in reading position; that is, the watermark must be across the page in the same direction as the typewritten material. If the watermark is hard to see, hold the paper up to the light.

379
Supplies

Finishes

Bond paper may have a smooth, cockle, or some type of easy erase finish or texture. Print is clearest on paper with a smooth finish. Paper with a cockle finish is slightly rippled. Paper with the added erasability finish is generally referred to by brand name, such as Type-Erase or Ezerase, and the brand name is usually the watermark. Although errors can be corrected readily with a soft eraser, many executives do not like the erasable paper because the ink is gradually absorbed and smears easily until it dries. Some carbon ribbons are not compatible with the erasable paper and the copy may not be clear.

Copier and Duplicating Paper

Either sulfite or fiber content bond paper can be used with most duplicating and copying equipment. Extra smoothness is needed for some copiers and a porous paper is needed for the mimeograph. Copying machine manufacturers provide instruction manuals that include suggestions concerning the type of paper to use.

Second Sheets

The paper (second sheets) used for multiple copies of letters, forms, and other documents prepared on the typewriter usually is known as onionskin or manifold.

Onionskin paper comes in 7-pound to 13-pound weights, but it frequently is 9-pound weight and has a 25 percent rag content for strength. The finish may be smooth, glazed, cockle, or erasable. Second sheets often are colored and may be labeled "Copy."

Lightweight manifold papers are made from wood fiber and are frequently used for snap-out forms. Most companies utilize copiers now and the amount of onionskin used has decreased.

Carbonless Paper

The carbonless type of paper is especially popular for forms. Carbonless paper has an invisible coating. The obvious advantages to using this type of paper are that no messy carbon paper is involved and no assembly is required. The disadvantage is its sensitivity to scuffing or marring.

380
Secretarial
Procedures:
Office
Administration and
Automated Systems

Carbon Paper

The weight and finish of the carbon paper to use depends on the type size, the number of copies to be made, and whether the typewriter is electric or manual. The finishes of the carbon usually are classified as soft, medium, and hard; the weights are classified as light, medium, and standard.

You may need to experiment with carbon of different finishes and weights to determine the one appropriate for the type of work to be performed.

Carbon Copy Sets

Preassembled copy sets, such as those illustrated in figure 16-1, consisting of second sheets interleaved with one-time carbon are faster, cleaner, and easier to use than carbon paper.

The copy sets may be tipped or perforated at the bottom, leaving the top open for easy erasing. The copy sheets are available in smooth, cockle, and erasable finishes, as well as in different colors.

Forms

Many large organizations employ experts in the area of forms design and control and have established procedures to be followed when printed

FIGURE 16-1. Preassembled copy set.

forms are needed. If the organization for which you work does not have procedures for developing and using forms, you usually can obtain many of the forms you need at an office supplies store.

When the use of a form would simplify recurring tasks and the type of form you need is not available, you can demonstrate creativity and initiative by designing a form to submit to your supervisor for approval.

Mailing Supplies

Envelopes

Envelopes are normally made of the same color, weight, finish, and type of paper as used for the letterhead. The name of the company and the address usually are printed in the upper left-hand corner of the envelopes.

Postal approved special green diamond border envelopes that are imprinted with "First-Class Mail" often are used to ensure the proper handling of important unfolded mail.

Window envelopes can be used to save time addressing the envelopes when large mailings are involved. Envelopes used for bulky mail may be made of 28-pound or heavier paper and come in numerous sizes. Envelopes used for international mail normally are made of lightweight paper.

Reusable interdepartment envelopes allow the sender, the receiver, and the department concerned to be identified. The envelope usually has a pressure-sensitive closure.

Since the price varies with the size and the type of paper, be careful in selecting the appropriate envelopes to use.

Labels

Mailing labels may be prepared in several ways. Rolls of labels and single labels can be used when multiple copies are not needed. Sheets of labels that are imprintable by mimeograph, multilith, spirit duplicator, letterpress, and copiers are available for repeat labeling jobs. When some types of duplicating processes are used, the typewritten master list may be used repeatedly to print the labels. Several carbon copies can be made when typing some label sheets. The pressure-sensitive labels do not require moistening, and they adhere to a wide variety of surfaces.

Visual Aid Supplies

Many types of pens and film are available for use with the overhead projector. The waterbase ink can be removed from the acetate film with a

382
Secretarial
Procedures:
Office
Administration and
Automated Systems

damp cloth. A correction marker is needed to remove the permanent ink. The pens come in a variety of colors and with fine, medium, and broad points.

Black images are produced on thermal and copier film; however, the film is available in several colors. The thermal film comes in four weights: light, medium, standard, and heavy. The heavy weight film lays flat on the overhead and other surfaces and is easy to write on, but it is considerably more expensive than film of other weights.

Typing Supplies and Accessories

Ribbons

Typewriter ribbons are available on spools and in cartridges and are of three types: fabric, one-time film, and multiuse film. Whether a spool or cartridge ribbon is used depends, of course, on the typewriter; however, the type of ribbon depends on the quality of work desired.

Since fabric ribbons are reusable, they are the most economical and often are used for memorandums, reports, and other documents that are prepared for in-house use.

The film (carbon) ribbons are used when superb sharpness and clarity are desired; thus, they are ideal when typing correspondence or work that is to be copied, printed, or microfilmed.

The one-time carbon ribbons are coated strips of film that advance one space each time a character is typed. The multiuse ribbons are also made of film, but they move slowly and several impressions are made from the same ribbon area. Since several characters are typed in the same area, what has been typed cannot be read by looking at the ribbon; therefore, this ribbon is often used when confidentiality is required. All carbon ribbons are used once and then discarded.

Corrections Supplies

Most executives prefer that typewritten work going outside the company not have any noticeable corrections. Regardless of how neat the correction may be, generally it is noticeable unless something is typed in the space where the error occurred; therefore, some errors, such as a word typed in the margin, should not be corrected. The page should be retyped.

The correction technique to be used depends on the work being prepared, the type of paper, the type of typewriter ribbon, and the preference of the typist and supervisor.

Erasers may be used to correct errors made with all types of ribbons and on all types of paper. A soft typewriter or pencil eraser should be used on sulfite and erasable bond paper and a hard typewriter eraser should be used on cotton-fiber bond paper.

Correction tape can be placed over the space where errors occur, and corrections may be typewritten on the tape. Liquid paper correction fluid also can be used to cover errors. The correction tape and opaquing fluid can be used effectively on work that is to be photocopied and on draft work, but they should never be used on work where the appearance of the original copy is important.

Sheets of rub-off letters, available in different type styles, can be used to correct an error after the page has been removed from the typewriter.

Corrections made with lift-off tape are least noticeable, but the tape must be used on self-correcting typewriters. Lift-off tabs can be used with some correctable typewriter ribbons and cover-up tabs can be used with all types of ribbons.

Since new correction supplies are constantly being introduced, you should periodically look at catalogs and visit supplies stores to select the correction aids most appropriate for your office.

Type Cleaners and Brushes

No work that has dirty type should ever leave the office. Solvents or plastic cleaners can be used to dissolve dried ink, and nylon filament brushes can be used to remove gummy deposits. Some cleaners can also be used to restore the resiliency in the rubber platen roll.

Typing Elements and Print Wheels

In addition to the pica and elite type, typing elements and print wheels are designed with other type styles. Some elements provide different options for punctuation characters, symbols, and numerous special characters. Contact the typewriter equipment companies when you have the need for different type styles.

Desk Accessories

Appointment Calendars

Appointment calendars are available in dozens of different designs. Consider the following characteristics as you select the calendar on which to schedule the appointments and record the tasks that must be completed:

384
Secretarial
Procedures:
Office
Administration and
Automated Systems

- Loose-leaf or spiral
- Intervals of 15 or 30 minutes
- Pages for daily, weekly, or monthly appointments
- Dated or undated
- Refillable or nonrefillable

Desk Drawer Organizer

Organizers with compartments for scissors, pencils, clips, rubber bands, and other small items can be used to keep things off the top of the desk but in a convenient place.

Telephone Shoulder Rest

When lengthy messages must be taken over the telephone, a shoulder rest can be helpful. The rests are available in different colors, are adjustable for use on the left or right shoulder, and are easy to install.

Telephone Lock

A telephone lock for push button or dial phones prevents unauthorized calls being placed from your phone.

Collator

Lightweight collapsible racks with as many as 24 sections that accommodate full-size and larger size sheets can be used to simplify collating tasks. When pages must be collated frequently, you may need an electric collator.

Pencil Sharpener

An electric sharpener should be used when the work of those in the office requires the use of well-sharpened pencils. The electric sharpeners automatically stop when the pencils are fully sharpened; thus, waste is reduced. The suction feet hold the sharpener firmly in place on the desk or table.

A stationery tray can be used to organize letterheads, envelopes, and other paper in the desk drawer. Stackable trays can be used to keep letters and other correspondence conveniently and neatly organized on the desk.

Numerous devices used to sort, store, and file papers and documents are available. Look at a catalog or visit a supplies store to select those devices that will help you perform your work efficiently.

Rotary and Business Card Files

Most secretaries like to have a rotary file on the desk for the names, addresses, and telephone numbers of those frequently contacted. A business card file can be helpful in many office situations.

Equipment and supplies are designed for filing and storing all types of cards, letters, documents, magazines, and so forth. They should be selected with your particular needs in mind.

Copy Holders

Various types of copy holders are available for shorthand pads, standard- and legal-size paper, and books. Many of the copy holders, such as the one shown in figure 16-2, have magnetic line guides that are especially useful when typing statistical copy. Copyholders are also available with a flexible arm that turns and stretches up, down, and around.

Staplers

When papers must be stapled frequently, an electric stapler makes the task easy. Electric staplers can be calibrated to give precise staple placement. They have nonskid suction cups, and they staple rapidly. If the stapler does not function properly, several holes make the page unattractive; therefore, a good-quality stapler of the electric or hand-operated type is essential.

Shredder

When you frequently need to destroy confidential documents, you may need a portable shredder that can be placed on the desk, as shown in figure 16-3. When selecting a shredder, consider the number of pages

386
Secretarial
Procedures:
Office
Administration and
Automated Systems

FIGURE 16-2. Oxford™ Flexible Arm Copyholder. (Courtesy of Esselte Pendaflex Corporation)

that can be shredded at one time and whether the staples must be removed.

Letter Opener

A standard blade-type letter opener is adequate for most offices; however, if a large volume of mail is received daily, an electric opener can speed the process. Since the electric opener makes a clean cut, it is especially useful when the envelopes must be attached to the correspondence or kept for a period of time.

References

The references the secretary should have available in the office depend somewhat on the type of work performed, but in almost all offices the following references are used frequently and should be kept handy.

Dictionary

For everyday needs, the standard abridged desk dictionary is used to find a word's meaning, spelling, syllabication, and pronunciation. Since the meaning, spelling, and usage of words change, the dictionary should have a recent copyright date.

Webster's New Collegiate Dictionary, Webster's New World Dictionary, The American Heritage Dictionary of the English Language, and *Funk and Wagnalls Standard Dictionary* are the abridged dictionaries frequently found in the office.

Even though abridged dictionaries are adequate for finding the use of most words, one of the following unabridged dictionaries should be available in the office area: *Webster's Third New International Dictionary of the English Language, Funk and Wagnalls New Standard Dictionary,* or *The Random House Dictionary of the English Language.*

Thesaurus

A thesaurus is needed when you know the meaning you want to convey, but you do not know the appropriate word to use. Many secretaries have *Webster's Collegiate Thesaurus* or *Roget's Thesaurus* available in the office.

Secretarial Manuals

Your references should include two or three secretarial manuals. One of these manuals should be *The Gregg Reference Manual,* published by the Gregg Division/McGraw-Hill Book Company. This manual thoroughly covers the basic secretarial rules and includes numerous examples and illustrations.

Directories

The *National ZIP Code Directory* and the local telephone directory must be readily accessible since they are used often during the day. Other directories may also be needed. For example, the *Congressional Staff Directory* may be needed in offices where executives communicate frequently with government officials.

Style Manuals

When reports are prepared from secondary data and footnotes and a bibliography are required, you should have one of the following manuals available:

A Manual for Writers of Term Papers, Theses, and Dissertations, published by The University of Chicago Press.

388
Secretarial
Procedures:
Office
Administration and
Automated Systems

FIGURE 16-3. Desktop paper shredder. (Courtesy of Shredex™ Inc.)

A Manual of Style, published by The University of Chicago Press.

Form and Style, published by Houghton Mifflin Company.

Atlas

The *Hammond World Atlas,* or one similar to it, is detailed enough to meet the needs of most offices.

Manuals for Machines

The manuals that explain the use and operation of the office machines should be studied carefully and be available for reference purposes.

Other References

Handbooks, such as the *Legal Secretary's Complete Handbook* and the *Modern Accountant's Handbook,* are available for almost all areas of business. You should have copies of those that relate specifically to your work.

If meetings are conducted according to parliamentary law, a copy of *Robert's Rules of Order* is needed.

You should also have one or more business writing textbooks. As you read and study other chapters in this textbook, you probably will become aware of other references that will be helpful in your work.

Summary

The secretary's responsibilities in the supplies area depend on the organization. They can range from the simple task of requisitioning the supplies from a central stockroom to the more involved steps leading up to and including placing orders with suppliers.

In addition to being knowledgeable about the numerous types of supplies available, the secretary needs to be aware of the many desk accessories and references that can be used to improve the quality of her work and increase her productivity.

Questions

1. Discuss the factors that should be considered when deciding on the quality of supplies to order.

2. What are the possible results of inadequately describing the supplies ordered?

3. Name the different ways of identifying the sources of supplies.

4. Since the unit cost of many supplies is less when large quantities are purchased, should a large volume of all supplies be purchased? Discuss.

5. Define "lead time."

6. When should the price of supplies be negotiated?

7. Define "purchase requisition" and "purchase order."

8. When is a supply requisition used?

9. In what type of organization is the secretary most likely expected to prepare the purchase order?

10. Explain the purpose of a receiving report.

11. List the factors that should be considered when storing supplies.

12. Discuss what the secretary may do to avoid having an inadequate quantity of supplies on hand.

13. Name the properties of paper the user may consider important.

14. What are the two types of bond paper?

15. When should paper with a high cotton content be used?

390
Secretarial
Procedures:
Office
Administration and
Automated Systems

16. What is the weight of a ream of 8½-inch by 11-inch paper made of 20-pound paper?

17. Why do some executives not like to use erasable paper?

18. What should the typist remember when using watermarked paper?

19. Name the advantages of using NCR paper.

20. Are envelopes used for international mail normally made of 20-pound paper?

21. Discuss the types of errors that make work that is to be sent outside the company unmailable.

—————————————————— Projects ——————————————————

1. Visit an office supplies store and complete the following projects:

   a. Compare the cost of several kinds of typing paper.

   b. Make a list of the correction supplies and indicate when each should be used.

   c. Compare several types of carbon paper and determine when each should be used.

   d. List several printed forms that you believe would be used in a typical office.

   e. Compare the cost of the different kinds of typewriter ribbons.

   f. List ten items that you did not previously know about and tell how each item could be used by the secretary.

2. Examine the letterhead of several companies and list the distinctive features of each.

3. Design letterhead for a hypothetical company and explain why you decided on the format.

4. Visit the offices of five secretaries and list the desk accessories and references they have readily accessible.

5. List the specific references (by name) you would select for an office and tell why you would select them.

—————————————————— Cases ——————————————————

1. Even though many of the supplies could be purchased for considerably less, your boss insists that they be purchased from a local supplier. Should you tell your boss that you believe this to be a poor business practice, report the matter to a higher-level executive, or take some

other action? If you do not report this situation to a higher-level executive, should you do anything to protect yourself should you be questioned?

2. The representatives of some of the companies from which you purchase large quantities of supplies send you Christmas gifts (in the $50 to $75 range). You are convinced that you buy the supplies that are best for your company and that you buy them at the lowest possible price. Should you keep the gifts?

3. Assume that you are responsible for ordering and storing supplies for 25 employees. A notice is clearly visible on the door of the storeroom asking employees to notify you when supplies reach a certain point. For example, you are to be told when only five reams of paper and two boxes of pencils are in stock. Some of the employees do not follow the instructions and as a result the supply of some items is sometimes depleted before you realize the need to place an order. What are some possible actions that can be taken to ensure an adequate stock of supplies at all times?

4. One of the executives frequently asks you to order large quantities of a certain type of expensive pen. You know that the executive never uses a pen of this type on the job. You suspect that he gives the pens to his son who is attending college and needs pens of this type for one of his technical courses. What should you do?

PART VII

CHAPTER 17

Human Relations

INTRODUCTION

Since much of your time as a secretary is spent interacting with other individuals, your ability to skillfully develop and promote human relationships is an important part of your job. Good working relationships in the office are dependent on being understood and perceived accurately by others, as well as by understanding and perceiving others accurately.

We communicate in many ways. Everything we do when we are around others is a form of communication and contributes to how we are understood or perceived. We are always telling somebody something, whether we intend to or not.

Many of the bases on which impressions are formed will be discussed in this chapter. You will observe that impressions are influenced by what we think, by what is said, by how it is said, and by observable nonverbal ways.

TACT

Secretaries are continually faced with situations that require a keen sense of what to do or say to maintain good relations, both with the public and with those inside the organization. The secretary's expertise in demonstrating tact can do much to create and maintain goodwill for the organization and keep the organization operating smoothly.

The secretary is confronted with many situations that require noncompliance with a request, that require pointing out errors that have been made by others, and that require finesse in getting others to respond in a positive way to her desires or needs.

The good secretary learns the art of saying "no." The refusal must be worded in such a way that the other person will not believe that he should not have made the request or that the refusal is personal. You might say "No, I will not help you with the assignment." However, the other person will have a much better feeling when your response is "I wish I could help you, but these letters I am typing must be ready for Ms. Buck's signature within an hour." Telling a client that "Mr. Jones has an appointment with an important client and can't see you" is not nearly as effective as "I'm sure Mr. Jones would like to see you; however, he has appointments scheduled all afternoon."

Should someone outside your organization ask for confidential information, your saying "Those data are confidential and I cannot give them to you" is apt to cause the person to believe he should not have asked. On the other hand, a response such as "I cannot tell you the specific salaries of the salespersons, but the range is from $30,000 to $50,000" will give the person the impression you are doing all you can to help. Always try to support your refusal to comply with a request by using facts, fairness, and sound business judgment or by citing a prior agreement.

Perhaps someone in the organization has been slow in submitting reports to your office. Your reminding the person that he is late may antagonize him. A request such as "May we have your report so that it can be presented to the Board at the June 15 meeting?" will get results in many instances because the coworker will realize that you have a need for the information and are not merely trying to intimidate him for being late.

Instead of telling a supervisor "You told me to do it this way," the capable secretary will say "I understood that this was the way you wanted it; I'll be glad to type the letter again." "Would you please check the total?" is certainly more tactful than saying "You made a mistake when you added the column."

Help the other person overcome his or her feeling of rejection by demonstrating that his or her needs are important and that you would sincerely like to meet those needs.

LISTENING

Listening is an important phase of the communication process; however, most training in the communication area in schools involves only writing, reading, and speaking. Yet from the time we start communicating, we spend at least as much time listening as we do on all the other three. According to some experts, the average adult spends about one-third of his time listening.

Many of your duties as a secretary will involve the use of listening skills. Much of your work will involve receiving instructions, using the telephone, and communicating with callers and coworkers. Learning to listen well is one of the most important things you can do as a secretary to improve your efficiency on the job and to develop your personal and business relationships.

Listening is crucial because it

- *Saves time.* If you hear something correctly the first time, you will not have to ask for information to be repeated.
- *Avoids confusion.* If you listen well, you will comprehend the entire message and it will not have to be repeated.
- *Creates a favorable impression.* You will develop a reputation for capability when you develop the skill of taking messages accurately; furthermore, the work of the office will flow more smoothly.

Barriers

To improve your listening skill, you need to be familiar with the following barriers that may interfere with the listening process.

Physical distractions.

Noise, interruptions, and physical discomfort may distract you or another person. Tapping a pencil, doodling, shuffling papers, looking away from the speaker, and other such activities may be disturbing factors. The speaker's appearance, voice, or speech characteristics may also impede the communication process.

Preoccupation.

People usually speak at a rate of under 200 words a minute; however, people think at somewhere between 600 and 800 words a minute. What one does with this time differential determines to a great extent how effective one is as a listener.

Ignorance.

If you know nothing about the topic, you probably will not be a good listener. You may hear and understand the speaker well, but you may still have no way of knowing the importance or relevance of what he or she is saying. Most people have difficulty listening when they are not interested in the topic being discussed. Frequently this lack of interest is a result of the person not being knowledgeable about the topic.

398
Secretarial
Procedures:
Office
Administration and
Automated Systems

Message length.

The longer the message, often the greater the risk of losing information and accuracy. Listeners tend to eliminate many details from the messages they receive.

Antagonism.

When we dislike someone, we have difficulty listening to him or her objectively and either consciously or subconsciously have as our primary objective the desire to end the conversation as quickly as possible.

Removing Barriers

Here are several pointers that will help you remove or minimize the barriers to effective listening.

- *Be prepared.* When you know in advance the topic of the conversation, frequently you can learn something about it. If correspondence has been received relating to the topic, perusing the files may help you become familiar with the matter to be discussed. Other office personnel may be able to brief you on the subject.

- *Remove distractions.* You may be able to close a door to eliminate noise. A coworker may be willing to answer the telephone while you are engaged in a conversation. An office machine may be turned off. An adjustment of the thermostat may add to physical comfort.

- *Be patient.* Give the speaker the opportunity to finish; do not interrupt at inopportune times. Try to put yourself in the other person's position and encourage him or her to say what he or she has to say. Any sign of impatience will often stop the communication process. When the speaker has finished is the appropriate time for you to ask questions to clarify the message.

- *Be interested.* Look and act interested by maintaining good eye contact, sitting in an alert position, and using facial expressions.

- *Take notes.* Skill in listening and taking notes simultaneously can make you a better listener and provide a written record of information for use at a later time. However, attempting to record a message verbatim frequently causes frustration and results in the listener missing the real significance of the message.
The fact that we listen a major part of the time we are on the job does not guarantee that we listen well. Being an effective listener is not an easy task; however, we can improve our listening techniques when we develop and practice proper habits.

Many ways of communicating nonverbally exist. Sometimes the nonverbal medium is the sole means of communication; at other times, it complements the language symbol. One must make certain the two are not contradictory.

Nonverbal communication may often be more expressive than verbal communication and when used in conjunction with it can powerfully strengthen or weaken the intended meaning of the verbal expression. Nonverbal communication may be as deceptive as words; therefore, we need to give serious consideration to the impression we are making on others—both verbally and nonverbally.

Have you ever walked into an office and even before a single word was spoken you experienced a positive feeling? What causes us to have that good feeling may be the physical setting, such as the decor of the office or the arrangement of the furnishings. More often, however, the feeling is caused by the body language of someone in the office. The posture, appearance, gestures, or facial expression of the person or persons you first encountered probably contributed to the impression. A person may give you the feeling that "I'm glad you're here" without saying a word. This nonverbal form of communication is known as kinesics and is shown by the secretary in figure 17-1.

FIGURE 17-1. A smile can help make a visitor feel welcome.

400
Secretarial
Procedures:
Office
Administration and
Automated Systems

The eyes are the most important part of the human body that is used to transmit information. Eye contact is crucial for establishing rapport with others. The way we look at other people can let them know we are paying attention to what they are saying. We can also look at a person and give the impression we are not hearing a word. Probably all of us have been guilty of looking directly at someone and not hearing a word while he or she was talking because we were thinking about something totally unrelated to what was being said.

Eye contact allows you to pick up visual clues about the other person; likewise, the other person can pick up clues about you. Studies of the use of eye contact in communication indicate that we seek eye contact with others when we want to communicate with them, when we like them, when we are hostile toward them (as when two angry people glare at each other), and when we want feedback from them. Conversely, we avoid eye contact when we want to avoid communication, when we dislike them, when we are trying to deceive them, and when we are uninterested in what they have to say.

By controlling the length of a glance, by shifting the eyes, by opening the eyelids, by squinting, by winking, and by manipulating the eyes in numerous other ways, we can transmit almost any meaning desired.

We can use other facial expressions to communicate. A smile can do much to make others feel comfortable. A smile can tell the other person "I like you." On the other hand, a smile may be used to indicate "I don't believe what you are saying." A frown may mean that you disapprove of what is being said, or it may mean that you are having difficulty understanding. Whatever expressions we use, we must be sure we convey the intended message.

Gestures may play an important part in communicating. A nod may say to the speaker "I hear you; I understand and agree with what you're saying." The folded arms may mean you are shutting out the other person. A pat on the back may indicate a warmth that would be difficult to verbalize; in other instances, it may indicate undue familiarity. The frequent shifting of position may mean lack of attentiveness or discomfort. You may lean forward to indicate you are paying close attention to what is being said. By standing up or shuffling papers, a person may be signaling that he or she wants to end the conversation.

The hands are used to communicate. For example, a clenched fist may indicate hostility or disagreement. The use of the hands to play with things while the other person is talking may suggest you are nervous, uncomfortable, or not attentive.

Our posture frequently tells others how we feel about ourselves. When we feel good about ourselves, we have a tendency to want to stand and sit erect. Most of us like to be around people who have good posture. Have you ever noticed that when you are with someone who is sitting or standing in an erect (not rigid) position, you almost invariably improve your posture? When we see someone slouching or stooped, we often assume that the person does not have a good self-image or that the person is physically ill or tired.

We have all followed someone upstairs and, even though no physical impairment was evident, the person was moving so lifelessly we were afraid he or she might fall on us. The way we walk indicates, at least to some extent, the enthusiasm we demonstrate in our other activities. While no one likes working in an office with those who dash from place to place, we have a better opinion of the person who moves with some vigor than we do of the one who acts tired or unmotivated most of the time.

In the business world, how we mesh our activities with the activities of others is extremely important. To others, our punctuality can reveal things about our personality. The length of time involved before we recognize a visitor to the office or the number of times the telephone rings before we answer may give the caller an indication of our concern for others and of our efficiency. Most of us are annoyed when we enter an office and are ignored while the receptionist continues to type several lines before recognizing us. An even more annoying situation is to have to wait while some of the employees discuss a topic that is obviously unrelated to the business activities of the office. When we are not recognized soon, we conclude that the person does not believe we are very important or, perhaps even worse, does not want to be interrupted. Since almost all visitors eventually are recognized and the telephone is almost always answered, nothing is to be gained by keeping the person waiting. Furthermore, your prompt response can show respect and concern for the person.

The formality or informality of a situation may be indicated by the seating arrangement. The student government president of a large university was impressed when the president of the university came from behind his desk and joined him in an informal setting around a coffee table. Obviously, the two had better rapport than if the president of the university had remained seated behind the desk. A good working relationship appears to exist between the executive and secretary shown in figure 17-2.

Where you are expected to sit when you take dictation or work on projects with your supervisor is an indication of the degree of formality practiced in your office. Many executives prefer that the secretary sit beside them when they dictate. Others prefer that the secretary sit on the opposite side of the desk. The secretary has little control over the seating arrangement in the executive's office; however, in many office situations, the secretary does have some control over the arrangement of his or her work area.

The use of space often communicates. The location of one's office or desk is frequently an indicator of status within the organization. Ask yourself, for example, whether the president or a lower-level executive has the corner office with windows and a good view. Generally speaking, the higher the level of the executive the more inaccessible he is. To get to the office of the highest level executive in the company, one almost without exception has to go around other desks.

Status symbols represent still another type of nonverbal communication to people inside and outside the firm. The president or chief executive

402
Secretarial
Procedures:
Office
Administration and
Automated Systems

FIGURE 17-2. A good working relationship between the executive and the secretary is important.

officer of the company has a large expensive desk; those with less status have smaller and less expensive desks. One must be especially careful, however, in evaluating others in terms of status symbols. Dress, for example, is not always an indication of an individual's wealth or position. What is important to one person simply may not be important to another.

Nonverbal communication alone will not enable us to fully understand others or to be fully understood; however, it can be used as a definite communication tool. In all types of communication, a positive approach should be used and we should be cognizant of the impact the things we say and do may have in establishing and maintaining a positive relationship with those involved.

ETHICS

Ethics may be described as the principles of conduct governing an individual or group. Each of us has a value system that has been developed over a long period of time, and our value system does not necessarily remain static. What we may consider unethical today we might not have considered unethical a year ago and vice versa. We must remember, too that other people also have value systems, and their values may be different from ours. A secretary is indeed fortunate when her values and the values of those with whom she must work are reasonably compatible. When the values of the secretary and those of others in the organization—and especially those of her superiors—are in conflict, a serious problem may exist. What is considered ethical and unethical varies so widely among individuals that in many cases no clear-cut solutions may exist.

Let's consider first some personal situations that you may need to resolve. Are you being unethical when you

- Lead the employer to believe you are more qualified than you are?
- Make personal telephone calls on company time and at company expense?
- Arrive at work a few minutes late and leave a few minutes early?
- Take sick leave when you are not sick?
- Spend more than the stipulated time on coffee or lunch breaks?
- Arrange an appointment for your boss's friend, but have told someone else your boss was not available?
- Accept a gift from a client who believes that you may be able to enhance his position with your supervisor?
- Use company postage to mail a personal letter?
- Take office supplies for personal use?
- Use the copying machine for personal use? (See figure 17-3.)

Now let's consider some situations you may need to resolve that involve your coworkers and subordinates. How should you respond when you

- Are asked to cover for others when they are away from their offices on unauthorized business?
- Are asked to relate confidential information to unauthorized persons?
- Are told rumors or information that you have no need or right to know?
- Are asked to corroborate something that you know is not true?
- Observe coworkers using office supplies for personal use?
- Observe coworkers' disloyalty to their supervisor or the company?
- Observe coworkers violating company policy or rules?

Finally, let's consider some situations you may need to resolve that involve your superiors. How should you respond if a supervisor

- Asks you to perform duties that are not a part of your job?
- Asks you to tell a caller he is not in the office when actually he is?

404
Secretarial
Procedures:
Office
Administration and
Automated Systems

FIGURE 17-3. Should copiers and other business machines and supplies be used for personal purposes?

- Asks you to tell a spouse something that is untrue?
- Asks you to do something that violates your values?
- Asks you for confidential information about others in the organization?
- Fails to recommend you for a higher-level position because he does not want to train a new employee?
- Receives money, goods, or services as "kickbacks"?
- Apologizes for a mistake by unfairly placing the blame on you?
- Leaves the office to play golf, but asks you to tell the president of the company that he has a dental appointment?

One would have difficulty gaining a consensus among a group of secretaries or executives concerning the answer to many of the previous questions. Some would say that taking a pencil for personal use, telling a little white lie, or typing a Do Good Garden Club program for the boss's wife is acceptable. But what about taking a dozen pencils for personal use, covering for unauthorized absences of coworkers on numerous occasions, and typing a 30-page term paper for the son of the boss?

At what point does something become unethical? You may decide that an act is not unethical when it is relatively insignificant and no major harm will be done. You must live with yourself; therefore, you must make your decisions in terms of your value system. No one can decide for you whether something is right or wrong. Certainly you want to draw the line when some act ceases to be merely unethical and becomes illegal, but in many cases this line is not clearly visible.

When you make decisions that involve a consideration of ethics, keep in mind that you must maintain a working relationship with others. Don't underestimate the power that peers and superiors can exert. However, just because everybody else is doing something does not make it right and should not be reason enough for you to make a decision that conflicts with your values. When you have a more stringent value system than those with whom you work, you should avoid being judgmental unless, of course, their actions adversely affect you or your work.

EMPATHY

When you empathize, you concern yourself with your feelings as they relate to the feelings of other people. We need to constantly consider how we would behave if we had others' responsibilities, interests, and experience. The good secretary follows the adage, "Put yourself in the shoes of the other person," and the Golden Rule, "Do unto others as you would have them do unto you." Empathy does not mean that we necessarily agree with the other person; however, we need to have an open mind and sincerely try to see why one believes as he or she does. The result should be that we are more capable of maintaining good relations with that person.

Perhaps the best way to develop empathy is to become truly interested in the other person. In working with others, you will find that the more you know about a person the easier you will be able to develop empathy for him or her. For example, when you know that your supervisor has unusual personal or business pressures, you may be able to better understand his or her behavior. You realize that perhaps his or her curt response to one of your questions is not caused by anything you have done but rather by other totally unrelated factors.

By reading the incoming correspondence, and especially by reading "between the lines," you can often gain valuable information about the correspondent. By meeting and speaking with others, you develop face-to-face impressions that may help you develop empathy. By becoming familiar with the businesses, the economic environments, and the geographical locations of those with whom you come into contact you may be able to more readily develop empathy.

REMEMBERING NAMES

Your ability to remember names will do much to help outsiders form a favorable impression of you and your office. Visitors who have previously been in your office are impressed when you are able to remember their names. A frequent visitor will question your competency if you have to ask his or her name on each occasion. Lack of interest in others is one of the greatest barriers in remembering names.

When you are not sure of someone's name, you should ask rather than guess. You may insult a person by calling him or her by the incorrect name. When you cannot remember someone's name, you may say "I'm sorry, I should know your name; but I can't think of it at the moment."

Although no formula will work for everyone as a technique for re-membering names, the following suggestions usually help:

- Make sure you understand the name initially.
- Repeat the person's name in your acknowledgment or silently.
- Ask the person to spell the name if it is unusual or may be spelled different ways. For example, verify the spelling of Smith by asking, "Is that spelled with an I or a Y?"
- Associate some facts about the person with his or her name.
- Make some notes (never anything uncomplimentary, such as fat or unkempt) about the person on his or her business card and review the card occasionally, especially before a person arrives for a scheduled appointment.

VOCAL PRESENTATION

Voice

Your voice is you! Your personality affects your voice. When you are in a good mood, your voice will reflect your happiness. When you are ill or when things have not been going well, your voice will also reflect this feeling. A good voice is both pleasant to listen to and effective as a communication medium. Although physiological and functional disorders may sometimes suggest the need for the services of a professional, there are certain qualities of voice we can vary easily and over which we have considerable control. Two of the most important voice characteristics are enthusiasm and energy. By putting forth some effort, we can change our rate of speaking; we can adjust the loudness; we can speak at different pitch levels; and we can make sure we pronounce and enunciate correctly and clearly.

Pronunciation

Pronunciation is the acceptable way of sounding the parts of the word by selecting the proper consonant and vowel sounds and by stressing the proper syllables. Examples of words commonly pronounced with misplaced accents are *comparable, preferable, presentation,* and *telegraphy.* The correct syllabications of these words are *com/pa/ra/ble, pref/er/a/ble, pre/sen/ta/tion,* and *te/leg/ra/phy.* When you hear or read a word of which you are not sure or when you hear a word pronounced in a different way to which you are accustomed, you should always refer to a dictionary. Do not automatically assume that you have been mispronouncing the word; the other person may be wrong. Variations from standard pronunciation may lead to misunderstanding, but more frequently they distract the person with whom you are talking and may interfere with communication. The pronunication guide and the diacritical system are thoroughly explained in the introduction to most dictionaries.

You may talk with people from all parts of the United States and, in some cases, the world. Even though these people are using the English language, you may find that they are using regional dialects. The minute some people speak, one can immediately know the section of the country of their origin. In the United States, three recognized standards of pronunciation are used: Eastern Standard, Southern Standard, and General American Standard. The General American Standard is used by the majority of the people.

Since correct pronunciation and language usage should be natural rather than conspicuous, you should adhere to the standard of your native area. If you attempt to change your speech to that of some other area, chances are you will make errors, some of which may cause you considerable embarrassment.

An exception to this rule is the pronunciation of geographical names. In general, you should attempt to pronounce geographical names the way they are pronounced in that area, which may be quite different from the way they are pronounced in your area. For example, a city in Missouri is pronounced Nevāda; the state is pronounced Neväda. By listening closely or by asking someone who knows the correct pronunciation, you can usually learn to pronounce the name of the town the same way as those who are natives of the area.

Enunciation

Enunciation is the precision or exactness of articulating a word or group of words spoken in sequence. Enunciation is concerned more with the clarity of speech in general than with the conventional accuracy of a single word. Poor enunciation is often associated with one's background or with carelessness. Poor enunciation may be classified under the four headings of additions, omissions, reversals, and substitutions.

408
Secretarial
Procedures:
Office
Administration and
Automated Systems

When an *r* is added to *idea* so that it becomes *idear* and an additional *e* to *athlete* so that it becomes *athelete,* an addition enunciation error is made. Omissions of sounds and syllables are rather common. For example, the letters in parentheses indicate sounds that are frequently omitted in the following words: *exper(i)ment, fam(i)ly, insi(st)s, lit(er)ature, pi(c)-ture, pop(u)lar, reco(g)nize,* and *temper(a)ture.* Reversal errors occur when sounds and accents are reversed, such as saying "perscription" instead of "prescription" and "tradegy" instead of "tragedy." Examples of substitution errors include pronouncing *heinous* with an *he* rather than an *ha* sound and pronouncing *Baptist* with a *b* rather than a *p* sound.

Pitch

Simply defined, pitch refers to the highness or lowness of the voice. The level of pitch can reveal your emotional and physical condition. A high pitch level may suggest anger, nervousness, or uncertainty. Conversely, a low pitch level may suggest relaxation and confidence. The pitch of the voice is not consciously noticed unless it is unusually extreme. A football player with a high pitch voice will obviously draw attention, as will a female fashion model speaking in a baritone voice. People usually prefer the lower rather than the higher pitch voice; but, in most cases, people should not attempt to force the voice into an unnatural lower pitch range. Rather, if the high pitch is the result of some emotional or physical condition, one should work to correct the disorder.

Loudness

How loud should you talk? Certainly you should not talk so loud that others will be uncomfortable or so low that others may have to strain to hear you. When you share an office, you must pay particular attention to your loudness level. When others are working, a conversation in an unusually loud voice may be distracting and annoying. On the other hand, if the person with whom you are conversing cannot hear what you are saying and frequently has to ask you to repeat, you may not be able to effectively convey a message. Not being able to hear what is being said can be very frustrating; therefore, in face-to-face conversations look for feedback when you are talking. Is the other person showing signs of having to strain to hear? Is he withdrawing? You may ask those with whom you work closely whether they believe you use the proper loudness level.

Rate

Rate is the speed with which we speak. We have all listened to those who talk "a mile a minute" as well as to those who appear to ponder over each word and idea. What is a good speaking rate? The answer, of course, depends on the situation.

Here are some guidelines for you to consider when selecting a speaking rate. When what you are saying is complex and involved and when the person with whom you are talking is not familiar with the content, you should use a slower rate. When the content is simple and the person is knowledgeable about the topic, you may wish to use a faster rate. We all use a faster rate to express excitement, joy, and similar types of emotions. We use a slower rate to express reverence and serenity. To avoid a monotonous sound, you should vary your rate by using pauses, such as before or after a key word or idea, to separate items or ideas in a series, and to indicate a major break in your thought.

Words

Choose words appropriate for the person with whom you are communicating. When you are talking with someone who is a specialist in your area of work, you can demonstrate your knowledge by using technical terms. On the other hand, you may make the listener uncomfortable by using a vocabulary with which he is not familiar; and the message you are trying to communicate may not be fully understood. For example, if you are talking with someone unfamiliar with data/word processing equipment, a reference to cathode-ray tubes and shared-logic systems may have little meaning.

A language of acronyms and initials has evolved in our society. Be sure that when you are writing or speaking you use words, initials, or acronyms that will be fully understood by the other person.

When you begin work in a new position, you should make a list of the words that are peculiar to the organization you are joining. Most business organizations have terminology that is unique to the industry. You may identify many words you will be using by reviewing material in the files, by reading professional journals, and by scanning advertising material. You should learn the correct spelling, pronunciation, and usage of the words you will be using frequently.

The appropriate level of language is highly variable. What is appropriate and effective in one situation may not be suitable in another. What is acceptable usage when talking with one of your coworkers may be totally unacceptable when talking with one of your superiors. The formal level of language is used in speeches and in job interviews, for example.

Although the formal level of language may be used in some business settings, such as when you are talking with high-ranking officials with whom you do not have frequent contact, the informal level is used in most business situations and in conversations with your coworkers and most of your superiors. Common sense dictates that even though you are using the informal level you still must follow the rules of etiquette and show courtesy and respect to those with whom you are communicating.

Expressions, such as "yeah," "okay," and "nope," are casual and should **never** be used in the office. Speech habits, such as inserting "you know" or "and uh," can annoy the listener. Language is important in the business world, and your mastery of it will have much to do with your success on the job.

OFFICE ETIQUETTE

Introductions

As a secretary, you will be responsible for making some introductions. The person given the greater courtesy is named first. The following general rules apply for introductions in social situations:

1. A man is introduced to a woman:

   "Ms. Riney, I'd like you to meet Mr. Wilson."

2. A young person is introduced to an older person:

   "Mr. Sexton, I'd like you to meet Johnny Chambers."

3. A lower ranking person is introduced to a higher ranking person:

   "Dean Coleman, may I present Professor Brady."

The general rules for making introductions in social situations are followed in making many introductions in a business environment; however, you will be faced with exceptions. What if Mr. Greenley, an older person, comes to your office to see Mr. Hanks, your boss? The proper introduction would be "Mr. Hanks, meet Mr. Greenley." When the executive introduces Ms. Watts, his secretary, to Henry Wilson, a client, business position takes precedence and the executive would say "Mr. Wilson, I'd like you to meet Ms. Watts, my secretary."

When introducing a person to a group, you should mention the newcomer's name first and name the others in the order in which they are sitting or standing. For example, "Mr. Hicks, I would like you to meet Ms. Schreck, Ms. Carr, Mr. Savage, and Ms. Highley."

If you introduce a senator or other high-ranking politician or religious leader and your employer, you should mention the name of the visitor first. If you were introducing your mother and your employer, the business environment would again prevail and you would mention the name of your employer first, even though your employer may be a male and much younger than your mother.

In introductions, always state your boss's title (e.g., Mr., Mrs., president) even though you may normally use a first name when addressing him or her. When a person has a professional title, such as senator, professor, general, bishop, you should mention the title in the introduction. Sometimes the person will prefer to be called by his or her first name. If the person does, after the introduction has been made, a statement such as "Please call me Mary" is appropriate.

Even though visitors to the secretary's office will introduce themselves, the secretary is not expected to respond by telling the visitors her name. However, when the executive introduces the secretary to a client, the secretary should respond in a natural way by saying "hello."

Although you should be well-versed in the rules to be followed in making introductions, if a situation arises in which you are not certain of the proper procedure, do not become overly conscious and place yourself and others in an embarrassing situation. Simply follow the procedure you believe to be appropriate and be sure you pronounce the names correctly and distinctly. In most cases, those being introduced will be making sure they understand the other's name and will not notice whether the introduction is made properly.

Handshaking

In social situations, when a man and a woman are introduced, the woman must make the first move by extending her hand. In a business environment, the person whose name is mentioned first should offer a hand first. However, common courtesy dictates that an extended hand is always accepted. Men usually make the gesture simultaneously, and professional women are learning to do the same.

Men should stand when they shake hands, unless standing would be awkward. For example, a man sitting in a booth in a restaurant may have difficulty rising. Women are not expected to stand when they shake hands, but when they are introduced to those in high-ranking positions they may show respect by standing.

A handshake, like other forms of nonverbal communication, may tell the other person a great deal about your personality. You should shake hands enthusiastically, but reasonably, and look pleasantly at the person whose hand you are shaking.

Standing

In a social situation, men who are aware of the social amenities stand when a lady first enters the room; when they are introduced to others; and, of course, any time they shake hands (such as when a man is leaving the

412
Secretarial
Procedures:
Office
Administration and
Automated Systems

group). Women are not expected to stand. In today's business environment, women are generally extended and are extending the same courtesies as men. For example, if a committee of peers is assembling for a meeting and a female member of the committee enters last, the men are not expected to stand.

In organizations where a formal atmosphere prevails, everyone in the room normally stands when the highest-ranking executive enters. In some companies, everyone in the room will stand when the president or chief executive officer enters.

As a secretary, you are not expected to stand when your supervisor comes to your desk, unless for practical reasons standing would appear to be appropriate. Sometimes the communication process is enhanced when you are both sitting or both standing.

When a first-time or infrequent visitor comes to your office, you are expected to leave your desk, open the door to your supervisor's office, and introduce the visitor. Merely pointing to the door places the visitor in an awkward position and indicates you are lacking in social awareness.

Sincerity

Most people think of sincerity as meaning honesty and lack of hypocrisy. When actions do not validate what has been said, the person's sincerity is questioned. For example, let's imagine a situation in which Sally has worked hours to prepare a 25-page report for Mr. Winter. When she places the report on Mr. Winter's desk he says, "Fine, Sally, keep up the good work," but does not look up from his desk. Will Sally believe that Mr. Winter's compliment is sincere? Even if Mr. Winter does believe that Sally has prepared a good report, he has not communicated this feeling to her. We can effectively communicate sincerity by praising specifically—not generally—the things others do well.

You should, of course, compliment coworkers when they look unusually attractive or when they have completed a task especially well. However, compliments lose meaning when they are tossed out indiscriminately or too often.

Excessive politeness may suggest insincerity. You may sound gushy when you use too many adjectives and adverbs. "Ms. Smith will be pleased to see you" sounds more believable than "Ms. Smith will be especially delighted to see you, one of our highly valued customers." To avoid sounding gushy, don't overuse words such as *extremely, very, truly, sincerely,* and *genuinely.*

People like to be recognized by name; however, by referring to someone by name repeatedly during a brief conversation may indicate you are overly solicitous.

One especially important way to demonstrate sincerity is to follow through on commitments. When you tell a customer you will check on his order and call him back, be sure that you do what you say. When you tell your supervisor that you will have a project completed by a certain time, make sure you meet the deadline. Do not attempt to "look good" by accepting an assignment even though you know you cannot or will not be able to complete it.

Consistency is important when you are developing a reputation for being sincere. All of us have known people who can be especially nice when they want something. Is the secretary reflecting sincerity when she appears eager to take on additional assignments or to work overtime when she knows that her evaluation appointment is near and at other times throughout the year does only what is absolutely necessary? A reputation for sincerity does not come about as the result of a single act; rather, it is developed over time.

Demonstrating sincerity can do much to build goodwill both within the company and with outsiders. As a secretary, you will have many opportunities to relate your genuine concern for others. Once you have established a reputation for being honest and sincere with others, you'll often find that others will be responsive and will return mutual respect.

Summary

Since a large percentage of the secretary's time is spent in working with others, your skills in the human relations area are critical to on-the-job success. As a secretary, you must remember that everything you do has an impact on others. Those with whom you come in contact are forming an impression of you, and in many instances what you do and say influences their image of your boss and the entire organization.

A secretary needs to be aware of the importance of being tactful in sensitive situations. She needs to realize that the backgrounds and experiences of those with whom she comes in contact may be quite different and that what is appropriate in one situation may be inappropriate at other times.

Others identify us by our voices, and they develop a mental image of us based in large part upon the sounds they hear as they listen to us talk. The principal ways in which we can vary our voices are in volume, pitch, and rate. And if we are to be understood and are to make a favorable impression on others, we must pay close attention to the way we pronounce and enunciate the words we choose to use in our conversations.

Listening is an integral part of communicating and is the most used communication skill. Understanding the barriers that may interfere with the listening process, and then acting appropriately, will help increase your effectiveness as a secretary.

The nonverbal elements of communication are especially important in understanding the other person's feelings. Sometimes body language is very clear; however, at other times it can be difficult to understand and can sometimes be totally misleading.

414
Secretarial
Procedures:
Office
Administration and
Automated Systems

The secretary is in a position to help create a favorable image for herself, for her boss, and for the entire organization. The importance of establishing and maintaining good human relationships should not be minimized.

 Questions

1. Discuss some techniques that may be used in an attempt to be tactful.

2. As a good listener, what can you do to avoid misunderstandings and mistakes?

3. How does being a good listener save time?

4. Do you believe that being a good listener helps make a favorable impression on the person with whom you are carrying on a conversation? Why?

5. Do you agree that the good secretary should usually record all messages verbatim to eliminate the possibility of leaving out something important? Discuss.

6. Discuss the statement, "It is easier to lie with words than with our body."

7. List five common hand gestures.

8. Explain why the eyes are the most expressive part of our body.

9. Why do we prefer to watch the person with whom we are talking?

10. What is the difference between something being unethical and illegal?

11. Are you unethical when you present only one side of an issue? Discuss.

12. Explain the difference between empathy and sympathy.

13. How can we develop empathy for others?

14. What is one of the greatest barriers in remembering names?

15. How may you develop a list of the words unique to the industry with which you are associated?

16. Do you agree that the formal level of language is always appropriate in the business office? Discuss.

17. What is the difference between initials and acronyms?

Eastern Standard _General American_
Southern "

18. Name the three recognized standards of pronunciation in the United States.

19. Which of the standards of pronunciation is the most commonly used?

20. How is the correct pronunciation of words determined?

21. How can one translate technical language or trade jargon without talking down to the listener? _use informal_

22. _Data_ and _status_ are common business terms that are frequently pronounced in two different ways. What is the preferred pronunciation of each?

23. What is the real test of sincerity?

24. What is the result of complimenting a person too often?

25. How should the introduction be made in each of the following situations?

    a. Your mother and your teacher (a male).

    b. Your mother and your teacher (a female).

    c. One of your friends (a male) and your mother.

    d. One of your friends (a female) and your mother.

    e. One of your friends (a female) and your father.

    f. Your friend (a female) and your mother's secretary (a female).

    g. Your friend (a male) and your father's secretary (a male).

––––––––––––––––– Projects –––––––––––––––––

1. For one week, list the situations in which you observe tact being demonstrated effectively. Prepare another list of the situations in which you observe the lack of tact.

2. List the impressions you form of ten people with whom you have had no prior contact. Identify the reasons for forming the impressions of each.

3. Identify the qualities possessed by someone for whom you have much respect. Rank the qualities according to the importance you place on each.

4. Record your voice as you carry on an informal conversation with a friend. Listen to the recording and pay particular attention to your pronunciation and enunciation and to the volume, pitch, and rate. List the particular strengths and weaknesses.

416
Secretarial
Procedures:
Office
Administration and
Automated Systems

5. Listen to a television talk show and list the words you believe to be misused or mispronounced. Use a dictionary to determine the correct usage and pronunciation.

6. Make a list of ten words you hear pronounced in different ways and then refer to a dictionary to determine the preferred pronunciation.

7. Read a daily newspaper and list the abbreviations and acronyms used. Place a check mark by those with which you are not familiar.

8. Read a professional journal article on the area of business in which you are most interested. Make a list of the words you believe to be unique to that area of business. Write the definition of each of the words.

9. View a television program without the sound. List the different types of nonverbal symbols used.

10. Observe people in a library, restaurant, or some other public place. Make a list of the nonverbal communication symbols you observe.

11. Record a speech, lecture, or newscast, but avoid making any written notes. After the recording is completed, list the items covered with as many of the details as you can remember. Listen to the recording and check the accuracy of your notes.

12. Make a serious attempt to remember the names of the next five people to whom you are introduced. List the techniques you used to remember the names.

Cases
---

1. You are the supervisor of the workers in your office. One of the young men is an expert typist and his written work is always of high quality. However, he consistently mispronounces words and you have heard several people comment on this weakness. How can you tactfully resolve the situation?

2. You frequently observe some of your coworkers leave the office with typewriter ribbons and other office supplies. A directive was recently distributed throughout the company urging all employees to help reduce the cost of supplies. Although you never take any supplies from the office, you are afraid your supervisor will notice others leaving with supplies and may think that you, too, take things for personal use. What should you do?

3. You recently attended a social function and noticed that one of those under your supervision at the office was wearing an especially attractive dress. When you complimented her, she told you that she couldn't afford such an expensive dress and intended to return it to the department store the next day. Do you believe this is unethical? If so, as her supervisor should you let this outside-of-work event influence your evaluation of her at the office?

4. A supervisor frequently comments on the good quality of your work and suggests that he is completely satisfied with your performance. When the yearly formal evaluation takes place, he gives you only average ratings on most factors and recommends that you receive only a modest pay increase. How can you tactfully discuss your disappointment with the supervisor?

CHAPTER 18

Appointments

The time an executive spends with others must be carefully planned. One of the secretary's major tasks is usually making sure the executive is where he or she is supposed to be at the correct time.

Once the executive establishes guidelines to be followed in scheduling appointments, the secretary normally plays a major role in determining those with whom the executive will meet and where and when the meetings will take place.

As a secretary, you have an excellent opportunity to help create goodwill for your boss and the company by demonstrating a thorough knowledge of good public relations skills as you carry out the activities involved in scheduling and canceling appointments, coping with unusual situations, greeting visitors, and maintaining a businesslike appearance and office atmosphere.

Many factors the secretary must consider when working with executives and coworkers within the company and people from outside the company will be discussed in this chapter.

APPOINTMENTS

Understanding the Executive's Scheduling Preferences

When you first begin your job as secretary to an executive for whom you must schedule appointments, you must learn from the executive or someone else in the office the answers to the following questions:

420
Secretarial
Procedures:
Office
Administration and
Automated Systems

- For what times of the day should appointments be scheduled?
- What procedures are to be followed to avoid conflicts when both you and the executive schedule appointments?
- How much time should be allocated for each appointment?
- Which appointments should be given priority?
- What types of statements are to be made when refusing to make an appointment for someone who insists?
- How should visitors be announced?
- What procedures are to be followed in providing refreshments?
- How should meetings that extend beyond the allocated time be terminated?
- What type of information is considered personal or confidential and should not be divulged when canceling an appointment?

Length of Appointments

The executive may want you to schedule the same amount of time for each appointment; however, when this plan is followed, visitors frequently will have to wait unless the time scheduled for each one is unusually long. When the time scheduled is longer than necessary, obviously fewer appointments can be made for each day and the result may be that you cannot make appointments for some people who may need to talk with the executive. Until you have been on the job long enough to learn through experience the amount of time to schedule for each appointment, you may need to ask the executive or the caller the amount of time to allocate.

When to Schedule Appointments

Some executives may not have any preferences concerning the time of day they will talk with visitors; others follow an established routine and may prefer to talk with visitors only during certain times of the day or on certain days. Many executives prefer to start their work day by reading the mail, making telephone calls, dictating correspondence, or performing other types of routine tasks. Some prefer that appointments not be scheduled for the day before or after a vacation or a business trip. You should know the executive's preferences and the procedures to follow when exceptions are to be made.

Preparing the Appointment Calendar

The appointments may be made over the telephone, in writing, or in person; and they may be made by the secretary or by the executive.

A complete written record must be made each time an appointment is scheduled to avoid forgetting some of the relevant information. Consider the following questions each time an appointment is scheduled:

- Who is involved? Unless the executive knows the person with whom the appointment is scheduled, note the business affiliation. Usually note the names of all of those who will attend the meeting.

- What is the date, time, and length of the appointment?

- Where is the meeting to take place? If the meeting is to be held at another location, indicate the street address and room number. A map or detailed instructions may be needed.

- Why is the meeting being scheduled?

The secretary normally uses a desk calendar similar to the one shown in figure 18-1 on which to record the name of the person and the company with which he or she is affiliated. After noting the appointment on the calendar, you may need to type the name, company affiliation, date, and additional information on a 3-inch by 5-inch card and then place the card in a tickler file similar to the one shown in figure 18-2. Where you place the card in the file depends on whether or not you or the executive must do some work in preparing for the appointment. For example, if the executive

FIGURE 18-1. Desk calendar.

422
Secretarial
Procedures:
Office
Administration and
Automated Systems

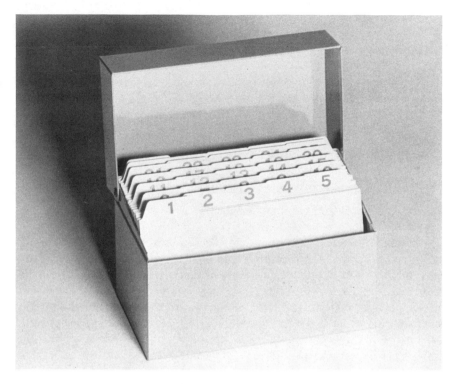

FIGURE 18-2. Tickler file.

must read a report or proposal prior to a meeting on July 18, you may need to file the card behind the July 15 guide so that he or she will have ample time to prepare.

When you have the responsibility of scheduling appointments for more than one executive, you normally should use a form similar to the one shown in figure 18-3.

Appointments must also be recorded on the executive's appointment calendar. Dozens of different types of appointment calendars are available and the following features need to be considered when selecting one:

- Loose-leaf or spiral.

- No intervals or intervals of 15, 30, or 60 minutes.

- Pages for daily, weekly, or monthly appointments.

- Ruled or blank space provided for comments.

- Refillable or nonrefillable.

- Dated or undated.

So that the appointments for an entire week may be observed at one time, many executives prefer to use an arrangement similar to the one shown in figure 18-4.

Tuesday, October 9

	Adams	Bell	Hanks
8:00			
8:30			
9:00			
9:30			
10:00			
10:30			
11:00			
11:30			
1:00			
1:30			
2:00			
2:30			
3:00			
3:30			
4:00			
4:30			

FIGURE 18-3. Appointment sheet for more than one executive.

If the executive also schedules appointments, you and the executive must understand the procedures to be followed to avoid scheduling conflicting appointments. When the executive travels and frequently makes appointments while away from the office, he or she should carry a small pocket-size calendar such as the one shown in figure 18-5.

When both of you are in the office, you should periodically check to make sure the calendars are up to date. If the executive checks with you while away from the office, you may discuss the appointments that have been made.

You may learn about professional meetings, community activities, and other events that should be listed on the calendar in a number of ways, including the following:

• Calendars distributed by professional organizations.

• Letters, newsletters, and magazines.

• Announcements appearing in the newspaper or on the radio and television.

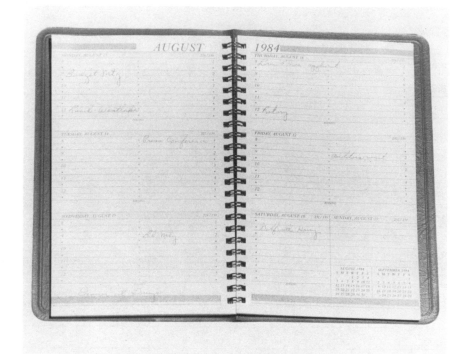

FIGURE 18-4. Executive's weekly appointment calendar.

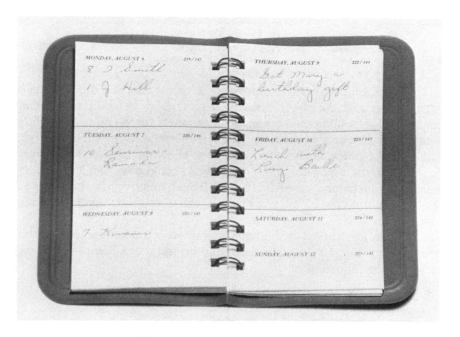

FIGURE 18-5. Pocket-size calendar.

- Comments made during a meeting.

- Announcements appearing in the formal minutes of a meeting.

In addition to the appointments, meetings, and other business-related activities, some executives like to have the birthdays and anniversaries of family members and friends listed on the calendar.

Arranging for Subordinates to See the Executive

When your boss asks you to have subordinates come to the office, you should usually indicate the purpose of the meeting unless the meetings are somewhat routine. Employees sometimes experience anxiety when they are requested to see the boss; therefore, if you indicate the purpose of the meeting, the subordinates are often much less apprehensive. Furthermore, they may be able to do preliminary work and come to the meeting prepared so that time may be saved.

You should not, however, pass on confidential information or indicate the meeting is going to be unpleasant. If the subordinate asks the purpose of the meeting and you believe you should not tell, simply say "Ms. Logan just asked that I see if you can meet at 10 o'clock." If true, you may say "Ms. Logan did not tell me" or "I'm not sure." You should not give any of the following responses:

"Ms. Logan asked me not to tell you."

"Ms. Logan wants to talk to you about the report that you failed to submit last week."

"She wants to tell you about a big pay increase she is recommending for you, but she asked me not to tell you."

Should the employee insist, you may need to say "Shall I ask Ms. Logan if you need to bring anything to the meeting?" or "Would you like to call Ms. Logan and ask her?"

Canceling Appointments

You may occasionally have to cancel an appointment that has been made with your boss. Since most business people experience situations that necessitate changes in their schedules, they are usually understanding when an appointment must be changed.

As soon as you realize an appointment must be canceled, you should call, apologize, and offer an explanation. The explanation need not be

426
Secretarial
Procedures:
Office
Administration and
Automated Systems

lengthy and should never include confidential or embarrassing information. Statements such as the following are usually appropriate because they give the person the impression the executive wants to talk with him or her, but cannot do so at the time initially scheduled:

> "Ms. Tyler asked me to call and tell Mr. Cohn that she is sorry she will not be able to meet with him at 10 on Friday morning. She has to make a trip to one of the branch offices, but she expects to be back the first of next week. We will call Mr. Cohn as soon as she returns."

> "Ms. Tyler very much wants to meet with Ms. Nance, but because of an emergency she must cancel the appointment scheduled for 3 o'clock tomorrow afternoon. Could Ms. Nance meet with Ms. Tyler at 11 on Wednesday morning?"

Use discretion when deciding on the reason to give for the cancellation. For example, "Mr. Boessen has to appear in court" would be totally inappropriate; but "Mr. Boessen has jury duty" would be acceptable. The fact that the executive must visit a branch office is an acceptable explanation, but to say that the executive must visit the New Orleans office because they have some serious personnel problems is inappropriate.

You may write, rather than call, if the person who has the appointment lives in another city and would be sure to receive the letter in advance of the time of the appointment.

When an appointment with an important client or a high-level executive is to be canceled, the executive usually writes the letter or makes the telephone call to explain why the cancellation is necessary. Sometimes, however, the executive may be away from the office and you will be expected to take the initiative in canceling the appointments.

Those who have appointments with your boss may also occasionally have to cancel. Express appreciation to the person for having notified you and offer to schedule the appointment for a later time. Expressions similar to the following are usually appropriate:

> "I appreciate your calling. May I schedule another appointment for Mrs. Luebbert?"

> "Thank you for calling. Please call when you want to reschedule the appointment."

Never say anything to make the person feel guilty for being unable to keep the appointment. Expressions such as the following are always inappropriate:

> "I wish I had known earlier that Mr. Brown couldn't keep the appointment; I could have scheduled someone else."

"I know Ms. Luebbert will be disappointed since she came in an hour early so she would be prepared for the meeting with Mr. Hannah."

"Ms. Luebbert has an extremely full schedule. I'm not sure we can reschedule the appointment."

A few people may consistently not cancel their appointments; they simply may not keep them. Even though your boss may have been inconvenienced, maintain goodwill by being pleasant if they call later to seek other appointments. Follow the established procedures in deciding whether the appointment should be made. You may, however, want to write a letter confirming the appointment or call prior to the time of the appointment to remind the person. The following statement is reasonably tactful, if the right tone is used:

"I notice that Miss Jones has a 1 p.m. appointment with Mr. Cramer. Is Miss Jones going to be able to keep the appointment?"

VISITORS

Receiving Visitors

In many companies, a receptionist has a desk near the front entrance and greets all visitors. The visitor may be asked to sign a guest register and indicate the person he or she would like to see, or the receptionist may ask the visitor for the information. When you are expecting an important client or someone who deserves or expects special attention, you should always notify the receptionist prior to the time of the appointment. In some companies, the receptionist is given a list of all appointments.

The receptionist may direct the visitor to the appropriate office or notify the office that a visitor is waiting.

If the executive's office cannot be seen from the reception area and the visitor has never been to your office, you should go to the reception area and greet the visitor by saying something such as "Good morning, Mr. Mueller. I'm Ruth Hutchinson, Mr. Richmond's secretary." You are not expected to initiate a handshake; but if the visitor extends his or her hand, you must shake hands. If the passageway is wide, walk beside the visitor; otherwise, lead the way by walking slightly in front of the visitor.

If the company does not have a receptionist and the visitor comes directly to your office, you should give him or her your complete attention. Even if you are talking on the telephone, you can smile and perhaps motion

428
Secretarial
Procedures:
Office
Administration and
Automated Systems

for the person to be seated. If you anticipate the telephone conversation will be lengthy, you should offer to return the call or interrupt long enough to assist the office visitor.

Smile, be pleasant, appear alert, and let all that you say and do make the visitor feel welcome. Each visitor should be greeted with "Good morning" or "Good afternoon." When you know the name of the visitor, you should include it in the greeting. You are not expected to stand, shake hands, or tell the visitor your name; however, you should have a nameplate on the desk. The greeting is followed by whatever is appropriate.

The visitor will judge you not only by how you look but also by what you say and how you say it. You should talk in a natural tone, enunciate clearly, pronounce words correctly, use a vocabulary the visitor will understand, and speak at a reasonable speed. Talk with enthusiasm and keep your voice cheerful. Look at the caller and listen closely. Never attempt to do other things as you talk with the visitor.

The person entering your office should find a businesslike atmosphere. Your appearance and attitude, as well as the office environment, should reflect favorably on the company.

You should always be well groomed and your attire should be appropriate. Rather than call the visitor's attention to the clothing, jewelry, or makeup you are wearing, you want the visitor to have the impression you are efficient. Nothing about your appearance should be so conspicuous that the visitor will find it distracting.

Never apply makeup or comb your hair in front of visitors in the office. Candy bars, potato chips, pretzels, or other food should never be eaten at the desk. The chewing of gum is considered inappropriate in many offices and should never be noticeable to the visitor. Some people consider smoking at the desk to be unprofessional.

You should look alert and interested. Never yawn or in any other way give the visitor the impression you are tired or bored. Sit erect and appear poised.

Your desk should be well-organized. Although you may perform many different tasks during the day, you can do only one or two things at a time. You should have facilities available to conveniently store the material on which you are not working. A cluttered desk does not give the caller the impression you are well-organized and efficient.

Try to keep the noise level low. If you need to use a particularly noisy machine, perhaps the task can be postponed until the visitor has left.

The office area should be kept well-organized and clean. A coat rack and comfortable seating should be provided, as well as a current newspaper and a magazine or two. Outdated newspapers and periodicals should be discarded. If you or the executives provide personal copies of periodicals, remove the mailing labels.

An attractive reception area is shown in figure 18-6.

The ashtrays should be kept clean, all extraneous papers and items (coffee cups, gum wrappers, etc.) should be picked up, and the lights should be working properly. The furniture and equipment should be dusted frequently.

FIGURE 18-6. Formal reception area. (Courtesy of Waddell & Reed, Inc./United Investors Life)

Everything the visitor observes should reflect efficiency.

If you believe the person will be visiting your office again, note some characteristics about the person on his or her business card and then file the card. Never write anything uncomplimentary, but notes about the approximate age, height, weight, color of hair, or other features may help you recognize the person at a later time. When a name is difficult to pronounce, ask the person to pronounce it slowly and then pronounce it to make sure you understood correctly. Write the pronunciation phonetically on the card. If the person does not give you a business card, you may note the information on a 3-inch by 5-inch card as shown in figure 18-7. Should the person make a subsequent appointment, review the card before he or she arrives so that you can use the name in the greeting.

Visitors with Appointments

Visitors who have appointments will not always arrive at the exact time scheduled. Those who arrive early should realize that they may have to wait. When the executive is in a meeting with someone else or is occupied in some other way, you may indicate to the visitor that you expect the executive to be available at the time scheduled. Never tell the visitor that the executive is free unless you are confident he or she will want the

430
Secretarial
Procedures:
Office
Administration and
Automated Systems

```
Ann Doerhoff      (pronounced Dearhoff)

Represents the Donley Equipment Company.

Wants to discuss the lease of the copying
machine illustrated and explained in the
attached promotional material.
```

FIGURE 18-7. Maintain a file of information that will help you properly greet visitors.

visitor admitted at that time; instead, simply indicate to the executive that the visitor has arrived. If the executive does not want to see the visitor at that time, you may say "Ms. Toler will be able to see you in about 15 minutes." To say "Ms. Toler will be *ready* to see you in about 15 minutes" may lead the visitor to believe the executive does not consider him or her very important.

Those who have appointments should not be kept waiting, but realistically an executive may occasionally not be able to stay on a precise schedule. A meeting may have taken longer than expected, someone with an earlier appointment may have arrived late, a higher-level executive may have made an unplanned call, or any number of other things may happen to disrupt the schedule. If almost all visitors are kept waiting, you should discuss the scheduling procedures with the executive. Some of the following actions may be appropriate:

- Allocate more time for all appointments or more realistically allocate the time for specific appointments.

- Allow more time between appointments.

- Arrange for some of those who want appointments to see other executives in the organization.

- Schedule appointments for approximate rather than exact times. For example, you may say "Mr. Lund has a full schedule, but I believe you will be able to see him sometime between 10 and 10:30 Thursday morning."

When a visitor must wait, try to be positive. Give the visitor some indication of when you expect the executive to be available. Say "Mr. Payne will be able to see you in about 15 minutes," rather than "You will have to wait 15 minutes." You usually should offer some explanation, such as the following:

"I'm sorry, but one of Ms. Adler's meetings lasted longer than expected. I believe she will be able to see you in about 10 minutes."

"I'm sorry, but Mr. Childs is still in a staff meeting. I'll take him a note to let him know you are here."

"Mr. Snyder was caught in a traffic jam on the way to work this morning. All of his appointments have been delayed a few minutes."

A statement such as "An important client dropped in unexpectedly this morning" may lead the visitor to believe he or she is less important than others. No statement should be made that will indicate a lack of concern or inefficiency on the part of the executive. The following types of statements are never appropriate, even though they may be true:

"Miss Hicks took a two-hour lunch today, so all of her afternoon appointments have been delayed."

"One of Mr. Hoffman's college fraternity brothers dropped in unexpectedly this morning."

"Mr. Reed went to a retirement party last night and didn't get to the office until late this morning."

If the visitor appears annoyed, you may suggest that another appointment be arranged or perhaps you or someone else may provide the assistance that is needed. You may offer to get the visitor a cup of coffee and indicate that the latest issue of a magazine or the morning newspaper is on the table in the waiting area. Show concern, but do not let your actions or what you say reflect exasperation or nervousness.

While the person is waiting, you should maintain a businesslike attitude. The secretary is usually not expected to entertain or converse with those who must wait. Once you have done all that you can to assist the visitor, you should continue with your work. You can be pleasant without carrying on a conversation. For example, when you change the paper in the typewriter, answer the telephone, or for some other reason interrupt your work, you can smile and appear pleasant should the visitor look your way. By continuing with your work, you are avoiding the possibility of divulging confidential information, becoming involved in a discussion of controversial subjects, or encouraging the visitor to ask personal questions. Furthermore, the time spent in carrying on a conversation with the visitor can probably be used more profitably in other ways.

Demonstrate a positive and pleasant attitude. Your day may be particularly frustrating and hectic, but you should not let anything you say or do reflect negativism. Expressions such as the following should never be used while the visitor is in the office:

"This just isn't my day."

"That person is always a problem."

432
Secretarial
Procedures:
Office
Administration and
Automated Systems

"A dozen salesmen have been here today."

"Mr. Swank always stays too long."

"My! I'm tired today."

When you need to discuss confidential matters while a visitor is waiting in your office, you may go to another office, ask the other person if you may contact him or her later, or unobtrusively write a note. Never give the visitor the impression that you are being secretive, that you believe he or she is trying to eavesdrop, or that you are talking about him or her. Avoid making the visitor uncomfortable by whispering, talking in a hushed tone, or saying something such as "I can't talk now; someone is in my office."

When a visitor arrives late for an appointment, you should be pleasant; but you do not have an obligation to readjust the executive's schedule in a way that will inconvenience the executive or visitors who have appointments for later in the day. If the executive will not be able to see the visitor for quite some time, you may need to schedule another appointment or suggest that the visitor talk with someone else.

Visitors Without Appointments

When you do not recognize those who come to your office without appointments, you need to determine who they are and what they want. They will usually introduce themselves and hand you a business card. If visitors do not introduce themselves, you should say something similar to the following:

"I am Ms. Magady, Ms. Kuster's secretary. May I tell Ms. Kuster your name and what you would like to talk with her about?"

"I'll see if Mr. Gaines will be able to see you. Do you have a business card I may give to him?"

The visitor will usually provide you with the information you need; however, occasionally the visitor may say something such as:

"I know she will want to see me. I'm an old friend."

"I'd rather surprise her."

"He will want to see me; I'm going to show him how he can save a lot of money."

If you know that your boss would be uncomfortable or annoyed having the visitor admitted unannounced, you may go to the boss's office or telephone and repeat the response the visitor gave you, ask the visitor to write a message for you to give to the boss, or firmly state that you are not allowed to admit visitors unless they give their name and the purpose of the call. The visitor usually has no reasonable response to the following question: "You wouldn't want me to get in trouble with Mr. Loftis by admitting you unannounced, would you?" If you happen to work in an office where visitors sometimes become belligerent, you should be familiar with the action to take to get someone removed from your office.

In some offices, sales representatives and business acquaintances of the executive may frequently come to the office without appointments. The representatives and business people may incorrectly assume you remember their name. To avoid the embarrassment of asking the name when you recognize the visitor, keep a card file arranged according to company names and have the names of the people listed on the cards. "I'm sorry I don't remember the name of your company" is sometimes less embarrassing than saying "I'm sorry I don't remember your name." Frequently, the representative will respond by giving his or her name as well as that of the company; but if only the name of the company is given, you can look at the card to determine the name of the individual.

When you believe the executive should not talk with the visitor, do not mislead the person by suggesting that he or she call for an appointment at a later time. Instead, you should try to maintain goodwill by using expressions such as the following:

"Mr. Knapp has a full schedule; perhaps someone else or I can help you."

"Ms. Judson has appointments all day. Would you like to leave a message?"

"We recently purchased a new copier, but I'll be glad to give Ms. Lea any promotional material you may have on the Copyrite."

"All applications for employment are processed in the Human Resources Department in Room 203. I am sure Ms. Runyon or one of her assistants will be glad to talk with you."

"All adjustment requests are handled by the Customer Service Department in Room 505. I'll call and tell them you want to talk about the microwave you recently purchased."

Do not become intimidated into arranging a meeting—even on a tentative basis—for someone you are confident your boss does not want to see. If you make a tentative appointment, you may have difficulty tactfully canceling it at a later time. You can sometimes appease the person by saying "I will talk with Ms. Huston when she is free and if she will be able to see you I will call." If Ms. Huston does not want to talk with the person, you are not obligated to call; and the person may not pursue the matter

434
Secretarial
Procedures:
Office
Administration and
Automated Systems

further. Never fail to call if you have promised to do so, but before you place the call rehearse what you plan to say.

Embarrassing situations may result from untrue statements concerning why the executive cannot see a visitor. Imagine the awkwardness of the situation created if the visitor has been told that the executive is out of town and the executive then walks through the office and is recognized by the visitor.

Your boss may want to be available to some people at all times. Certainly, higher-ranking executives and their secretaries do not need permission to enter your boss's office, but they usually ask or give you an opportunity to indicate whether he or she is busy. Relatives, close friends, and executives on the same level generally have access to the boss's office. If your boss is talking with an important client or a higher-level executive, you should mention that fact; but do not try to keep the person from entering.

Introducing Visitors

If the visitor has not been in your office or met the executive, you should lead the way to the executive's office and make the proper introduction. You should then close the door and return to your desk unless you believe the executive may want you to assist in some other way. The executive may, for example, ask you to get coffee.

Many executives prefer to come to the secretary's office and greet the visitor. In this situation, the executive and the visitor frequently introduce themselves. Visitors may be uncomfortable when they are told that "Mr. Jones' office is the third door on the left. You may go right in." The caller may not know whether he or she should knock and may interpret the executive's "Come in" response as somewhat impersonal.

Problem Visitors

If a visitor to your office becomes irate, you must do all you can to maintain goodwill. One of the best ways to avoid becoming defensive is to remember that unless you are the one whose actions created the problem, the visitor's remarks are not about you. Be attentive; listen carefully until the visitor has finished talking. The problem may not appear significant to you, but to the visitor it is important; otherwise, he or she would not be upset. Remain noncommittal; do not tell the visitor you believe he or she has a right to be angry. Do not argue, emphasize the problem, or make caustic remarks, even though you may believe the visitor is wrong.

After you have listened to what the visitor has to say, you may know how the problem can be resolved. For example, you may suggest that the person talk with your supervisor or someone else, leave a message, or take some other action. If you know that the person simply wanted to express his or her views, you can usually placate the person by sincerely asking "What would you like for me to do?" In many instances, the visitor will respond with "Nothing this time, but ...."

Occasionally, visitors may be inquisitive and ask personal questions. You may indicate you do not know the answer, give a vague answer, counter with a question, or suggest that the questions be asked during the meeting with the executive or in some other department.

Some of the types of questions that may be asked and some possible responses are given in the following examples:

Question: "How many units (of some product) did you sell last month?"

Possible
answers: "I haven't seen the sales figures for April."
  or
"You'll have to ask in the Sales Department; we don't have those figures in this office."

Question: "Isn't your company planning to lay off several employees?"

Possible
answers: "Mr. O'Hern hasn't discussed any reduction with me."
  or
"Where did you hear something like that?"
  or
"I don't know. I suppose you should ask in the Personnel Department since they handle all personnel matters."

Question: "I understand Ms. Smith recently had surgery. What was the problem?"

Possible
answers: "I didn't ask."
  or
"She didn't tell me, and I didn't think I should ask."
  or
"I understand it wasn't anything serious."

436
Secretarial
Procedures:
Office
Administration and
Automated Systems

Question: "Are you married?" or "How old are you?"

Possible answers:

"Why would you possibly be interested in knowing that?"

    or

"I can't imagine your being interested in knowing that."

    or

"I'm not sure how that relates to the purpose of your meeting with Ms. Halstead."

The previous responses are not particularly subtle and even though the questions should not have been asked, the visitor may be offended or embarrassed. Thus, as suggested earlier in the chapter, you should continue with your work and not provide the opportunity for questions of these types to be asked.

MEETINGS

Preparing for Meetings

You may need to do several things, such as the following, prior to or during a meeting:

- Reserve a conference room.
- Provide files of correspondence or other material concerning the topic to be discussed.
- Obtain information from other executives or departments.
- Determine that adequate seating is available and the office or room is properly arranged.
- Arrange for special equipment that may be needed.
- Study the file cards so that you will be able to recognize the visitors when they arrive.
- Arrange for someone to answer your calls if you are expected to attend the meeting.
- Make arrangements for refreshments.

At the end of each day, you should check the calendar and tickler file concerning the appointments scheduled for the next day. The information you have recorded on the card will aid the executive in preparing for the meeting. In addition to the card, you may need to provide a file or documents for the appointment. Whether you place the information on the executive's desk at the beginning of the day or follow some other plan depends on the preference of the executive.

A more in-depth coverage of arranging meetings is given in Chapter 5.

Delivering Messages During Meetings

When the executive or the visitor receives a telephone call during the meeting, you should offer to take a message. If the call is for your boss and you believe the call is urgent, you may use the intercom to announce who is calling and tell the purpose of the call.

If the call is for the visitor, you may enter the office and say something, such as "Mr. Hawkins, your secretary is on the telephone and would like to talk with you. Would you like to use the telephone in the reception area?" Hand the visitor a typewritten note if several people are participating in the meeting.

When a telephone is not available in the reception area or a nearby unoccupied office, you should offer to let the visitor sit at your desk. Be sure you have covered or removed confidential material prior to delivering the message. Try to perform some work away from the desk area while the visitor is talking so that you will not appear to be listening to the conversation. Needless to say, you should never comment on anything you may overhear.

Terminating Meetings

Some executives are able to tactfully terminate a meeting by their actions or by what they say. They may place papers in a folder, stand, or walk toward the door. They may say "Thank you for coming in" or "I'll study your proposal and get in touch with you soon" or by some other statement or action indicate the meeting is to end. To cope with the occasional visitor who may be reluctant to leave, you and the executive may have an

438
Secretarial
Procedures:
Office
Administration and
Automated Systems

understanding that after a specified time you are to telephone, deliver an "important message," or announce that he or she has a meeting. The interruption will give the executive an opportunity to terminate the meeting or to let you know that he or she wants to continue the conversation.

Summary

Most executives do not have the time, need, or desire to talk with all of those who may seek appointments; therefore, the executive's work day must be planned carefully if the time is to be used wisely.

Accuracy is essential when recording information concerning the appointment. Tact must be exercised when refusing to make an appointment for someone and when canceling an appointment.

The secretary must be aware of the importance of maintaining good public relations as she assists the executive in planning the appointment calendar and in making those who visit the office feel welcome. The secretary's voice, appearance, and attitude, as well as the office environment, are used by the visitor in forming an impression of the company.

Questions

1. What are the disadvantages of scheduling the same amount of time for each appointment?

2. List the preferences the executive may have in regard to the times for which appointments are scheduled.

3. Why should a written record be made each time an appointment is made?

4. Should the executive's appointment calendar always have 15-minute intervals printed on it?

5. Discuss the procedures that should be followed when both the secretary and the executive schedule appointments.

6. When must the secretary shake hands with the visitors?

7. Discuss the things that contribute to a businesslike atmosphere in the office.

8. List the types of information to consider when making appointments.

9. What things, other than appointments, are often listed on the executive's calendar?

10. Should subordinates always be told why the executive wants to see them? Discuss.

11. Explain the steps to be followed in canceling an appointment.

12. Should you refuse to schedule an appointment for someone who has already canceled or not appeared for three appointments? Discuss.

13. Discuss the things the secretary may need to do to help the executive prepare for an appointment.

14. Does a secretary always introduce herself to the visitor?

15. Name some techniques that may be used to help remember names of people who visit your office.

16. If most visitors who have appointments with the executive must wait for several minutes, what changes in the scheduling procedure should be considered?

17. What actions may need to be taken when someone arrives late for an appointment?

18. When you recognize a visitor to the office but cannot remember his or her name, what should you do?

19. If you believe the executive does not want to talk with someone who telephones and insists on an appointment, should you tentatively schedule the appointment and then later cancel it? Discuss.

20. What may be done to avoid being asked personal questions by visitors to the office?

440
Secretarial
Procedures:
Office
Administration and
Automated Systems

———————————————— Projects ————————————————

1. Visit an office supplies store and prepare a list of the various types of appointment calendars available. Write a brief description of each type.

2. When you shop, observe the things you believe the employees do to help create goodwill for the company. Write a report telling how these effective principles can be applied in office situations.

3. Ask your friends and relatives who work as secretaries to tell you about problems they have experienced in scheduling appointments and in working with visitors in the office. Write a report telling how the problems were resolved and goodwill was maintained.

———————————————— Cases ————————————————

1. While you were talking on the telephone scheduling an appointment for an important client, a visitor walked into the office. When you finished talking with the client, you immediately assisted the visitor and forgot to list the client's appointment on the calendar and did not think of it again until the client appeared in your office at 10 a.m. on Thursday, the time of the appointment. Your boss is in a staff meeting that is scheduled to last until noon. What should you do?

2. You are secretary to Mr. Nellis, vice president of marketing. Mr. Nellis is meeting with an important client and Mr. Dillinger, president of the company, walks into your office while you are talking on the telephone. You know that Mr. Nellis should not be interrupted. What action should you take?

3. Your boss frequently schedules appointments and fails to record them on the calendar. As a result, you are often faced with the task of having to ask the visitors for whom you have scheduled appointments to wait; and you believe they think you are at fault. Should you tell the visitors what happened, tell your boss he simply must record all appointments, tell your boss that the people you schedule should have precedence since you had no way of knowing the others had been scheduled, or take some other action?

4. Your boss's wife and five-year-old son come to your office each Wednesday about 11:45 so they can accompany your boss to lunch. The son "takes over" your office the minute he enters. He picks up papers on your desk, turns on machines, and in general causes havoc. The wife makes no attempt to control the youngster. How should you cope with this situation?

5. The ashtrays in your office are frequently full, even though the office is cleaned each night. You do not believe you should have to clean the ashtrays and pick up gum wrappers and other items left on the tables and floors. What should you do?

6. John Hendrix, who has told you he is a representative with the Tolar Product Company, arrived in your office at 11:50 without an appointment. He wanted to talk with your boss, Mr. Mayer, whom you expected to return to the building soon; therefore, you suggested that Mr. Hendrix wait. Mr. Mayer does not return by 12 o'clock when all of the other people on your floor of the building are leaving for lunch. You do not object to postponing your lunch, but you do not particularly want to be left alone on the floor of the building with Mr. Hendrix, especially since he did not have a business card. What are some possible actions you may take?

7. Assume that you are secretary to Mr. Bailey, principal of the high school. A senior girl is in Mr. Bailey's office at 5 p.m. when you are ready to leave the office. All of the other school personnel have left the building. What should you do?

CHAPTER 19

Interoffice Relationships

During the work week, you will be spending as much time with your boss and coworkers as with your spouse or family; therefore, your happiness depends to a considerable extent on your relationships at work.

Since at work you are part of a team or you would not be there, your success is dependent upon the cooperation of those with whom you work. The success of the organization depends on how effectively the individuals work together as a team.

Many of the things you need to consider as you begin a new position and work with your boss and others in the organization will be discussed in this chapter.

STARTING A NEW POSITION

First impressions are important. When you begin working in a new position, you want others to form a favorable opinion of you. You want others to perceive you as being friendly, efficient, cooperative, courteous, considerate, dependable, enthusiastic, and interested. When others like and respect you, they usually will want you to be successful and will be eager to assist you in adjusting to the position.

Coworkers and superiors probably will compare you to your predecessor. When you are replacing an efficient secretary, you will realize the advantages of entering a well-organized office; however, others will tend to expect the same level of performance from you. They may fail to realize that the one you are replacing reached her high level of efficiency only

443

444
Secretarial
Procedures:
Office
Administration and
Automated Systems

after having gained considerable experience in the position. An efficient predecessor who is available to give you some on-the-job training can do many things to contribute to a smooth transition and to your success.

If you are replacing an inefficient secretary, you may experience many frustrations, but at the same time you may be able to easily create a favorable impression on the executive and others with whom you work. Some suggestions that will help you effectively adjust to the new environment are given in the following sections.

Listen for Clues

In addition to listening to the instructions concerning the tasks you are expected to perform, you should listen for clues regarding the following:

- Who is highly respected in the company?
- What are possible areas of conflict?
- What types of relationships exist between different executives?
- What types of relationships exist between personnel in different departments?
- How do the employees view the company?
- Does a formal or informal atmosphere prevail?
- What type of relationship did your predecessor have with coworkers and executives?

Study Files

As you look through the files, you should seek to determine the following:

- What is the writing style of the executive for whom you work?
- What type of relationship does the executive have with superiors and subordinates?
- What was the quality of the work completed by your predecessor?
- What is the quality of typing and other technical aspects of the correspondence originating in other offices in the company?
- Are words and phrases with which you are unfamiliar used in the correspondence?

Study Manuals

One way to demonstrate your eagerness to learn is to ask to borrow an office manual so that you may study it before assuming your duties.

Become thoroughly familiar with the content of the manual. Even though you may not be able to retain everything covered in the manual, you should be able to remember where to look when questions arise.

When you are expected to operate equipment with which you are not familiar, ask for permission to borrow the operator's manual for a night or a weekend. The instructions presented in the operator's manual frequently are more detailed and easier to understand than those given by someone who regularly uses the equipment. Furthermore, if some aspects of the operation are complicated, you can review the instructions as many times as needed without being embarrassed. $\times$

Ask Questions

When you begin a new position, you will probably need to ask numerous questions. Since the questions you ask will tell others much about your ability, consider the following when you believe you need to ask a question:

- *Should you know the answer or know where to find the answer without asking?* Do not ask questions concerning subjects that are explained in detail in the office manual or those things that can be readily found in the file. Try to avoid asking questions for which you should have learned the answer during your professional training. Do not ask technical questions when the answer can be found in a reference manual.

- *Are you asking the appropriate person?* When you have a question for which you cannot find the answer, ask the person whom you believe will be the most willing and likely to provide the answer. For example, if you have a question concerning mail, you may need to check with someone in the mail department of your company or the Postal Service. By checking with those who are thoroughly knowledgeable, you may be able to learn things that will improve the operation of your office. Your boss may not necessarily be the person you should ask and may sometimes be uncomfortable if asked a question he or she cannot answer.

- *Is the question stated intelligently?* Give thought to the question before asking it. Do not, for example, say "I have no idea where to get the sales data." Instead, say "Should I check with the sales or accounting department for these financial data?"

Do small things well. Do not assume that you must be given challenging tasks to perform in order to prove your ability. By doing small things quickly and well, you can demonstrate your dependability, your ability to pay attention to details, your ability to organize, and your willingness to do work that may be menial but necessary.

FORMALITY

The degree of formality found in the organization depends on the people involved, and it is usually established by those in high-level positions. In some organizations, an informal atmosphere prevails and most or all people are on a first-name basis; in others, courtesy titles are used when addressing those in superior positions.

Your coworkers may use the superior's first name, but generally you should use a courtesy title until the person asks you to use his or her first name. Imagine the embarrassment you would experience should a superior whom you have called by her first name say "I prefer that you refer to me as Mrs. Smith." You should not, however, be embarrassed should the superior whom you referred to as Mrs. Smith say "Please call me Susan."

Even though you may initially be uncomfortable addressing a superior who is considerably older than you by his or her first name and someone younger by using a courtesy title, you should do so if that is what the person prefers.

FORMING OPINIONS

Form opinions of others objectively. You should always be appreciative of advice or background information volunteered by your coworkers, but you should listen to their comments about others with an open mind. Objectively arrive at your opinion of others in the organization. If a coworker comments that "Mr. Bates is impossible to work for; nothing pleases him," you should postpone forming an opinion of Mr. Bates until you have had an opportunity to learn first-hand what he expects. The coworker may have a biased opinion.

Some people who do good work and expect others to also do good work are sometimes not well-liked by those who are only marginally qualified and not highly motivated. Generally, your opportunities for success are greatly enhanced when you work for and with those who are capable, dedicated, and hard working and expect others to possess the same qualities.

The people with whom you associate during rest periods and at lunch can have an impact on your success. Be friendly and show respect for your coworkers, but be slow to form close relationships. Try to associate with those who have a positive attitude toward the company and the people who work for the company. Associate with those who are respected by the successful people in the company.

In many companies, a secretary works for more than one executive. One of the executives may be higher-ranking than the others and, therefore, may be the one to whom the secretary is primarily responsible. Sometimes, however, the executives are of equal rank and the secretary is expected to be equally responsible to each of them.

Ideally, executives who must share the services of a secretary are considerate of each other and do all that they can to make the work environment pleasant. Nevertheless, the secretary who must work for more than one executive of equal rank should be prepared to cope with the executive who may expect her to spend an inordinate amount of her time performing his or her work and who may insist that his or her work be given priority.

To avoid showing partiality, you should ask the executives to establish guidelines you are to follow in determining the order in which the work is to be completed. The executives may decide that the work should be completed in the order in which it is assigned, that certain tasks should be given priority, that you should use your judgment, or that some other procedure should be followed.

If one of the executives frequently insists that you not follow the established procedures and that you complete his or her work before completing the work of others, you should not argue. Simply state the facts, such as the following:

> "Miss Jones and Mr. Day have given me work that they expect me to have completed by noon. Will you please ask them if I may complete your work first?"

> or

> "I'll have to first check with Miss Jones and Mr. Day. I am working on projects they indicated they need by noon."

You may be able to equalize your work load by alerting the others when you know that one of the executives has a major project pending or by encouraging the executives to give you work well in advance of the time it must be completed. You may be able to demonstrate initiative and your ability to plan by saying something such as "During the first week in July, I will have to spend most of my time working on the quarterly report for Miss Tilton. Do you have some work that you may need me to complete at that time which I could be working on now?"

You should give the executives your work schedule for each day or have the schedule on your desk where it is readily accessible to them so that they may check on your work load and know that you are spending your time wisely.

448
Secretarial
Procedures:
Office
Administration and
Automated Systems

An executive may be especially cooperative and considerate, and you may enjoy working for him or her more than for the others. You should attempt to conceal your feelings and concentrate on the good qualities of each of the executives rather than on the things that may annoy you or make your work difficult. You should never be critical of one executive for whom you work while talking with another one.

LOYALTY

You have an obligation to be loyal to your company and your boss. You also have an obligation to be loyal to yourself, your family, and your friends.

All employees need to believe in the goals established for the company and be willing to work toward accomplishing those goals. You need to be able to morally support the products the company manufactures, the services it provides, or the activities in which it is engaged. The company has a legitimate claim to your time during the normal work day, but it does not have a claim to all of your time. You owe yourself time to have a life that is totally apart from your professional life.

Your boss has a legitimate right to make demands on your time and the right to expect you to comply with reasonable instructions and requests. Your boss has the right to expect you to be on the job every day and to arrive on time. Your boss has the right to expect you to spend your time on the job working on business-related tasks.

Your boss does not have the right to expect you to support policies or perform tasks that you believe to be unethical or illegal. Your boss does not have the right to expect you to do something that is contrary to the policies of the company or that will benefit his or her area of responsibility but be detrimental to the organization as a whole.

Loyalty to the company and loyalty to your boss should never be allowed to become a conflict of interest. The secretary owes her primary loyalty to the company that pays her salary and not to the person for whom she works. You should not be loyal to your boss if you have to be disloyal to the company. Be sure, however, that you have all of the facts before you decide that a conflict exists.

You owe your coworkers a degree of loyalty. Take advantage of opportunities to help them avoid mistakes or to protect them from the effects of honest mistakes. Show them the same consideration you would expect and appreciate if you were in their position. For example, if one of your coworkers submits a report that contains an obvious error, you may want to give him or her an opportunity to correct the error before submitting the report to your boss. If you believe someone has overlooked an assignment or forgotten a scheduled meeting, you can show consideration by reminding the person. Much more is accomplished by doing all that you can to help others look good than by making them look inferior. As a secretary, you have numerous opportunities to help others look good. Take advantage of those opportunities; perhaps they will reciprocate. Even if they do not, keep in mind that someone who is at an equal or lower level at this time may become your superior at a later time.

Should others in the organization be in the wrong ethically or legally, they may expect you to assist in concealing their actions. You should consider the possible consequences before getting involved with a cover-up.

When conflicting demands are placed on your loyalties, you will probably have to make compromises. You may need to consult with others who can often offer suggestions that may help you reach acceptable solutions.

Let us assume that you are asked to work overtime. You need to consider your loyalty to your boss, to your family and friends, and to yourself. Consider the impact your decision will have on each one. Will your not working late inconvenience a number of people in the company or jeopardize a major project on which your boss may be working? Will your not working late be a negative factor when the boss is considering you for a pay increase or promotion? Will your working late create a hardship on members of your family or friends? Will your working late create personal problems that will be difficult to resolve?

You may need to let the people involved know of the conflicts and seek their suggestions regarding possible solutions. Instead of saying "You are unreasonable in expecting me to work overtime tonight," you perhaps should explain by saying "Unless I am able to leave at 5, I will not be able to join my car pool and will have to take a bus. The bus stop is five blocks from my house." The executive may offer to pay the taxi fare or may decide that you should not work overtime.

PERFORMING QUESTIONABLE TASKS

You may be asked to perform what you consider to be unprofessional tasks, such as serving coffee or straightening the room before or after a meeting. If the tasks need to be performed and only you and your boss are available to perform them, you need to consider the cost of your time and the cost of the executive's time. Obviously, the cost of your time to the company is less than that of your boss.

You may also be asked to perform personal tasks, such as running errands, paying bills for the boss, and so forth. You may have a perfect right to not want to do them, but before you refuse to comply with the

450
Secretarial
Procedures:
Office
Administration and
Automated Systems

request you should remember that your success in the company depends to a considerable extent on the impression you make on the person for whom you work.

If you agree to perform personal tasks, do not do so grudgingly. You may, however, need to remind the executive that you may not be able to complete some of the office-related work by the time it is needed. If you are asked to select a birthday gift for a family member or perform other personal tasks for your boss, you may need to indicate you will be late returning to the office after lunch. You should not be expected to work late to complete company work when you had to spend the time during the day performing personal tasks.

If you do not object to performing certain tasks but do object to being asked, change your behavior. For example, you may resent your boss's lack of courtesy when he or she says "Get me some coffee." Avoid the annoyance by saying "Would you like for me to bring you some coffee?" before he or she has the occasion to ask.

BECOMING COMPATIBLE WITH THE BOSS

You need to attempt to determine what the executive likes and dislikes and structure your behavior in the office accordingly, as long as your principles are not violated. You can learn much about the executive by observing his or her behavior. You should usually try to emulate the good qualities of the executive and perhaps attempt to set an example so that the executive will want to improve in other areas.

Here is a list of the types of things you can observe in an attempt to avoid doing things that may annoy the executive:

- Do you arrange papers on the executive's desk the way he or she wants them?
- Do you frequently have difficulty finding documents?
- Are you ready to begin work in the morning and after lunch, or do you simply arrive on time and make the boss wait until you get organized before he or she can give dictation or ask you to perform other tasks?
- Is your appearance sometimes unkempt even though that of the executive is always impeccable?
- Do you carry on lengthy conversations even though you know the executive is a person "of few words"?
- Are you sometimes late in meeting assignments even though the executive is always punctual?
- Do you forget to follow through on assignments?

- Is your work station sloppy even though the executive keeps his or her desk arranged neatly?

- Do you volunteer for assignments for which you are not qualified and then find that you are unable to complete them?

- Do you fail to write down instructions and have to ask for them to be repeated?

- Do you plan your vacation for a time when you are needed in the office?

- Do you practice good health habits so that you are seldom absent from work because of ill health?

Your boss may not complain about your work or behavior; however, he or she may not be completely satisfied with what you do. You should look for verbal and nonverbal clues that may suggest changes are desired. For example, a frown may indicate that a letter was not transcribed exactly the way he or she wanted it even though you may not be asked to retype the letter.

The successful secretary makes a concerted effort to do those things that please her boss and to avoid doing those things that her boss finds annoying.

CONFIDENTIAL INFORMATION

Discretion should be used in revealing work-related information about your boss and the company. The information should be shared with only those who have a right to know.

Someone who has line authority over your boss has the right to know work-related information about your boss; but a subordinate does not necessarily have the same right. For example, an executive who has line authority over your boss has the right to know the whereabouts of your boss; an inquisitive subordinate does not. Neither has the right to non-work-related information, such as family or financial matters, that your boss may have shared with you in confidence or that you may have learned through correspondence you may have read or conversations you may have overheard.

Use good judgment in deciding what information you should reveal. Here are some examples of appropriate and inappropriate dissemination of information about your boss:

Inappropriate: "Mr. Hicks is appearing in traffic court this morning."

Appropriate: "Mr. Hicks is away on personal business."

Inappropriate: "Mr. Hicks is in an alcoholic rehabilitation center."

Appropriate: "Mr. Hicks is on sick leave."

452
Secretarial
Procedures:
Office
Administration and
Automated Systems

Inappropriate:	"Mr. Hicks is vacationing in Europe."
Appropriate:	"Mr. Hicks is on vacation."
Inappropriate:	"Mr. Hicks is at lunch (if the person calls at 2 p.m.)."
Appropriate:	"Mr. Hicks is meeting with a client."

Since a secretary is in a position to know many things about her boss, the boss must be able to trust her completely. The personal information you may know about your boss or his or her family should not be of concern to others and should not be discussed with others at work or away from the office.

Be confident you are not betraying the confidence your boss has placed in you before you reveal personal information to his or her family. For example, assume that your boss, Mr. Hilyard, does not want his wife to know that he is having lunch with a female friend. Should Mrs. Hilyard inquire, you could respond by saying "He left the office alone and he didn't tell me where he was having lunch." "He was at the office when I left at 5" could be given in reply to her question regarding whether he was at the office until 9:30 the previous night.

Do not put yourself in an awkward position by making untrue statements, but at the same time do not feel obligated to tell all that you may know. Discourage your boss sharing things about his or her personal life that may place you in an awkward position by saying "Perhaps you should not discuss this subject with me."

Your boss may make uncomplimentary remarks about acquaintances or people within the organization directly to you, or you may overhear the remarks as your boss makes them to someone else. You should refrain from expressing your opinions concerning the individuals. Any comments you make in response to a direct question should be based on factual evidence that you have a right to know through the performance of your duties. Uncomplimentary remarks should be made about others only if you have an obligation to share the information with your boss.

ACCEPTING CRITICISM

When someone criticizes you or your work, you should listen and assume that the criticism is intended to be constructive. The person who tells you about a mistake you have made may be doing you a favor. Do not immediately become defensive; instead, consider what is said and try to objectively determine whether the criticism is justified.

You may want to respond to criticism by saying "I appreciate your calling this to my attention. I'll certainly consider what you have said." If your boss criticizes some aspect of your work, you should conscientiously consider what you can do to improve. Perhaps you can ask your boss for suggestions. Some of your coworkers may suggest better ways of doing things. If you believe the suggestions have merit, try to apply them.

EXPRESSING OPINIONS ABOUT OTHERS

Use caution in expressing opinions about others. Your boss or others in the company may ask you questions about a previous employer or perhaps some mutual acquaintance, such as a particular college professor. You should respond by saying something complimentary about the person, if at all possible. Even if your experiences with the individual were not pleasant, you should not make derogatory remarks. Those who are seeking your opinion may be related to or be close friends with the individual, or their experiences may have been totally pleasant. Thus, they may assume that you were the cause of any problems you experienced. Furthermore, they may wonder whether you will describe them in the same uncomplimentary way at a later time.

MUTUAL CONSIDERATION AND RESPECT

In building a positive work relationship, everyone in the organization should show consideration and have respect for others. When your boss shows consideration, let him or her know you appreciate it. For example, if your boss tells you on Monday that he would like for you to work overtime on Friday, you may comment that "I appreciate your asking me now. I can make arrangements for John to meet me here so we can have dinner downtown." You may prefer to take dictation in the morning, but your boss may normally dictate in the afternoon. If he or she happens to give dictation some morning, you may encourage the practice by saying "I'm glad you dictated these letters this morning. I'll have time to have them ready for your signature by the end of the day."

Considerate executives remember to ask rather than demand and show courtesy and appreciation by saying "please" and "thank you." Thoughtful executives also offer to assist the secretary when she is rushing to meet a deadline by perhaps offering to get her a cup of coffee or answering the telephone. Many executives offer to assist the secretary in serving refreshments to visitors in the office and in performing similar types of tasks.

454
Secretarial
Procedures:
Office
Administration and
Automated Systems

Be sure you conform to the rules of the company. Never place your boss in the position where he or she may be embarrassed by your behavior or be unable to support you. Assume, for example, that your boss issues a directive stating that vacations can be taken only during June, July, and August. You should not expect your boss to make an exception and permit you to take your vacation at some other time.

Most companies have established personnel policies, and the executives in the various areas are expected to enforce them. Do not annoy your boss by approaching him or her about concerns over which he or she has no control. For example, you may believe you should have a pay increase, should be permitted to begin the work day at 7 a.m. and leave at 4 p.m., or be given compensatory time rather than overtime pay. Even though your boss may agree with you, he or she may not be able to take any action.

Never embarrass your boss by pointing out errors. If he or she uses an incorrect word or grammar in what is being dictated, correctly transcribe the material and be prepared to show him or her the appropriate rule in a reference manual should you be questioned.

When coworkers have a rush assignment to complete, you should offer to assist if you have the time. Perhaps you can offer to duplicate or collate material for them, or perhaps you can offer to answer the telephone.

Have respect for everyone in the organization. Workers at all levels are important, and the work they perform is necessary if the goals of the organization are to be accomplished. Those in positions at levels lower than yours can often help make your work easier and help you look good. For example, if those in maintenance know that you respect them, they may respond more readily if you need a chair repaired than they would if they had the feeling you consider yourself superior. Someone in the mail room may call you when an important letter arrives rather than wait until the regular time to deliver it.

If you work for a high-level executive whose work has priority, you should show consideration for others. For example, if you know that a service department must assist you in carrying out a task, you should alert the department as soon as you learn of the project. Remember, that the work they may need to do for others may be important, too.

PLAN YOUR SUGGESTIONS

Well-thought-out suggestions are often accepted by the executive and result in changes that contribute to a more desirable work environment. Before approaching the executive, view the situation from his or her standpoint. How would you react if you were in the position of the executive? What are the facts? Do you have all the facts needed to make an intelligent decision? What are the ramifications of the suggestion? Is implementing the suggestion possible under existing company policies?

Whether your boss is receptive to your ideas depends to a considerable extent on the timing. After you have experience in working with your boss, you will know the times when he or she is approachable. When deciding on the most appropriate time to approach your boss with a suggestion, you should consider the following questions:

- *Does your boss have time to listen?* Even though what you want to discuss may be important, decide whether it is more important than a major project on which your boss may be working or perhaps a meeting with an important client.

- *Can the discussion be held without interruption?* A telephone call or a visitor to the office can destroy the effectiveness of your presentation. Try to select a time for the discussion when interruptions are least likely to occur or arrange for someone to answer your telephone and meet visitors. You may want to arrive early or stay a few minutes late so that the conversation will not be interrupted.

- *Are you and the boss in a mental state that is conducive to objectivity?* If you or your boss is emotionally upset or extremely tired, you should postpone the discussion until a time when you are both relatively calm and relaxed.

- *Does the discussion relate to only one issue?* If you approach your boss with several suggestions at one time, he or she may be overwhelmed and as a result may not act favorably on any of the suggestions.

You and your boss should meet for at least a few minutes each day to discuss routine matters. The meetings should encourage two-way communication that is necessary if you are to work as a team. Your boss needs to share with you his or her objectives and explain how your combined efforts can accomplish the objectives. You both need to have the opportunity to ask questions, make requests, and collectively establish priorities. The meetings should provide for feedback by both you and your boss.

MAKING DECISIONS

As a secretary, you will need to make many decisions. Do not be afraid to use your good judgment and make decisions that do not involve legal matters or large sums of money. You may occasionally have to say "I'm sorry," but your boss will probably respect you for having taken the initiative in deciding what should be done.

456
Secretarial
Procedures:
Office
Administration and
Automated Systems

Even though you have been given explicit instructions, you may have to use your judgment in deciding whether to carry out those instructions. For example, your boss may tell you that he or she does not want to be disturbed under any circumstances. Obviously he or she should be disturbed if an emergency should arise or if a higher-level executive comes to the office and insists on seeing him or her.

CONFRONTATIONS

Almost invariably when people work together as closely as they do in a business, conflicts will occasionally arise. When they do, you should carefully consider what, if any action, you should take.

Remember that the impact of a confrontation at work may be quite different from one with an acquaintance. You will likely have to continue working with the person on the job, whereas you may seldom see the acquaintance. The atmosphere in the work environment is not desirable when several people have an intense dislike for others or do not communicate with each other.

Confrontations should be avoided under the following conditions:

- When you do not have a good opportunity of obtaining positive results.
- When your purpose is simply to "gripe."
- When the other person is under stress or pressure.
- When the other person will not be able to resolve the problem.
- When the condition is only temporary.
- When you are unwilling or unprepared to accept criticism the other person may give concerning you or your work.

If a problem with your boss arises only occasionally, you may be wise to cope with it rather than try to solve it. For example, if the executive occasionally asks you to work overtime and the overtime does not create a hardship for you, you may be wise to work overtime even though may prefer not to.

Summary

Teamwork in an organization is essential if the work to be carried on is to flow smoothly. The secretary's actions are important in developing a good working relationship with her boss as well as with the others in the organization. The secretary's actions and attitude influence to a considerable extent the impression others form of her; thus, the secretary should be concerned with the impression she first makes on the others in the organization when she becomes a part of the team.

In many offices, the secretary works for more than one executive. She needs to be aware of some of the actions she can take to cope with difficult situations and conflicts that almost invariably occasionally occur.

The secretary is in a position to have knowledge of much information about her boss, others in the organization, and the organization. She must realize the importance of considering the information confidential and of using discretion in sharing the information with others.

In building a positive work relationship with her boss and coworkers, the secretary must avoid challenges or confrontations, especially on petty issues that may be temporary.

––––––––––––––––––– Questions –––––––––––––––––––

1. Discuss the importance of having good work relationships.

2. Do you believe others in the organization are fair when they compare a new secretary to her predecessor? Discuss.

3. List several of the things that can be done to create a favorable first impression.

4. When you do not know the answer to a question, should you always ask your boss or someone else who may know the answer? Explain.

5. Should a secretary memorize the contents of the office manual?

6. Which is the better way of learning how to operate office equipment: have someone familiar with the equipment explain the operation or read the manual provided by the manufacturer of the equipment? Discuss.

7. What should be considered when you must ask questions?

8. Should a courtesy title be used when referring to those in superior positions in the organization? Discuss.

9. If a secretary works for three executives, should she allocate one-third of the time to each one? Explain.

10. Explain what is meant by being loyal to the company.

11. Discuss what is involved in being loyal to your boss.

12. What should a secretary do when a conflict arises in terms of loyalty to the boss and loyalty to the company? Explain.

13. What should the secretary consider when asked to perform personal, or what she considers to be unprofessional, tasks? Discuss.

14. Should the secretary always assume that the boss is satisfied with her work if he or she does not complain? Explain.

458
Secretarial
Procedures:
Office
Administration and
Automated Systems

15. Discuss the need for confidentiality in a work environment.

16. Define constructive criticism.

17. If all people in the organization are important in accomplishing the organization's goals and objectives, why are they not all paid the same salary?

18. Discuss the factors to be considered before approaching an executive with suggestions.

——————————————————— Projects ———————————————————

1. Look at office manuals your instructor may have available or that you may be able to borrow from a friend who works as a secretary. Prepare an outline for the portions of a manual that you believe would be helpful to secretaries in all offices.

2. If you have worked in an office, make a list of the ways you and your boss worked as a team.

3. Talk with your friends who work for more than one executive and ask them to share with you problems they have experienced and how the problems were resolved.

4. Think of things your friends or members of your family do that you find annoying. Consider how you might change your behavior and as a result eliminate the annoyance. For example, if a friend consistently borrows money from you, you may change your behavior and have only the amount of money you need for your own purposes.

——————————————————— Cases ———————————————————

1. Roger Page often asks his secretary, Janet Peterson, to purchase gifts for different members of his family during her lunch period. Occasionally, Janet returns to work late when she has to shop for the gifts. Mr. Page sometimes appears annoyed. How should Janet cope with this situation?

2. Diana Osborn performs many personal tasks for her boss. She does not object, but her boss never says "thank you" or expresses appreciation in any other way. Should Diana refuse to perform the tasks, indicate she resents not being thanked, consider these tasks just part of the job, or take some other action?

3. Anita Owens works as secretary to the executive vice president of the Crocker Company. Anita has excellent secretarial skills and does outstanding work. The quality of her work is superior to that completed by Lori Patton, secretary to the president. When particularly important

work must be completed, the president often asks Anita to do the work. Is Anita justified in resenting being asked to complete the work since the president's secretary is paid considerably more than she? What should Anita do or say?

4. One of the three executives for whom Judy Markle works never refers to her by "Judy"; rather, he uses "girl," "young lady," and occasionally an expression such as "good looking." Judy likes her job, but she objects to the executive not calling her by name. Should Judy ignore the situation, ask the executive to call her "Judy," or take some other action?

5. When Ramona began working for the Pilyard Company, Wilma who had worked as a secretary for the company for several years was eager to help her adjust to the new work situation. Ramona appreciated Wilma's willingness to help, but after only a day or two she began to realize Wilma was not very efficient and was not well-liked or respected by others in the company. What should Ramona do?

6. When Beth started working as a secretary at the Kimberly Company, her boss and others often made remarks regarding her predecessor's ability, such as her being able to type 95 words and take dictation at 200 words a minute. Beth is well-qualified, but her typing and shorthand speeds are not as high as those of her predecessor. As a result, she feels somewhat inferior. What should Beth do to overcome this feeling of inferiority? What should she say when others comment on the efficiency of her predecessor?

7. While several secretaries were eating lunch, Mary commented on a confidential matter that only she and Becky knew about. Becky realized that Mary should not be discussing the confidential information. What should she do?

CHAPTER 20

Financial and Legal Assistance

Many of the duties performed by a secretary may have legal implications. Although no attempt is made in this chapter to present legal advice, you will be introduced to some general information about laws and several areas in which caution should be exercised.

Most companies and agencies either employ attorneys as members of their staff or retain legal firms. As a secretary, you need to be able to recognize the special situations related to your office responsibilities that require you or your supervisor to seek advice from the legal source available to your company or agency.

NOTARY PUBLIC

A notary public is a commissioned officer of the state and is authorized to administer oaths, take acknowledgments, and certify to the genuineness of documents. The administering of oaths or affirmations will not be discussed in this chapter since most secretaries outside the legal profession do not perform these functions.

A notarization is an act of certifying that a person appeared before the notary public and, after being properly identified, signed an acknowledgment of his or her free will. The notary public in essence certifies to the genuineness of the signature.

Secretaries often accept the responsibility of becoming notaries public at their supervisor's request on behalf of the company or to increase their qualifications.

461

462
Secretarial
Procedures:
Office
Administration and
Automated Systems

Qualifications

In most states, a notary public must be a citizen of the United States. In addition, state and county residency requirements must sometimes be met. The minimum age qualification varies from 18 to 21, depending on the state. Some states have other specific qualifications that must be met.

Procedure

An application form can be obtained from the office of the Secretary of State or other appropriate official. The completed form must be submitted along with a filing fee. In some states, one or more citizens must sign affidavits concerning the character of the applicant. In a few states, the applicant must be endorsed by a member of the legislature, a judge, or some other designated official. Certain states require that the applicant take an examination before a commission is granted.

The appointment as a notary public is granted by the governor or secretary of state in the vast majority of the states. The term of office varies from two to ten years, except in Louisiana where the term is indefinite. The notary public may be commissioned for the county in which he or she resides and can perform duties as a notary public in that specific county.

Often, evidence of issuance of bonding must be obtained to fully meet the qualifications for a notary public commission. Bonding is an agreement by a surety company that it will pay damages in the event of misconduct on the part of the notary public. In other words, a bond is a form of insurance based on the notary public's honesty and character. The bonding fee charged usually is a percentage of the amount of the bond. A related benefit for the notary public is that acceptance by a bonding company usually helps establish personal credit.

After the commission has been received and properly recorded by the county clerk (or other appropriate official), you should order a notary seal and stamp. This can be done through almost any stationer. The statutes may specify what should be included on the seal.

Responsibilities

A commission as a notary public is a public trust. You must perform your duties with this thought constantly in mind.

Even though your supervisor may have requested that you obtain a notary public commission and paid all fees, you are the one legally responsible for the transactions you conduct. Your supervisor cannot force you to perform an illegal notarization.

Your most important duty as a notary public, then, is to attain proper and complete evidence of identification when you do not know the person. Usually, a driver's license or some other similar document is sufficient to establish identification. You must remember that Social Security cards are not to be used for identification purposes. When you have any reason to doubt that the documents submitted are valid, you should refuse to perform the notarization. As a notary public, you are responsible under the law in cases of false certification. The penalty can be quite severe—fines from $50 to $5,000 or imprisonment—depending upon the state and the offense.

A notary public does not read the document to be notarized, but the acknowledgments should be carefully read and all blanks in both the document and the acknowledgment should be completed.

If a document states that it is "under seal," you should be sure that the signature is followed by the letters "L.S." (an abbreviation for the Latin term *locussigilli,* meaning the place of the seal) or the word "Seal." If a corporation is party to a document, the corporate seal should be imprinted after the officer's signature.

All transactions should be recorded in the notary's journal. Depending upon the state involved and the type of notarization completed, the notary public may require the person to sign the entry in the record book or journal to give the notary public additional protection if a problem should arise.

Notaries public are permitted to charge fees for their services; however, when the company pays all of the cost involved in the notary obtaining the commission, a fee is not charged when notarizing documents for the company. You should clearly understand company policy regarding whether you should charge when notarizing documents for employees and those not associated with the company.

Acknowledgments

The term *acknowledgment* has been referred to earlier in this chapter. An acknowledgment is an act by which a person signs an instrument before an authorized official, such as a notary public, and vows that he or she executed the document of his or her free will. The notary public then signs the certification.

Uniform Acknowledgment Act

Although not all states have accepted the Uniform Acknowledgment Act, the acknowledgments generally follow a similar form. Under the provisions of the Act, the accepted forms are shown in figure 20-1.

You will note that acknowledgments contain the following information:

- Name of state and county in which the acknowledgment is made. In Kentucky, Massachusetts, Pennsylvania, and Virginia, *commonwealth* is used instead of *state;* in Louisiana, *parish* is used instead of *county.*

464
Secretarial
Procedures:
Office
Administration and
Automated Systems

By individuals:

STATE OF _____)
: SS.
COUNTY OF _____)

On this the _____ day of _____ , 19 ____ , before me,

_____ , the undersigned officer, personally

appeared _____ , known to me (or satisfactorily proven) to be

the person whose name is subscribed to the within instrument and acknowledged

that he/she executed the same for the purposes therein contained.

IN WITNESS WHEREOF, I hereunto set my hand and official seal.

_____

Notary Public

My commission expires _____ 19 ____ .

FIGURE 20-1. Acknowledgments.

- Date of acknowledgment. If predated or antedated, the action is fraudulent.
- Signature of person or persons making the acknowledgment.
- Signature and designation of officer taking the acknowledgment.
- Date of expiration of commission. This is not required in all states; however, if the document is to be recorded out of state, the expiration date must be noted.
- Notary's seal. This, too, is not required in all states.

Affidavits

On an affidavit, which is a statement containing certain facts sworn to by a person before a notary public, a common notary's certification is called a jurat. The jurat format shown in figure 20-2 is almost universally used.

By a corporation:

STATE OF_____)
                             :
COUNTY OF_____)

On this the _____ day of _____ , 19 _____ , before me,

_____ , the undersigned officer, personally

appeared _____ , who acknowledged himself to

be the _____ of _____ a

corporation, and that he, as such _____ ,

being authorized to do so, executed the foregoing instrument for the purposes therein

contained, by signing the name of the corporation by himself as _____ .

IN WITNESS WHEREOF, I hereunto set my hand and official seal.

_____
Notary Public

My commission expires_____ 19 _____ .

FIGURE 20-1. Continued

Subscribed to and sworn to before me, in my presence,

this _____ day of _____ , 19 _____ , a Notary Public

in and for the (county) (state) of _____ .

_____
Notary Public

My commission expires _____ , 19 _____ .

FIGURE 20-2. Jurat format.

466
Secretarial
Procedures:
Office
Administration and
Automated Systems

FIGURE 20-3. A notary public should observe the person signing his name.

Caution

Many people are not fully aware of the function of a notary public and requests may be unusual. Often, buyers will submit to the notary public motor vehicle titles already signed by the seller who may live in another state or even another country. You must refuse to notarize such documents. People may appeal to you on the basis of friendship to bend the law. Remember, you alone are responsible for the legality of the certification of signatures as being genuine; and the only way you can be certain of the genuineness of the signature is to observe the person signing his name, as illustrated in figure 20-3.

Often, people mistakenly believe that, because you are commissioned as a notary public, you are qualified to offer legal advice. A notary public commission does not give you the right to give legal advice of any type.

SIGNING THE SUPERVISOR'S NAME

A secretary often is given limited authority to sign her supervisor's name to correspondence. No secretary should assume that she has been granted this authority; it should be explicitly authorized by the supervisor.

If the supervisor has given you permission to sign his or her name to correspondence, under "common law" you have become an agent for your supervisor. In other words, you are generally recognized as a person who has the authority to make commitments for your supervisor. Others generally recognize that your supervisor is legally responsible for your actions on behalf of the company or agency for which you work.

The person who receives correspondence signed by you for your supervisor has the right to assume that the supervisor and/or company has made a bona fide (genuine) offer or statement on which he or she can rely. The supervisor is expected to follow through with the commitment, even though it may have been made in error, unless the parties mutually agree to terminate the offer or it can be proved that the secretary signed the correspondence with the intent to defraud.

Although a secretary should carefully proofread all correspondence and other typed material, she should be especially cautious when she signs her supervisor's name. Never sign your supervisor's name unless you are confident he or she would also be willing to sign.

Usually, a secretary is not given authority to sign her supervisor's name on legally binding documents, except those of a routine nature. When you are given authority to sign routine documents, you should never be intimidated into signing something that may be costly or embarrassing to your supervisor or company. For example, assume that you are given authority to sign your supervisor's name on routine absence and expense forms for company personnel. If a senior staff member asks you to sign your supervisor's name to an untrue statement that would allow him to list an expenditure as a tax deductible item on his income tax return, you should refuse. Your abuse of the signatory authority could result in considerable time loss and embarrassment for your supervisor should he have to appear before Internal Revenue Service representatives in regard to the matter.

The supervisor's name may be signed in several ways. The most frequently used method is to write the supervisor's name in the signature space and place your initials inconspicuously beneath it.

Other methods are

Julie Delaney
DK
Julie Delaney
Vice President for Operations

Julie Delaney by Debra Kaiser,
Secretary
Julie Delaney
Vice President for Operations

Debra Kaiser, Secretary,
for
Julie Delaney
Vice President for Operations

468
Secretarial
Procedures:
Office
Administration and
Automated Systems

FINANCIAL RESPONSIBILITIES

Cash is highly susceptible to improper diversion and use. If your work involves handling or controlling cash, you must maintain documentary evidence to minimize the possibility of being suspected of inefficiency as well as of fraud.

In most large companies, the accounting department is responsible for maintaining all financial records. In some sole proprietorship and partnership forms of business organizations, the secretary's duties may include some accounting functions, especially the depositing of funds and the reconciling of the bank statement.

Even in a large company, one executive may control a special checking account. For example, in some companies the salaries of high-level executives are known by only the top executive. To ensure the individuals' salaries remain confidential, the top executive may maintain a special payroll checking account. As secretary to the executive, you might be expected to write the checks for the executive's signature and reconcile the bank statement.

The duties you may be expected to perform in regard to a checking account and a petty cash fund are discussed in the following sections.

Deposits

All cash and checks received should be deposited promptly. The money the checks represent cannot be used by your company until the checks are cashed. The company may need to use the money to meet some of its obligations or may want to invest the money. Furthermore, should the person who signed the check die before the check is cashed, your business may have to wait a considerable period of time until a will is probated to receive money from the estate.

All of the currency and checks to be deposited should be listed on a printed form called a deposit ticket or deposit slip. The form will vary from bank to bank, but most deposit tickets provide space for the name, date, account number, and a list of the items you are depositing. If numerous items are to be deposited, you may need to use more than one deposit ticket or list the currency and coins and the total of the other items and attach an adding machine tape. The deposit ticket should always be prepared in duplicate so you will have written evidence of the deposit.

The bank will usually provide you with a bag to use for night deposits. The bag should be locked. You may give permission for the bank personnel to unlock the bag and make the deposit, or you may ask that the bag be kept locked until you arrive to make the deposit in person. When a deposit is not made in person, the bank will mail the deposit ticket.

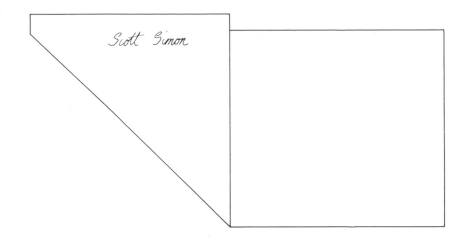

FIGURE 20-4. Endorsement in blank.

Endorsements

The one to whom a check is made payable must endorse the check by writing or stamping his or her name on the back of it. After a check has been endorsed, it may be cashed, deposited in a bank, or transferred to another person or business.

An endorsement on a check shows that payment has been received for it or that the check has been transferred to someone else.

The three principal kinds of endorsements are blank, full, and restrictive.

You can endorse a check by signing your name on the back of the check, as shown in figure 20-4. This endorsement in blank should be used only when you are at the bank to cash or deposit the check. A check endorsed in blank may be cashed by anyone who may get possession of it; therefore, should the endorsed check become lost or stolen, an unauthorized person may be able to cash it.

A check should be endorsed exactly the way the name is written on the face of the check. If you receive a check on which your name is misspelled and you are sure the check is intended for you, first sign your name as it is written on the check and then write it correctly. Assume that Deborah MacLaren received a check on which her surname was spelled "McLaran." The check should be endorsed as shown in figure 20-5.

A full endorsement is one in which the endorser indicates to whom the check is to be transferred. A check made payable to Henry Kenmore could be transferred to Tom Webster by using the full endorsement shown in figure 20-6.

An endorsement of this type means that Kenmore wants the check paid to Webster. No one but Webster may endorse and cash the check.

470
Secretarial
Procedures:
Office
Administration and
Automated Systems

FIGURE 20-5. When your name is spelled incorrectly, first sign your name as it is written on the check and then write it correctly.

Checks received by a business are seldom transferred to another business or individual.

A restrictive endorsement limits the use of a check to the purpose stated in the endorsement, as shown in figure 20-7.

A check endorsed in this way can only be credited to the depositor's account at the bank. Should someone else get possession of the check, he or she could not cash it. When you mail a deposit, always use a restrictive endorsement for the checks.

If you are responsible for the checks your company receives, you should endorse the checks as soon as you receive them. When several checks are received, you should obtain a rubber stamp to use in endorsing the checks.

Postdated Checks

You should never accept a postdated check—one that has a future date—unless you have been given permission to do so by your supervisor. A postdated check will not be honored by the bank prior to the date on the check; therefore, the check is not negotiable until that date.

Writing Checks

When a check-writing machine is not used, checks should always be typewritten or written in ink since those written in pencil or erasable ink

FIGURE 20-6. Full endorsement.

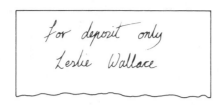

FIGURE 20-7. Restrictive endorsement.

can be changed easily. Should you make a mistake in writing a check, write a new one. Never cross out or erase words or figures on a check. A blank check should never be signed.

Most businesses use prenumbered checks. To account for all checks, you should write "void" on spoiled checks and file them with the canceled checks returned by the bank.

A bank ordinarily has to reimburse the depositor if a forged check is paid; however, if you have been unduly careless in preparing the check, the bank may not be responsible for reimbursement and your employer may have to suffer the loss.

Stop Payment

Occasionally a check may be lost or stolen and you may want to request that the bank not honor the check should it be presented for payment. To stop payment on a check, the depositor must fill out and sign a stop-payment request form at the bank. A form of this kind is shown in figure 20-8.

As you can see, the account number, date, amount, date of the check, date of the stop-payment order, and the name of the person to whom the check was written are shown on the form. The one who signed the check must sign the form. Banks usually charge for stopping payment on a check.

Bank Reconciliation

The bank reconciliation is important because it is a means of comparing the checkbook balance with the cash reported on the bank statement. The checkbook balance is seldom equal to the bank statement balance. Some checks that have been written may not have been presented to the bank for payment and a deposit made late in the day or mailed may not have been recorded by the bank by the date the statement was prepared. The bank may have deducted amounts of which you may not be aware, such as a service charge or a dishonored check, until the statement is received. And, of course, errors may have been made by either party in recording transactions.

ORDER TO STOP PAYMENT

UNITED MISSOURI BANK OF WARRENSBURG
WARRENSBURG, MISSOURI 64093

ACCOUNT NO.: 220-1196

DATE: September 11, 1984

TIME: 12 Noon

Please stop payment on the following-described check.

Number of Check	Date of Check	Payable To	Amount	Reason for Order
79	9/1/84	Leslie Squires	$75.50	Check lost.

Depositor agrees to hold the bank harmless for said amount and for all costs and expenses incurred by the bank by reason of its refusal to honor said check and depositor further agrees that if, contrary to such stop payment order, payment is nevertheless made through inadvertence, accident or oversight, the bank's liability shall be limited to the amount of actual loss sustained, and the bank shall not be liable with respect to other checks drawn by depositor which are returned for insufficient funds because of such payment. This order shall be effective for 6 months from the date hereof if it has been made in writing by the depositor or an authorized signatory. If not so made in writing, this order shall be effective only for 14 days from the date hereof. It is acknowledged that this order cannot be put into effect until at least 90 minutes after it has been received by the bank.

☑ Written Request

☐ Oral Request Phone No. 429-7071

Depositor John McKee

Address 135 North Market Street

By John McKee
(Authorized Signature)

UMB 01912

FIGURE 20-8. Stop payment order.

The bank reconciliation form consists of two major sections. One section begins with the bank statement balance and the other section begins with the checkbook balance. Both sections end with the adjusted balances, which must agree. A typical reconciliation form is shown in figure 20-9.

You should start the bank reconciliation process by checking to see that the deposits you have made are recorded on the bank statement. The canceled checks (those that have been paid by the bank) returned with the bank statement should then be arranged in numerical order. Any deposits not recorded by the bank and the checks that have been written but not presented to the bank for payment (outstanding) should be listed on the bank statement section of the reconciliation form.

All deductions the bank has made on the statement and that you have not previously recorded should be listed on the checkbook balance part of the reconciliation. After the mathematical computations have been made, the bank statement and checkbook adjusted balances should be equal. If the balances do not agree, you should be able to locate the error by considering the following questions:

1. Did you add and subtract correctly on the reconciliation?
2. Have you added and subtracted correctly in the checkbook?
3. Did you balance the statement at the end of the last month?
4. Have you deducted your checkbook charges (e.g., for printing, stop-payment, or dishonored checks) shown on the bank statement?
5. Are all deposits and checks entered in your checkbook?

Balance as shown on bank statement . . . . $ 7,225.25

Add deposit made but not shown on
   bank statement 8,918.25

                                                   $16,143.50

Subtract checks issued but not
   presented to the bank

     1,372.25

      720.25

     1,200.50

                                             3,293.00

Adjusted bank balance $12,850.50

- -

Balance as shown in checkbook $12,863.00

Subtract items deducted on the
   bank statement but not recorded
   in checkbook

  12.50 Service Charge

                                              12.50

Adjusted checkbook balance $12,850.50

FIGURE 20-9. Bank reconciliation.

6. Are any checks that were outstanding from previous statements still outstanding?

7. Do the amounts written on the checks and in the checkbook agree?

Petty Cash

Most payments for business expenditures are made by check; however, to avoid the delay of processing a check each time a small amount may be needed, most businesses establish a special cash fund that is designated "petty cash." The cash may be needed for payment of relatively small amounts, such as for delivery charges, for supplies that may be purchased

474
Secretarial
Procedures:
Office
Administration and
Automated Systems

at a nearby store, or for the supervisor to take a client to lunch. Although the petty cash fund is usually small, management may want to have ready access to several hundred dollars. As a secretary, you may be responsible for maintaining the petty cash fund.

A check to establish or replenish the fund is written in the accounting department. The money obtained from cashing the check should be placed in a safe or a locked box.

Guidelines should be written and should specify who is authorized to disburse money from the fund, the purposes for which the money may be used, and the maximum amount that may be disbursed at one time.

If you are responsible for the fund, ideally you are the only one who has access to the money. If others also have authority to take money from the fund, you should check at the end of each day to make sure that the money and receipts are equal to the total for which you are responsible and to determine whether the fund needs to be replenished.

Each time a disbursement is made from the fund, a receipt form similar to the one illustrated in figure 20-10 should be completed.

If someone must approve your disbursing money from the fund, space should be provided on the receipt for his or her signature. All people, including your supervisor, to whom you or others disburse money should immediately initial or sign the receipt. You should describe the purpose for which the money was disbursed.

When the amount of money in the petty cash fund is reduced to a predetermined minimum amount, you should prepare a form similar to the one shown in figure 20-11. You should then present the form and signed receipts to the accounting department and ask that a check be written to replenish the fund.

RECEIVED OF PETTY CASH

No. _____   DATE _____

DESCRIPTION OF ITEM / SERVICE PURCHASED	AMOUNT
CHARGE TO ACCOUNT **TOTAL**	

_____   _____
RECEIVED BY   APPROVED BY

TOPS ⬥ FORM 3008   LITHO IN U.S.A

FIGURE 20-10. Petty cash receipt. (Courtesy of Tops Business Forms)

PETTY CASH RECONCILIATION

*TOTAL AMOUNT $ _____   DEPT./BRANCH _____   DATE _____

| Cash On Hand | | Summary Of Transactions—Reconciliation Period From _____ To _____ | | | | | | | | | | |
Currency	Amount	Account	Date	Amount	Date	Amount	Date	Amount	Date	Amount	Total
$20.00 Bills											
10.00 Bills											
5.00 Bills											
2.00 Bills											
1.00 Bills											
Checks											
$1.00 Coins											
.50 Coins											
.25 Coins											
.10 Coins											
.05 Coins											
.01 Coins											
Total Cash											

SUMMARY

Total Cash											
Total Petty Cash Slips											
*Total Amount											
Overage											
Shortage											

Disposition of Over/Short:

☐ Overage: Sent Herewith

☐ Shortage: P/C Slip Prepared

TOTAL

Accounting Department

Audit/Review: Date	By:
Account Distribution: Date	By:
Petty Cash Reimbursement: Date	By:
Check Number:	Amount Reimbursed: $

_____   _____
Signature of Person Reconciling   Signature of Supervisor

TOPS FORM 3210   LITHO IN U.S.A.

FIGURE 20-11. Petty cash reconciliation voucher. (Courtesy of Tops Business Forms)

476
Secretarial
Procedures:
Office
Administration and
Automated Systems

At all times, the amount of money you have on hand and the signed receipts must be equal to the amount of the fund when it was initially established. If a shortage occurs, you should immediately notify your supervisor.

RECORDS RETENTION

Although business records may need to be kept for several reasons, the most important one is legal. The federal government requires that certain records be maintained. For example, income and expense records must be kept for so long as they may become material in the administration of any Internal Revenue Law. The *Guide to Record Retention Requirements* is a useful reference published annually by the federal government. The guide is published by the National Archives and Records Service and is available from the Superintendent of Documents, U.S. Government Printing Office, Washington, DC 20402.

The digests of recordkeeping provisions constituting the guide are grouped under the departments or independent agencies that impose or administer regulations. The digest illustrated in figure 20-12 was included in the guide under the Treasury Department and the Internal Revenue Service subheading.

All states have developed statutes of limitations that stipulate the time after which legal rights cannot be enforced by civil action in the courts.

4.103 Employers liable for tax under the Federal Insurance Contributions Act. [Amended]

To keep records of all remuneration, whether in cash or in a medium other than cash, paid to his employees after 1954 for services (other than agricultural labor which constitutes or is deemed to constitute employment, domestic service in a private home of the employer, or service not in the course of the employer's trade or business) performed for him after 1936; and records of all remuneration in the form of tips received by employees after 1965 and reported to him. Records shall include information specified in section cited.

Retention period: 4 years after the due date of such tax for the return period to which the records relate, or the date such tax is paid, whichever is later. 26 CFR 31.6001-1, 31.6001-2

FIGURE 20-12. Entry from *Guide to Record Retention Requirements*.

Most large companies have developed a records retention schedule to meet the legal requirements, as well as the other needs of the company. If the company for which you work does not have a schedule, you may need to discuss the need for one with your supervisor.

DESTROYING CONFIDENTIAL INFORMATION

Personnel records, financial and product data, computer printouts, mailing lists, and many other types of information may become obsolete or of no value to your company, but the consequences may be disastrous if the confidential data become available to competitors or even someone outside your office in your organization. With the emphasis on privacy rights, companies must be concerned not only with current data but also the security of outdated confidential information.

Espionage is a reality, not only in the government but also in industry. When confidential data are no longer needed, they should be destroyed. Since many people may have access to papers in the wastebaskets and burning records is not permitted or practical in most office buildings, shredders are an essential piece of equipment in most companies. Microfilm and microfiche may be destroyed chemically and by some types of shredding equipment.

In addition to the original and duplicated copies, all rough drafts, carbon paper, used carbon typewriter ribbons, and shorthand or longhand notes of sensitive material must be destroyed. Desk-top shredders are convenient when materials must frequently be destroyed.

Tapes on which confidential material has been recorded should be kept in a secure place. The material should be erased when it is no longer needed.

PRIVACY

During the past several years, concern over potential invasion of privacy has become widespread, and information about employees has become one of the issues. The procedures practiced by the company in regard to the collection, maintenance, and dissemination of information about employees often involve serious legal questions.

Federal and state laws designed to protect the privacy of personal information have been passed. The major law is the Federal Privacy Act of 1974, which applies to federal agencies and the private companies supplying services to them. Several states have enacted laws giving employees in the private sector the right to see their personnel records and spelling out rules of confidentiality for personnel record handling.

478
Secretarial
Procedures:
Office
Administration and
Automated Systems

The company for which you work probably has a written policy concerning the data about employees. Become thoroughly familiar with the policy and conscientiously adhere to it.

If a policy has not been established in your company, seek approval from your supervisor before disclosing any information about employees to anyone within or outside the organization and before letting employees look at the information your office may have on file concerning them. Releasing some types of information may result in legal actions being taken against the company.

Many companies will release only "directory information" about employees. The directory information may consist of only the job title and the dates of employment. The individuals within your organization should know what your company considers directory information and should be given the opportunity to request that information not be released without their consent.

SUBPOENAS

In your capacity as a secretary, you may receive a subpoena, which is a legal order signed by an attorney directing that a person testify at a particular time and place as a witness. In many states, the subpoena must also be signed by a judge before it is served.

Subpoenas are of two common types: The "judicial subpoena" requires the witness to appear in person at a trial, and the "subpoena duces tecum" requires the witness to bring documents or other records in his or her possession to be used as evidence at the trial. The need to maintain complete and accurate records, especially those that may have some legal significance, cannot be overemphasized.

If you receive a subpoena, you are bound by law to appear and testify; however, you should not become excessively apprehensive at the time you receive the subpoena. The company attorney can assist you in complying with the action stipulated.

CAUTIONS

Any action you take that may have legal implications for your company should be undertaken conscientiously. What may appear to be unimportant at the time may later be extremely significant from a legal standpoint. Assume, for example, that you work for a governmental agency which is required to advertise for bids on equipment to be purchased or work to be completed. The notice normally will state that the bids must be submitted by a specific time. If you are responsible for accepting the bids, you must meticulously record the exact time they are received. An error involving only a few minutes may be very important from a legal standpoint.

Many situations arise in the office when the secretary may financially obligate the company even though a formal legal contract may not be signed. For example, the secretary may request that work be done, such as the repair of a typewriter or other office equipment, or she may quote prices to customers. Never take any action or make any statement unless you are positive your supervisor would do the same.

If you are expected to sign for deliveries or work that has been done, you should use caution. When you are asked to sign for a package, you normally should not expect the carrier's representative to wait until you check the contents. Even if you have been given the authority to accept deliveries, if you believe something is wrong you may want to sign your name and add the statement "Received but not inspected." If an equipment service representative has performed maintenance and you are unable to check the machine to make sure it is operating properly, you may want to sign your name on the work order and indicate "John Wheeler arrived at 9 a.m. and left at 1 p.m."

When you believe that something may be questioned at a later time, always keep the evidence or make a written record of what happened and give a copy to your supervisor. For example, if you open some correspondence and the letter mentions enclosures but they are not received, make a notation on the letter that the material was missing when the letter was opened. Sometimes an envelope may need to be stapled to a letter or document received. The postmark may be important as evidence. The dates and times when certain telephone calls were made or received may be important, as well as when certain people visited your office.

Privileged information is secret or confidential information that should be discussed only with those who have the right to know about it. You can always decide whether the information is privileged by asking "Would I have known it had I not been working in this office?"

If someone asks you to take an action that you believe to be questionable, you should not argue with the person but instead suggest that the person talk with your supervisor. If your supervisor asks you to do something that you believe to be illegal, you should express your concern to him or her and suggest that the company attorney be consulted.

Summary

Although a secretary is not expected to be a legal authority, she should be familiar with the legal implications of many of the decisions she will need to make while performing her duties. Not only must the secretary take precautions to avoid having her integrity questioned, she must make sure that her actions do not intentionally or inadvertently result in her superior and the company becoming involved in embarrassing and costly legal entanglements.

480
Secretarial
Procedures:
Office
Administration and
Automated Systems

—————————————— Questions ——————————————

1. Why should the secretary consider the legal implications of the actions she may take or the statements she may make in performing her duties?

2. What governmental unit grants notary public commissions?

3. Why do many secretaries obtain notary public commissions?

4. Must a notary public carefully read each document to be notarized?

5. May the Social Security card be used for identification purposes when notarizing a document?

6. If the company pays all of the secretary's fees and expenses involved in becoming a notary public, does she have an obligation to notarize all the documents the executives may present to her?

7. What is a "commonwealth"?

8. Is the notary public who charges a fee obligated to give legal advice?

9. What is a "bona fide" offer?

10. What question should the secretary always ask before signing her supervisor's name to a letter or document?

11. Why is cash often more difficult than other assets to control?

12. Postdated checks should not be accepted. Why?

13. What is the purpose of the endorsement on a check?

14. Explain the three most frequently used types of endorsements for checks.

15. Must all checks be endorsed in ink?

16. What should be done when an error is made while writing a prenumbered check?

17. Explain why the bank reconciliation is important.

18. Should the bank be notified immediately when the adjusted checkbook balance does not agree with the adjusted bank statement balance?

19. Are petty cash funds always $100 or less?

20. Explain the steps involved in controlling the petty cash fund.

21. Should the petty cash fund be replenished at the end of each day?

22. Discuss when and how records should be destroyed.

23. Discuss "statute of limitations" in terms of records retention.

24. Define "directory information."

25. Explain the two common types of subpoenas.

26. Is the person who accepts a subpoena admitting that he or she has violated a law?

27. What is privileged information?

28. What should the secretary do if she is asked to take an action that she believes to be illegal?

——————————————— Projects ———————————————

1. Assume that when you begin your position as a secretary for the Westwood Company, you find that you are responsible for the soft drink, cigarette, and candy machines located in the employee lounge. You are told that your predecessor conducted the operation on a cash basis. The vendors were paid in cash when they filled the machines. The money collected from the machines was kept in an unlocked box in the desk drawer. The profit from the operation of the machines was used to buy wedding gifts for employees, to send flowers to those hospitalized, and so forth. This vending machine operation involves several hundred dollars a year, and you believe this informal arrangement could result in your being accused of misappropriating some of the money. Prepare a detailed list of procedures that you believe should be followed to ensure proper accounting for the money involved.

2. Use the following information to prepare a back reconciliation for the Weatherford Company for April 30:

   a. Bank balance shown on the statement at April 30: $750

   b. Balance of cash shown on the Weatherford Company records: $848.25

   c. Deposit in transit not recorded by the bank: $125

   d. Checks outstanding: $10, $25, and $40

   e. Service charge shown on the bank statement: $3.25

   f. Discovered an error made by the bank in recording a deposit: Deposit was for $250 and the statement shows $205

——————————————— Cases ———————————————

1. Nancy Walker has a notary public commission. Since the company for which she works paid the fees and reimbursed her for the cost of the notary public seal, naturally she is expected to notarize business-

482
Secretarial
Procedures:
Office
Administration and
Automated Systems

related documents for the executives. Should Nancy be permitted to charge employees of the company when she is asked to notarize nonbusiness-related documents?

2. Assume that your boss has been asked to submit a written statement concerning a legal matter. As he dictates the statement, you realize that he is making several untrue statements. After you have transcribed the statement the way it was dictated, he signs it and asks you to notarize it. Should you comply with his request?

3. Kristine is in charge of the petty cash fund. Occasionally coworkers ask to borrow money from the petty cash fund for lunch or some other purpose. They are willing to sign a receipt for the money, and they usually repay the loan the next day or two. However, because of this practice, Kristine sometimes does not have sufficient petty cash funds to pay for the things for which the fund was established. What should Kristine do?

4. Karen and Kianne have control of a petty cash fund of several hundred dollars. In addition to making some payments from the fund, they are expected to cash personal checks of $50 or less for the employees. Kianne is very efficient and is confident she is not responsible for the $20 shortage that is noticed at the time the fund is to be replenished. What action should be taken this time and what action should be taken to avoid future errors?

PART VIII

CHAPTER 21

Selecting and Securing a Position

Employment of secretaries is expected to increase faster than the average of any other occupation through the 1980s. Automated office equipment has enhanced the need for skilled office workers, and this trend will continue for several years.

Well-qualified candidates will obtain positions offering excellent opportunities. Such candidates should follow a systematic approach in locating a position for which they are personally, socially, and professionally prepared. Many office positions are available for candidates with entry-level skills, but you should continue your training to prepare for the better-paying, more advanced levels.

The job search is an involved process that you should begin by looking at yourself from the standpoint of others since much of your work will involve interacting with superiors and coworkers. Consider the secretarial tasks you enjoy and analyze your qualifications in terms of the contributions you can make to a potential employer. After completing this, consider the types of businesses that interest you and locate job openings. Learn all you can about yourself, about the possible jobs, and about the companies. You will then be ready to prepare your resume and letter of application.

The next step in the employment process is the interview, where you and the potential employer will have an opportunity to evaluate your qualifications in terms of the company's needs.

The employment process culminates in the offer of a job that you accept or reject. Most companies also notify applicants when they are not selected for a position.

All of these steps will be discussed in detail in this chapter. By conscientiously completing each of the steps, you should be able to approach the interview with confidence.

485

486
Secretarial
Procedures:
Office
Administration and
Automated Systems

SELF-ANALYSIS

Your obtaining the position you want and achieving the success you desire depends to a considerable extent on the impression you make on other people. Place yourself in the position of someone, such as a professor or former employer, who might be asked to evaluate you. Assume the role of the other person, and look at yourself from his or her viewpoint. Then rate yourself above average, average, or below average on each of the factors listed in figure 21-1 that will have a definite impact on your success as a secretary.

As you continue the steps in the employment process, try to use concrete evidence to reflect your strengths in those areas in which you rated yourself *above average.*

IDENTIFYING DUTIES

You now need to identify the tasks you are qualified to perform and those you enjoy the most. Spend time looking at the *Occupational Outlook Handbook* under the various headings relating to secretarial and clerical work. You will find dozens of duties you might be asked to perform. Categorize the duties under major headings, such as the following, to identify the areas of work you find most desirable:

- Use of the telephone
- Work with the public
- Dictation and transcription
- Computers and word processors
- Travel arrangements
- Mail functions
- Meetings
- Creative work
- Communication

A job description for a secretary who reports to a mid-management level supervisor in a major corporation is shown in figure 21-2. Prepare a description for what you consider to be an ideal job.

	Above Average	Average	Below Average

Relationships with Others

	Above Average	Average	Below Average
Displays poise and self-confidence	_____	_____	_____
Demonstrates tactfulness	_____	_____	_____
Works cooperatively with others	_____	_____	_____
Accepts criticisms and suggestions gracefully	_____	_____	_____
Speaks correctly and clearly	_____	_____	_____
Has good command of the language	_____	_____	_____
Appears emotionally mature	_____	_____	_____
Is friendly and courteous	_____	_____	_____
Demonstrates loyalty	_____	_____	_____
Makes favorable impression	_____	_____	_____
Makes friends easily	_____	_____	_____
Is reliable	_____	_____	_____
Has a sense of humor	_____	_____	_____

Intellectual Ability

	Above Average	Average	Below Average
Applies common sense when solving problems	_____	_____	_____
Identifies the important factors of a particular situation	_____	_____	_____
Establishes priorities	_____	_____	_____
Analyzes a situation objectively	_____	_____	_____
Grasps instructions quickly	_____	_____	_____
Thinks systematically and logically	_____	_____	_____
Recognizes factors involved in difficult situations	_____	_____	_____
Solves problems with clear, decisive thinking	_____	_____	_____

FIGURE 21-1. Rating scale.

	Above Average	Average	Below Average
Motivation and Initiative			
Desires to accomplish objectives	_____	_____	_____
Reflects enthusiasm	_____	_____	_____
Shows ambition — has a high level of desire or drive	_____	_____	_____
Carries out assignments with little guidance	_____	_____	_____
Meets deadlines	_____	_____	_____
Recognizes things that need to be done and completes them without having to be asked	_____	_____	_____
Leadership Qualities			
Assumes a leading role in group activities	_____	_____	_____
Gets jobs done with and through others	_____	_____	_____
Is honest and sincere	_____	_____	_____
Follows through with confidence, without fear of making a mistake	_____	_____	_____
Is asked for assistance or advice	_____	_____	_____
Organizes work efficiently	_____	_____	_____
Accepts responsibility	_____	_____	_____
Does more than is required	_____	_____	_____
Personal Qualities			
Appears well-groomed	_____	_____	_____
Dresses appropriately	_____	_____	_____
Shows energetic attitude	_____	_____	_____
Possesses those qualities others look for in those they enjoy being around	_____	_____	_____

21.1 cont.

Classification: Secretary

Reports to: Supervisor

Summary:

Performs general secretarial duties for a supervisor who reports directly to a manager.

Duties and Responsibilities:

1. Performs varied clerical and secretarial duties requiring a knowledge of office routine and understanding of the organization, programs, and procedures related to the work of the office.

2. Originates periodic record changes and accomplishes other general office work which relieves the supervisor of routine administrative duties.

3. Receives visitors, answers inquiries, and makes necessary appointments.

4. Answers telephone and opens and distributes incoming mail.

5. Types, takes dictation, and maintains proper filing systems and adequate personnel records.

Qualifications

Typing 55 wpm/Shorthand 80 wpm

FIGURE 21-2. Job description for a secretary to a mid-management level supervisor.

IDENTIFYING STRENGTHS

As you continue completing the steps involved in the employment process, you need to keep in mind that you will be hired only if the employer believes you have the qualifications needed to do the job more effectively than others who may be applying. List concrete examples of your strengths as you consider the areas of education, experience, and activities. Remember that the employer will be interested in the following qualities:

- Ambition
- Cooperativeness
- Dependability
- Health
- Industriousness
- Maturity

490
Secretarial
Procedures:
Office
Administration and
Automated Systems

- Self-respect
- Skills

  Communication
  Management
  Organization
  Planning
  Technical

- Teamwork
- Tenacity
- Time management

Education

When you complete your college degree and seek your first full-time position, your strongest selling point will probably be your education. The fact that you have some college credit or have earned a degree will make you more employable than others who may be competing for the position. As you consider your education, identify those aspects that make you unique.

Most colleges require several of the same courses for a particular degree; therefore, completing introductory courses will not be a distinguishing factor. Perhaps you took some advanced or elective courses relevant to the position demonstrating that you did more than meet the minimum requirements. Did you enroll in accounting, economics, management, statistics, or other related business courses that were not a required part of your degree? Did you have a course in public speaking, human relations, or other relevant areas?

Should you apply for a position with a company that is involved in international trade, your knowledge of a foreign language may be of considerable value. Sometimes courses in technical areas can add an important dimension to your total preparedness for a secretarial position within a particular industry. One applicant was favorably considered for a position in the aircraft industry because she had studied aviation courses and had obtained a private pilot's license.

Everyone applying for the position will have a knowledge of shorthand and typing; but your shorthand, typing, and transcription speeds may be superior to those of many others. Be factual and specific as you list your qualifications. Do not say that you are an expert typist; instead, give your typing, shorthand, and transcription speeds as a specific number of words per minute.

You may want to capitalize on what you have learned in some courses. For example, you may want to indicate that while enrolled in the office procedures class you attended meetings and compiled and typed the minutes; worked on realistic problems that involved making car, hotel, and air reservations; prepared itineraries; prepared graphic aids; edited and typed business reports; planned meetings and programs; took and transcribed office style dictation; and worked on other practical projects relating to office situations. Specify the office machines you can operate and mention any expertise you have in using word processing machines and computers.

As indicated earlier in this chapter, you should stress the positive aspects of your qualifications. You may want to include the grade-point average in your major or your overall average when you believe it is high enough to set you apart from others who are competing for the same position. If your grades are low, you should not mention them.

Experience

Show how your experience has helped prepare you for the job for which you are applying. When you have related work experience, identify the duties by using action words and, when possible, show how well you accomplished the tasks. Do not merely list the titles of the jobs you have held. Job titles do not have standard meanings; therefore, instead of stating that you worked as a secretary, you should use action words to describe your duties, such as "typed reports and letters, prepared agenda, planned itineraries, performed writing and editing functions on IBM and Wang word processing equipment, received visitors, made appointments, operated a Dimension PBX system, typed confidential letters and reports, and opened and routed mail."

Whether or not your experience relates specifically to the position for which you are applying may not be as important as evidence indicating you possess the qualities important for all types of office employment. For example, you may have demonstrated ambition and a willingness to work hard by earning enough to pay for part or all of your education; learned how to get along well with all types of people by working as a waitress; or developed your ability to work as part of a team by serving on committees. Perhaps you proved you are honest by having the responsibility of recording receipts and depositing large sums of money. Or your work may have involved supervising others. You may have learned the importance of establishing priorities and budgeting your time. Your dependability may be reflected by the fact that you were not absent or late.

Evidence of your growth and success on the job may be shown by promotions, pay increases, and assignment of additional responsibilities.

Extracurricular Activities and Hobbies

Many of the things you gained from your work experience may also be applicable when you consider your activities and hobbies. For example,

492
Secretarial
Procedures:
Office
Administration and
Automated Systems

by participating in sports, you may have demonstrated your ability to work as part of a team. As secretary of an organization, you may have written letters, prepared reports, and recorded the minutes. Perhaps by serving as chair of the social committee you became more aware of the social amenities and learned to become comfortable in a variety of situations.

Mere membership in an organization is not considered significant by most employers, but election to an office indicates you are liked and respected by your peers. Also, as an officer or chair of a major committee you developed leadership and management skills.

By actively participating in organized activities, you show that you are interested in working with people. The activities in which you are involved and the hobbies you pursue give the employer some indication of your range of interests. List only hobbies you actively pursue; otherwise, you may be embarrassed during the interview. If you have listed reading as one of your hobbies and you cannot name the last novel you read, the employer may conclude that you have not been totally honest in presenting your qualifications.

SELECTING BUSINESSES

Before you start identifying and contacting companies concerning employment possibilities, you need to consider the following questions and others that may be particularly important to you:

- Do you prefer a particular type of industry or business?
- Do you prefer to work for a large or a small company?
- Do you prefer a particular location?
- Do you prefer to work in an office with many employees or in a small-group environment?
- Do you prefer a well-established company or one that is relatively new?
- Do you prefer to work for a sole proprietorship, partnership, or corporation?
- Do you prefer to work for only one executive?

SOURCES OF JOB OPENINGS

As you seek to identify the businesses that need the knowledge and skills you have to offer, you may need to consider some or all of the following sources.

Most colleges have a career planning or placement office that provides free services for their graduates. In addition to offering counseling services, serving as a depository for credentials, maintaining a list of job openings, and arranging interviews, the placement office often maintains files with information about the companies that use the services of the office.

Several months prior to the time you plan to seek full-time employment, you should file your credentials with the placement office. The credentials you file normally include recommendations from professors and previous employers, as well as much of the information asked for on application blanks. Get to know someone in the placement office so that you can be kept informed about openings for which you are qualified. Many of the placement offices have professional counselors who can give assistance in helping you evaluate your qualifications in terms of the needs of the employers.

Several companies have recruiters who regularly interview on campus. Check frequently with the office so that you can arrange to have on-campus interviews with the recruiters representing the companies in which you are interested.

Even after obtaining full-time employment, many people continue to keep up-to-date credentials on file with the placement office so that they may be notified of openings for experienced secretaries.

Friends, Acquaintances, and Relatives

Your professors can be an excellent source of information about job opportunities. Do not minimize the importance of getting to know them well and making a favorable impression on them. Business executives frequently contact their former professors when they have job openings. Department heads are often contacted by employers, especially when a company has previously hired well-qualified graduates from the college. The professors can serve as effective intermediaries by asking questions about the position and company and by providing meaningful first-hand information concerning your qualifications.

You may be able to make contacts and learn of job openings by attending meetings of professional organizations and getting to know the officers. When business people speak at business club meetings, they often mention their employment needs and supply information about the company.

Your friends and relatives may be able to provide you with information concerning the employment needs of the companies with which they are associated or those they may know about. Since a large percentage of the job openings are never advertised, you greatly improve your likeli-

494
Secretarial
Procedures:
Office
Administration and
Automated Systems

hood of learning about job openings by letting as many people as possible know about your qualifications and the type of position you are seeking.

Newspapers

A good source of job openings is the classified section of the newspaper, especially the Sunday edition of the metropolitan newspapers. When you are interested in a position being advertised, you should respond promptly.

In addition to the positions advertised in the newspaper, you can learn of potential openings by reading articles in the business section. When new businesses are locating in your area or established businesses are planning to expand, you may logically assume that they may need employees who possess your skills. You may demonstrate initiative and enhance your employment opportunities by contacting the company before the job openings are announced.

Even when you are not actively seeking employment, you should frequently look at the jobs advertised to stay abreast of the type and number of jobs being advertised, the specific skills being requested, and the salaries and benefits being offered.

Private Employment Agencies

Since private employment agencies are dependent on bringing together employers and applicants, they are eager to be helpful. In the process of acting as an agent for the one seeking a job and as a recruiter for the employer, the agency often performs many functions for the employer. The staff of the agency usually screens the applicants on the basis of the information provided on the registration form, administers skill tests, and conducts interviews. Carefully plan your visit to an employment agency, since only those candidates the agency personnel believe meet the qualifications specified are referred to the company for consideration.

A fee is charged for the services provided by the agency; therefore, you should select an agency carefully. Fully understand the amount of the fee being charged and whether the employee or the employer pays the fee. Be sure to read and understand all parts of the contract before you sign it.

Public Employment Agencies

State- and city-operated employment agencies provide essentially the same services as private employment agencies, except the services are free to both the employers and the applicants.

Government Positions

All levels of government have positions for secretaries. Information about examinations, applications, and employment procedures for federal employment can be obtained by contacting the Office of Personnel Management. In metropolitan areas, you can find the proper government office to contact for positions at the state and local levels by looking in the telephone directory. Your college placement office and professors should also be able to provide you with the names and addresses of the offices to contact.

Direct Inquiry

Most companies are eager to have well-qualified secretaries apply. A direct inquiry made by writing a letter or by walking in often can be effective. When you walk in, you probably will be given an application blank to take with you or to complete at that time.

Should the company have an immediate opening for a secretary with your qualifications, you may be given screening tests and be interviewed at the time you make your first contact. Therefore, you should be dressed appropriately and be well-prepared.

If the company does not have a position open at the time, the personnel office will keep your application on file for consideration when a vacancy occurs.

LEARNING ABOUT THE COMPANY

After you have completed all of the preliminary research, you need to identify the particular companies you want to contact. Before contacting them, consider the following questions to find out all you possibly can about the company:

- Where are the offices, stores, or branches located?
- What does it produce or what services does it provide?
- What has been its growth pattern?
- What are the prospects for the industry and for the particular business?
- Is the business financially sound?
- Does the company produce a product or provide a service of particular interest to you?
- What is the reputation of the company in terms of the quality of products or services provided?

496
Secretarial
Procedures:
Office
Administration and
Automated Systems

- What is the history of the company in regard to employer–employee relations?
- Is the company respected in the community?
- Do the employees speak highly of the company?

You may have difficulty finding answers to all of the questions, but by using all the resources you have available you should be able to learn much about most companies.

A company's annual report provides information concerning its past, present, and projections for the future. The college placement office or the library probably has the annual report on file, or you may obtain a copy by writing to the company. The placement office may also have brochures and other literature giving useful information about the company.

The business section of metropolitan newspapers, *The Wall Street Journal,* business magazines, and trade journals have numerous articles concerning industries as well as specific businesses. Moody's manuals and Standard and Poor's manuals provide a wealth of information concerning the large corporations.

If possible, talk with several people who work for the company; do not form an opinion of a company on the basis of what only one person may tell you. Try to find out what the employees like most and least about the company. Perhaps your professors, friends, relatives, or other people with whom you come in contact have first-hand information they will share with your.

THE RESUME

After you have done the preliminary work of visualizing yourself as others see you, identifying the types of duties you are primarily interested in performing, listing your qualifications, considering the type of businesses for which you would like to work, and collecting information about the company, you are ready to start developing your resume and letter of application.

Although some guidelines should be followed in preparing the resume and letter of application, you should not use resumes or letters written by someone else. The resume and letter of application must present an accurate picture of you.

A data sheet or resume is a concise and orderly listing of information about yourself that will help the potential employer evaluate your qualifications in terms of the position or positions available. Although you and other applicants may be equally qualified, you may get an interview and the others may not simply because of the way you prepare the resume. Present your qualifications in a way that will make you appear superior and that will enable the employer to differentiate you from other applicants.

The resume is written after you have analyzed your skills and abilities in terms of the particular position for which you are applying. To a considerable extent, as long as the rules of effective writing are observed, the effectiveness of a resume depends on who reads it. What particularly appeals to one person may not be important to someone else. Nevertheless, you need to consider the following sections normally found in resumes.

Title

As a minimum, the title should include your name, address, and telephone number. You may individualize the resume by including the name of the job sought and the name of the firm, as shown by two of the examples presented in figure 21-3. You want the resume to be visually appealing to the employer.

Job Objective

Professional resume writers do not unanimously agree that the job objective should be a separate part of the resume, but obviously the reader needs to know the type of position you are seeking. The objective may be written in specific or general terms, such as the following:

A secretarial position requiring a high degree of skill in taking dictation and transcribing.

To work as a private secretary to a senior-level officer.

Entry-level position that will lead to development as an executive secretary or office manager.

Entry-level position that offers development opportunity for a career in office administration.

Secretarial position that requires expert shorthand and typing skills that will lead to an executive secretary or office manager position.

Education

Include the names and location (city and state) of the institutions (after high school) you have attended, the dates you attended, the degree or degrees you earned, and the main areas of study not reflected by the

498
Secretarial
Procedures:
Office
Administration and
Automated Systems

```
1012 Maguire Street
Kansas City, MO 64101                                    (816) 254-2777

                          R E S U M E

                              of

              SUSAN WILSON'S QUALIFICATIONS AS A SECRETARY
```

```
                          QUALIFICATIONS OF

                            Susan Wilson
                          1012 Maguire Street
                          Kansas City, MO 64101
                            (816) 254-2777
```

```
1012 Maguire Street
Kansas City, MO 64101                                    (816) 254-2777

              SUSAN WILSON'S PREPARATION FOR WORK AS AN EXECUTIVE

                   SECRETARY WITH THE ABC COMPANY
```

```
                          R E S U M E

                            Susan Wilson
                          1012 Maguire Street
                          Kansas City, MO 64101

                            (816) 254-2777
```

FIGURE 21-3. Resume titles.

degree title. List your most recent education first. The unique aspects of your education should be stated in specific terms. Mention unusual skills you attained or knowledge you acquired that may be particularly related to the position. However, listing all of the courses you have studied may diminish the impact of those that are significant and may indicate your lack of ability to separate the important from the unimportant. Several arrangements that can be used to present your education are shown in figure 21-4.

September 1980-   Elite University, Westphalia, IL.
May 1984   Bachelor of Science with a major in Office Administration.
                  Earned 9 semester hours in accounting, 6 hours in finance,
                  and took electives in business report writing, computer
                  programming, and human relations; grade-point average of
                  3.4 (4.0 scale) in major.

Bachelor of Science, Elite University, Westphalia, IL, May 1984
    Major: Office Administration
    Professional Skills: Typewriting, 80 wpm
                          Shorthand, 140 wpm
                          Transcription, 25 wpm
                          Can perform all functions on the Wang word
                              processor.

Graduated, Elite University, Westphalia, IL. Bachelor of Science with
    a major in office administration. May 1984. Grade-point average: 3.5.

Earned 9 semester hours in accounting, 6 hours in computer programming,
and 9 hours in Spanish.

Graduated, Elite University, Westphalia, IL, Bachelor of Science degree with
    a major in office administration, May 1985. Electives in public speaking,
    statistics, and German.

Attended Harper Valley Community College, Springfield, MO, September 1981-
May 1983.

FIGURE 21-4. Arrangement of educational data.

Experience

The experience section of the resume should give the name and location
of the companies for which you have worked, the dates on which you
began and terminated the job, and your responsibilities or duties on the
job. You should list all of your full-time experience and your meaningful
part-time experience. Use the term *present* to indicate current employment. You need not include the street address or telephone number of the
company or the name of the supervisor, but such information assists the

500
Secretarial
Procedures:
Office
Administration and
Automated Systems

Cross-Country Transportation, Kansas City, MO, Summer 1983
Worked for three senior-level managers while the secretaries
were on vacation. Scheduled appointments, greeted visitors,
took dictation and transcribed, attended meetings and
recorded the minutes, routed incoming mail, answered the
telephone, and placed outgoing calls.

Summer   Food Service Department, Hilarious Amusement Park
1983   Kansas City, MO

          Started as a clerk and was promoted to supervisor after
          five weeks; ordered supplies; planned schedules for
          10 workers; opened and closed the snack bar.

FIGURE 21-5. Arrangement of experiential data.

reader in verifying your experience. List the work experience in reverse
chronological order. Be consistent and include the same type of information for all the facts you list.

The examples in figure 21-5 illustrate how your experience may be
listed. Notice that the personal pronoun *I* is not used.

Activities, Hobbies, and Honors

You may choose to use separate headings for your activities, interests, and
hobbies, or you may decide to omit them completely. One reason for
including them is to convey the image of being a well-rounded individual.
Also, by listing the offices you have held in organizations you can show
that you coped with many of the same types of situations found in the office. Spell out the names of all organizations. When listing Greek-letter
groups, be sure to indicate whether they are service, honor, or social. If
you have received the same honor on several occasions, simply use an
expression such as "Consistently on the Dean's List" rather than listing it
several times.

Personal Data

The laws relating to equal opportunity employment prohibit prospective
employers from discriminating for reasons of age, color, creed, race,
religion, and sex. So that they may not be accused of using it, some
employers prefer not to have the information. Therefore, you may decide
to omit this section of the resume.

When personal data are given, they usually involve the age or birth date (not both), family or marital status, height, weight, and health. Some applicants include hobbies, interests, date of availability for employment, travel, and memberships in this section.

References

For many years, references were listed on the resume. Now, however, some prefer to omit the list and simply add that "References will be furnished upon request" or "References on file with the Placement Office, Elite University, Westphalia, IL." Even though you may not list the references on your resume, you need to be prepared to make them available.

The best references are those people who know well your personality, your education, and your job performance. Although someone's title may appear impressive, you may make a mistake by listing the person as a reference unless he or she knows you well enough to make meaningful comments about your qualifications by using specific statements rather than generalities.

You should always get permission before using someone as a reference. This is not only the courteous thing to do since the person will be doing you a favor, but you can also provide information about the job for which you are applying and things about yourself that may help the person cover points that are especially important for a particular job. Also, the person you ask may not want to serve as a reference and may, as a courtesy to you, suggest that you ask someone else. You should give a copy of your resume to each of the references.

THE LETTER OF APPLICATION

Although the letter is seen first, it should be written after the resume has been prepared. The information you present in your letter concerning your education, experience, and activities should summarize or draw attention to the data presented in the resume.

Your primary objective when writing a letter of application and submitting a resume is to be granted an interview. You should try to make the same favorable impression with the letter that you expect to make in the interview; therefore, the letter must sound like you. You should not attempt to give a complete history of your background; rather, you should concentrate on presenting those qualifications that you believe to be superior to those of others who may be applying and those you believe the

502
Secretarial
Procedures:
Office
Administration and
Automated Systems

employer will consider most important. You want to whet the interest of the employer so that he or she will want to learn more about you.

The letter of application normally identifies the position for which you are applying, summarizes your education and experience in terms of the position, and ends by asking for an interview. Carefully consider the following as you write your letter of application.

Inside Address

The letter should be addressed to an individual, except when you are responding to a blind ad in the newspaper. When you do not know the name of the person to whom the letter should be addressed, call the company and ask. Be sure to spell the name correctly and use the proper title.

Body

The letter of application usually begins by telling the reader how you heard of the opening (when you know an opening exists), what position you are seeking, and something to indicate you can make a positive contribution to the company. When someone has told you of the opening, be sure you do not use the name of the individual without first obtaining permission.

"My part-time work as a secretary in a law office and four years of college should enable me to be an effective secretary at Harms and Harms" identifies the position and shows possible reader benefit. Using "My name is _____ and I'm applying for ...," "Please accept my application for ... ," and "May I please be considered for ..." will not generate much enthusiasm on the part of the reader.

You should continue the letter by highlighting your education or experience. The coverage of your education may include the name of the institution you attended or from which you received your degree, the date you received the degree, the main areas of study, and those things that you believe are particularly appropriate for the position for which you are applying.

Be factual and specific as you relate how your work experience has helped you prepare for the position. Do not simply list the companies for which you have worked and the titles of the jobs held. Use action words as you refer to your qualifications and keep in mind that all your qualifications must be presented in such a way that the reader will see that what you have to offer will be valuable to the company.

After you have highlighted your education and experience, you may want to tell what you gained from participating in activities or organizations that can be applied on the job.

You should end the letter by asking for an interview. "I look forward to meeting you so that you may further evaluate my qualifications. My telephone number is (816) 429-6200, and I am usually at home after 4 p.m." ends the letter with the action you desire and makes the response easy. Do not say "Call anytime" or "I'm always there." Also, avoid using expressions such as "Please call ...," "Please write ...," "At your convenience," "At a mutually convenient time," and "Personal interview." You are not in a position to tell the reader to write or call, most employers will not plan an interview at an inconvenient time, and all interviews are personal. At the time you write the letter, you have no assurance the reader will respond; therefore, never say "Thank you in advance."

Closing

Be sure to type your name and to use proper business format in the closing lines. Check with a secretarial reference manual to verify formats.

TYPING THE LETTER AND RESUME

The physical appearance of your letter of application and resume is important. The appearance may tell the employer as much about you as what you write. Technical errors in your letter and resume can destroy the effectiveness. Errors in content, style, organization, and mechanics are always inexcusable, especially for someone applying for a secretarial position.

One applicant indicated in the first paragraph of the application letter that she could "... offer enthusiasm and competentcy ..." and later in the same letter stated she had "wom third place in a contest" and had experience as a "cler-typist." The applicant was not granted an interview even though she was not applying for a position in the secretarial area.

The letter and resume should be typed on the same good grade of 8½-inch by 11-inch bond paper. The letter should be one page. Whether you should use a one- or two-page resume depends on the amount of relevant data you have to present. When you use a second page, you should place your name and the page number about an inch from the top.

A resume is ordinarily arranged in some type of tabulated format. Remember that layout, margins, headings, centering, capital letters, spacing, and underlining can be used to highlight the information you want to emphasize. You should avoid using paragraphs and complete sentences in the resume. Items of a similar nature, such as duties performed on the positions you have held, should be listed in parallel form. Use action

504
Secretarial
Procedures:
Office
Administration and
Automated Systems

words in phrases as you list the specific facts concerning your qualifications; and, as noted earlier, avoid using *I.*

Since you are applying for a secretarial position, you should type original letters and resumes. If you have access to word processing equipment, you can easily make the necessary changes as you prepare letters and resumes for various employers.

After you have prepared your letter and resume in final form, you should proofread them and be certain you have not made errors in the content or in the typing. Have another person proofread your letter and resume to help guarantee accuracy. Use the questions listed in figure 21-6 as you evaluate your letter and check it for accuracy. You should also ask many of the questions as you evaluate and check your resume.

The letter of application and resume presented in figure 21-7 reflect the qualities necessary to make them effective.

INTERVIEWING

When you are invited to visit the company for an interview, your confidence should be bolstered by the fact that your letter of application and resume were effective. Remember that the purpose of the interview is not only to give the interviewer an opportunity to evaluate you in terms of the company's needs, but also to give you the opportunity to evaluate the job and the company.

The best way to be relaxed during the interview is to be convinced that you are the best person for the position. To have that feeling of confidence, you must have thoroughly and carefully considered all important facts about yourself, about the type of position for which you are applying, and about the specific company with which you are interviewing. Having conscientiously completed this task, you will have fresh in your mind and on paper the facts needed to prove that you are the right person for the job.

Preparation

As part of your preparation for the interview, you should think of questions you are likely to be asked and form answers to them. In addition, you should think of questions you may ask the interviewer. The types of questions you ask and the answers you give can tell the interviewer that you have carefully prepared and that you have a sincere interest in a position with the company.

Here are some questions frequently asked during the interview. You should be prepared to answer them.

_____ Type the letter as an original?

_____ Type the letter on a good grade of bond paper (at least 50 percent rag content)?

_____ Type the letter without making any errors?

_____ Use a dark black ribbon?

_____ Place your return address approximately 10 lines from the top of the page?

_____ Include your street name and number, city, state, and ZIP in the return address section?

_____ Use the reader's name and title in the inside address?

_____ Spell the reader's name correctly?

_____ Use the reader's name in the salutation?

_____ Include the following in the body of the letter?

   _____ Tell how you heard of the opening?

   _____ Identify the position for which you are applying?

   _____ Lead the reader to believe you can help the company?

   _____ Tell the name of your degree?

   _____ Tell your major?

   _____ Tell the names of the courses you have taken that might help you be more prepared than others with a similar degree?

   _____ Tell your grade average if it is 3.0 or higher?

   _____ Tell what you learned from your education that can be applied to the job?

   _____ Tell about your work experience?

   _____ Tell what you learned from your work experience that can be applied to the job?

   _____ Tell about your participation in activities?

   _____ Tell what you learned from your participation in activities that can be applied to the job?

   _____ Emphasize your strengths by mentioning facts?

   _____ Refer to your resume by mentioning some important data included?

   _____ Ask for an interview?

_____ Type your name in the closing section?

_____ Sign your letter?

FIGURE 21-6. Checklist for letter of application and resume.

- What do you know about our company?

- Why do you want to work for us?

- Why did you decide you wanted to work for a (small-, medium-, or large-size) company?

- Why are you particularly interested in a business engaged in our line of work?

10 West Prestige Lane
St. Charles, MO 63301
April 15, 1984

Ms. Cynthia Fitzsimmons
Managing Partner
Fitzsimmons, Smith and Harding
15 Oak Park Place
St. Louis, MO 63290

Dear Ms. Fitzsimmons:

Your ad in today's <u>St. Louis Post-Dispatch</u> for a legal secretary interests me. I offer you background preparation that includes degrees in business and two years of meaningful part-time experience in a legal office.

My secretarial training at the junior college level gave me a thorough knowledge of legal terminology and forms and experience in taking and transcribing legal dictation accurately. While completing my Bachelor of Science in Office Administration degree at Hillside University, I have studied several relevant elective courses, which are listed on the enclosed resume.

During the past two summers and during the school year, I have worked in a law firm where I have been able to apply many of the skills and much of the knowledge I learned in the classroom. My duties evolved from those of a file clerk and typist to those of a secretary.

In addition to working approximately 20 hours per week to help pay for my education, I was able to maintain a high grade average, actively participate in campus activities, and hold leadership positions.

Now that I will complete the degree requirements in May, I am eager to become part of the working team that has made Fitzsimmons, Smith and Harding one of the leading corporate and defense firms in the St. Louis area. I will appreciate your giving me the opportunity to discuss further my qualifications for a secretarial position. I can be reached after 4 p.m. at (314) 421-1156.

Sincerely,

Brenda Lawson

Enclosure

FIGURE 21-7. Letter of application and resume.

QUALIFICATIONS OF BRENDA LAWSON FOR A POSITION AS SECRETARY

FOR FITZSIMMONS, SMITH AND HARDING, ATTORNEYS AT LAW

10 West Prestige Lane
St. Charles, MO 63301   (314) 421-1156

Job Objective

Position that requires expert shorthand and typing skills and that will
lead to an executive secretary or office manager position.

Professional Education

1982-1984   Hillside University, St. Louis, MO
              Bachelor of Science in Office Administration, May 1984

              Grade-point average: 3.6 (4.0 scale)

              Relevant elective courses:

                   Report Writing   Small Group Communication
                   Human Relations   Business Communication
                   Public Speaking   Computer Science

1980-1982   Three Rivers Junior College, Ferguson, MO
              Associate of Science with a major in legal secretarial
              practice, May 1982

              Earned six semester hours in business law in addition to
              the required hours in the secretarial area.

Professional Skills

              Typing: 80 wpm
              Shorthand: 140 wpm
              Transcription: 30 wpm
              Functional knowledge of the following:
                IBM and Wang word-processing equipment
                Copying and offset printing machines
                Teletypewriter
                Transcribing equipment
                Computer terminals

Work Experience

May 1982-   Wise and Smith, Attorneys at Law, Florissant, MO
  present
              Worked full-time as a file clerk and typist the first
              summer and part-time during the school year. Replaced
              vacationing secretaries the summer of 1983. Keyboarded
              and edited on Wang word-processing equipment; took
              dictation and transcribed; greeted clients; scheduled
              appointments; opened and logged incoming mail.

FIGURE 21-7. Continued

```
QUALIFICATIONS OF BRENDA LAWSON


Experience (continued)

  May-September    The Steak House, Brentwood, MO
      1981
                   Started as a waitress; was promoted to cashier after four
                   weeks.

Activities and Honors

                 Phi Beta Lambda business organization

                 President
                 Secretary--Edited and typed quarterly newsletter;
                         composed business letters; prepared
                         news releases

                 Beta Gamma Sigma honor business fraternity

                 Intramural Softball

                   Captain

                 Dean's List--All semesters

References

    Furnished upon request.
```

21.7 cont.

- What do you believe to be your real qualifications for this job?
- Why should we hire you?
- What are your greatest strengths? weaknesses?
- What is important to you in a job?
- If we employ you, how long would you plan to stay?
- What do you expect to be doing five years from now?
- What kind of salary do you expect now? five years from now?
- Why did you choose a secretarial career?
- Should the relationship between a supervisor and the secretary be formal or informal?
- In what kind of work environment are you most comfortable?
- How do you spend your spare time?
- What classes did you enjoy most? least? Why?

- What is your attitude toward working for a woman? a man?
- What was the last book you read?
- Do you regularly read a daily newspaper? a news magazine?
- Do you plan to take additional courses?
- What features of your previous jobs have you liked? disliked?
- Why did you leave your last job?
- Can you work under pressure and meet deadlines?
- Do you object to working overtime occasionally?

You may want to consider asking the interviewer some of the following questions:

- May I see a copy of the job description?
- Does the job description adequately cover the duties I would be asked to perform?
- May I see an organization chart?
- What qualities do you want most in the person who fills the position for which you are considering me?
- What would be my main responsibilities?
- How often are formal evaluations given?
- Would I be expected to work many hours of overtime?
- How many have held this position during the last five years?
- When would I be expected to report for work?
- Why don't you promote someone from within the company (if you are not applying for an entry-level position)?
- What do you like most about the organization?

Supplies, Data, and Reference Material

You should anticipate the things you may need before, during, or after the interview and take them along in a small attache case or in a purse and file folder. Do not, however, take notes during the interview. The following should be included in what you take to the interview:

- Questions you want to ask.
- Resume.
- Transcript.
- Pencil and pen.

510
Secretarial
Procedures:
Office
Administration and
Automated Systems

- List of the names, addresses, and telephone numbers of the places you have worked. Include the names of the supervisors and the dates you worked.

- Names, addresses, and telephone numbers of those who have given you permission to use their names as references.

- Small notebook for dictation should you be given a test.

- Pocket-size dictionary.

- Eraser.

Arrival

Arrive approximately 10 minutes early for the interview. If you are going to an unfamiliar area, you should allow plenty of time to travel, park, and locate the office. By arriving a few minutes early, you can prepare mentally to enter the interview relaxed and with a positive attitude. Also, by observing the activity in the office you may learn something about the organization. Are people friendly? Are they businesslike? Are they appropriately dressed? Do they appear happy? Do they appear to be competent?

Be sure you pleasantly greet the receptionist and everyone you meet. The interviewer may ask for their impressions after you leave.

You should know the interviewer's name so that you may use it when you meet. If you do not know the name, you may ask the secretary or receptionist. Know how to pronounce the name correctly. Even though you may observe others referring to the executive by his or her first name, you should use a courtesy title during the interview. If the interviewer initiates the handshake, you should apply a firm handshake, indicate you are pleased to meet him or her (mention the name), and then wait to be asked to be seated. Sit erect and lean slightly forward to express interest.

Your appearance is extremely important. You want to give the appearance of a successful secretary. The instant you walk into the office, the interviewer will start to form an impression of you. Conservative suits, well-made skirts and blouses, and simple jewelry are considered appropriate attire when applying for most secretarial positions.

During the Interview

Even though you have a selfish motive for being interested in the job, you need to demonstrate by your comments, questions, and answers that you are most interested in finding out how you can help the company.

You can improve the impression you make in an interview situation by listening closely and showing an interest. Look at the interviewer and give him or her your complete attention. Answer questions completely, but avoid extraneous information. Do not assume that you have to do all of the talking to make a favorable impression. You can convey sincerity by paying attention and responding honestly and briefly. Smile, act natural, and convey the impression that you would be pleasant to work with.

The interviewer should initiate the salary topic or mention that the salary will be discussed by those in the personnel office. You should know the range for applicants with your qualifications so that your response to a question about how much you would expect is reasonable. By talking with your professors and friends and by looking at published salary data for secretarial positions in different geographical areas, you should know the salary you have the right to expect. If your qualifications are about the average for the job, you can indicate that you would expect to be paid the going rate or within the normal range. If you have added qualifications, you might say "With my two years of work experience, I would expect to start at the upper end of the normal range." You may not want to state an exact figure, but you should never state that you do not know what salary you expect since that would indicate you have not adequately prepared.

Closing the Interview

The interviewer may place papers in a folder, make a comment about the next step to be taken, ask if you have any further questions, or simply rise from the chair to indicate the interview is completed. Unless you have some further questions or information to supply that you believe will enhance your employment opportunities, do not prolong the interview. Accept the handshake if offered, thank the interviewer, and close by saying you look forward to hearing from the company.

Remember to be pleasant to the receptionist as you leave. You may simply smile or make some sincere complimentary remark about her or the company.

APPLICATION BLANK

You will probably be asked to complete an application blank either before or after the interview. The way you complete the application can have a definite impact on your being given serious consideration for the position.

Someone must have thought the information asked for on the application was important; therefore, you should carefully and accurately complete all items. Read the form before you start completing it and follow the instructions. The neatness and accuracy you demonstrate in completing the form may be one factor in the total evaluation process.

The application form shown in figure 21-8 is typical. Observe that the applicant is asked not to supply any information that may be contrary to federal, state, or local laws. Note, too, that most of the information requested is the same as that shown in the resume.

HALLMARK CARDS INCORPORATED
Application For Employment

Date _____ 19 ____ — —

42-202-9430 REV. 5-82

ADMINISTRATIVE USE ONLY

EEO-1 FILING CODE

SOCIAL SECURITY NO.

PERSONAL

NAME   FIRST   MIDDLE   LAST

PRESENT ADDRESS   CITY   STATE   TELEPHONE NO.   ALTERNATE TELEPHONE NO.

PREVIOUS ADDRESS   CITY   STATE   ZIP CODE   HOW LONG LIVED HERE?

PREVIOUS ADDRESS   CITY   STATE

HOW DID YOU BECOME INTERESTED IN EMPLOYMENT HERE?

HAVE YOU PREVIOUSLY BEEN EMPLOYED BY THE COMPANY? IF YES, PLEASE SHOW IN EMPLOYMENT RECORD   ☐ Yes ☐ No

WHAT TYPE OF WORK DO YOU PREFER? (STOCK, PRODUCTION, ORDER SELECTING, CLERICAL, RETAIL SALES)

TYPE OF EMPLOYMENT DESIRED:
☐ Full Time   ☐ Part Time   ☐ Temporary
☐ Permanent

PREFERRED HOURS

DO YOU HAVE ANY PHYSICAL, MENTAL OR MEDICAL IMPAIRMENT OR DISABILITY THAT WOULD LIMIT YOUR JOB PERFORMANCE FOR THE POSITION FOR WHICH YOU ARE APPLYING
☐ Yes ☐ No If yes please explain

ARE YOU COLOR BLIND
☐ Yes ☐ No

ARE YOU A U.S. CITIZEN?
☐ Yes ☐ No

IF NOT, WHAT TYPE OF VISA DO YOU POSSESS?   DATE OF ISSUANCE   CARD NUMBER   PLACE OF ISSUANCE

HAVE YOU EVER RECEIVED WORKER'S COMPENSATION? IF YES, EXPLAIN DETAILS
☐ Yes ☐ No

HAVE YOU EVER BEEN CONVICTED OF A FELONY?
☐ Yes ☐ No

BE SURE YOUR EMPLOYMENT RECORD ACCOUNTS FOR ALL TIME SINCE LEAVING SCHOOL

Please include any U.S. military service in this record, including the Vietnam era. If you have been married or remarried, please write (in the margin) the name under which you were employed by each of the following:

EMPLOYMENT RECORD

GIVE COMPANY NAME OF LAST OR PRESENT EMPLOYER   ADDRESS   CITY   STATE

DATE STARTED (MONTH & YEAR)   DATE LEFT (MONTH & YEAR)   PAY RATE   POSITION HELD   NAME OF SUPERVISOR   PHONE NO.

PREVIOUS EMPLOYER   ADDRESS   CITY   STATE

DATE STARTED (MONTH & YEAR)   DATE LEFT (MONTH & YEAR)   PAY RATE   POSITION HELD   NAME OF SUPERVISOR   PHONE NO.

PREVIOUS EMPLOYER   ADDRESS   CITY   STATE

DATE STARTED (MONTH & YEAR)   DATE LEFT (MONTH & YEAR)   PAY RATE   POSITION HELD   NAME OF SUPERVISOR   PHONE NO.

PREVIOUS EMPLOYER   ADDRESS   CITY   STATE

DATE STARTED (MONTH & YEAR)   DATE LEFT (MONTH & YEAR)   PAY RATE   POSITION HELD   NAME OF SUPERVISOR   PHONE NO.

It is our custom to inquire for further details at the schools you indicate. It will be helpful in identifying your record if you will give as accurate information as possible on dates, degrees, and (if a married woman applicant) your name while attending the school.

EDUCATION RECORD

NAME OF SCHOOL	LOCATION	MAJOR COURSE OF STUDY	YEARS ATTENDED From	YEARS ATTENDED To	DID YOU GRADUATE	DEGREE
HIGH SCHOOL(S)			19	19		
COLLEGE(S)			19	19		
			19	19		
BUSINESS TRADE OR TECHNICAL SCHOOL			19	19		

ARE YOU NOW ATTENDING ANY SCHOOL? ☐ Yes ☐ No

SCHOOL ACTIVITIES

SPECIAL ABILITIES THAT SUPPORT YOUR EMPLOYMENT INTEREST

SCHOOL HONORS

GRADE AVERAGE (LETTER) Major ____ Overall ____

IN WHAT SUBJECTS DID YOU MAKE YOUR BEST GRADES

HOBBIES, AND SKILLS (TYPING, SHORTHAND, ART, MECHANICAL, WOODWORKING, PHOTOGRAPHY, ETC.)

IMMEDIATE FAMILY

NAME	ADDRESS
FATHER	
MOTHER	
HUSBAND OR WIFE	
BROTHERS OR SISTERS	

PERSONAL REFER.

IN CASE OF EMERGENCY CONTACT:

NAME (Do not give names of former employers or relatives)	STREET AND NUMBER	CITY AND STATE	OCCUPATION	PHONE

Have you signed a secrecy agreement in favor of a previous employer? _____

Are you under any obligation to a previous employer through a secrecy and invention agreement or otherwise restricting employment with a competitive firm? _____ If so, give name of employer _____

In the event I become an employee of the company, or any of its subsidiaries, I agree in consideration of such employment, to disclose fully all ideas, designs, inventions, developments, new processes, or improvement of existing ideas or processes which I may originate, develop, or discover during my employment, I further agree that I will not, directly or indirectly, disclose to any competitor any process, design, trade secret, or other information during such employment or within two years following termination of my employment, nor will I, directly or indirectly, accept employment or compensation from any competitor of the company during such employment or within two years following termination of my employment.

I authorize investigation of all statements in this application. I understand misrepresentation or omission of facts called for is cause for dismissal.

Date _____ Signature _____

PERSONNEL DEPT.

THIS SPACE FOR USE OF PERSONNEL DEPARTMENT

PLACEMENT RECORD

DATE	BRANCH		
DEPARTMENT		SHIFT	
CLASSIFICATION			

FIGURE 21-8. Application form. (Courtesy of Hallmark Cards, Inc.)

514
Secretarial
Procedures:
Office
Administration and
Automated Systems

FOLLOW-UP PROCEDURES

Thank-You Letter

Common courtesy requires that you write a thank-you letter after you have been granted an interview. The potential employer did you a favor by talking with you; furthermore, the letter can be used to reinforce the areas of your preparedness that you learned through the interview were of greatest interest to the employer. The letter should be short, courteous, and personal. The letter should sound like you.

An effective thank-you letter is illustrated in figure 21-9.

```
                                            15 Spruce Lane
                                            Cedar Rapids, IA  52407
                                            May 15, 1984



    Ms. Judy Jette
    Office Manager
    Prospect Bank
    1000 Main Street
    Cedar Rapids, IA  52407

    Dear Ms. Jette:

    Thank you for meeting with me yesterday to discuss the secretarial
    position.  The friendly and helpful attitude reflected by you and
    the others I met convinced me that Prospect Bank is the type of
    organization with which I want to be associated.

    I am confident that my experience in a position where a high degree
    of accuracy was required, together with my formal education, has
    given me the background needed to be an effective member of your
    staff.

    I look forward to hearing from you soon.

                                    Sincerely,



                                    Helen Strobel
```

FIGURE 21-9. Thank-you letter.

ACCEPTING A POSITION

When you decide to accept an offer, you should write a letter and say so enthusiastically. Sometimes you may be asked to telephone your acceptance. In that case, you should write a letter confirming the telephone conversation. The following example illustrates how you can start the letter by accepting the offer, continue by including something to reassure the employer a wise decision was made, and close by confirming the date you are to report to work:

> I am pleased to accept the position as secretary. I am confident I have much to offer Hart and Hart.
>
> Early next week I will come by the office to visit with Miss Brooks and obtain a copy of the office manual. I look forward to beginning my career with you on September 5.

REJECTING A POSITION

If you are offered a position and choose not to accept it, you must honestly respond to the offer. Promptly answer and give the reason for the refusal (perhaps you have already accepted another position) and express appreciation for the confidence the company placed in you.

Summary

The employment process involves identifying your qualifications in terms of the contributions you can make to potential employers and deciding how to act on that information in the most positive way possible. Remember that you will not be hired because you need a job or because you feel qualified. You will be hired because you have shown the potential employer that you can do more for the company than others who may be applying.

Completing all steps of the employment process is not an easy task, but the process is well worth the time and effort involved if you are to obtain the most satisfying job possible. You need to keep in mind that you will be spending as much time on the job as with your family; thus, how you feel about your job is extremely important.

The job search involves your conducting an in-depth study of how you affect others, what you enjoy and are qualified to do, what and where

516
Secretarial
Procedures:
Office
Administration and
Automated Systems

opportunities exist, and finally presenting yourself in the most favorable light possible. Only after you have thoroughly completed the preliminary work are you prepared to develop the resume and letter of application and to present yourself favorably in an interview situation. The follow-up to the interview can make a difference when you and others may be about equally qualified.

———————————————— Questions ————————————————

1. Since experts predict that a shortage of secretaries will exist throughout the 1980s, well-qualified applicants should be able to obtain a position. Why, then, should the prospective secretary need to complete the time-consuming steps of the employment process discussed in this chapter?

2. You will not be hired simply because you are qualified. Why will you be hired?

3. What is probably more important in terms of your success on the job than your typing and shorthand skills?

4. Why may the fact that you studied statistics or accounting as electives be important when you are being considered for a position, even though the position for which you are applying may not require you to use what you learned in the courses?

5. Do you agree that you should list on the resume all of the courses you have studied in college? Discuss.

6. List the possible sources of job openings and give the primary advantages of each.

7. Is the resume or the letter of application written first? Why?

8. What is the essential question all interviewers are trying to answer?

9. The most qualified persons do not necessarily get the best jobs. Discuss.

10. What is the primary reason for applicants being nervous during the interview?

11. What are the twofold objectives of the interview?

12. What is a job description?

13. Why do you believe typing and shorthand are listed last on the job description shown in figure 21-2?

14. Since everyone applying for a secretarial position will have a knowledge of shorthand and typing, how can you use your skills in these areas to enhance your employment opportunities?

15. When only strengths are mentioned in the resume and letter of application, is the applicant being unethical? Explain.

16. How can your work experience be a factor in your favor even when the work has not been in the secretarial or clerical area?

17. What is the purpose of listing hobbies on the resume?

18. Why may the employer be interested in knowing about the activities in which you have been involved in the community or school?

19. Why should those who are employed look at the help wanted section of the newspaper periodically?

20. What is the primary difference between private and public employment agencies?

21. If the applicant is to be interviewed by the employer, why does the employment agency conduct interviews, too?

22. Why should applicants not use resumes or letters of application written by someone else?

23. Since data concerning education, experience, and activities are almost always listed on the resume, what can you do to entice the employer to notice your resume?

24. What is the primary objective of the letter of application and resume?

25. How can you arrive at a salary you have the right to expect?

26. Should the application blank be completed in pencil, ink, or typewritten? Explain.

27. Why should you seek a position you will enjoy?

28. Why will an organization normally request an applicant to complete an application form when the person has already submitted the information in the resume?

29. What information about an applicant can an interviewer learn through the interview that cannot be learned from the resume or letter of application?

—————————————— Projects ——————————————

1. Complete all steps of the employment process discussed in the chapter.

2. Assume that you are a prospective employer. Ask yourself the question, "Why should I hire you?"

   Use a tape recorder as you answer the question, then play back the answer and critique it. Continue to do this until you are satisfied that the

518
Secretarial
Procedures:
Office
Administration and
Automated Systems

answer would be appropriate in an actual interview. Follow the same procedure as you ask yourself the other questions listed in the section on preparing for the interview.

3. If your library has an actual or mock interview film on file, arrange to view it.

4. Write out the information asked for in the application form shown in figure 21-8. Obtain application forms from several businesses and discuss the types of information to be supplied.

5. Prepare a detailed budget and determine the minimum amount of pay you must have to live comfortably. Compare this amount with the prevailing rate of pay for secretaries in the area where you want to work.

6. Conduct library research and prepare a report on the types of information the employer cannot legally seek during the interview.

7. All students in the class should wear attire they believe to be appropriate for an interview. Have a discussion concerning what is worn that day.

8. Obtain a copy of the salary survey conducted by the Administrative Management Society chapter (or other such agency) for your area.

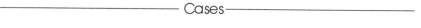

Cases

1. Mary Wilson went to the personnel office of a company to obtain an application form. The Director of Personnel briefly talked with her and believed she was qualified for a position open at that time. The Director asked Mary to take a shorthand and typing test and have an interview with the supervisor of the department in which the vacancy existed. Mary realized she was not dressed appropriately for an interview. What should Mary have done?

2. During the first week of May, Susan Stith sent a letter of application and a resume to three different companies. She was offered a position at the Holt Company when she went for an interview on May 9. She had not received a response from the other two companies; therefore, she accepted the offer and agreed to report for work on May 20. On May 12 the Best Way Company contacted Susan and asked that she come for an interview on May 15. She went for the interview and was offered the position, which appeared to be considerably more attractive than the position she had accepted at the Holt Company. She accepted Best Way Company's offer and notified the Holt Company on May 19. Is Susan's action ethical? Discuss.

3. The instructor of your office procedures class announced that a local company had an opening for a well-qualified secretary. One of the students in the class told you she planned to apply for the position and she would like for you to not apply since you are more qualified than she and would probably get the job. What should you do?

CHAPTER 22

Career Goals

Just as you set goals while enrolled in school, you need to set goals for professional growth once you begin working in a full-time position.

This chapter offers suggestions for developing professionally, for preparing for a higher-level position in the secretarial area, and for preparing for a change in your career path.

PROFESSIONAL DEVELOPMENT

The secretary has many opportunities to demonstrate initiative and to grow professionally, including membership in professional organizations, professional accreditation, reading, seminars, and formal education.

Professional Organizations

Professional organizations for secretaries can be found in almost all cities. Sometimes the organizations are for those working in specialized areas, such as legal and medical, but usually at least one organization can be found that has members who work in various types of offices. These organizations provide excellent opportunities for secretaries to interact and grow professionally.

522
Secretarial
Procedures:
Office
Administration and
Automated Systems

Certification

Several professional accreditation programs, including the following, are available to those who meet the qualifications.

The basic objective of the Institute for Certifying Secretaries, a department of Professional Secretaries International, is to upgrade the secretarial profession by encouraging secretaries to raise their standards of professionalism. The Institute has the major goals of preparing and administering the annual Certified Professional Secretary (CPS) examination program and promoting the CPS program.

The CPS examination has been administered since 1951. The two-day examination is given annually in approximately 250 centers. The examination covers six areas: behavioral science in business; business law; economics and management; accounting; communication applications; and office administration and technology.

Other professional associations also provide testing programs and professional certification. The National Association of Legal Secretaries (International) provides several services for the members and administers the Professional Legal Secretary examination and certification program. The two-day examination covers legal secretarial skills and exercise of judgment, legal terminology and techniques, secretarial procedures and office management, written communication skill and knowledge, human relations, and accounting.

The National Association of Education Office Personnel sponsors a Professional Standards Program that provides for different types of certificates based on experience, education, and professional activity.

Reading

You can increase your knowledge about the business, the industry, and your profession and as a result become a more valuable employee by developing a reading program. As a minimum, you should read a daily newspaper and a weekly news magazine, as well as the following magazines:

The Office

Office Administration and Automation

The Secretary

Modern Office Procedures

Modern Office and Data Management

Your boss or the company library will probably subscribe to several magazines, *The Wall Street Journal,* and trade and professional journals that relate specifically to your area of work. You may be able to borrow the publications for a night or a weekend.

In addition to newspapers and periodicals, you should read books that will help you become more knowledgeable about your work. Your boss may be able to recommend books or other material that relates to your company's operation and will be pleased to learn that you are eager to stay abreast of the changes occurring in the area. You should always follow through on the suggestions that are made to indicate that you are sincere in your desire to improve your qualifications.

As you read the newspapers and periodicals, pay particular attention to the business news items and the advertisements and consider how what you learn can be used to make your job easier or improve the operation of your office.

Seminars

Universities and other organizations frequently sponsor seminars for professional secretaries. Since the seminars are designed to increase your worth to your company, the company will often pay the fee and give you released time to attend. Those attending the seminar are usually given useful reference material that supplements the course presentation.

When considering a seminar, you should look at the outline of the material to be covered and select a seminar that includes topics of particular interest to you. The content of seminars varies considerably, as indicated by the following topics that were listed in recent announcements of seminars:

- Your Role in the Organization
- Techniques for Planning and Control
- Improving Interpersonal Skills
- Strategies for Effective Time Management
- Strengthening the Boss/Secretary Team
- Assertiveness Training
- Effective Business Writing
- Effective Communication in the Office
- Increasing Job Effectiveness Through Time Management

A seminar may be designed to cover a single topic in depth or may include several unrelated topics.

Education

Your formal education need not stop when you become employed or when you complete a particular degree. Many companies will pay the tuition when the employees enroll for job-related courses.

524
Secretarial
Procedures:
Office
Administration and
Automated Systems

If colleges or universities are located in the community where you live, you should consider enrolling for courses that will help you in performing your job or in making you more promotable. A knowledge of a foreign language may qualify you to work in a branch office of the company located in another country. A computer course may enable you to make better use of the computer in your office. Courses in the technical area in which you work may prepare you to assume additional responsibilities.

PROMOTIONS

A promotion may result in your obtaining a better secretarial position or a position in a different job area with the company where you are now working or with a different company.

Many secretaries are content with their jobs and have good reasons for not wanting the additional responsibilities that would be associated with a promotion. Before deciding that you are not interested in a promotion, however, you should consider several questions, including the following:

- Will I possibly become bored with this job?
- What will I need to do to remain proficient in my present position?
- How will my job change as a result of technology?
- Will my salary continue to be acceptable?
- Would I enjoy my job if my boss should leave and I were to have to work for a different executive?
- What are the possibilities for a promotion at a later time?

Seeking Promotions

You had the basic knowledge and skills necessary to be successful in your present position before you were hired. Likewise, you should prepare for the higher-level positions you may seek and should be fully qualified before seeking the positions.

When you are seeking a promotion, you should ask a number of questions, including the following:

- Am I performing my present job competently?
- Am I 100 percent dependable?
- Do my actions reflect that I have an interest in my work and the company?

- Have I demonstrated that I can be an effective team member?
- Am I better qualified than anyone else for the promotion?
- Have I done all that I can to prepare for the promotion?

Sometimes qualified people are not promoted because they are not as visible as others and because their qualifications are not known to those who make decisions regarding the promotions.

Keep your boss and the personnel department informed about your accomplishments. For example, if you complete a college course or attend a seminar, you should send a memorandum to the personnel department and ask that the information be included in your personnel file. If your boss does not know of the accomplishment, give him or her a copy of the memorandum.

Becoming expert in your area of responsibility is important, but you should not allow yourself to become indispensable. Have your area of responsibility so well-organized that someone else could easily assume your duties. For example, teach others how to operate the equipment in your office, keep an up-to-date list of frequently called numbers, prepare written procedures to be followed in performing routine tasks, and so forth.

Learning of Job Openings

In addition to learning of openings by following the suggestions presented in the preceding chapter, you may learn of openings in other ways when you are an employee of the company.

Your boss may be in a position to initiate changes in your area of responsibility or may know of anticipated changes in the organization that will result in your being promoted to a higher-level position.

In many companies, announcements of openings are posted on the bulletin boards or printed in the company newsletter. You can let the personnel office staff know that you are interested in being considered for certain positions.

The contacts you have with executives at various levels as you assist your boss in carrying out his or her functions provide you with opportunities to make a favorable impression on people who are in positions to assist you.

People frequently learn of potential job openings through the "grapevine" or informal communication channel. For example, during lunch you may hear someone comment that his or her spouse is being transferred to another geographical area in six months. Although your coworker may not notify the personnel office for several months, you may be able to learn a skill or in some other way become fully qualified so that you will be favorably considered when the opening is announced.

526
Secretarial
Procedures:
Office
Administration and
Automated Systems

DETERMINING YOUR CAREER DIRECTION

When you want to stay in the secretarial area and move up in the company, you need to consider the number of positions at the higher levels, whether the positions will likely become available, and the competition for the positions.

If you believe you have little opportunity for advancement in the secretarial area within the company, you may decide to seek a position in another company where the opportunities for advancement are greater.

You will probably not be familiar with the structure of the company with which you may be seeking a position; therefore, you should ask about opportunities for advancement by asking "What are the advancement possibilities for someone who does well?" or "What are the positions now held by those who previously held this position?"

Changing Careers

A secretary who is considering a change in her career path has many options, including a change to another area of work, such as accounting, finance, personnel, or marketing, or a change to a supervisory position.

A change in your career may have a considerable impact on your personal and professional life. You need to be aware of changes, such as the following, which may occur:

- You may be expected to relocate.
- You may be required to work overtime.
- You may have to travel.
- You may be confronted with pressure situations.
- You may be working with employees who have educational and experience backgrounds that are different from those with whom you normally work.

Becoming Familiar With Work Areas

When you consider changing your career path, you need to explore the area thoroughly and consider carefully the ramifications associated with the change. You should consider whether you are qualified and, if not, what you must do to become qualified. If you need additional formal education, can you become qualified by attending night school or will you have to resign your position and attend school full time?

Here are some questions you should ask as you talk with people who are employed in the occupation area you are considering:

- Why did you choose this line of work?
- What do you like most about the work?
- What do you like least about the work?
- What qualities are needed in addition to the training and education?
- What is the employment outlook for this area now and five years from now?
- What are the advancement possibilities?
- What changes are anticipated?

In addition to talking with people employed in the area of work you are considering, you should investigate the area further by

- Reading an elementary textbook relating to the area.
- Enrolling for a course or two in the area.
- Reading magazines specifically relating to the area.
- Looking at the want ad section of the newspaper to determine whether positions appear to be available.
- Talking with someone in the personnel department of your company.
- Talking with instructors at the college you attended.

Deciding to Change Careers

Before you decide to change your career direction, prepare two lists. One list should contain your reasons for wanting to make the change. The other list should contain the advantages of remaining in the secretarial field. After you have prepared the lists, make your decision by carefully considering the reasons that have the greatest impact on your personal and professional life. Usually, the decision to make a change in the direction of your career should not be based on only one reason, such as higher pay.

When people seek a new position because they are unhappy in their present position, they should attempt to identify the real reasons for their unhappiness. The reasons for their unhappiness may not be job related and a change in positions will not necessarily result in their being happy. Even if the reasons are job related, a change in positions will not necessarily solve the problem. A person who has difficulty working with co-workers in a particular office often encounters similar difficulties in working with the personnel in a different work environment.

Understanding Supervisory Functions

As a secretary, you have assisted the executive in carrying out the management functions and have developed many skills that will be helpful to

528
Secretarial
Procedures:
Office
Administration and
Automated Systems

you as a supervisor. You need to realize, however, that as a supervisor you will not necessarily have the same degree of authority as the executive for whom you have been working and may not have access to many of the executives with whom you worked in carrying out the executive's directives. As a supervisor, you will be working at the lowest management level; thus, most of your work will be with those in your line of authority and your immediate superior who will probably be a middle-level manager.

If you move to a supervisory position in an established department, you will have people working for you whom you did not hire and might not have hired had you been in the supervisory position at the time they were considered for employment. Also, if the position is in the company where you have worked as a secretary, you will be supervising those who were formerly your coworkers and perhaps some of them had anticipated they would be selected for the supervisory position.

When you decide to seek a supervisory position, you should be qualified to perform the planning, organizing, controlling, staffing, and directing functions discussed in chapter 1. A major part of your work as supervisor will involve making decisions, communicating with subordinates and superiors, and delegating work.

The steps in the decision-making process are interrelated; however, most management experts identify separate steps in the process:

1. Identify the problem or situation.

2. Identify possible solutions.

3. Analyze and evaluate the alternatives.

4. Select an alternative.

5. Implement the selected alternative.

The supervisor is held accountable for the results of decisions made in his or her area of responsibility; however, the supervisor frequently seeks the advice and support of superiors and subordinates in identifying and analyzing the situation or problem and in arriving at a solution.

A supervisor is responsible for deciding what tasks are to be completed and selecting the people to whom the tasks are to be assigned. A good supervisor does not attempt to do all of the work required in his or her area; instead, the supervisor should make sure the assignments are fully understood, delegate the authority the subordinates need, and offer to provide assistance when needed. The subordinates should then be expected to assume the responsibility for successfully completing the tasks.

The supervisor is held accountable for his or her performance, as well as the performance and actions of subordinates.

The effective supervisor must be able to communicate with superiors, other supervisors, staff personnel, and subordinates.

The supervisor's communication with superiors involves keeping them informed, responding to their requests, making suggestions, seeking assistance in solving problems, and so forth.

As a supervisor, you must be able to interpret correctly the messages received from higher-level management and transmit those messages accurately to your subordinates in understandable language; thus, good communication skill is essential.

Identifying Your Supervisory Abilities

When you are preparing to seek a supervisory position, you need to make a list of your abilities. Consider the responsibilities you have in your present position and what you have accomplished. Ask yourself the following questions in an attempt to determine whether you qualify for a supervisory position:

- Can I give directions clearly?
- Do I accept responsibility?
- Do I assume authority when necessary?
- Do I show concern for the welfare of others?
- Do I get along well with others?
- Do I have the necessary technical knowledge?
- Do I have a positive attitude and believe in the goals and objectives of the company?
- Do I show initiative by seeking better ways of doing things?
- Am I dependable?
- Do I accept criticism gracefully?
- Am I cooperative?
- Can I adapt to changing situations?
- Do I listen carefully?
- Do I show respect for others?
- Do I take a sincere interest in my work?
- Do I take the time necessary to ensure the satisfactory completion of assignments?
- Do I take advantage of opportunities to improve?
- Am I tactful and considerate when pointing out errors others have made?

Before you approach employers, you should make a list of what you have done to demonstrate you are skilled in the above areas.

530
Secretarial
Procedures:
Office
Administration and
Automated Systems

LEAVING A POSITION

You want people to speak favorably of you after you have left a position. You also want to leave feeling confident that you would be considered favorably should you decide to seek employment with the company at a later time.

Unless ample notice is given, your leaving may create a hardship on the company. Your new employer should understand your desire to give your present employer 30 days' notice. If your new employer insists that you assume your duties immediately or you will not be hired, you may want to consider whether you want to work for someone who appears inconsiderate of the needs of others.

Even though you may not have liked certain aspects of your job and all of the people with whom you worked, you have nothing to gain by making uncomplimentary remarks at the time you leave. Do not mention how glad you are to be leaving or overemphasize what appear to be favorable aspects of the new position.

You should continue to be dependable and conscientious while you are serving out your notice period. Do not arrive at work late, leave early, or take unnecessary sick or personal leave. If you are involved in a major project at the time you submit your resignation, try to complete the task during the notice period.

If your replacement reports for work before you leave, do all that you can to assist her in successfully adjusting to the work environment. Perhaps the person you are replacing will do the same for you. You should alert your replacement to the likes and dislikes of those for whom she will be working. Do not, however, make derogatory remarks about the individuals or say anything that will cause your replacement to question whether she should have accepted the position.

Summary

Secretaries who want to be considered professionals should stay abreast of the happenings in the secretarial field. A secretary should consider joining professional organizations, becoming certified, enrolling for additional college courses, attending seminars, and reading as she develops professionally.

A qualified secretary may be promoted to a higher-level secretarial position within the company or, when the advancement opportunities are limited, she may need to consider joining another company where the opportunities appear greater. A secretary may consider changing the direction of her career and seek a supervisory position or a position in another profession. Before making a change in her career path, however, the secretary needs to carefully consider the reasons for wanting to make the change, as well as the advantages and disadvantages associated with the contemplated change.

––––––––––––––––––––––––––– Questions –––––––––––––––––––––––––––

1. What are the major goals of the Institute for Certifying Secretaries?
2. Does the CPS examination cover only shorthand and typing skills? Discuss.
3. Define "seminar."
4. List some courses that you believe might be helpful for a secretary to study as electives while in college or after completing a degree.
5. Discuss reasons a secretary who is well-satisfied with her job might not be satisfied with the job at a later time.
6. Should a secretary who desires a promotion become qualified for the higher-level position before or after receiving the promotion? Discuss.
7. Do the best qualified individuals always receive the promotions? Discuss.
8. List several ways of learning of job openings.
9. Discuss the career options a secretary may consider when planning to leave the secretarial field.
10. List the steps involved in the decision-making process.
11. Discuss things the person who is leaving a position may do to maintain the respect and goodwill of those with whom she has been working.
12. If a secretary has worked long enough to earn a 15-day vacation, should she consider the 15 days as part of the 30-day notice period? Discuss.

––––––––––––––––––––––––––– Projects –––––––––––––––––––––––––––

1. Read at least one newspaper each day and one news magazine each week for a month. Prepare a bibliography of the articles you find particularly interesting and write at least one paragraph on each of the five articles you find most interesting.
2. Talk with friends or acquaintances who have changed careers. Discuss the reasons why they changed careers and the procedures they followed in making the change.

532
Secretarial
Procedures:
Office
Administration and
Automated Systems

3. Talk with friends or acquaintances who have made a career of working in the secretarial field. Discuss with them the reasons why they decided to remain in the secretarial field.

4. Look at the want ad section of the Sunday edition of a metropolitan area newspaper. List the titles of the secretarial jobs, the skills required, and the salaries mentioned.

5. Assume that you supervise five people in the word processing center. According to a report distributed by the Personnel Department, absenteeism in your department is 10 percent higher than the company average. Your boss has sent you a memorandum asking for an explanation and what you plan to do about the situation. Write a report in which you identify the problem, evaluate possible solutions, and explain the solution you plan to implement.

--- Cases ---

1. Assume that you have worked as a private secretary for a vice president of the company for five years. An opening for a supervisor is announced and you believe you are fully qualified. Should you seek the position if other secretaries who have been with the company much longer than you are also interested in the position?

2. You supervise five workers in the word-processing center. Two of the workers are often slovenly attired. When you discuss their appearance with them, they point out that they do not have contact with people outside the company; therefore, they do not believe their appearance is important. How should you respond?

3. You supervise eight workers. How should you handle each of the following situations?

   a. Shelly does outstanding work but frequently comes to work late and wants to leave early. She explains that she is paid the same as the others and she can do the same amount of work as the others in much less time.

   b. Laura is absent frequently and tells you that she is sick. Her co-workers tell you that she frequently tells them she has been shopping, has taken a short trip, or has done something else that would indicate she was not too ill to report for work.

   c. John has body odor.

   d. Jean and Lois spend several minutes a day socializing and frequently do not get their assigned work completed.

   e. Lori had applied for the supervisory position for which you were selected. She appears to resent working for you and often does not follow your instructions.

INDEX

Acknowledgments, 463
Affidavits, 464
Application letter, see employment
    process
Appointments, 419–438
    Calendar, 420
    Canceling, 425
    Length, 420
    Scheduling, 419
    Tickler file, 422
    Timing, 420
    With subordinates, 425
Atlases, see library resources
Automobile rental, 121

Biographical directories, see library
    resources
Business Organizations
    Departments, 9–14
        Administrative services, 14
        Finance, 12
        Marketing, 12
        Personnel, 12
        Production, 14
        Purchasing, 11
    Legal forms
        Corporations, 4
        Partnerships, 4
        Sole proprietorships, 4

Career changing, 526–530
Central Exchange (Centrex), 169
Certified professional secretary
    (CPS), 522
Charts, see reports
Chief executive officer (CEO), 6
Compatibility, 450
Computer applications, 38–41
    Appointment calendar, 38
    Communication links, 40
    Directory, 38

Electronic mail, 39
Phone message log, 39
Reminder file, 38
Reports, 39
Secretarial, 40
Computer-Output-Microfilm (COM),
    45
Confidentiality, 451, 477
Confrontations, 456
Copiers
    Features, 41
    Intelligent, 43
Criticism, 452
Custom calling services
    Call forwarding, 168
    Call waiting, 168
    Speed calling, 168
    Three-way calling, 168

Data bases, 341
Decision-making, 455
Delivery services
    Bus, 202
    Emery Worldwide, 202
    Federal Express, 202
    Taxi, 202
    United Parcel Service (UPS),
        201
Departmental functions
    Administrative services, 14
    Finance, 12
    Marketing, 12
    Personnel, 12
    Production, 14
    Purchasing, 11
Desks
    Accessories, 383–387
        Appointment calendars, 383
        Card files, 385
        Collator, 384
        Copy holder, 385
        Drawer organizer, 384

534
Secretarial
Procedures:
Office
Administration and
Automated Systems

Letter opener, 386
Pencil sharpener, 384
Shredder, 385
Sorters and trays, 385
Stapler, 385
Telephone lock, 384
Telephone shoulder rest, 384
Types
    Pedestal, 51
    Word processing and
        computer, 52
Direct Distance Dialing (DDD), 149
Directories, see library resources
Domestic Mail Manual, 183
Dun & Bradstreet, Inc., see library
    resources

Electronic typewriter, 33
Empathy, 405
Employment process, 484–516
    Application blank, 511
    Application letter, 501–504, 506
        Body, 502
        Closing, 503
        Inside address, 502
        Typing of, 503
        Typing of, 503
    Follow-up, 514
    Identifying duties, 486
    Identifying strengths
        Education, 490
        Experience, 491
        Extracurricular activities, 491
    Interviews
        Arrival, 510
        Closing, 511
        During, 510
        Preparing for, 504
        Supplies, 509
    Job description, 489
    Resume, 496–505, 507
        Activities, 500
        Education, 497
        Experience, 499
        Job objective, 497
        Personal data, 500
        References, 501
        Title, 497
        Typing of, 503

Selecting businesses, 492
Self-analysis, 486
Sources of job openings, 492
Envelopes, addressing, 218
Ergonomics, 49, 54
Ethics, 402, 449
Etiquette
    Handshaking, 411
    Introductions, 410
    Sincerity, 412
    Standing, 411
Executive's preferences
    Appointments, 419
    Mail, 215
    Telephone calls, 138
Exhibits, see reports
Expense reports, 127, 129
Extended Direct Distance Dialing
    (EDDD), 150

Facsimile, 173
Fact books, see library resources
Files, 37, 54
Financial responsibilities, 468–476
    Bank reconciliation, 471
    Cash, 468
    Checks, 469
    Deposits, 468
    Endorsements, 469
    Petty cash, 473
    Postdated checks, 470
    Stop payment orders, 471
Furniture, see office furniture

Government publications, see
    library resources
Graphic aids, see reports

International Direct Distance
    Dialing (IDDD), 152
International travel
    Passports, 122
    Visas, 123
Interoffice relations, 442–457
    Formality, 446
    Opinions, 446
    Working with more than one
        executive, 447

Interviewing, see employment
  process
Introductions, 410
Invitations, 280
Itineraries, 124, 126

Job description, 18–22, 489
Job openings, sources of
  Direct inquiry, 495
  Employment agencies, 494
  Friends, acquaintances, and
    relatives, 493
  Government positions, 495
  Newspapers, 494
  Placement office, 493

Letters
  Annotated, 217
  Application, see employment
    process
  Appreciation, 478
  Claim, 273
  Congratulatory, 277
  Order, 261
  Request, 265
  Thank-you, 279, 514
Libraries, 326
Library resources, 327–343
  Atlases
    New York Times Atlas of the
      World, 336
    Rand McNally Commercial
      Atlas & Marketing Guide, 335
  Biographical directories
    Biography Index, 337
    Current Biography, 337
    Who's Who in Finance and
      Industry, 337
  Card catalog, 327
  Data bases, 341
  Directories
    Ayer Directory of Publications,
      336
    Congressional Directory, 336
    Congressional Staff Directory,
      336
    Directory of Directories, 336

    Directory of Special Libraries
      and Information Centers,
      326, 336
    Guide to American
      Directories, 336
    National ZIP Code and Post
      Office Directory, 200
  Fact books
    Britannica Book of the Year,
      335
    Encyclopedia Americana, 335
    Encyclopedia Britannica, 335
    Facts on File, 335
    Information Please Almanac,
      334
    International Yearbook &
      Statesmen's Who's Who, 335
    Stateman's Yearbook, 335
    World Almanac & Book of
      Facts, 334
    World Book Year Book, 335
  Financial information
    Dun & Bradstreet, Inc.
      Million Dollar Directory,
        338
      Reference Book of
        Corporate Managements,
        338
    Moody's Investor Service, 337
      Handbook of Common
        Stocks, 338
      Manuals, 338
    Standard and Poor's
    Corporation
      Corporation Records, 337
      Industry Surveys, 338
      Register of Corporations,
        Directors and Executives,
        338
  Government publications
    Domestic Mail Manual, 183
    GPO Sales Publications
    Reference File (PRF), 340
    Monthly Catalog, 340
    Statistical Abstract of the
      United States, 340
  Indexes
    Books in Print, 334
    Business Periodicals Index,
      329

536
Secretarial
Procedures:
Office
Administration and
Automated Systems

Cumulative Book Index, 334
New York Times Index (The),
331, 333
*Readers' Guide to Periodical
Literature,* 329
Vertical File Index, 330, 332
*Wall Street Journal Index
(The),* 329, 331, 333
Librarians, assistance of, 341,
344
Microform, 343
State publications
*Monthly Checklist of State
Publications,* 340
*State Government Reference
Publications,* 340, 342
Listening, 137, 396–398
Long-distance calls, 149–154
Calling card, 151
Collect, 150
Conference, 151
Direct dial, 149
International, 152
Operator-assisted, 150
Person-to-person, 150
Station-to-station, 149
Third-number charge, 151
Time and charges, 150
Time zones, 154
Toll-call records, 151
Long-distance services
Combined Network's All-net, 172
Federal Telecommunications
System (FTS), 172
MCI Telecommunications
Corporation, 172
Southern Pacific
Communication (SPRINT),
172
Tie-lines, 173
United States Transmission
Systems, 172
Western Union (Micro), 172
Wide Area Telecommunications
Service (WATS), 161, 171
Loyalty, 448

Mail
Classes
Electronic Computer-
Originated (E–COM), 188
Express Mail, 184
First-class, 184
Fourth class (parcel post),
186
Mixed classes, 187
Official, 188
Priority, 184
Second class, 185
Third class, 185
Equipment
Folding and inserting
machines, 199
Postage meters, 198
Scales, 198
Incoming
Annotated, 217
Dating mail, 211
During executive's absence,
216
Envelopes, 208
Incorrectly delivered, 210
Mail digest, 211, 213
Mail expected register, 211,
213
Mail register, 211
Packages, 210
Personal mail, 208
Presenting mail, 215
Publications, 210
Routing, 212, 215
Sorting, 207
Internal pickup and delivery,
200
Interoffice, 224
Metered mail, 198
*National ZIP Code and Post
Office Directory,* 200
Optical character recognition
(OCR), 218
Outgoing
Addressing, 218
Arrangement of address, 217
Folding and inserting letters,
222
Placement of address, 218
Typing the address, 219
Window envelopes, 223
Special services
Ancillary, 196
Certificate of mailing, 194,
196
Certified, 192, 194

Collect on delivery, 192
Insured, 190, 193
Registered, 189, 191
Restricted delivery, 194
Return receipt, 192, 195
Special delivery, 195
Special handling, 196
Zone Improvement Plan (ZIP)
Code system, 200
Management
Authority
Functional, 9
Line, 7
Span of control, 9, 11
Staff, 8
Functions
Controlling, 5
Directing, 5
Organizing, 5
Planning, 5
Staffing, 5
Levels
First-line, 7
Middle, 6
Top, 6
Meetings
Agenda, 95
Equipment, 97
Follow-up, 101, 104
Interruptions, 103, 437
Notification of participants, 88
Preparing for, 436
Programs, 100
Refreshments, 100
Scheduling, 87
Selecting a place, 96
Supplies, 98
Terminating, 437
Micrographics
Aperture card, 44
Cartridge, 44
Computer-Output-Microform
(COM), 45
Jacket, 44
Library resources, 343
Microfiche, 44
Microfilm, 43
Readers, 45
Ultrafiche, 44
Minutes
Assisting others, 360
Content

Adjournment, 359
Amendments, 356
Announcements, 359
Attendance, 353
Corrections, 354
Discussion, 357
Headings, 352
Main motion, 355
Minutes of previous meeting,
354
Reports, 357
Resolutions, 357
Follow-up, 364
Index, 366, 368
Prior planning, 349
Recording the proceedings, 350
Robert's Rules of Order, 351,
389
Typing, 360
Modem, 40
Moody's Investors Service, see
library resources

Names
Pronouncing, 407
Remembering, 406
*National ZIP Code and Post Office
Directory,* 200, 387
News releases, 282
Nonverbal communication, 399
Notary public
Procedures, 462
Qualifications, 462
Responsibilities, 462

*OAG Travel Planner & Hotel/Motel
Guide,* 113, 123
Office environment
Air quality, 59
Color, 58
Lighting, 58
Noise, 59
Privacy, 62
Safety, 61
Temperature, 59
Office furniture
Chairs, 56
Desks
Pedestal, 52

538
Secretarial
Procedures:
Office
Administration and
Automated Systems

Word processing and
    computer, 52
Modular, 51
Partitions, 56
Storage
    Credenzas, 54
    Files, 52, 54, 56
    Tables, 53
Office layout
    Open, 49
    Traditional, 49
Official Airline Guide, 113
Open office, advantages, 51
Optical character recognition
    (OCR), 40, 218
Organizational charts, 7, 10, 13, 16
Organizations, see business
    organizations

Petty cash, 473
Planning, priority tasks, 79
Preferences of the executive
    Appointments, 419
    Mail, 215
    Telephone calls, 138
Primary data, 289
Privacy, 451, 477
Private Branch Exchange (PBX)
    Account coding, 170
    Automatic callback, 170
    Automatic hold, 171
    Call forwarding, 170
    Call hold, 170
    Call pickup, 169
    Call transfer, 169
    Camp-on call, 170
    Conference call, 171
    Discriminating ringing, 169
    Speed call, 170
    Trunk queuing, 170
Professional development
    Certification, 522
    Education, 523
    Organizations, 521
    Reading, 522
    Seminars, 523
Promotions, 524
Proofreading, 252

Rail, bus, and automobile travel,
    120

Records
    Destruction, 477
    Retention, 476
References, desk
    Atlases, 335, 388
    Dictionaries, 386
    Directories, 387
    Manuals, 387
    Robert's Rules of Order, 351,
        389
    Thesaurus, 387
Remote Meter Resetting System
    (RMRS), 199
Reports
    Data, 289
    Graphic aids
        Charts
            Bar, 301, 303–305
            Line, 303, 305
            Map, 306
            Pie, 300
        Exhibits, 307
        Parts
            Appendix, 315
            Bibliography, 315
            Letter of transmittal, 313
            List of illustrations, 313
            Summary, 315
            Table of contents, 313
            Title page, 312
        Tables
            Amounts, 293
            Boxed, 298
            Column heads, 292, 297
            Continued, 299
            Footnotes, 295
            Format, 295
            Number and title, 291
            Percentages, 294
            Spacing, 297
            Stubs, 292
            Ruled, 296
            Unruled, 296
            Wide, 299
        Types
            Formal, 309
            Letter, 316
            Memorandum, 317
        Typing
            Footnotes, 309
            Headings, 310
            Indentions, 309

Margins, 309
Pagination, 310
Spacing, 309
Reprographics
Copiers, 41
Intelligent copiers, 43
Offset, 41
Respect, 453
Resume, see employment process
Robert's Rules of Order, 351
Room reservations, 120

Secretarial
Positions
Administrative assistant, 15
Executive secretary, 15
Lead word processing
operator, 15
Secretary—level A, 15
Secretary—level B, 15
Word processing operator, 15
Role of, 17
Self-analysis, 486
Signing documents, 467
Speaking
Enunciation, 407
Loudness, 408
Pitch, 408
Pronunciation, 407
Rate, 408
Voice, 406
Standard and Poor's Corporation,
see library resources
Subpoenas, 478
Suggestions, 454
Supervisory abilities, 528
Supervisory functions, see
management functions
Supplies
Ordering, 375
Price, 375
Quality, 374
Quantity, 374
Receiving, 376
Storage, 377
Types
Desk accessories, 383
Files, 385
Forms, 280
Mailing, 381
Paper, 378

Typing, 382

Tables, see reports
Tact, 395
Teleconferencing, 40
Telegraph services
Mailgrams, 175
Telegrams, 174
Telex and Telex II (TWX), 175
Telephone directories
Blue pages, 162
Business listings, 162
Dialing instructions, 164
Directory assistance, 164
Emergency numbers, 164
Maps and charts, 164
Rate information, 164
White pages, 162
Yellow pages, 163
Telephone use
Answering, 140
Direct dialing, 149
Ending conversations, 148
Extended Direct Distance Dialing
(EDDD), 150
International Direct Distance
Dialing (IDDD), 152
Listening, 137
Long-distance, see long-distance
calls
Personality, 135
Placing calls, 138
Planning calls, 137
Preferences of executive, 138
Screening calls, 143
Taking messages, 146
Transferring calls, 147
Unattended telephone, 143
Telephones, types of
Key, 166
Mobile, 167
Rotary dial, 165
Speakerphone, 167
Touch-A-Matic, 167
Touch-Tone, 165
Tickler file, 422
Time log
Analyzing, 76
Recording, 76
Time management
Biocycles, 72

540
Secretarial
Procedures:
Office
Administration and
Automated Systems

Crises, 70
Delegating work, 72
Office visitors, 68
Paperwork, 70
Planning, 79
Procrastination, 71
Relaxation, 74
Repetitive tasks, 73
Secretarial skills, 74
Stress, 73
Telephone use, 67
Thinking, 75
Waiting, 71
Travel agencies, 11
Travel arrangements
Financial
Cash advances, 127
Reimbursement, 127
Reservations
Air, 112, 118
Automobile, 121
Canceling, 124
Room, 120

Uniform Acknowledgment Act, 463

Visitors
Problem visitors, 434
Receiving visitors, 429
Terminating visits, 437
See also appointments
Voice, see speaking

Wide Area Telecommunications
Service (WATS), 161, 171
Word processing
Electronic typewriters, 33
Features of word processors, 36
Functions of word processors, 35

Hardware
Central processing unit (CPU), 29
Display screen (CRT) (VDT), 28
Keyboard, 28
Printer, 30
Software, 31
Work stations
Centralized, 27, 32
Centralized with satellites, 27, 32
Decentralized, 33
Shared logic, 27, 32
Standalone, 27, 32
Work interruptions
Office visitors, 68
Telephone calls, 67
Writing
Grammar
Modifiers, 246
Parallelism, 249
Pronouns, 244
Subject-verb agreement, 242
Principles
Archaic expressions, 234
Conciseness, 238
Concrete words, 241
Courtesy, 230
Empathy, 230
Expletives, 236
Negative words, 231
Redundant expressions, 238
Substitutions, 239
Tone, 229
Voice, 235
You attitude, 230

Zone Improvement Plan (ZIP) Code system, 200